The German Opposition to Hitler

THE GERMAN OPPOSITION TO HITLER

The Resistance, the Underground,
and Assassination Plots, 1938–1945

MICHAEL C. THOMSETT

McFarland & Company, Inc., Publishers
Jefferson, North Carolina, and London

The present work is a reprint of the illustrated case bound edition of The German Opposition to Hitler: The Resistance, the Underground, and Assassination Plots, 1938–1945, *first published in 1997 by McFarland.*

LIBRARY OF CONGRESS CATALOGUING-IN-PUBLICATION DATA

Thomsett, Michael C.
    The German opposition to Hitler : the resistance, the underground,
and assassination plots, 1938–1945 / Michael C. Thomsett.
        p.   cm.
    Includes bibliographical references and index.

    ISBN-13: 978-0-7864-3027-7
    softcover : 50# alkaline paper ∞

    1. Hitler, Adolf, 1889–1945 — Assassination attempts.   2. Heads of
state — Germany — Biography.   3. Germany — Politics and government —
1933–1945.   4. Anti-Nazi movement — Germany.   I. Title.
DD247.H5T52   2006
943.086'092 — dc21   97-18933

British Library cataloguing data are available

On the cover: Adolf Hitler (Clipart.com)

Manufactured in the United States of America

McFarland & Company, Inc., Publishers
  Box 611, Jefferson, North Carolina 28640
    www.mcfarlandpub.com

To my mother, Karin Glasgow,
and the memory of my grandfather,
Friedrich R. Walbaum

$\mathcal{A}$CKNOWLEDGMENTS

This book would not have been possible without the dedicated line editing of Jean Freestone Thomsett. Her suggestions focused the book in a manner that I could not have achieved on my own.

Additional thanks are offered to Dr. Paul Roley for his suggestions on point of view and reporting in the context of the times. My appreciation also to Karin Walbaum for editing of translations and German text, as well as general recommendations.

Michael C. Thomsett
Spring 1997

TABLE OF CONTENTS

PROLOGUE: THE GROWTH OF CONSPIRACY

> It is the nature, and the advantage, of strong people that they can bring out the crucial questions and form a clear opinion about them. The weak always have to decide between alternatives that are not their own.
>
> Dietrich Bonhoeffer, *Resistance and Submission*

This book presents a history of the active resistance of German citizens against the Nazi government and the tragedy of their failure to change or eliminate it. Theirs was, by necessity, a hidden resistance. Its members were German citizens uniting against their own country's government with the intention of assassinating its leader, Adolf Hitler.

Although Hitler was a charismatic leader who was able to consolidate his power to the extent of nullifying opposition, he was not entirely unopposed. If it seemed that no cry was raised against Hitler, it was because all the usual outlets — newspapers, radio, books — were closed to the voices of dissent.

All forms of opposition to Hitler had to take place in secret. There was no political debate in Germany. The personal danger to anyone who disagreed with Hitler made joining the resistance extremely serious. Nevertheless, thousands of people did join. And eventually, it was not just a resistance of words; their intention was to remove their country's leader from power, by assassination if necessary.

The experience of the German opposition demonstrates that becoming a member of a conspiracy to remove a nation's leader is a step not taken lightly or impulsively. An individual passes through three phases on the way.

The first phase is alienation, the experience of those who cannot agree with the philosophy of their government. The feeling that their views are unrepresented in the important decisions and actions of the day may lead to a sense of helplessness.

The second step is resistance itself, which may take many forms. A person may simply talk quietly with others about the problems they share. Another may simply slow down his or her work, or purposely sabotage government operations through poor performance.

1

The bravest individuals may publish their thoughts boldly and willingly pay the consequences.

The third step is conspiracy. When people recognize that resistance is not enough to solve the problems, they come to believe that they have no choice but to conspire with like-minded people and make plans for the removal of the government.

In occupied countries, resistance is against an invader, a foreign force in the home country. Acts of resistance are attempts to boost the morale of fellow citizens against the common enemy, and those who act are often heroes to their fellow countrymen. But resistance against one's own government might be called treason. Thus those who oppose the government of their own countrymen must belong to a secret group, a hidden resistance.

This point is critical. Resistance to a foreign invader provides certain advantages gained through the support and sympathy of fellow countrymen, whereas Germans in resistance to the Nazi regime experienced extreme isolation. F. L. Carsten, professor of Central European history at the University of London between 1961 and 1978, expresses it well: "While members of the French or Norwegian resistance always knew that they could find shelter and succor almost anywhere among their compatriots, the exact opposite applied to the German Opposition. Its members were increasingly thrown back upon their own resources, confined to minute circles of conspirators...."[1]

There were three primary sources for resistance to Hitler and his regime, which overlap in several ways. The first was political groups. Hitler gained power as a politician and was able to win out over a wide number of other interests who had hoped to gain control. Political opponents recognized that Hitler intended to use his power to strengthen the German military for the purpose of war.

Yet the military, too, was a source of resistance. Because the conspiracy would need troops to enforce the authority of a newly declared government, military involvement was absolutely necessary. Army generals were essential to the very idea of resistance and became leaders of the opposition.

The third source of resistance was individuals with moral objections to Hitler's tactics. Hitler consolidated his power by fanning the flames of German anti–Semitism to make the Jews a scapegoat for Germany's loss in the First World War as well as all of the problems that arose in the postwar period. Many who witnessed the treatment of European Jews during Hitler's reign were forced by conscience to join the resistance. A number of church leaders, in addition to military and political leaders, actively opposed Hitler.

Resistance was not without its price. Between 1933 and 1945, more than 500,000 non–Jewish German civilians were imprisoned for so-called "political crimes." These crimes included being a Communist, making statements critical of the government, or being perceived as a threat to the state. Among the German armed forces, where resistance was widespread, 24,559 members were sentenced to death for refusing to go along with the programs of the Nazi government.[2]

Those who joined in the anti–Hitler conspiracy were often driven by their conscience to do so; yet because conscience also dictated loyalty to country, the decision to conspire against the government involved a struggle between conflicting ideals. For members of the military, who had personally sworn an oath of loyalty to Hitler, the problem of joining the resistance was yet more complicated. To a German officer of that time, the oath was a matter of the utmost seriousness. It trapped many officers into blind obedience, perhaps offering an excuse for some to simply follow orders, while presenting a true moral dilemma for others.

The Nazi leadership revealed itself as so completely evil and ruthless that men and women of conscience were compelled to act — even though they realized that the consequences could be dire. The deep concerns that brought together large numbers of conspirators from many backgrounds and disciplines, and the events that prevented them from achieving their goals, make an amazing and tragic story.

The history of the German resistance culminates with the bomb plot of July 20, 1944. This attempt nearly succeeded, but its failure led to the arrests and executions of many of Germany's finest and bravest patriots. Hitler's uncanny sense of self-preservation was evident well before the final assassination attempt, even in how he dealt with nonviolent opposition, which many in the resistance favored.* He proved remarkably effective at isolating opposing voices and rendering them impotent, so that by the time his regime was firmly entrenched, removing him by nonviolent opposition was out of the question. By the time assassination became imperative, Hitler had surrounded himself with a tight net of security.

This is more than a story of people opposed to state policy. It is a chronicle of citizens who had to face the ugly truth that their country was enthralled by evil leaders. The members of the hidden resistance realized that historians would judge all German citizens of the time, including themselves, according to the position they took. They also recognized that, even with their efforts, some historians would be suspicious of their motives. Their very association with Hitler's government would condemn them as ambitious, self-serving, or opportunistic. At the same time, they knew that failing at least to try to remove Hitler from power would be seen as a form of acceptance and approval, a perception they could not allow.

Those who joined in the plots to remove Hitler were true heroes. They listened to their conscience, and the majority of them paid for their decision with their lives. In many cases, friends and family members who were not directly involved in the plots were punished as well. Being a part of the hidden resistance was not a decision that anyone took lightly. They knew the risks, but they also believed that their actions were necessary. This is the story of those actions and the people behind them.

---

*An important distinction has to be made between nonviolent opposition by means of passive resistance and opposition backed by force of arms. Passive resistance was used effectively by the German clergy, for example, to register protest against the regime. Those in the civilian and military opposition who favored the nonviolent approach supported Hitler's enforced arrest and the installation of a replacement government backed by the power of the army.

Chapter 1

ROOTS OF THE NATIONAL SOCIALIST PHILOSOPHY

The great masses of the people ... will more easily fall victims to a big lie than to a small one.

Adolf Hitler, *Mein Kampf*

The decade of the 1930s was one of extreme turmoil in Germany. It was a country deeply affected financially and socially by the loss of the First World War. Political chaos bordered on civil war, currency lost its value in the severe inflation, and burgeoning unemployment embittered the working person against the failure of the government in the years preceding Hitler. The turmoil enabled Hitler to rise to power, even though his party never held a majority and he was personally distrusted and disliked by many Germans. His was a compromise government, put together in an environment in which a number of factions competed with one another, preventing any one group from holding a singularly strong position with voters.

It was the very factionalism of German politics that provided Hitler with his opportunity. The diverse political groups trying to gain power were unable to unite to solve Germany's severe economic and social problems, and Hitler succeeded by creating a coalition. That coalition was based on the idea of anti–Semitism as a uniting theme. His views, however, were not new or original. Hitler focused the ideas of anti–Semitism that had been expressed over a long period of time and was able to build a power base on the back of those ideas.

An overview of the history of German anti–Semitism will help one to understand the basic Nazi political platform. The conflict between the Nazi regime as the official government of the nation on the one hand and the anti–Nazi movement on the other has to be perceived against the base of a society in which anti–Semitism was tolerated and had a long-standing history of its own. The Nazi goal of destroying the Jews in Europe was not developed in isolation. The policy developed by appealing to the social elements embracing anti–Semitism, by strengthening their position politically through the Nazi political machinery, and eventually by electing Nazi officials.

Adolf Hitler was able to rise to power on the wings of an idea — that Jews were separate from Germans and that social coexistence between these two groups was not possible. In fact, the Nazi philosophy rests on the dynamic that the existence of a Jewish "race" is a threat to the existence of the German "race." To effect this distinction, it was necessary for the Nazis to invent racial terms for groups that were not actually racially distinct.

In his 1925 book *Mein Kampf,* Hitler incorporated popular German folklore into the notion of an "Aryan" race. According to the dictionary, an Aryan is actually any descendant of prehistoric people who spoke an Indo-European language. A person of Iranian or Indian descent is Aryan in the linguistic sense. The legend, however, made Aryan a Nordic and racial concept, a pure Caucasian race of people whose racial purity needed to be preserved and protected from "lesser" races, most notably of Slavic and Jewish origin.

The Nazi* regime is closely associated with the policy of genocide of the Jews in Europe. They were chillingly effective in putting into practice the theory that one race is superior to another. This "Aryan" concept was taken quite seriously and became state policy in Germany in 1933, when it was made legal and legitimate by the force of law. Many Germans were shocked and disturbed by this legitimization, and their opposition was the core conflict that drew many people to the resistance. Members of the resistance held onto the moral perception that genocide was disgraceful and criminal, whether carried out unofficially or as part of a "legal" program by the ruling government.

The roots of German anti–Semitism can be traced back at least 400 years to Martin Luther, the German founder of the Protestant Reformation movement. He suggested the proper treatment for Jews: burn their synagogues, tear down their houses, take their books, forbid the rabbis to teach, and deny them access to public roads. Expulsion of Jews was a common occurrence in medieval times; Jews had been expelled from most European countries, and Luther's sentiments were typical of the time. But the ideas expressed by Luther were followed through with tragic effectiveness by Hitler.

Luther also voiced a theme that later became a key theme in Nazi rhetoric. He recommended that: "their usury be forbid them and all their gold and silver specie and treasure be seized and set aside. This being the cause: Whatever they have is … stolen and robbed from us by usury, for they have no other living."[1]

Luther was even more specific as to how Jews should be treated for their crimes: "We must drive them out like mad dogs, lest we partake in their abominable blasphemy and vices, deserving God's wrath and being damned along with them. I have done my part. Let every man look to doing his. My hands are clean."[2]

The idea that Jews brought wrath upon themselves was a recurring theme of the Nazis. Just as Luther claimed, "My hands are clean," a number of Nazis responsible for the atrocities against the Jews claimed that they were merely doing their duty as obedient Germans and that the Jews had brought destruction upon themselves. Many murderers

---

*"Nazi" is an abbreviation of the longer, official party name, Nationalsozialistische Deutsche Arbeiterpartei, or the National Socialist German Workers' Party, also abbreviated as the NSDAP.

of Jews viewed themselves as patriotic Germans, able to do the distasteful job of elimination and still remain "civilized."

This attitude among those charged with implementing the holocaust was widespread. Many expressed a sense of pride in their role of ridding the world of Jews. It was their mission and privilege, their patriotic duty. This view was expressed by one physician who worked in the concentration camps: "Of course, I am a doctor and I want to preserve life. And out of respect for human life, I would remove a gangrenous appendix from a diseased body. The Jew is the gangrenous appendix in the body of mankind."[3]

Such sentiments were not new. Many of the ideas expressed by the Nazis had their roots in the German nationalistic movement underway since the late eighteenth century. German philosopher Johann Gottlieb Fichte was known as the father of German nationalism. He had advised Germans, *"Charakter haben und Deutsche sein"* (Have character and be German). Fichte saw Jews as a threat to the German state, and helped solidify the idea of German nationalism as an ideal of racial purity. In 1793, Fichte had described Jews as a state within the state and warned that allowing their presence to continue would eventually destroy Germany. He said of the Jews that he would prefer "to cut off all their heads in one night, and to set new ones on their shoulders, which should contain not a single Jewish idea."[4]

The theories Fichte taught became especially popular to many Germans of the late nineteenth and early twentieth centuries. To them, the term *Volk* meant much more than just "the people." A derivative of the word, *völkisch,* literally means "ethnic." The idea of Volk implied a distinction that was racial in its nationalistic fervor and depth. The word encompassed the entire fiber of the German way of life: culture, territory, morality, attitudes, and the heritage (both historical and racial) of Germany. George Mosse defined Volk as being "fused to man's innermost nature ... the source of his creativity, his depth of feeling, his individuality, and his unity with other members of the Volk."[5]

Friedrich Ludwig Jahn, disciple of the poet and pamphleteer Ernst Moritz Arndt, described Volk as being essential to the survival of a nation. He, along with Arndt, is known for the development of the nationalism generally associated with the concept of Volk in German culture and especially as used with anti–Semitic belief. Jahn explains the importance of Volk: "A state without Volk is nothing, a soulless artifice; a Volk without a state is nothing, a bodiless airy phantom, like the Gypsies and the Jews. Only state and Volk together can form a Reich, and such a Reich cannot be preserved without Volkdom."[6]

In such circles of belief, the exclusionary nature of Volk takes on a mysticism of its own, to the point of religious fervor. Being German becomes the same thing as having a sense of Volk. Thus, being non–German (or, more to the point, non–Aryan) means that one cannot have Volk. In this view, Jews did not have any validity as people, nor did they have character as individuals.

Anti-Semitic racial theories were well documented by Bruno Bauer in 1842, when he published an article describing Jews as the ultimate capitalists. The following year, Bauer published a book, *Die Judenfrage* (The Jewish Question), in which he claimed that Jews had contributed nothing to civilization. This theme was central to the Nazi movement, which expanded upon it.

Another influential book of the time was *Die Naturgeschichte des deutschen Volkes als Grundlage einer deutschen Sozialpolitik* (The Natural History of the Volk as the Foundation of a Germanic Sociopolitical System). Written by Wilhelm Heinrich Riehl, historian and novelist, it praised the ideal of the pure German society and condemned modern commercial developments as corrupting influences.

Also writing on the subject of race was Christian Lassen, a professor at the University of Bonn who died in 1871. In his work, *Indische Altertumskunde* (Indian Antiquities), he claimed that the only Caucasian races to have created civilizations were Semites and Aryans. He also claimed that history established the Semitic inability to live cooperatively and harmoniously with others, a virtue Lassen attributed to the Aryan race.

Agreeing with this assessment was Wilhelm Marr, who coined the term *anti–Semitism*. Marr was an unsuccessful journalist who blamed his failure on the Jews. In 1873 he published a pamphlet entitled *Der Sieg des Judentum über das Germantum* (The Victory of Jewry over Germandom).

Like Marr, Karl Eugen Dühring also blamed his career failures on Jewish influence. A professor at the University of Berlin until he was forced to retire in 1877, Dühring described the Jews as a "counterrace" apart from the rest of mankind.

Publishing of pamphlets and public speaking to convey anti–Semitic ideas gave way to more organized movements in 1878, with the formation in Berlin of the first overtly anti–Semitic political party. Adolf Stöcker, a chaplain, founded the Christian Social Worker's Party. His theme: everything that was wrong in the world was a consequence of an international Jewish conspiracy.

Stöcker addressed a party meeting on September 19, 1879, on the topic, "What We Demand of Modern Jewry." He offered three anti–Semitic proposals: (a) taking a denominational census to compare the disproportion between Jewish capital and Christian labor, (b) placing a limitation on appointments of Jewish judges, based on the size of the Jewish population, and (c) removing Jewish teachers from elementary schools. Hitler later embraced these ideas and carried them out.

Paul de Lagarde took anti–Semitism yet further. He suggested that all Jewish elements should be permanently removed from German society. This was essential, he believed, if Christianity were to survive and regain its purity. He stated: "Every Jew is proof of the enfeeblement of our national life and of the worthlessness of what we call the Christian religion."[7]

With this background of political and social sentiments against the Jews and with the emergence of a strongly anti–Semitic form of nationalism, the momentum and social acceptability of anti–Semitism grew throughout the late nineteenth century. In 1879, Heinrich von Treitschke, a professor of history at the University of Berlin, began publishing a series of articles in the *Preussische Jahrbucher* on the subject of Jews in German society. He wrote: "Even in circles of the most highly educated, among men who would reject with disgust any ideas of ecclesiastical intolerance or national arrogance, there resounds as if from one mouth: '*Die Juden sind unser Unglück*'" (The Jews are our misfortune).[8]

By the following year, the movement had gained many converts. A petition submitted to Bismarck with 225,000 signatures stated that the Jews were the masters of the German worker, were determined to control property, and would destroy the nation. The petition, influenced by the demands made the year before by Stöcker, stated that steps were needed to prevent Germany from falling into economic slavery. Four steps were suggested: (a) restrictions on Jewish immigration, (b) removal of Jews from government positions, (c) reform in school programs to instill a "Christian" character, and (d) a census of the Jewish population.

The petition drive had been organized by three people: two schoolteachers, Ernst Henrici and Bernhard Förster, and an aristocrat, Max Liebermann von Sonnenberg. Hitler was later to institute racial laws based on the ideas expressed in the petition.

One of the petitioners, Ernst Henrici, later became a leading anti–Semitic politician. He founded Soziale Reichspartei (Reich* Social party). As a public speaker, Henrici was known for inciting violence at mass meetings. After his speeches, mobs ran into the streets, where they broke windows of Jewish-owned shops, beat Jews, and on at least one occasion, set fire to a synagogue. These extremes led to a forced disbanding of the party two years after it had been founded. But in its short history, Henrici's party foreshadowed the fate of the Jews under Hitler's regime approximately 50 years later.

Anti-Semitism did not die when Henrici's political party was disbanded. In 1881 the Deutsche Reformpartei was founded in Dresden and soon became an anti–Semitic propaganda group organized through a series of reform unions, or *Reformvereine*, throughout Germany. By 1885, fifty-two chapters had been opened, and by 1890 there were 136 such chapters.

As anti–Semitic political parties gained strength, their champions began winning elections. In 1887, Otto Böckel was elected to the Reichstag, the German parliament. He promoted the notion that Jewishness could not be diminished by intermarriage and that the Jew deserved only the rights of aliens. Böckel organized a new party three years later that was called the Antisemitische Volkspartei (Anti-Semitic People's Party). Its primary position was to favor "the repeal, by legal means, of Jewish emancipation."

In the election of 1892, Böckel's success was followed by the victory of Hermann Ahlwardt. A schoolteacher, Ahlwardt had two years earlier published a book, *Der Verzweiflungskampf der arischen Völker mit dem Judentum* (The Despairing Struggle of the Aryan People with Jewry). In the book, he described Jewry as an octopus with tentacles going into all sectors of German life. Ahlwardt later published two exceptionally offensive pamphlets, for which he was sentenced to prison. He had meanwhile, however, won election to the Reichstag in 1892 and accordingly was immune from having to serve time.

A political force called *Mittelstand* (middle class) was growing in Germany in the 1890s and supported candidates who expressed anti–Semitic ideas. Between 1887 and 1914, ninety Mittelstand deputies gained Reichstag seats. Most were small business owners, craftsmen, lower-level civil servants, teachers, and lawyers. These were the same social groups that later provided primary support to the Nazi party during its genesis and early growth period of the 1920s. No Mittelstand deputies were elected from labor, and only two were elected from the aristocracy.

The Mittelstand movement was represented by three primary groups, all founded in 1893. First was the Alldeutscher Verband (Pan-German League), which started in Austria. Members wanted to cultivate "German national values all over the world." The

---

*The German word Reich *means realm, empire, nation. References to the Nazi regime as the "Third Reich" were Hitler's invention, the "Reich that would last one thousand years." The First Reich refers to the Holy Roman Empire, and the Second Reich is the German Empire from the reign of Kaiser Wilhelm I in 1871 through the abdication of Wilhelm II in 1918.*

league became overtly anti–Semitic under the leadership of Georg von Schönerer. Membership totaled 20,000, and Jews were not allowed to join. Schönerer stated that "the removal of Jewish influence from all sectors of public life is indispensable."

To Schönerer, it would not be enough for Jews to abandon their beliefs and way of life. In the past, the option of conversion to Christianity had provided a means of escape from discrimination for Jews in German society. But Schönerer asserted there could be no conversion for the Jew. He proclaimed: *Aus der Rasse kann man nicht austreten* (One cannot resign from one's race).

The Deutschnationaler Handlungsgehilfenverband (National Germanic League of Clerks), the second of three Mittelstand groups, was founded in Hamburg. By 1913 it claimed 150,000 members. The third quasi-political Mittelstand organization, and the most influential, was the Bund der Landwirte (Agrarian League). By 1890 its membership had risen to 250,000. The organization stated that its primary mission was to be "an opponent of Jewry, which has become altogether too mighty in our country and has acquired a decisive say in the press, in trade, and on the exchanges."

The momentum of anti–Semitism was picking up toward the turn of the century. The movement was bolstered by the work of Ernst Haeckel, a biologist, philosopher, and popular writer of the day as well as the leading German Social Darwinist. He wrote in 1900: "Thousands of good and beautiful and admirable species of animals and plants have perished ... because they had to make room for other and stronger species, and the victors in this struggle for life were not always the nobler or morally more perfect forms. Precisely the same applies to the history of nations."[9]

Anti-Semitic politicians at the turn of the century seem to have been more willing than ever to express a desire for drastic measures. Jews were increasingly described as nonhuman, alien, not deserving of life, and clearly not deserving of the treatment a native German might receive. Houston Stewart Chamberlain, an Englishman who died in 1927, adopted the anti–Semitic view and became one of the leading heroes of the Nazi movement. He wrote in 1901: "The entrance of the Jew into European history ... meant the entrance of an alien element — alien to that which Europe had already achieved, alien to all it was still destined to achieve."[10]

Another writer, Heinrich Class, published in 1912 a widely read anti–Semitic book, *Wenn Ich der Kaiser Wär* (If I Were Kaiser), which went through five editions before the outbreak of the First World War. Anti-Semitism has always been a cyclical phenomenon in Germany. It was rampant at the start of the twentieth century, as witnessed by the popularity of books such as that written by Class. The mood of anti–Semitism diminished as the First World War approached, but it found fresh life when the war began to go badly for Germany. The combination of military setbacks and severe food shortages led to the anti–Semitic forces blaming the Jews for the misfortunes the nation suffered.

By 1920 anti–Semitism was again popular. That year the *Protocols of the Elders of Zion,* a book originally intended to bolster anti–Jewish sentiment in Russia and to provide an excuse for pogroms there, was published in a German translation. It sold 120,000 copies by the end of the year. A common slogan of the day was *Deutschland erwachen, Jude verrecken* (Germany awaken, Jews perish).

The decade of the 1920s was significant for anti–Semitic literature. In 1925, Hitler's *Mein Kampf* (My Struggle) was first published; it was destined to become the political landmark book of the Nazi movement. And in 1930 the ideological tome *The Myth of the 20th Century,* by Alfred Rosenberg, was published. Rosenberg was a pseudo-philosopher and one of Hitler's earliest mentors.

Not only was anti–Semitic literature widely published, elements in the scientific community became interested in the concept of racial purity. By 1923 such concepts had caught the interest of Fritz Lenz, a physician and geneticist who criticized the lack of laws designed to protect racial purity. He lauded legislation enacted in the United States that prohibited people with epilepsy or mental retardation from marrying and, in some states, banned interracial marriage. Lenz advocated sterilization and was later to become a leading proponent in the development of Nazi laws protecting "racial hygiene."

The reasoning Lenz expressed, founded in the theory of eugenics, was that the state has the right, if not the outright responsibility, to decide who should be allowed to procreate. The Nazis embraced this argument to support their policy of genocide for the good of the Aryan race.

The expression of theoretical laws to protect racial hygiene advanced under Nazi rule to the actual extermination of millions. The gradual evolution of the genocidal policy was based on this "scientific" eugenic presumption and progressed over a period of years in five sequential steps: (a) coercive sterilization of the mentally ill, the retarded, and other "undesirable" people, (b) the "mercy killing" of crippled or deformed children in hospitals, (c) the "mercy killing" of impaired adults, the mentally ill, and the aged in centers especially designed for the purpose and equipped with carbon monoxide gas, (d) killing by various methods of so-called "impaired" adult prisoners in labor, concentration, and extermination camps, and finally, (e) mass killings in extermination camps.[11]

The very idea of anti–Semitism, expressed as an acceptable social force, is alien to many people today. Racial prejudice in a democratic society may be widespread and even tolerated, but it is viewed as an invisible force. Even when it was practiced openly in the United States, its most extreme proponents wore hoods to hide their identities. The German tolerance of Nazi anti–Semitism developed not suddenly, but as a culmination of decades of justification for those beliefs. Author Richard Grunberger provides an excellent explanation of anti–Semitism and Nazism:

> Without anti-semitism, Nazism would have been inconceivable, both as an ideology and as a catalyst of the emotions. As for German society only two of its many sub-groups, the cultivated liberal minority among the bourgeoisie, and the politically educated segment of the working class, were relatively immune to anti-semitism. Ranged in the opposite camp were the partly dispossessed military and land-owning élite, the educated and property-owning bourgeoisie, disoriented by defeat and social change, and the huge, economically vulnerable petit bourgeoisie of shopkeepers, craftsmen, farmers and white-collar employees, whose backward-looking anti-capitalist yearning predisposed them towards the "socialism of fools," as August Bebel had described anti-semitism.[12]

Grunberger explains further that the outbreak of the Second World War did not significantly impact the German attitude toward the Jews: "The stress of war partly accounted for public indifference to Jewish sufferings, but basically the holocaust was not a real event to most Germans, not because it occurred in wartime and under conditions of secrecy, but because Jews were astronomically remote and not real people."[13]

The disintegration of Germany at the close of World War I helped accelerate the mood of anti–Semitism. A large part of the political problem grew from the way in which Germany was treated in peace negotiations.

U.S. president Woodrow Wilson in October 1918 demanded the abdication of Kaiser Wilhelm II as one condition of signing the armistice. Wilson communicated through his emissary, Colonel Edward House, the United States representative to the Allied Supreme War Council. House, in this powerful position, had great influence in negotiating with the political and military leadership in Germany.

President Wilson offered an armistice on the principles of his famous Fourteen Points, first expressed in a speech to Congress on January 8, 1918. While this plan was most often associated with the last of the points, a call for the formation of a League of Nations,* the Fourteen Points had other specific features as well. These included the repudiation of secret treaties, establishing absolute freedom of the seas for all nations, and the declaration that vanquished nations should not be punished through the "loss of populations."†

When Wilson communicated to Germany through Colonel House that he wanted an armistice based on the principles of his Fourteen Points, the response was predictable. General Erich Ludendorff, head of the German High Command, considered Wilson's offer to be an assurance that Germany would be granted peace while also being allowed to maintain its territorial integrity and even its military power. When, on October 4, 1918, Chancellor Prince Max of Baden opened negotiations for an armistice, German leadership believed that Wilson had made assurances.

Then on November 5, Wilson qualified his offer. The peace terms were still to be based on the Fourteen Points, but with two exceptions. First, the Allied powers expected to be compensated for war damages through reparations. And second, Great Britain insisted on reserving its right to control of the seas.

What Wilson failed to communicate to the German leaders was that Colonel House had attended a meeting on October 29 with Georges Clemenceau and David Lloyd George, the leaders of France and England. At that meeting, they expressed to Colonel House their reservations concerning Wilson's assurances to the Germans. Thus, armistice negotiations were entered by Germany on the presumption of guarantees which, in truth, had been secretly withdrawn.

Negotiations for the treaty took place at Versailles, the palace of the French kings, in the Hall of Mirrors. It was, ironically, the very spot where the birth of the German

---

*Wilson represented the United States in proposing formation of the League of Nations. The United States never joined the League, however, as Congress did not ratify the agreement. The League, never effective as a world peacekeeping organization, had no effect on German policy between the wars.

†The reference to populations implied agreement to not reduce Germany's territories and to continue recognition of Germany's colonial claims.

Empire had been proclaimed in 1871. Hostilities had ceased, and the business at hand was to formalize the peace — on terms dictated by the victorious powers. The onerous restrictions on Germany contained within the Versailles Treaty were to become a rallying point for the entire German nation.

The most stinging clause in the peace treaty, and the most controversial, was number 231, the War Guilt Clause. It read: "The Allied and Associated Governments affirm and Germany accepts the responsibility of Germany and her allies for causing all the loss and damage to which the Allied and Associated Governments and their nationals have been subjected as a consequence of the war imposed upon them by the aggression of Germany and her allies."[14]

The War Guilt Clause set up a justification for charging Germany reparations for the costs of the First World War. Because Germany was not allowed to participate in the peace discussions, however, it had no way to protest either the clause or the amount of reparations it would have to pay. Over the years between the two wars, the issue of *Kriegsschuldfrage* (the war guilt question) became one of endless debate, not only within Germany but throughout Europe. For Hitler, it became one of the major political rallying points of his career. He promised to rectify what he called the *Versailler Diktat* (dictate of Versailles) and punish those responsible for creating it. This is one of the foundations of the Second World War.

Even before the infamous Versailles Treaty was signed, however, conditions in Germany had deteriorated to serious levels. When the kaiser abdicated on November 9, 1918, as demanded by President Wilson, chaos overtook the German government. In Berlin, which was at a standstill because of a general strike, civil unrest and discontent prevailed, and the Communists tried to establish a new government. Many Germans, having witnessed the consequences of Communism in Russia, found these developments alarming.

In December 1918, the First Soviet Congress of Germany met in Berlin and made demands on the government. These demands included dismissal of General Paul von Hindenburg as army commander, abolition of the regular army, and the creation of a civil guard under control of the Soviet Congress, operating through a Council of People's Representatives.

On December 23, 1918, an armed group calling themselves the Sparticists attempted to seize power and proclaim a socialist republic. They broke into the Chancellery and could not be dislodged by regular army troops. They were led by Rosa Luxemburg and Karl Liebknecht. They and their followers had virtually taken over not only the streets, but essential services as well — newspapers, telegraph offices, government printing offices, and railway stations.

To combat these conditions of virtual civil war, the *Freikorps* — political opponents of the Sparticists — organized to fight. Its membership was dedicated to saving Germany from Communism and other threats. An urgent call to arms by the military in newspapers and on billboards brought out hundreds of young men, mostly from the middle classes. Counteraction by the Freikorps prevented Germany from becoming a Communist country in 1919.

In the week of January 10 through January 17, 1919, referred to as "Bloody Week," the Freikorps destroyed the Sparticist threat. Sparticist leaders Luxemburg and Liebknecht were captured and murdered. But conditions in Berlin were still not considered safe by

January 19, when elections were held for the National Assembly. It was so dangerous in Berlin that the newly elected Reichstag deputies considered meeting in the capital too risky.

The National Assembly met not in the capital, but 150 miles to the southwest, in Weimar, away from the continuing threat of riots and street fighting. By February 11, a new government had formed, the so-called Weimar Republic. The constitution was passed July 31, 1919, and was ratified by President Hindenburg on August 31. A key clause in the new constitution was later to be used by Hitler in seizing total control: Article 48 gave the president dictatorial powers during an emergency.

No one party or political point of view won a majority in the new government, and the compromise government that was put together pleased no one. Of a total 421 seats, the Social Democrats won 185; middle-class parties won 166; conservatives, 44; the right-wing, 19; and all others, 7.

The new constitution granted Jews complete equality in society, a feature that caused many Nazis to refer to the government over the following 12 years as a "Jew Republic." In spite of the Weimar social guarantees, a recurring theme emerged more strongly than ever in German public sentiment: the Jews were responsible for Germany's defeat in the war and equally responsible for the punitive Versailles Treaty. Within a short time, it was publicly acceptable to tout the line of Jewish responsibility for Germany's postwar problems and economic conditions.

The creation of a new republic did not end Germany's problems. The German people concluded the First World War believing that they were entitled to peace and that they had been assured of peace. The peace conference included representatives from 27 separate nations, but Germany was excluded from the conference. The Allied Supreme War Council, which had directed the war, now became the "Supreme Council," appointing itself to draft the peace agreement. The Council's membership included representatives of the five victorious nations: Great Britain, France, the United States, Italy, and Japan. The five delegation leaders, plus foreign ministers from each nation, constituted what came to be known as the Council of Ten.

The scope of problems to be addressed at the peace conference was enormous. In addition to specific economic and military matters, the attendees undertook the task of redrawing national boundaries and had to deal with an array of technical issues. At least 52 commissions were created to deal with the many aspects of peace. By May 1919, the terms of the German treaty were agreed upon, and only then were German delegates invited.

The German delegation, upon reviewing the terms presented to it, registered its protest, but to no avail. Germany was given a short time limit to sign and no room to negotiate. When the terms of the proposed agreement were published in Germany on May 7, 1919, mass demonstrations broke out along with demands that Germany not sign. Treaty terms included disbanding the Austria-Hungary empire, disposal of all of Germany's colonies, a division of the state of Prussia by creating a Polish corridor, and punitive reparations.* Germany's armed forces were also limited to no more than 100,000,

*The question of reparations was not set at Versailles. In July 1920, at the Spa Conference, the Allies agreed to divide reparations among themselves as follows: France would receive 52 percent of the total; Britain, 22 percent; Italy, 10 percent; the remainder going to other Allied powers. In 1921 the Reparation Commission set total reparations at 150 billion gold marks.[15]

and they were not allowed any planes or tanks. The navy would not be allowed to build any ships exceeding 10,000 tons. Even though the proposed terms were unpopular with the German nation, its leaders had no choice, and the treaty was signed on June 28, 1919.

Hitler was to point constantly to the Treaty of Versailles as a "stab in the back" of Germany. There was an element of truth in this accusation; the Allied powers made promises and then failed to keep them. It is also important to acknowledge, however, that Germany had, indeed, lost the war militarily. The German forces were not able to continue in the battlefield, nor to break the blockade imposed by their enemies. So the "stab in the back" was a diplomatic problem and not, as Hitler was to claim, a ruse that tricked Germany into surrender.

The Versailles Treaty was extremely punitive, and every German knew it. Hitler's appeal lay largely in this fact, and he used it effectively. Widespread bitterness over the punitive treaty only added to the political and social turmoil in Germany. Even after the Sparticists had been quelled, outbreaks of violence continued in the streets of German cities, notably in Berlin. Numerous factions clashed for control. Anti-Semitism became a focus for the right wing, and even the unsettled, unhappy people of the middle classes, longing for pride and national identity, were increasingly attracted to the Nazi party line. Harold Laswell observed at the time:

> Insofar as Hitlerism is a desperation reaction of the lower middle classes, it continues a movement which began during the closing years of the nineteenth century.... The psychological impoverishment of the lower middle class precipitated emotional insecurities within the personalities of its members, thus fertilizing the ground for the various movements of mass protest through which the middle classes might revenge themselves.[16]

This trend continued for the next decade, in which the Nazi voting trends gradually broadened to include a wide segment of the German voting public. In 1923 the Nazis won 800,000 votes. In 1930 that number rose to 6.5 million. And in 1932, out of a total of 45 million voters, 14 million chose Nazi deputies.[17]

The Nazi rise to power was not sudden, nor did the deputies of that party ever represent a majority. They were, however, able to accumulate blocks of power influential enough that a government was forced to reckon with them. This occurred through coalition, compromise, and eventually, capitulation of their opponents. The percentage of the total votes won by the Nazis in the five years ending with Hitler's becoming chancellor reveal the dramatic changes. In 1928 the Nazis won 2.6 percent of the total; in 1930, 18.3 percent; in July of 1932, 37.3 percent; in November of 1932, 33.1 percent; and in 1933, 43.9 percent.[18]

In 1919, it seemed a very real threat that Germany might become a Communist-controlled nation; indeed, it very nearly did happen. The Nazi movement and its supporters confronted Communist groups in endless street brawls, eventually gaining the upper hand. To Hitler, the need for control existed on two levels. First, he would have to take control of the streets, recognizing that it is better to disrupt the opposition's rallies with force, than to have the opposition doing the same. Second, he would need to take legitimate control of the government. Gaining control of the streets while also becoming a recognized legitimate political authority were the essential ingredients of Hitler's rise to power. Only by achieving both could Hitler ever hope to gain the support of the military, which was essential to his longer-term intentions.

The severe unemployment level — about 40 percent — in Germany of the early 1930 depression years was a golden opportunity for Hitler. In January of 1928, the registered unemployment total in Germany was 1.862 million. The true picture was far worse, since so many unregistered unemployed were not included in the official statistics. By January of 1932, the registered unemployment figure had risen to 6.042 million.[19]

The conditions of chaos and unemployment, in which about four in ten people in the German workforce were unemployed, contributed to Hitler's appeal and rise to power. He deflected power from the Communist political interests by scapegoating the Jews. He was also able to direct the energies of his supporters, to make it seem plausible that somehow the Jews had "stabbed the country in the back" and were now making a profit from German misery. (How German unemployment was profitable to anyone was never explained.) This theme, which was hammered into the minds of the people again and again, became seemingly less ludicrous and more acceptable over time. Ultimately it became an unchallenged and universally known truth in the minds of the people.

The appeal of the Nazi movement grew from several social and political issues. Most obvious to the historian is wide acceptance of anti–Semitism and the scapegoating of the Jews. It is easy to see how anti–Semitic sentiment progressed to action of law between 1933 and 1945, and civil rights eroded away in the name of the law itself. The legitimization of anti–Semitism did lead to the loss of millions of lives, the near-total destruction of European Jewish culture and society, and the emergence of a German resistance based on revulsion at what was being done.

It was through the legal system that Hitler first put his campaign against the Jews into effect. He became chancellor of Germany on January 30, 1933. Within six months, the first sterilization law was enacted. Wilhelm Frick, minister of the interior, introduced the law on June 22 and warned at that time that Germany was under threat of *Volkstod* (death of the people), making the new law necessary. This law is significant because it gave the government the legal right to medical control over the decision as to what constituted *lebensunwertes Leben* (life unworthy of life).[20]

The eventual genocidal policies grew from the basis established in law, and it is of historical interest to note that the first of these laws concerned a medical issue: the governmental right to determine whether or not a person or a class of people should be prevented from procreating. Applied to the case of congenital defect, the law makes a certain biological sense; but as the history of the Nazi regime proves, allowing a government such power leads to abuses, potentially on a large scale. From this early law, a series of additional laws were developed, leading to just that: genocidal policies on a large scale.

Prominent in the early sterilization program was Ernst Rüdin, a psychiatrist with an international reputation. He is credited with much of the claim to legitimization of the Nazi racial policies. He praised the first sterilization law of 1933 and later laws as valuable and important for "preventing the further penetration of the German gene pool by Jewish blood."[21]

A number of laws passed in 1933 strengthened the Nazi government's rights to solidify its position. First was the Enabling Act, passed on March 23, 1933. This law gave the government the right to pass future laws without Reichstag approval. The effect of this law was to give virtual total control to Hitler and at the same time to nullify the democratic rights as well as any checks and balances of the Reichstag, the German parliament.

Eight days after the Enabling Act was passed, Hitler dissolved the legislatures of all German states, with the exception of Prussia. He directed that Communist-held seats were not to be filled. Yet another law was passed April 7, appointing *Reichsstatthälter* (Reich governors) in all states. The new governors were all Nazis, and they were given sweeping powers to appoint or remove judges and other officials. The appointment of these governors, with their new powers, gave weight and meaning to the Enabling Act.

Also on April 7, the Law for the Restoration of the Professional Civil Service passed, which made provisions for dismissal of non–Aryan civil servants. Just prior to this, on April 4, President Hindenburg registered a protest with Hitler concerning the treatment of Jewish war veterans in anticipation of this new bill:

> The President   Berlin, April 4, 1933
> Chancellor Adolf Hitler, Berlin
> Dear Mr. Chancellor:
>
> In recent days, a number of cases were reported to me in which judges, lawyers, and justice officials who are wounded war veterans, and whose conduct of office has been flawless, were forcibly retired and are to be dismissed because of their Jewish descent....
>
> This sort of treatment of Jewish officials, wounded in the war, is quite intolerable. I am convinced, Mr. Chancellor, that you will share this human feeling with me.... If they were worthy of fighting and bleeding for Germany, they must be considered worthy of continuing to serve the fatherland in their professions....
>
> s. von Hindenburg

> The Chancellor   Berlin, April 5, 1933
> Dear Mr. President:
>
> There are two reasons for the defense of the German people against the inundation of certain professions by the Jews.
>
> The first is the glaring wrong created by the incredible discrimination against the German element that supports the state. For there are a whole number of intellectual professions today — medicine and the law for instance — where ... the Jews hold up to 80 per cent and more of all positions.... The second is the great shock to the authority of the state which has been caused by the fact that an entirely alien body ... is pushing its way into government positions....
>
> I have already been discussing the preparation of a law with minister of the interior Frick which would remove the solution of these questions from individual arbitrariness and subject them to general applicable legislation. And in these discussions, I directed the minister of the interior's attention to those cases where you ... would like to see exceptions made....

Work on the law in question will proceed as quickly as possible, and I am convinced that this matter, too, will then find its best possible solution....

s. Adolf Hitler[22]

The law under discussion passed two days later, the same day as another that was entitled Law Regarding Admission to the Bar. This law removed the right of Jews to practice law in Germany. This was followed quickly on April 11 by a law defining "non–Aryan" status, which required proof of genealogy as a prerequisite for obtaining a civil service job.

On April 25, the Law Against the Overcrowding of German Schools and Institutions of Higher Learning was placed on the books. This law limited non–Aryan school attendance to no more than 1.5 percent of the total.

Hitler had a free hand in the sense that he didn't need Reichstag approval. The legislative branch of government had ceded its powers to Adolf Hitler. Now the only political threat might come in the form of opposition parties. This problem was eliminated on July 14, 1933, with enactment of the Law Against the New Formation of Parties. It stated in part, "The sole political party existing in Germany is the National Socialist German Workers' Party." Anyone attempting to form an opposing party could be punished by up to three years' hard labor or more "unless other regulations provide for heavier punishment."[23]

As each of these laws was placed in effect, a systematic exclusion of Jews from mainstream society was achieved. This set the country on the path to the actual removal of Jews from society through expulsion and, finally, relocation. Throughout this period, many Germans began to recognize that the removal of Jewish civil rights was a destructive and immoral process, but Hitler had convinced the Reichstag that the times demanded a quickening of the political process. So great was the "danger" that there was not time for political debate. Tragically, a majority of the Reichstag deputies agreed.

It was important for Hitler to proceed through the power of law. This is not to say that he or his fellow Nazis had any respect for civil rights or liberties or for the law itself. He realized, however, that he needed a broad base of support — from industrialists, the military, and the middle classes of the country. Once there were laws on the books, it was easier for Hitler to develop his political and military coalition.

The scope of laws passed in 1933 was one symptom of a massive social change being engineered by Hitler. In historical context, we can see where these trends led. At the time, however, the changes were widely viewed, particularly by the non–Jewish segments of the German population, as positive and necessary. One term promoted by the Nazis to describe the social changes of 1933 was *Volkwerdung,* which means "a people becoming itself."

Hitler was aware of international reaction to his Volkwerdung policies. The German government had put a great effort into building and maintaining goodwill through diplomatic channels. The emissaries were given the mission of explaining to foreign governments the need for anti–Jewish legislation. This diplomatic effort was increased by the government after extremely negative reaction overseas to the infamous Nürnberg (Nuremberg) Laws of 1935.

The popular President Hindenburg died in 1934, and Hitler no longer had to worry about internal opposition to his plans. As long as Hindenburg was alive, Hitler was forced to move slowly, so as not to anger the respected, aged president. Hindenburg held the power of demanding the resignation of a chancellor, and Hitler had to move slowly and cautiously to avoid jeopardizing his position. After Hindenburg's death, however, anti–Jewish legislation and other measures accelerated.

At a Nazi party congress rally held in Nuremberg (in German: Nürnberg) on September 15, 1935, a series of new and drastic laws set a precedent in German legal history. Certain acts or even the status of individuals and families were declared illegal, in many cases retroactively. Thus Hitler's legal minds set a precedent by determining that the Jewish "problem," specifically, had to be dealt with by a significant change in the structure of the law itself.

The first of two laws passed at the Nuremberg rally was the Reich Citizenship Law. This law declared that only individuals of "German or kindred blood" could be citizens. An additional decree of November 14, 1935, dealt with the problem of marriages between Jews and non–Jews, couples described as *Mischlinge* (hybrids). It would eventually become illegal to have such a marriage, regardless of when it was entered.

The second was the Law for the Protection of German Blood and German Honor. Provisions of this law forbade marriages and sexual relations between Jews and "Germans or kindred blood." Furthermore, Jews were no longer allowed to hire German citizens under age 45 as domestic help or to display the German flag.

On October 18, 1935, an ordinance arose from the Nuremberg laws that regulated sterilization and the issuance of marriage licenses. The regime set up a system for creating a national card index to track people with specific hereditary traits. Special research institutes for the study of hereditary biology and "racial hygiene" were established at several universities. Their purpose was to collect genetic information over a period of several generations. The physician would become a genetic counselor and policeman and "protector of the family that is free from hereditary defects."[24]

In 1938 several new laws were enacted which further restricted the rights of Jews. On March 26, the Decree Regarding the Reporting of Jewish Property mandated that all Jews were to assess and report the value of their property no later than June 30. This law aided the Nazis in the near future, when the government expropriated Jewish-owned property.

On August 17 the Second Decree for the Implementation of the Law Regarding Changes of Family Names and Given Names was implemented. (The First Decree had been issued January 5, 1938, and had established governmental authority over the changing of names.) Provisions of the latest decree included the following: Jews were forbidden to take Aryan names; all Jewish men were required to add the name Israel to their name, and all Jewish women were required to add the name Sarah to their name.

This law was designed to identify the large number of people of Jewish descent who had taken Christian-sounding names in order to pass in German society without the restrictions and problems that had become widespread. It also was aimed at those who baptized their children in Christian churches, at the time giving them Christian names for the same purpose.

The round of 1938 legislation gave Hitler and the Nazi government virtual control over the Jewish community. Jewish civil rights were almost totally extinguished. Starting in that year, Jews were arrested without due process, without even the commission of a crime. Their property could be seized, their children kept out of school, and their rights to operate businesses restricted and finally taken away.

On September 1, 1941, the Police Decree Concerning the Marking of Jews represented a final step in the complete removal of Jewish civil rights. This decree specified that Jews over the age of six were no longer allowed in public without displaying a yellow Star of David, worn visibly with the word "Jew" in black letters. Furthermore, Jews were forbidden to leave their neighborhoods without carrying written permission to do so from the local police. They also were not allowed to wear medals, decorations, or insignia.[25]

The culmination of Nazi efforts to destroy the Jews in Europe was spelled out at the Wannsee Conference of January 20, 1942. Reinhard Heydrich, head of the SS Intelligence Service, reported to several top-ranked ministers of the government his appointment of a "Plenipotentiary for the Preparation of the Final Solution of the European Jewish Question." He quite accurately described the process that had been taking place since 1933. It had begun, he stated, by expelling Jews "from various spheres of life of the German people." Following that was expulsion of Jews "from the living space of the German people." Finally, the step he was announcing at the conference was the "evacuation of the Jews to the East."[26]

Thus was the stage set for the destruction of European Jewry. It was more than theory. By 1942 the Nazis had already had direct experience in putting their plans into practice. The most unimaginable and large-scale acts of destruction were now occurring within the law as the law existed in Germany. The entire Nazi movement was based on the conflict between Aryan and Jew. The Nazi regime put tremendous effort into legalizing the removal of civil rights for the Jews and, eventually, into their removal and murder.

In embarking on this course, Hitler had made enemies. Motives varied for opposing the Nazis, but everyone in the resistance movement agreed without hesitation that the policies against Jews and other civilians were reprehensible, illegal, and immoral. Those who could not support the regime in good conscience could not simply go along with the policies and were likely to join or at least to support the hidden resistance.

Chapter 2

THE RISE TO POWER

It can be observed in many instances that persons who are not Nazis nevertheless defend Nazism against criticism because they feel that an attack on Nazism is an attack on Germany. The fear of isolation and the relative weakness of moral principles help any party to win the loyalty of a large sector of the population once that party has captured the power of the state.

Erich Fromm, *Escape from Freedom*

The 1920s was one of the most troubled decades in the history of Germany. The country was hit especially hard by high unemployment, and the spirit of nationalism smoldered under the indignation of Versailles. Germany was like a man who has not eaten anything for three days and is not especially discerning about what kind of food he receives, as long as he is fed. The German people in the 1920s were starving for leadership. They came out of the First World War spiritless, lacking direction, and wanting desperately to reestablish a belief in their own greatness.

Recognizing this, Hitler was able to gain the power he craved. From complete obscurity at the beginning of the decade, he ended it well on his way to becoming chancellor of the nation. A man whose party had never received a true mandate from the voters ended up with complete control.

By 1923, the Nazi party's membership was growing rapidly. But outside of Bavaria, Germany's southern state, and its capital Munich, the Nazi party was virtually unknown. In that year, Hitler came to believe that it might be possible to seize power in Germany, even though his party was small and obscure. He believed that he could lead a coalition of anti-government interests in Bavaria and wrest power from the government in Berlin. Hitler was no doubt influenced by Mussolini's march on Rome the year before, using a similar tactic of political deal making. As Mussolini had bluffed the government with a series of demands, so Hitler hoped to gain power quickly and without serious opposition.

In February 1923, four paramilitary groups in Bavaria called "patriotic leagues" joined with the Nazis and formed the Arbeitsgemeinschaft der Vaterländischen Kampfverbande (Working Union of the Fatherland Fighting Leagues). Hitler was declared the leader of this association. By September, Hitler consolidated yet more fighting power with

21

formation of the Deutscher Kampfbund (German Fighting Union), under the leadership of three individuals, of whom Hitler was one. The Union's declared purpose: to overthrow the government and do away with the Versailles Treaty.

At this early stage, Hitler was already cultivating the support of military leaders. At a rally in Nuremberg on September 2, 1923, from which the German Fighting Union was initiated, Hitler stood in the reviewing stand next to General Erich Ludendorff, one of the German heroes of the First World War. Ludendorff was a proponent of revolution and had supported a number of attempts at overthrow from the right. Hitler, knowing this, recognized the opportunity to align himself with the traditional German military, complete with a well-known sponsor.

In the turmoil of 1923, a number of uprisings placed the German government in serious jeopardy. The government depended upon the loyalty of General Hans von Seeckt, commander of the army. The army insisted on its independence from government control, however. When Germany's president, Friedrich Ebert, confronted the general by asking him whom the army would support in the event of revolution, Seeckt said, "The army, Mr. President, stands behind me."

Seeckt made it clear that the army wanted to retain its independence. Yet it did help the government by putting down a number of revolutions during this period. In late September 1923, a well-organized armed group called "Black *Reichswehr*" seized several forts east of Berlin. Seeckt used regular army troops to quell the threat. This was followed closely by threats of Communist takeovers in Saxony, Thuringia, Hamburg, and the Ruhr. In Bavaria, where the Nazi party operated, the state government was defiant of Berlin. Seeckt, sensing that the Bavarian government and Hitler, with his armed leagues, were a threat, issued a specific warning to them that any attempt at armed rebellion would be crushed by military force.

In 1923, in spite of warnings from Seeckt, it was apparent that anyone with the fire power and opportunity might very easily succeed in revolution. In this environment, Hitler decided to kidnap the triumvirate rulers of the state of Bavaria, Gustav von Kahr, General Otto von Lossow, and Colonel Hans von Seisser. This would be done in a dramatic moment, during a military parade scheduled for Germany's Memorial Day, Totengedenktag, November 4, 1923. Hitler's men would seize the three, and Hitler himself would jump onto the stand and proclaim the revolution. He would then call upon the Bavarian leaders, under threat of arms, to join him. This sort of drama appealed to Hitler, but on the day of the parade, the plot was abandoned upon discovery that a large number of well-armed police were on the scene.

A revised plan called for a march on the city of Munich, complete with armed announcement of the revolution. That was scheduled for November 11. This plan was also abandoned, however, when Hitler heard that Kahr (one of the three government leaders in Bavaria) was scheduled to deliver a speech at the Bürgerbräukeller, a large beer hall on the southern side of Munich, on November 8. The other two government leaders were scheduled to attend as well, providing Hitler an opportunity to take all three leaders at the same time.

Just before 9 P.M. on the evening of November 8, 1923, Hitler's storm troopers, the SA, or *Sturmabteilungen* (storm detachments, also known as the Brownshirts), surrounded the beer hall and Hitler entered the building. Jumping onto a table, he fired a pistol into the air. Kahr, who was delivering his speech, paused at the interruption. Hitler, with the help of a bodyguard, forced his way to the rostrum. Kahr stepped back as the pistol-waving Hitler took over, announcing:

> The national revolution has begun. This building is occupied by six-hundred heavily armed men. No one may leave the hall. Unless there is immediate quiet, I shall have a machine gun posted in the gallery. The Bavarian and Reich governments have been removed and a provisional national government formed. The barracks of the *Reichswehr* and police are occupied. The army and the police are marching on the city under the swastika banner.[1]

Hitler's bluff gained him the momentary confusion he sought. He ordered the three leaders to follow him to a private room, which they did. The three refused, however, to give in to Hitler's demands to support his revolution, even under threat of death. Regardless, Hitler ran back into the main hall and announced that the three leaders had agreed to join with him in a newly declared government.

Although Hitler had convinced those in attendance of the cooperation of the government's leaders, word came that fighting had broken out between storm troopers and regular army troops at the army engineers' barracks. As the beer hall meeting began to disperse, Hitler decided to investigate in person. This was an error fatal to the putsch, since no one remaining on the scene ensured that the "cooperating" government leaders stayed there. As soon as Hitler was gone, the three leaders escaped from the beer hall. By the time Hitler returned, they were gone and it was too late.

Meanwhile, Ernst Röhm, one of Hitler's lieutenants who was leading a contingent of Brownshirts, had occupied army headquarters at the War Ministry in Munich. Other strategic buildings were not occupied, however, and in a short time General von Seeckt was advised of the problem. He ordered the army to quell the revolution, and the War Ministry was surrounded by morning.

By now, the organization of the revolution had fallen apart completely. Hitler tried desperately to locate Kahr, Lossow, and Seisser, without success. He had always recognized that a successful revolution requires the support of the army, the police, and the politicians, and now he had none of these. Hitler had belatedly informed General Ludendorff of the putsch. Although angry at being told of it after the fact, he did lend his support and joined the rebels. But even Ludendorff's support of the plan didn't help at this point.

The general proposed to Hitler that the army and police would never fire on him because he was a war hero. He suggested that he and Hitler should march to the center of Munich and attempt a takeover. Hitler agreed. In the late morning of November 9, 1923, Hitler and Ludendorff led three thousand storm troopers from the beer hall to the center of Munich.

A detachment of police blocked a narrow street called Residenzstraße, through which Hitler and his group needed to pass. The Nazis tried to talk their way through, but it didn't work. No one is certain which side fired first, but gunfire was exchanged for about one minute. Sixteen Nazis and three policemen were killed, and scores were wounded on both sides.

Ludendorff alone did not fall to the pavement when the firing began. He marched forward through the cordon of police with his aide, Major Streck. No one followed, not even Hitler, who quickly escaped the scene. Witnesses later reported that Hitler was the first to flee, leaving his dead and wounded supporters behind. He escaped to the home of a supporter outside of Munich, where he was taken into custody by the police two days later.

Hitler was tried on a charge of treason. His trial began on February 26, 1924. He used the trial to gain a national reputation and to place guilt on the German political leaders for their lack of loyalty and nationalism. Sentences were announced on April 1, 1924. General Ludendorff, one of the ten people put on trial, was acquitted. The rest were found guilty of treason. Although the German constitution specified a prison term of life, Hitler was given only five years and he was released after serving only nine months.

The beer hall putsch made Hitler a national figure and, in the eyes of many Germans, a national hero. He had stood up against the weak and indecisive government, taken a stand for nationalism and against compliance with the Versailles Treaty. Although the putsch itself was an ill-planned, ill-executed effort, the Nazis enshrined the memories of those who lost their lives in the short volley of gunfire and transformed the brief battle into a rallying cry.

During his imprisonment, Hitler was treated in style and was given a private room in the fortress at Landsberg. He was allowed unlimited visitors during his stay and used his nine months to write his philosophy down in the form of a book, *Mein Kampf* (My Struggle).*

After his release from prison, Hitler had to rebuild his Nazi party. The party had been banned from most states in Germany at the same time that Hitler was found guilty of treason, and its assets had been seized by the government.

Upon release from prison, Hitler was faced with the task of putting the Nazi party back together. His short absence from the scene meant lost momentum (not to mention that the party itself was now illegal). Even displaying the swastika was against the law, and party membership fell to about 100. By February 1925, Hitler — now swearing to work within the system and the law from that point forward — was granted permission to resume publication of the Nazi paper, the *Völkischer Beobachter* (Popular Observer). The newspaper resumed publication on February 26.

Hitler rented the Bürgerbräukeller, scene of the putsch, and on February 27, 1925, held a meeting for the purpose of raising money and rebuilding his Nazi party. With many of the original leaders and supporters in exile or now disinterested altogether,

*Hitler wanted to entitle the book "Four and a Half Years of Struggle Against Lies, Stupidity and Cowardice." He was talked into the shorter and easier to market title by Max Amann, his publisher.

Hitler's new agenda included consolidation of all party power in his hands. He also intended to reestablish the party as a serious political organization.

More than 2,000 people attended (the hall had a capacity of 3,000). The response of the audience was so positive that the Bavarian government became concerned. The putsch, after all, was a recent memory. The government revoked Hitler's license to speak in public, and since he was still on parole, there was nothing he could do but comply. Hitler diverted his energies into articles, published in the newspaper which the government allowed to continue, and into the final stages of work on *Mein Kampf.* The book's first edition came out on July 18, 1925, and its 10,000 copies sold out by the end of the year.

One state where Hitler was not banned from public speaking was Thuringia. In July 1926, he held a mass meeting, the first of many Parteitage (Party Days), at Weimar. Hitler was attempting to build political momentum, but in the election of 1928, Nazi deputies received less than half the votes they had received four years earlier. Hitler's party held only 12 seats in the Reichstag. In comparison, the Communists held 54 out of a total of 491 seats. The Nazi party was too small to hold any political influence after the election of 1928. Always a primarily Bavarian party, the Nazis were not taken seriously outside of the southern regions. Membership in 1925 had been 27,000; by 1928 the party claimed 108,000 members. It is likely that these figures were exaggerated.[2]

During the late 1920s, Hitler took the steps necessary to organize his party into an effective political machine. He saw the necessity of gaining numbers of members and acquiring votes, but also keeping control and building momentum. The party was organized on two fronts, one to attack and criticize the government, the other to build internal power and control. The Hitlerjugend (Hitler Youth) was created to recruit young people into the party. Younger boys could join the Deutsches Jungfolk (German Youth) and girls were recruited into the Bund Deutscher Mädel (Union of German Girls). Even a woman's organization, the N. S. Frauenschaften (National Socialist Women's Group) was formed. Separate Nazi organizations were created for a variety of occupations, even for intellectuals and artists. The party moved away from a looseknit ideological group and gradually became a far-reaching society of its own.

The SA were also reorganized into bands for the purpose of protecting Nazi meetings and, of equal importance, to break up meetings of opposing forces and to terrorize attendees and speakers of those groups. Ernst Röhm, who had distinguished himself during the beer hall putsch by occupying the War Ministry, had broken ties with Hitler in 1925 and had left for La Paz, where he worked in 1930 as a military adviser to the Bolivian government. In October 1930, Hitler asked Röhm to return and head the SA. Röhm agreed on condition that he be given complete control regarding all internal SA matters. Hitler agreed, but his relationship with Röhm and the SA was a troubled one, and Röhm had an ongoing disagreement with Hitler concerning the SA and its role in the larger scheme of things. Röhm believed the SA should be incorporated into the army as a militia under his command. Hitler, though, always thought of the SA as a political force whose purpose should be to terrorize political opponents, break up meetings, and protect Nazis at their rallies.

Röhm was at this time also placed in control of the SS—*Schutzstaffel* (meaning, roughly, defense corps), an elite organization formed originally to serve as Hitler's

Adolf Hitler, although banned from speaking in public in most parts of Germany, rebuilt the Nazi party and was able to take command of the military in 1934 (Photo: National Archives).

personal bodyguard unit. Their uniform included a black shirt, an imitation of Mussolini's Black Shirts. The first SS leader had been a journalist named Berchtold, but he had been replaced by Erhard Heiden. Finally, in 1929, Hitler found a permanent SS leader in Heinrich Himmler, a soft-spoken chicken farmer who was to become one of the most feared and notorious of the Nazi leaders.

During this party building period, Hitler also put Paul Joseph Goebbels into a position of permanent power. Goebbels first met Hitler in 1922 and, upon hearing him speak, joined the Nazi party. A writer and gifted orator in his own right, Goebbels idolized Hitler completely. He was to become famous as minister of enlightenment and propaganda for the regime and was one of the few individuals to have Hitler's ear throughout the Nazi reign.

The third person involved in the organizational phase of the Nazi party was Hermann Göring, the most flamboyant of the Nazi leaders. He had gained a reputation as an ace flyer in the First World War and, as an early Nazi loyalist, had been one of those present at the beer hall putsch. At the famous minute of gunfire, Göring had taken a bullet in the leg. From 1923, following the beer hall putsch, until 1927, Göring had been in exile in Sweden, where he had worked for an aircraft company and had been cured of his

Ernst Röhm had ambitions of leading the SA as a special militia force in the army (Photo: National Archives).

addiction to drugs. Later, during World War II, Göring headed up the Luftwaffe (German air force) and was, along with Himmler and Goebbels, in the immediate circle of influence around Hitler.

Recruiting hundreds of thousands of devoted members and organizing them into controllable groups was an essential task for Hitler. He also needed, however, the right political climate and opportunity in order to put that organized party into the political mainstream. That climate arrived in the form of a severe depression.

The depression hit worldwide in 1929, and Germany was affected especially badly. There are a number of reasons for this, including the requirement that Germany pay punitive reparations under the Versailles Treaty. The country had been borrowing capital from other countries, especially from America, to keep its economy solvent. When the American stock market crashed in October 1929, the well of capital went dry. Germany was unable to export enough goods to pay for its own essential imports, and German industry was unable to continue operations and had to lay off thousands. Production between 1929 and 1932 was cut in half, and unemployment rose to exceed six million.

In May 1931, several large banks folded, including the Darmstädter und Nationalbank. This forced the government to close all banks temporarily.

The value of the German mark suffered as a result of the depression. The currency problem which became severe in 1929 had actually begun many years earlier, however. The German mark in November 1922 was valued at 7,000 to the dollar. Two months later in January 1923, it had tumbled to 50,000 to the dollar. The currency of Germany collapsed even further later the same year. By December, the mark was valued at 4,200,000 to the dollar.[3]

In late 1929, the depression made a bad situation worse. A worthless currency plus unrelentingly high unemployment enabled Hitler to point the finger of blame. The Versailles Treaty, by then a decade-old sore spot with all Germans, was to be brought up again and again by Hitler. The Jews, accused of engineering the "stab in the back" of the German nation, were to blame for all troubles, including the depression itself. And of course, the weakness and indecisiveness of the government, Hitler asserted, had played into the hands of the conspirators. Only he could change all of that.

As the weight of the economic crisis fell on Germany, political events worked to Hitler's advantage. The last Social Democrat chancellor of Germany, Hermann Mueller, resigned in March 1930 and was replaced by Heinrich Brüning, a leader of the Catholic Center party. Brüning asked President von Hindenburg to invoke article 48 of the constitution, granting the chancellor emergency powers. He wanted that power in order to put his financial program into effect quickly.

Members of the Reichstag objected to the idea of invoking emergency powers and demanded that the emergency decree be withdrawn. The impasse between the chancellor and the Reichstag — a pattern that became common in the next three years — led to the need for dissolving the Reichstag and calling for new elections.

On September 14, 1930, the new elections were held. Hitler had gone on the campaign, seeing his opportunity to increase the number of Nazi deputies in the government. He promised to abandon payments required under the Versailles Treaty, to ensure a job to every German, and to make Germany strong once again. His appeal to an impoverished nation on the soup line was strong indeed. The Nazis had previously held only 12 seats, but after these elections, they held 107. The change in popular vote was impressive as well. Four years before, Nazi deputies had received 810,000 votes; in 1930 they received 6,409,000. The Nazi party, previously the smallest in the nation, was now the second largest.[4]

For the business leaders of Germany and for the army, the surprise Nazi victory presented a dilemma. On the one hand, the power centers in German industry and the military found the Nazis to be vulgar and extremist; on the other hand, their rise in influence could not be ignored. Hitler clearly appealed to the spirit of nationalism in Germany, and of greatest political significance, he promised the German worker a brighter future. This, the German industrialists surely realized, meant that the Nazis were a force to be reckoned with, not only in 1930 but into the future as well.

By the middle of 1931, President Hindenburg began considering what should happen the following year when his seven-year term of office would end. Hindenburg, at the age of 84, had lost much of his mental alertness and was no longer the quick-minded hero of Tannenberg.*

On October 10, 1931, Hitler met with the president for the first time. As of this date, Hitler did not hold any political office (although Nazi deputies did and their loyalties were definitely to him). In fact, Hitler was not even a German citizen at that time. If he were to decide to run for public office, he would have to eventually file for citizenship.

Chancellor Brüning had ideas of his own. He wanted to restore the German monarchy as an alternative to the failures of the parliamentary government that had been in power since 1919. He proposed cancellation of the 1932 presidential election and extension of Hindenburg's term. This would require a two-thirds vote of the Reichstag. Brüning then proposed that the monarchy be declared, naming Hindenburg as regent. Brüning believed this plan was workable and would end the political threat of the Nazis.

Hindenburg was not interested in this plan. At this time, he declared that he did not intend to run for another term, but he was perplexed at the prospects of Hitler's rising power. He referred to Hitler as "the Bohemian corporal"† and vowed that he would never allow such a man to become chancellor. By the beginning of 1932, Chancellor Brüning still wanted to prolong Hindenburg's term of office and hoped the Nazi leader would agree.

Hitler was not in favor of the Brüning plan, however, even when Brüning offered to recommend Hitler to Hindenburg as his successor for the office of chancellor. Hitler did not respond directly to Brüning but went instead to Hindenburg with his answer. He declared that he thought Brüning's plan was probably unconstitutional, stating also that he would be willing to announce his support for Hindenburg's reelection if Hindenburg would publicly state his opposition to the Brüning plan.

Hindenburg would not agree to this proposal and instead indicated he would probably run for another term. Hitler now was faced with a difficult political question: should he himself run for president against the popular Hindenburg? Running and losing would almost certainly end his political prospects in the future, and if Hindenburg did not run again, Hitler's failure to enter the race might be seen as political weakness, a failure to take advantage of the party's momentum. And there was the further complication that Hitler was not a citizen of Germany.

During the months of January and February, 1932, Hitler struggled with this decision. Then on February 15, Hindenburg announced his own candidacy, and one week later Joseph Goebbels announced that Hitler, too, was a candidate for the top office. Two additional candidates assured that no one would be able to poll a clear majority. Theodor Düsterberg was the candidate of the Nationalist Party, and Ernst Thälmann ran on the Communist ticket.

Hitler became a citizen by arranging to have himself named as an attaché to the legation of the state of Braunschweig. This technicality made Hitler a citizen of Braunschweig

---

*Tannenberg was the site of a famous battle of 1914 in which Hindenburg and Ludendorff prevented an attempt by Russian forces to invade East Prussia.

†Hindenburg was confused in his reference to Hitler as "Bohemian." Hindenburg had spent time during his younger army days in Branau, an area of northern Bohemia quite different from Hitler's Austrian birthplace, Branau-am-Inn.

and thus a citizen of Germany as well. The candidate campaigned with gusto, using his well-organized party machinery to post one million boldly colored posters, eight million pamphlets, and twelve million copies of the party newspapers. For the first time in German history, a candidate made use of film and loudspeakers to get the word out.

The election took place on March 13, 1932. Hindenburg was barely short of the needed majority with 49.6 percent; Hitler was second with 30.1 percent. A second election was required, between Hindenburg, Hitler, and Thälmann, who had come in third. That election took place on April 10. Hindenburg polled 53 percent, and Hitler was second with 36.8 percent.[5]

While the constitutional process was underway, the Nazi SA was planning an armed overthrow of the German government. Immediately before the March 13 election, the 400,000 members of that organization were mobilized and placed strategically around Berlin. Röhm described this move as precautionary, although the police had seized documents showing that a takeover by force was in the plans.

On April 13, Hindenburg signed a decree to authorize suppression of the SA and SS. Röhm, reacting angrily, wanted to defy the order, but Hitler, recognizing that timing was essential to his plans, ordered that the decree was to be obeyed. There would be no armed rebellion and no resistance to the government at this point. Debate in the government over the decree helped create an environment of mistrust. When Chancellor Brüning suggested to the president that the government should take over several bankrupt Junker* estates in East Prussia and give the land to the peasants, Hindenburg was furious. Even though Brüning had been the president's staunchest ally in the recent political campaign, Hindenburg listened to his friends and political supporters, the aristocrats of Prussia, who referred to Brüning as an "agrarian Bolshevist."

Brüning's plan to distribute land to non–Junkers did not sit well with Hindenburg. On May 29, 1932, he summoned the chancellor and demanded his resignation. On May 30, the resignation was tendered. On the same day, Hitler met with Hindenburg, who asked for Hitler's support of a new government. Hitler promised that he would lend his support. On June 1, 1932, Hindenburg named Franz von Papen as new chancellor.

Papen was a relatively obscure 53-year-old politician, and his choice as chancellor surprised many. He had no backing as a politician; this was perhaps the very reason Hindenburg chose him. He instructed Papen to form a government above parties and politics. On June 4, Papen dissolved the Reichstag and called for new elections to be held July 31. Under pressure from the Nazis, Papen also agreed to lift the ban on the SA.

An unprecedented wave of violence and murder followed as the SA sought out Communist political meetings to break up. In the first three weeks of June, there were 461 pitched battles in the streets of Prussia, resulting in 82 deaths. Papen responded by invoking Article 48 of the constitution to give himself emergency powers. He banned all parades for the two weeks prior to the election, and on July 20, he declared himself Reich commissioner for Prussia, dissolving the existing Prussian government. At the same time, he declared martial law in Berlin.

The July 31 election, the third national election in less than six months, was a clear

---

*The Junkers were the nobility, or landed aristocracy, in Prussia. They are associated with extreme nationalism and German military traditions.

victory for the Nazi party. The Nazis won 230 seats in the Reichstag — not a majority, but the largest block in a house with 608 members. Hitler's deputies had won 37 percent of the popular vote, their best showing yet. The outcome put Hitler in a position, for the first time, of being able to make demands on the government.

Hitler's demands included appointment of himself as chancellor and enactment of a new enabling act giving him broad powers to rule by decree. He arrogantly warned that if the Reichstag did not grant him this power, it would be disbanded and the deputies sent home.

On August 13, Chancellor von Papen rejected Hitler's demands, stating that the most he could offer was the position of vice chancellor. Hitler refused to accept that post, vowing to take up the discussion with Hindenburg directly. The president, upon hearing that Hitler was making these demands, summoned him and responded that, in the volatile and tense times they faced, it would not be wise to transfer governmental power to a new party, especially one which had not won a majority and was known to be intolerant and undisciplined. He recommended that Hitler work with the other political powers, promising to listen to Hitler as a representative of a political coalition.

The meeting ended without any conclusive agreement, as Hitler refused to compromise. Hindenburg was not prepared to turn full control of the state over to Hitler, and Hitler would accept nothing less.

Furious at being rejected, Hitler met with his Nazi leaders to decide what to do next. He rejected a plan for an armed takeover by the SA, although that group had again mobilized and placed itself around Berlin. Reluctantly, Hitler decided the best course was political, and he took steps to create the appearance of a developing coalition with the Center party. Combined with the Nazi deputies, the two groups together commanded a majority in the Reichstag.

Hitler's tactic was not to create a true coalition but to place pressure on Papen. On August 30, the deputies of the two parties voted Hermann Göring as president of the Reichstag. When the Reichstag convened on September 12, a motion by Ernst Torgler, the Communist leader, was made to censure Papen's government. Without any objection from the floor, Göring called for a vote on the motion. The result was 513 to 32 to remove Papen from power.

The Reichstag was dissolved yet again, and new elections set for November 6. At that election, the Nazis lost 34 seats, being reduced down to 196. Following the election, it was clear that Papen would be unable to maintain any control over the government. He resigned on November 17.

On November 19, Hitler met with President Hindenburg, who offered two choices. First, he would grant Hitler the chancellorship if Hitler could construct a viable majority coalition in the Reichstag. Second, Hitler might serve as vice chancellor under a new government formed with Papen as chancellor, ruling under emergency decree. Over the next few days, they negotiated. Hitler knew he could not form a majority in the Reichstag, but he still wanted the chancellorship. In what Hindenburg thought was the only workable compromise, he appointed Kurt von Schleicher chancellor.

Schleicher, a close friend to Hindenburg's son Oskar, had been minister of defense in Papen's government. He had been influential in pulling political strings throughout the turmoil and intrigue of German politics in 1932 and had been one of the president's most trusted advisers for many months. Now, after having finally gotten the top spot for himself, he was destined to rule for only 57 days.

On January 23, Schleicher met with Hindenburg and advised him that a majority in the Reichstag was not forthcoming. He asked the president to grant him emergency power to rule by decree. He also asked for what he called "temporary elimination" of the Reichstag, advising the president that it would be necessary to create a military dictatorship. Hindenburg would not grant the emergency powers to Schleicher and suggested that he try again to create a majority.

Schleicher was undone by rumors circulating at the time. One rumor had it that Schleicher, in collusion with army leaders, was planning to place President Hindenburg under arrest and assume complete power. Such stories angered Hindenburg, who demanded Schleicher's resignation immediately.

On January 28, Schleicher resigned, knowing that his was an impossible task. The word was out that Papen would again be appointed chancellor by president Hindenburg. Rumors were flying. Hindenburg, referring to Hitler with disdain, again vowed he would never appoint him as chancellor.

Another rumor about Berlin at this time was that the Nazis were planning an armed takeover of the government. On January 29, a crowd of workers estimated at 100,000 gathered in Berlin's Lustgarten to proclaim their opposition to Hitler being named as chancellor. But Hindenburg, listening to the advice of his son Oskar and others, made his decision. The next day, January 30, 1933, Hindenburg, frustrated at the inability of anyone to effectively break the deadlock in the Reichstag, announced that Hitler was to head up a new government as chancellor of Germany.

On the very day he became chancellor, Hitler sent Göring to meet with representatives of the Center party, which held 70 seats in the Reichstag. Göring reported back to Hitler that the leaders of the Center party wanted concessions. Hitler was facing the same problem as his predecessors — the inability to obtain a majority through acceptable compromise.

Göring recommended dissolving the Reichstag and calling for new elections. Hitler agreed and conveyed the suggestion to Hindenburg. New elections were set for March 5. This time, though, conditions would be different. Hitler and the Nazis had at their disposal all of the resources of government, most notably the radio and the press.

On February 27, less than one week before the election, the Reichstag building was burned. It is virtually certain that this fire was set intentionally by the Nazis so that they could blame it on their primary election opponents, the Communists. The leaders of that party were quickly rounded up and put on trial.

Hitler made the most of the allegation that the Communists were behind the fire. He immediately asked President Hindenburg to sign a decree "for the Protection of the People and the State," citing the imminent threat of Communist takeover of the nation. Hindenburg agreed and signed the decree under authority of article 48. The decree remained in effect from this point through the end of Hitler's reign in 1945.

The decree suspended civil liberties, including freedom of expression, of the press, and the right of assembly in public. The wording of the decree was so vague that it gave the Nazis power to do whatever they wanted. The government was authorized even to impose death sentences for a number of crimes. The decree further enabled Hitler to prevent his opponents from campaigning and even to place them under arrest. At the same time, he fostered widespread fear among the people of a Communist plot to take over the government. More than four thousand people were arrested following the Reichstag fire, including several members of the Reichstag itself. They were taken away without due process under terms of the emergency decree, mistreated in captivity and in many cases murdered. The Communist newspapers and many publications of other liberal parties were banned; only the Nazis were allowed to continue publishing and campaigning at will.

Thus in the last week before the election, the opposition to the Nazis was crushed. At the same time, the Nazi propaganda machinery went into high gear. Streets were plastered with posters and swastikas, the radio constantly carried the voices of Nazi leaders, and storm troopers were out in force. The Nazis organized massive nighttime rallies, complete with torchlights, loudspeakers, and bonfires.

In spite of the Nazis having complete control of information, and in spite of their removal of much of the opposition, the Nazis were unable to win a majority of the vote. On March 5, 1933, Nazi deputies won 17,277,180 votes, only 44 percent of the total. The balance was split between the Center party, the Catholic Bavarian People's Party, the Social Democrats, and the Communists, who in spite of being accused by the Nazis of the plot to overthrow the government, still managed to poll just under five million votes.

Hitler's plan had been to gain control of two-thirds of the Reichstag vote, which he needed to get his new enabling act. It would grant him and his cabinet the power to rule exclusively for four years, effectively making the Reichstag nonexistent as a legislative body. But the election did not produce the majority Hitler needed. The 81 Communist deputies, Hitler and his cabinet decided, would not be allowed to take their seats in the Reichstag, and they further decided they could ban the Social Democrats. With his decree granting emergency powers, Hitler was in the position to exclude as many Reichstag deputies as he needed to get his two-thirds majority.

On March 24, 1933, the Enabling Act was passed 441 to 84 in a newly opened Reichstag assembled in the Kroll Opera House in Berlin. It gave Hitler all the power he needed to control the government completely. Essentially, this legislation legalized Hitler's dictatorship, turning over to him complete authority to control all legislative functions of the government. One by one, political opposition groups folded on their own accord or were crushed by Hitler's new "majority." Ultimately, all political parties except the Nazi party were outlawed in Germany, making it a virtual certainty that any serious opposition in the future would be impossible.

The only obstacle to unbridled power was Hindenburg. The president still had the constitutional authority to remove Hitler, and with the loyalty of the army, it would be possible to do so. There was much internal conflict between 1933 and 1934 as top Nazis vied with one another for power. Himmler and Göring were conspiring against Röhm, and the power of the SA was a source of concern for Hitler. Rumors of plots and conspiracies to overthrow the government continued in Berlin.

Army leaders, increasingly concerned about the growing power of the SA, recommended to President Hindenburg a declaration of martial law. They also suggested turning over control of the government to the army. Hitler met with Hindenburg on June 21 and was warned that unless tensions in the country could be controlled at once, he would be removed from power. Hitler, shocked at the threat of losing everything he had built up, acted quickly.

On June 30, Hitler initiated a purge of the SA and its leadership. Röhm was arrested and murdered, as were hundreds of other SA leaders and other enemies of the Nazis. This action became known as the Röhm Purge. The entire SA organization was disbanded and replaced now by the more controllable SS, which was placed directly under Heinrich Himmler's command.

On July 2, 1934, Hindenburg thanked Hitler for taking decisive action to rescue Germany from the threat of high treason. The president and the army leadership were extremely relieved at the disbanding of the SA, which had come to be perceived as the greatest threat to German security. Hindenburg sent a telegram to Hitler which read: "From the reports placed before me, I learn that you by your determined action and gallant personal intervention, have nipped treason in the bud. You have saved the German nation from serious danger. For this I express to you my most profound thanks and sincere appreciation."[6] Hitler's action convinced Hindenburg that it would not be necessary to declare martial law after all. The army's position was that removal of the SA also removed all threats to their power and prestige.

Pushing Hitler to do something about the SA was Hindenburg's last significant act. He died at the age of 87, on August 2, 1934. Three hours after the death of the president, Hitler announced that the office of president was abolished and declared himself to be commander in chief of the armed forces.

Hitler had arrived. Hindenburg had given him power because he yearned for a majority, a consensus, and progress in solving the economic and social issues important to Germany. He could not realize at the time that he had plunged his country into the new dark ages of Nazism.

Chapter 3

EARLY MILITARY RESISTANCE

Normal respect for authority is a necessary trait for any law-abiding
citizen; but the average German's lack of natural poise led him to the other
extreme: excessive civil and military obedience, with the inherent danger of
accepting and obeying any law and any authority, whether good or bad.
This trait was exploited by Hitler; it explains why his legal assumption of
power helped so much to strengthen his position.

Fabian von Schlabrendorff, *The Secret War Against Hitler*

Any study of the opposition to Hitler has to be understood in the context of the times. This is especially true concerning resistance in the military. Opinions of military leaders in Germany before World War II were vastly different than the opinions they developed as the war began to go badly for Germany. While army leadership generally mistrusted Hitler, it became increasingly easier for the military resistance leaders to attract new members as frustration increased at Hitler's mismanagement of the war. As matters deteriorated, so did military loyalty.

Hitler did have his supporters among the military, however. He had given many assurances to the army that he intended to restore its traditional position of power and prestige. Until the end of the First World War, the officer class had enjoyed great prestige but the Versailles Treaty curtailed Germany's armed forces in size and might.

To gain allegiance from the officer class, Hitler took several steps to enhance the prestige of its members. On July 20, 1933, Hitler proclaimed the Army Law, which did away with the jurisdiction of civil courts over the military, restoring the tradition of the army as separate under the law. This greatly pleased the officer corps.

At the same time, Hitler instituted a change in the loyalty oath required of all military personnel. The oath, once taken, demanded personal loyalty, regardless of one's dislike of the Nazis. From the very beginning of his plans to control Germany, Hitler recognized the need for loyalty from the army. The officer corps was a powerful political organization insofar as every politician was concerned. If the army was unhappy with the nation's leadership, especially in the turmoil of the 1920s and early 1930s, it was virtually impossible for a politician to remain in office. The army was aware of this, and its leaders often reminded the politicians of their power and independence. There were so many near-insurrections in Germany during this period that political dependence on the support and loyalty of the army was unavoidable.

High on Hitler's agenda for consolidating power was to reduce the army's power over political leadership. To achieve that, he needed to place the officer class in a position of loyalty to him. He recognized that to a professional German army man, an oath carried with it a moral obligation and duty. The German officer's oath had such power that many an officer felt obligated to remain true to his oath even when he disagreed completely with Hitler.

Only a few hours after the death of President Hindenburg on August 2, 1934, Hitler announced the requirement that every member of the army was to swear an oath of loyalty to him personally. The requirement was made into law with formal passage of the Law of the Oath of the *Wehrmacht* (defense force). The oath read: "I swear before God to give my unconditional obedience to Adolf Hitler, führer of the Reich and of the German people, Supreme Commander of the Wehrmacht, and I pledge my word as a brave soldier to observe this oath always, even to peril of my life."[1]

While obedience to a commander in chief is essential in every army, the loyalty oath presented a dilemma. For the first time, the German soldier was required to swear a personal commitment. The oath is often cited as a reason for not refusing illegal orders. Many an officer witnessing atrocities committed by the SS and Gestapo* at the front and at home in Germany pointed to the oath as the one reason for not taking a moral stand against the Nazis.

There is ample evidence of German military disdain for the Nazis, extending to a refusal to work directly with the SS or to support Hitler's genocidal policies in any manner. The claim that the oath prevented German officers from taking a stand cannot be substantiated. Thousands of members of the military were executed for refusing to participate in illegal acts such as genocide (see Prologue, Note 1). A number of military officers did, in fact, join the resistance, and not all only in response to battlefield reversals. Their reasons were often founded on a tradition of military behavior and responsibility not based on blind obedience.

Many of the officers in the resistance were overt in their opposition to Hitler and his regime; they were forced to resign or were reassigned and transferred. From Hitler's point of view, the loyalty oath, once taken, made any form of insubordination or criticism an act of treason. But the traditional standards of the Prussian officer class did not support that simplistic point of view. The Prussian Code of Military Law, the guiding source for military behavior and discipline prior to the Nazi era, specifically stipulated that orders that are against the law are not to be obeyed. The requirement of blind obedience, which was often cited after the war at the war crimes trials, was strictly a Nazi conception.[2]

---

*Gestapo is an abbreviated name taken from the official organization name, Geheime Staatspolizei, or Secret State Police. Göring established the Gestapo in Prussia on April 26, 1933. Under Himmler's command in 1934, the organization expanded its role as a department of the SS.

Hitler instituted the loyalty oath at the beginning of his regime, well before the atrocities and loss of civil rights that Germans and other Europeans were to suffer in the subsequent years of Nazi rule. By 1934, the German army, having sworn its loyalty to Adolf Hitler, had no legal basis on which to oppose the regime. A political distaste for the political leader and commander in chief is clearly no grounds for overthrow of the government.

Hitler had come to power through the system. His reign was legal, and he commanded personal loyalty from the armed forces. Considerable debate centering on the oath of loyalty went on throughout the Nazi years within the army itself. A number of officers believed it was their moral obligation to fight Hitler in every way possible.

A large number of officers, while expressing sympathy with the resistance, did not want to join actively. As General Adolf Heusinger, operations chief of OKH,* expressed it: "You must realize that the generals who occupied key positions refused to engage in any kind of subversive activity until they had made certain of Hitler's death."[3]

There was danger in resistance, from the moment Hitler came into power. And yet, the army was the backbone of the resistance in Germany. Without support of army leaders opposed to the Nazis, the civilian and political forces would never have been able to organize any serious resistance efforts. The well-planned efforts of the resistance were invariably centered in the army, where troops were at the command of a sympathetic general and would be able, by force of arms, to enforce a coup. Without army support, overthrow of the government, guarded by the SS and the Gestapo, would be impossible within Germany.

Even though the Versailles Treaty strictly forbade the arming of the country, Hitler kept his promise to tear up the treaty and to rebuild the country's army, navy, and air forces. As a result, professional soldiers were pleased at the return of Germany to its position of military might, and they credited Hitler with the strength of leadership to achieve that. Hitler had given assurances to the army leaders that he would enable them to rearm upon gaining power. On February 2, 1933, Hitler addressed a meeting of the country's top admirals and generals at the home of General Kurt von Hammerstein, then commander in chief of the *Reichswehr*, Germany's standing army. He promised the armed forces that they would be allowed to rebuild their forces to heights far above the restrictions imposed at the end of the First World War. The navy leaders in attendance, in particular, were pleased at the prospect of being allowed to rebuild, as the Versailles Treaty limited Germany to no ships above 10,000 tons — in other words, no ships large enough to be considered part of a naval power.

Rebuilding of the military was among Hitler's top priorities. On October 1, 1934, barely two months after assuming full control of the German government, Hitler ordered the army to triple its size, from the 100,000 maximum allowed under the Versailles Treaty to 300,000.

The German government quietly proceeded with its military build-up. The navy

---

Oberkommando des Heeres, or Army High Command.

began the process of constructing two battle cruisers of 26,000 tons, well above the 10,000-ton limit under the Versailles Treaty. Upon completion, these cruisers were to be named the *Scharnhorst* and the *Gneisenau*. The navy was also quietly constructing a number of submarines, also strictly forbidden by the treaty.

On March 16, 1935, Hitler announced a law establishing a military draft. His goal was to enlist half a million men, though he was prepared to back away if France or England raised serious objections. The English, French, and Italians jointly protested Germany's build-up in a statement of April 11, 1935, and the Council of the League of Nations in Geneva also voiced disapproval and appointed a committee to recommend steps to take if Hitler built up German military power again in the future. Beyond these meager gestures, however, no significant warnings were issued to Germany, so Hitler proceeded with his plans.

Among both military and civilians, Hitler's announcement of a military draft was seen as the event that ended the oppression of the Versailles Treaty. Hitler became a popular hero as the man who refused to go along with the treaty, who was finally doing something to restore German honor. The positive response in Germany to this step was expressed well by author Richard Grunberger: "Military service had been part of the German way of life as far back as men could remember. Conscription was not merely welcomed as begetting triumphs in foreign policy … it was part of popular folklore that no man's education was complete without the discipline of the barrack-square."[4]

On May 21, 1935, Hitler proclaimed the Reich Defense Law. As of that date, the Reichswehr's name was changed to the Wehrmacht, and all of the German armed forces were completely reorganized. Hitler named himself supreme commander of the armed forces and General Werner von Blomberg, minister of defense, became minister of war as well as commander in chief of the armed forces.

Blomberg, chosen for his loyalty to Hitler, was also respected by the officer class. The Reich Defense Law also had an economic purpose. Germany's recovery from the depression was largely based on an economy of rearmament. The country's economic policies were given the name *Wehrwirtschaft* (war economy). Hitler appointed Dr. Hjalmar Schacht as plenipotentiary-general for war economy as part of the newly proclaimed law. He authorized Schacht to act as minister of economics and to "direct the economic preparations for war."

Schacht achieved this through the simple printing of money to pay for materiel. He was able to convince foreign countries to extend credit to Germany by using so-called "Mefo" bills*— IOU's guaranteed by the state and used to make payments to manufacturers. As they didn't appear in the official government's budget, nor in the published statements of the national bank, the Reichsbank, which managed transactions in Mefo bills, they were not considered a form of deficit spending. They simply didn't show up at all on the state's books, so there was no immediate threat of currency devaluation as a consequence of this financial trick. Between 1935 and 1938, no less than twelve billion marks in Mefo bills were utilized to fund rearmament.[5]

---

*"Mefo" is an abbreviation of a dummy corporation called Metall-Forschungsgesellschaft A. G. whose ownership consisted of four armament firms; the company, however, was actually created by Schacht. The state took on responsibility for the corporation's debts. The effect was to provide the nation with virtually unlimited financing for rearmament while at the same time creating jobs in armament factories, thus dramatically reducing unemployment.

Hitler concentrated on quietly rebuilding Germany's military might through this form of creative capital between 1935 and 1937. Aware that France's armed forces were substantially more powerful than Germany's, Hitler did not want to do anything that might cause the French to move against him. Finally, on January 30, 1937, the fourth anniversary of his coming to power, Hitler believed that Germany's military had sufficient strength to make a bold move. Addressing the Reichstag, he announced that Germany was withdrawing its signature from the Versailles Treaty. At this occasion, Hitler was able to point to four years in office with many notable accomplishments. He had rebuilt the country's armed forces in complete defiance of the rules set down at Versailles. In the process, he had stamped out unemployment. Germany was a growing world power.

Hitler's popularity grew from these economic, political, and military accomplishments. All of his actions, however, were aimed at preparation for war. Hitler, managing the economy of Germany, was faced with the prospect of economic prosperity in what he himself termed a war economy, or continued unemployment and depression. The unfortunate consequence of the war economy was that, were prosperity to be continued, it would require actual war. If large segments of the public chose to ignore these realities, the military leaders were all too aware of where the country was headed.

The people were not ignorant of the military build-up. For the average citizen, the immediate need to put food on the table was of greater concern than where the country was heading, and under what sort of leadership. The fact that Germany was operating under the Versailles Treaty, which forbade rearmament, was discreetly ignored, especially by those who had been unemployed and were now at work.

A popular joke of the day illustrates this point. One worker tells another, "I'm employed now at the bicycle factory." The second one asks, "Is there much demand for such a product?" The first one replies, "I'm told there is. But each time I try to build a new bicycle, it comes out looking like a gun."

It was Hitler's success that caused many military leaders to back away from thoughts of resistance, including many generals who found the Nazi philosophy reprehensible. Even professional soldiers, although happy that the military no longer operated under the restrictions of the Versailles Treaty, were opposed to the prospects of another war in Europe.

One of the first to seriously consider overthrowing the Nazi government was General Hammerstein, who as commander in chief of the Reichswehr was in the best position to overthrow Hitler by force. The general was so alarmed at the prospect of Hitler gaining power that, early in 1933, he seriously considered using the Reichswehr to seize power to remove the risk of Hitler's being appointed as chancellor. He had even discussed the idea of armed overthrow with Chancellor Schleicher, as part of a proposal to depose Hindenburg and declare a military dictatorship.

Hammerstein didn't act, however, because of his loyalty to Hindenburg, who had personally reassured Hammerstein that he would never allow Hitler into a position of power. Hammerstein had been consistently outspoken in complete opposition to the Nazis and vowed in 1932, "The Reichswehr will never allow them to come to power."[6]

After Hitler's appointment as chancellor, Hammerstein again approached the president. He hoped that he would be able to influence Hindenburg to take action against Hitler, but Hindenburg coldly suggested to Hammerstein that he should not meddle in politics but instead concentrate on taking care of the army. Hammerstein's access to the president became increasing difficult, and in January 1934, he resigned his post as commander in chief of the army, to be replaced by General Werner von Fritsch. Although Hammerstein continued in his opposition to the Nazis, he no longer had the army at his disposal.

During Hammerstein's final year as head of the Reichswehr, the most important member of the resistance among the military emerged. General Ludwig Beck had been appointed in October 1933 as head of the Truppenamt (Department of the Army, also called the "shadow General Staff," since such a body was specifically forbidden by the Treaty of Versailles). Beck was to play a key role in coming years, not only as head of military-based resistance plans, but also as an important liaison between military and civilian opposition groups.

Throughout the 1930s, Beck stayed in touch with civilian resistance leaders and formed a small group called Mittwochgesellschaft (Wednesday Club) to meet and discuss ways of removing the Nazis from power in Germany. His original reasons for opposing Hitler were military. He recognized Hitler's war ambitions and believed that going to war would be disastrous for Germany. Over time, however, he adopted a strong moral opposition to the Nazis as well. Their increasing excesses and criminal behavior were repulsive to Beck, strengthening his opposition.

Beck was born in 1880 in the Rhineland. His father was an engineer and owner of an iron mine. His uncles on both sides of the family had fought in the Franco-Prussian War of 1870. Beck attended Wiesbaden University but decided to become a soldier in 1898. He studied at the Berlin War Academy for three years and showed an exceptional talent for military strategy and organization. During the First World War, he rose to the rank of major and after the war served in the Reichswehr. By 1930 he had attained the rank of major-general.

Beck was recognized as an exceptional leader with a keen and organized mind, a man whose character was unquestionable. He was liberal in his political philosophy and an exceptional writer on military matters. He suffered poor health, however. His ailments included chronic insomnia and tooth pain which doctors were not able to cure. In spite of his physical problems, Beck dedicated himself from 1938 onward to keeping military and civilian elements of the resistance in touch with one another.

Ludwig Beck impressed all with his personal integrity and had a powerful, commanding personality and a broad range of cultural and intellectual interests. To many, he seemed more of a philosopher than a military officer. No one in the resistance doubted that Beck was their leader. Many fellow opposition members described Beck as the "heart of the movement." He was invariably able to resolve conflicts in the ever-growing membership of the opposition when called upon to judge an issue. He was completely opposed to the Nazis and all they stood for and understood well before the beginning of the Second World War that Germany could never win. He was mistaken, though, in his initial judgment of Hitler, believing that the party could be reformed by removing the Gestapo and reestablishing law and order. Beck failed to recognize that this was impossible as long as Hitler was retained as head of state.

Beck disagreed with Hitler's war plans and said as much through meetings and verbal and written communication. He was only converted to active opposition in 1938, however, when it became clear that Hitler intended to go to war. In 1936, Schacht, Hitler's minister of economics, sent a friend to visit Beck with a discreet inquiry concerning military support for an overthrow of Hitler's government. Beck replied that the question was largely a political matter rather than a military one, but that if a civilian-led change of government were to occur, the army would not oppose it. The problem for Schacht, though, was that he knew such a move would be impossible without armed support. The SS and Gestapo were too powerful and would quickly crush any attempt at a civilian coup. In spite of Beck's desire for a political opposition with army support, politicians against Hitler came to depend more and more on the army and, in particular, on Beck as the most sympathetic army leader.

Beck was forced to admit by 1937 or 1938 that it was Hitler, and not just the Nazi party, who was instigating terror in Germany. By then it was apparent that Hitler was seriously planning to make war on Germany's neighbors. Hitler issued a series of directives on November 5, 1937, that led to Beck's decision to actively organize a resistance to the Nazi regime. The top secret directives to all commanders of the armed forces included orders for "preparations of the armed forces for a possible war in the mobilization period 1937-38."[7]

The armed forces must be ready, Hitler instructed, to use military power in attacking Austria and Czechoslovakia, if necessary. Hitler correctly predicted that France and Britain would not aid the Czechs, but he was fully prepared to go to war to gain territories targeted in his directives. His generals, stunned by the order to prepare for war, now realized that their leader's talk of war was not just politics. He actually meant to carry through.

Hitler's November 5 decision caused great alarm in military and diplomatic circles. Foreign Minister Konstantin von Neurath expressed alarm to General von Fritsch, commander in chief of the army, and to General Beck, chief of the general staff. Neurath told the generals that his entire foreign policy had relied on Hitler's repeated assurances to foreign governments that he was interested only in maintaining peace.

Fritsch agreed to meet with Hitler and make a case for backing away from a commitment to armed confrontation. He met with the Führer on November 9 and presented his arguments based on military considerations. Hitler was unwilling to hear any dissent, and Fritsch's attempts at reason were fruitless.

Neurath himself met with Hitler in January 1938, at which time he warned that Hitler's expansion plans could lead to a war with England and France. Neurath presented the ultimatum that if Hitler didn't change his mind, he would resign. That threat suited Hitler, who was planning to make changes, both in the Foreign Office and in the army. He distrusted the aristocratic element in the Foreign Office and was determined to replace several people with Nazis. On February 4, 1938, Neurath was removed from office and replaced by Joachim von Ribbentrop. On Göring's recommendation, Hitler established the Geheimer Kabinettsrat (Secret Cabinet Council) for the purpose of advising the

General Ludwig Beck was an early opponent of Hitler and the Nazi movement. He became the military leader of the resistance (Photo: National Archives).

government in foreign policy matters. Neurath was appointed as president of that council, and the move was announced in such a way as to make it appear that he had been promoted. In truth, the council existed in name only and never even held a meeting. At the same time that Neurath was dismissed, Hitler also fired Ulrich von Hassell (ambassador to Rome and later a prominent member of the active resistance), Herbert von Dirksen (ambassador to Tokyo), and Papen (ex-chancellor and ambassador in Vienna).

Hitler's directives also lost him the services of Dr. Hjalmar Schacht, minister of economics, as a result of his plans to pursue military action. Through Schacht's financial wizardry, Hitler had managed to finance his entire rearmament plan. But beginning in 1936, Schacht had begun complaining that the country's credit could be stretched only so far and was already at the limit.

The generals opposed Hitler's war plans, and they found in Schacht a credible ally. Throughout this period, Schacht had a series of heated disagreements with Hermann Göring, whose complete ignorance of economics didn't prevent him from believing he knew better than Schacht how the economy of Germany could and should work. The minister, entirely frustrated at Göring's far-fetched economic schemes, tendered his resignation on September 5, 1937. Hitler didn't want to accept Schacht's resignation, fearing negative reaction from Germany's overseas creditors, but Schacht was adamant. He agreed to remain in the cabinet as minister without portfolio and also to retain his position as president of the Reichsbank, steps intended to soften the shock of his resignation. His term of office was officially ended on December 8. Göring took over the post of minister of economics.

In 1938, Hitler made a number of significant changes in the top army positions. First to go was General Werner von Blomberg, commander in chief of the armed forces. The general's physical appearance was striking. The consummate field officer, he was tall, blond, and handsome. At the age of 59, he was dedicated to the ideals of traditional Prussian military power. He signified the dignity and honor of the officer corps and looked the part.

Blomberg's wife of 28 years had died in 1932, and the general was a lonely man. In 1935 he decided to remarry, but he knew that his fellow officers might disapprove of his union with his fiancée, a War Ministry stenographer much younger than he.*

A firm and loyal follower of Hitler, Blomberg approached Hermann Göring and asked for advice because he was concerned about how his remarriage might be seen in government and military circles. Göring gave his blessing, offering to put in a good word on Blomberg's behalf with Hitler. The wedding was held on January 12, 1938, with Hitler and Göring in attendance as witnesses. Almost at once, though, disturbing rumors began to circulate about the new bride, Erna Gruhn. The Berlin police vice squad, it was revealed, had a file on the young woman. She had a shady background, including a record of arrests for prostitution and posing for revealing photographs.

The Berlin president of police, Wolf Heinrich von Helldorf, decided to handle the matter discreetly and took the file on Gruhn to General Wilhelm Keitel. Keitel was on a fast promotion track in the army because of Blomberg's favor and influence, and his oldest son had in 1937 married Blomberg's youngest daughter. The police chief suggested

---

*By tradition, the professional officer was expected to marry within the officer caste. For example, Blomberg's first wife had been the daughter of a retired army officer.

General Werner von Blomberg, commander in chief of the armed forces, was removed from his post because of rumors concerning his wife (Photo: National Archives).

that the dossier be destroyed. He was surprised, though, when Keitel refused to handle the matter quietly and within the army. He suggested instead that Helldorf hand over the file to Göring, which he did.

Göring, having his own ambitions to be named as Blomberg's successor for the job of commander in chief of the armed forces, gladly showed the file to Hitler on January 25, 1938. Hitler was furious. Having stood up as a witness at Blomberg's wedding, he believed he had been made to look like a fool, and he was now determined that the general had to go.

Göring confronted Blomberg the same day. Upon hearing the charges for the first time, the general admitted he had known of his wife's background all along and offered to seek a divorce. Göring replied that a divorce wouldn't be enough; he would have to resign.

Blomberg was dismissed by Hitler, although with apologies and the assurance that he would be returned to his post as soon as the scandal had died down. Hitler suggested one year's absence and promised, "Everything that has happened in the past will be forgotten." On January 27, Blomberg left for Capri to continue his honeymoon.*

In spite of Hitler's assurances that Blomberg would be brought back into the army when things quieted down, he was never restored to duty, even when he offered to return following the outbreak of war. He returned to Germany in January 1939, after the year of exile that Hitler had proposed. With his new wife, he remained in retirement until his death in March 1946.

Also to find himself suddenly out of favor was General Werner von Fritsch, commander in chief of the army. Fritsch, approximately the same age as Blomberg, had been in the army since the age of 18. When he was only 31, he received an appointment to the General Staff Corps, a rare distinction for such a young officer. During the First World War, Fritsch held a series of staff positions and was known for his wide range of knowl-

---

*An aside to Blomberg's dismissal illustrates the extent of fanaticism found in the officer corps. Admiral Erich Raeder sent his aide, Lieutenant von Wangenheim, to Capri to track down the general, with orders to ask him, out of respect for the reputation of the officer corps, to divorce his wife. The lieutenant, however, brought an excess of zeal to his mission. He confronted Blomberg by offering him a loaded revolver. Blomberg refused to take the pistol, later writing to Keitel that Wangenheim "apparently had quite different views and standards of life."

edge and for his shrewdness. Fritsch had complete integrity and was a consummate professional, but he was also blunt and unyielding by nature. His complete dislike of the Nazis was intense, and he made no effort to conceal the way he felt. Fritsch had been in touch with Beck, and they had discussed the idea of removing the Nazis from power using the army. He also was in touch with many of the members of a growing civilian opposition. By 1938 the Gestapo was fully aware of Fritsch's overt opposition.

On January 25 (the same day Göring revealed to Hitler the police file on Blomberg's new wife), he also showed the Führer a paper supplied to him by Heinrich Himmler concerning Fritsch. The paper, prepared by Reinhard Heydrich, head of the Sicherheitsdienst or SD (SS Security Service) and Himmler's top aide, charged that Fritsch had violated Section 175 of the German criminal code, which concerned homosexual activity. The paper went on to say that Fritsch had been paying blackmail since 1935 to keep this information secret.

Fritsch hotly denied the charges as "stinking lies," and Hitler agreed to meet with the general to hear his side of the story. Fritsch was summoned to Hitler's office that evening, and the meeting was also attended by Göring and Himmler. Hitler confronted Fritsch directly with the charges, which Fritsch stiffly denied, on his honor as an officer. At that point, Himmler brought into the room a man named Hans Schmidt, who was a career criminal with a long record. His primary activity recently had been spying on homosexuals and blackmailing them. He identified Fritsch as a man who had been paying him money to keep his homosexual tendencies secret.

Fritsch, speechless at the charge, refused Hitler's demand for resignation. He insisted on a trial by military court of honor. Refusing this demand for the moment, Hitler ordered Fritsch to take indefinite leave. Not dropping the matter, Fritsch convinced the Ministry of Justice, in cooperation with an army inquiry, to investigate the matter.

Meanwhile, Hitler took over for himself Blomberg's previous position as commander in chief (added to his role as supreme commander) and did away entirely with the War Ministry. It was replaced with the OKW, Oberkommando der Wehrmacht (Command of the Armed Forces). This organization was charged with central oversight of the army, navy, and air forces. Keitel was named chief of the High Command of the Armed Forces, a position he held through the end of the Second World War.

Hitler publicly announced the resignations of Blomberg and Fritsch, both for "reasons of health." Another 16 generals were also relieved of their commands at the same time, and 44 others whose loyalty was questionable were reassigned.

Hitler chose Field Marshal Walther von Brauchitsch to succeed Fritsch as head of the army. Brauchitsch was about to get a divorce with the intention of marrying another woman. It seemed that this scandal would be his undoing until Göring intervened. The woman the general wanted to marry not only passed muster on the basis of her morals, she was also a dedicated Nazi. The trouble passed quickly.

On March 17, 1938, the Fritsch trial began. But previously, on February 4, Hitler had taken over full command of the military, so Fritsch's vindication was to come too late. By the following day, Fritsch was, indeed, cleared completely. Schmidt admitted he had been forced to lie in identifying the general; he was executed in Sachsenhausen concentration camp in the summer of 1942.

The Fritsch trial was not open to the public, so there was no publicity concerning

Fritsch's vindication. His life and career were ruined, and his reputation stained beyond hope in spite of his acquittal. He was quietly allowed to rejoin his old unit, the 12th Artillery Regiment, on August 7, 1939. He wrote at the time, "I shall accompany my regiment only as a target." And on September 22, 1939, he was killed in battle in Poland.

The purge of top generals in January 1938 was a turning point for resistance leaders, who were shocked at the lies the Nazis were willing to create to remove Fritsch from power and at the shabby treatment of both Blomberg and Fritsch. Both officers had reputations as distinguished career officers, and they were dispensed with in the cruelest way. Recognizing, perhaps for the first time, that the Nazis were capable of anything, General Beck became committed to the idea of resistance.

In the spring and summer of 1938, the military, led by General Beck, consolidated its plans with civilian opposition leaders for a coup d'état. For the military, the elimination of General Fritsch was the loss of an opportunity. Many, including Beck, had believed that Fritsch would eventually remove Hitler, using force if necessary. Once Fritsch was gone, Beck concluded that his own resignation was inevitable. He was so deeply opposed to Hitler's plans to invade Czechoslovakia and so concerned about the prospects of war that he determined to do all in his power to prevent Hitler from achieving his war plans. He believed at first that in his position as chief of staff, he might be able to influence General Brauchitsch, commander in chief of the army, to take a strong stand against Hitler. Beck realized that without cooperation from Brauchitsch, it would be impossible to sway Hitler. Beck's idea was to talk Brauchitsch into organizing a strike among the army leadership, but this idea never struck Brauchitsch as a practical one. He knew it would be impossible to get all of the generals to go along. There were plenty of ambitious officers available who would gladly take a promotion and step into vacated top positions.

Hitler had already demonstrated that he was willing to dispense with any dissenting generals, and this was widely recognized. The Führer's lack of tolerance for any dissent created an environment in which everyone was forced to be completely in support or completely opposed. There was no middle ground available, so the idea of a strike by all generals wasn't practical.

Brauchitsch also argued that it was improper for military leaders to become involved in political decisions. This remained the commander in chief's position. He might offer expert military advice against Hitler's plans, but once a political decision had been made, Brauchitsch believed it was his duty to go along. Beck disagreed. He began writing a series of memos intended to convince the commander in chief that a strong position taken by a majority of army leaders was the only way to influence Hitler. If a strike wouldn't work, perhaps the collective voices of disagreement would. Beck delivered his first memo to Brauchitsch on May 5, 1938. Recognizing that Brauchitsch would not respond to any political arguments, Beck confined his discussion to military points. Britain and France would not allow a shift in power in Germany's favor, Beck stated, and Germany did not possess the resources for a protracted war. A military move on Czechoslovakia would cause a response from its allies, so the only viable solution would be one acceptable to Britain.

Brauchitsch met with Hitler and presented Beck's memo. Hitler said Beck's views were pessimistic, and he rejected the arguments out of hand. Beck wouldn't give up, however. He prepared a second memo for Brauchitsch on May 29 and personally read it to the commander on May 30. In this memo, he expressed his agreement with Hitler that Czechoslovakia should be destroyed because it presented a threat to Germany. Beck repeated his previous argument, however, that Germany lacked the military strength to withstand a military response from France and Britain.

Beck warned that Germany might be able to win a fight against the Czechs but would then face the combined might of France, Britain, and perhaps even the United States, a confrontation Germany would obviously lose. Brauchitsch heard Beck out but took no action in response.

On the day Beck read his memo to Brauchitsch, Hitler announced a September deadline for invasion of Czechoslovakia, a decision he described as unalterable. Beck drafted a third memo in which he made technical military arguments against Hitler's invasion plans. Beck also complained that the invasion decision had been made without consultation with him as chief of staff of the army. Therefore, the General Staff could not be held accountable for the disaster which would result, Beck insisted. Brauchitsch read the latest Beck memo on June 3 but again did not respond. Brauchitsch never disagreed with Beck's views; he simply refused to contradict Hitler.

Beck next ordered indoor war games to study the likely course of the planned Czech invasion. His intention was to convince other army leaders that the outcome would be bad for Germany. The war games were based on the assumption that France would retaliate. In the war game, Czechoslovakia was easily defeated, but the French army had also made advances into German territory. It was clear that Germany could win the Czech battle but would lose the larger war. Even though the war games went poorly for Germany, a number of military experts disagreed with his conclusion that France would intervene. To many military leaders, Beck's fears were outdated.

Beck offered his resignation in June 1938, but General Brauchitsch asked him to reconsider. Beck wrote another memo on July 15, urging his superior to recognize the need to resist preparations for war. He again used a purely military argument, predicting that the course Hitler had chosen would probably lead to a worldwide conflict. Beck's memo concluded:

> I regard it as my duty today — in full knowledge of the significance of such a step but conscious of the responsibility laid upon me by my official assignment for the preparation and conduct of a war — to put forward the following urgent request: the Supreme Commander of the *Wehrmacht* must be induced to halt the war preparations which he has ordered and to postpone his proposed solution of the Czech question by force until the military conditions therefore have radically changed. At present I can see no prospects of success and this, my view, is shared by all my subordinate Deputy Chiefs of the General Staff and heads of General Staff sections, insofar as they are concerned with preparation for and conduct of war against Czechoslovakia.[8]

The following day, July 16, Beck prepared another memo, again urging Brauchitsch to assess the situation realistically: "Ultimate decisions concerning the survival of the Nation are involved. History will burden these leaders with a blood guilt if they do not act as their professional and political conscience dictates. Their obedience as soldiers has its limits at the point where their knowledge, their conscience, and their responsibility forbid execution of an order."[9]

Beck suggested again that a "collective step" be taken by the majority of generals who were opposed to Hitler's war plans. He suggested that if those generals met and agreed beforehand on their message, a meeting with Hitler would convince the Führer to change his mind. He approached Brauchitsch on July 19 to repeat this suggestion, referring to the plan as a chance for the generals to have a "showdown with the SS and the Party bosses." Brauchitsch did not want to hear of Beck's plans, which were sounding more and more like a coup d'état, and did not respond. Beck repeated his suggestion once again on July 29. He recommended that Brauchitsch should tell Hitler: "The commander in chief of the Army, together with his most senior commanding generals, regret that they cannot assume responsibility for the conduct of a war of this nature without carrying a share of the guilt for it in face of the people and of history. Should the Führer, therefore, insist on the prosecution of this war, they hereby resign from their posts."[10]

Beck was so insistent that at his suggestion, Brauchitsch called a meeting of group and corps commanders in Berlin, which took place on August 4. Beck's July memo was read, and attendees were asked to offer their own points of view. Only two generals sided with Beck, General Walther von Reichenau, commander of Army Group 4, and General Ernst Busch, commander of VIII Army Corps. The meeting convinced Brauchitsch that Beck's opinion was wrong.

Regardless, Beck still thought Brauchitsch should deliver his prepared statement to Hitler. He suggested the commander approach Hitler and read the statement on August 15 at a scheduled gathering Hitler had ordered for all senior generals. Brauchitsch refused to consider taking such a bold stand. Hearing of Beck's continuing protests, Hitler passed a warning through Brauchitsch that dissent must stop at once, that no further discussions were to be allowed. He, Hitler, knew best, and that was the end of it.

Beck, realizing he could not halt Hitler's plans and believing Brauchitsch too weak-willed to see the truth, resigned on August 18 and urged Brauchitsch to do the same. The commander refused. Considering the timing and pending move against Czechoslovakia, Hitler could ill afford news of dissent among his top generals. Although he accepted Beck's resignation, he forbade any press announcement. The top army leaders were ordered to keep Beck's resignation quiet, and Beck was temporarily placed in command of the First Army. The official admission of Beck's resignation as chief of staff was not made until October 1938.

Beck was not the only military figure to resign in protest. Chief of Naval Staff Vice Admiral Günther Guse protested the invasion plan and resigned his post shortly after writing to Hitler on July 17, 1938, to say:

> In a conflict European in scope Germany would be the loser, and ... the Führer's whole work so far would be in jeopardy. So far, I have not spoken to any ranking officer in any of the three branches of the armed services who did not share this opinion, or who did not fear that considering the political tension of the moment, an attack on the Czech state would develop into a European war. In this situation, the responsible advisors of the Führer

have not only the duty of obedience to his orders. They also have the duty to do all that is in their power, and that includes taking every necessary logical step, to see to it that a development which threatens the continued existence of the nation is stopped in time.[11]

While Beck was trying to make a difference from within the command structure of the army, he was assisted by the chief of the Abwehr (Army Counter-Intelligence), Admiral Wilhelm Canaris, and by General Hans Oster, Abwehr chief of staff. These two held extraordinary power because they were directly involved with the military's intelligence-gathering network. The value of their contacts was immense. Their participation in the resistance enabled the movement to operate efficiently and to establish contacts overseas. Their involvement eventually cost Canaris and Oster their lives.

The Abwehr, by the nature of its work, operated in absolute secrecy. This legitimate requirement enabled the resistance great operating room, and the entire system of counter-intelligence was put at the disposal of the resistance. Oster, protected by Admiral Canaris, was given all the freedom he needed to work with underground contacts, while Canaris used his position to save many resistance members who were arrested by the Gestapo.

The Abwehr was divided into three sections. Section I was charged with collecting information, Section II was responsible for sabotage in other countries, and Section III, headed by Canaris, was the counter-intelligence division. By the outbreak of war, none of the sections were headed by ardent Nazis, but only Oster, in Section III, was a member of the organized resistance. At its height, the Abwehr had 43,000 members, of which 8,000 were officers.

Canaris, a career naval officer, was picked to head the counter-intelligence department because he had a reputation as an absolute conservative and nationalist who despised the Versailles Treaty. The Nazi leadership believed Canaris would work faithfully for them because he was also a staunch anti–Communist. Throughout the period 1938 to 1944, Canaris was a valuable ally to the resistance, but he never took an active role. His discretion enabled him to maintain the appearance that he was a loyal supporter of the government. Oster, bolder and more imaginative than Canaris, held his superior in his sway. In terms of resistance activity, Oster was the leader. Canaris, with a flair for subterfuge, provided resistance members everything from desk space to false passports.

Oster was born in 1888 and was the son of a Protestant minister. He had served in the army in the First World War, and although an astute politician and military expert, he was also an intellectual, with a wide range of interests. Over the years between 1938 and 1944, Oster (working with the approval and help of Canaris) worked diligently with General Beck. Oster and Beck were the prime leaders of the military resistance.

It was a powerful combination. Oster was able to arrange travel overseas under the cover of intelligence investigations, to use the offices and technology of the Abwehr, and to deflect the Gestapo from prying into resistance activities too closely. Beck had the alliance of many top army leaders, the reputation as an honorable man, and the desire to overthrow the Nazi regime.

Chapter 4

RESISTANCE IN GERMAN CHURCHES

I must state that we Christians feel this policy of destroying the Jews to be a grave wrong, and one which will have fearful consequences for the German people. To kill without the necessity of war, and without legal judgment, contravenes God's commands even when it has been ordered by authority, and like every conscious violation of God's law, will be avenged, sooner or later.

Dr. Theophil Wurm, bishop of Württemberg, letter to state
secretary of the Reich Chancellery, December 20, 1943

While the Nazis were consolidating the support of the army and getting rid of dissenting voices within its ranks, a war against outspoken church leaders was also underway. Clergymen frequently were fearless critics against the crimes of the Nazis. Using the pulpit as a place to register and communicate protest, these clergymen themselves soon became targets of the Nazis. The persecution of Christian churches in Germany occurred because of the outspoken, moral protests. Hitler saw religion as a threat to the survival of the Nazi state, and for good reason. The church was a center of morality in the country, and its leaders in the towns and cities of Germany could not stand by quietly and without protest allow Hitler to carry out his plans against the Jews and, finally, against anyone who stood in his way.

Germany was, at the beginning of the Nazi era, a country divided along Catholic and Protestant lines. The Reformation, which started in Germany, actually led to the permanent religious division of the country, with a largely Catholic culture in Austria, Bavaria, and the Rhineland, and a largely Protestant culture in the rest of the country. Religion and politics were never far apart at the time. The Center Party was formed with the primary political purpose of defending Catholic interests in the policies of pre–Nazi Germany.

The Catholic and Protestant churches in Germany were split by the Nazi rise to power. Many leaders supported the Nazi movement, often even on Christian principles. Many others found it impossible to even consider lending their support and, to the contrary, felt morally compelled to speak out strongly against all that Hitler and the Nazis stood for.

With the Nazi rise to power came two disturbing trends in pro–Nazi ecclesiastic ideology. First was the belief in a form of Christianity completely free of Judaism, an expansion of Luther's own anti–Semitism. The second was an ideology called *Neuheidentum* (New Heathenism) that attempted to merge Nazism and Christianity. This included an Aryan Jesus who carried a sword rather than a crown of thorns and became a Nordic avenger rather than a peacemaker.

Both of these movements, affecting Christianity but based on nationalism, had the effect of damaging the independence of all churches and sects. The mixture of German nationalism and fervent belief was not a Nazi invention, however. It had preceded Hitler, and he only aggravated the tendency through his antichurch policies. Many deeply religious Germans believed in the period preceding the First World War that dying for the Fatherland was on a par with Christian martyrdom. To be reluctant to die for the cause was a question of loyalty among these believers, even becoming a question of religious faith. They labeled pacifism as blasphemy against God.

To the extent that new Christian ideologies tied to the political state were rejected or resisted, the Nazis began discrediting Christian churches in Germany as a means for removing their influence, especially on the young. Leading this effort was Julius Streicher, known to be primitive, gross, promiscuous, ill-mannered, and ruthless in manner. On one of his many antichurch campaigns, he compared the Christian Eucharist to Jewish "ritual murder." Streicher was ignorant on matters of basic theology, saying for example, "Christ mixed a good deal with women. I believe he stayed with one who was an adulteress, so I have heard."

Streicher is best-known as the publisher of *Der Stürmer* (The Stormer), a pornographic newspaper whose sole purpose was to attack enemies of the Nazi regime. While the Jews were especially degraded in the pages of the paper, the Christian churches were also its targets. One recurring theme was that of young girls or boys victimized by lecherous Catholic priests. Streicher also described life among Catholic clergy as highly sexual, with stories of nuns being raped by their father-confessors. Streicher's publication was cited as evidence for the prosecution in the trials of many priests arrested from 1935 onward. They were charged with smuggling, treason, or immorality, for the purpose of discrediting the church and sending them to concentration camps.

The Nazi regime wanted not only to discredit the churches in the minds of the people. They also wanted the weight of the law on their side. The regime created the *Volksgerichtshof* (People's Court) specifically to try cases of treason, crimes against the state, and other crimes committed by those deemed not to be among the *Treu und Glauben* (loyal and true). The roots of the People's Court preceded Hitler. In 1922, during the Weimar Republic, the Law Protecting the Constitution was passed as an emergency measure. This gave the government the power to punish without due process,* which gave the Nazi government a precedent for its later abuses against anyone they considered a "menace to the state." The use of such principles to silence and punish members of German religious faiths was widespread.

The passage of a law providing for punishment without the usual procedures of trial and presentation of evidence was a significant development, for which a price was paid under the Nazi regime. It violated one of the basic premises in law, that of nulla poena sine lege, *which means "no punishment without law."*

At the time that Hitler began building power, the Nazis needed to work with other political parties. Hitler knew he needed to entice votes from deputies of the Zentrum (Catholic Center Party) in order to produce a voting majority. Hitler was all too aware that there were millions of Catholics in Germany, and he could not simply abandon their interests politically.

Many church leaders supported Hitler's policies and ideologies, even before he came to power. The Catholic vicar-general of Mainz in 1930 said it was wrong for good Christians to hate members of other religions but then qualified this to say that Hitler was correct in complaining that there was too much Jewish influence in many segments of German society. The groundwork was being laid to make a case for Christians to hold true to their beliefs while supporting anti–Jewish ideas.

When Hitler spoke before the Reichstag on March 23, 1933, to ask for emergency powers, he stated it was his belief that the Christian faiths provided "essential elements for safeguarding the soul of the German people." He further promised that he would always protect the rights of Christian churches, declaring that it was his ambition to achieve a "peaceful accord between Church and State."[1]

Furthering this position, Hitler's government signed a Concordat* with the Vatican on July 20, 1933. This Concordat guaranteed freedom of the Catholic religion in Germany and its right to govern its own affairs. Terms the Vatican agreed to included the requirement that bishops in Germany would take a loyalty oath to Hitler. A treaty with the Vatican and the diplomatic recognition that accompanied it provided international respectability.

Many future protests by Catholic priests and bishops concerning Nazi policies were based on the government's violations of the Concordat's Article I, which specified:

> The German Reich guarantees the freedom of the profession and the public exercise of the Catholic religion. It recognizes the right of the Catholic Church, within the limits of the general laws in force, to regulate and to administer freely her own affairs and to proclaim in the field of her competence laws and ordinances binding upon her members.[2]

Catholic opposition in Germany intensified during 1933, when the first sterilization law went into effect. This idea was especially repellent to the Catholic church, even in light of the justifications put forth by the Nazi government supporting its reasons for the law. With 30 million members in Germany, the Catholic church was also in a position in 1933 to stand up to the Nazi government and to be heard. With its own political party and a large youth group, the Catholic church was a force to be reckoned with.

Hitler dissolved the Catholic political parties in 1933 as part of his plan to create a majority in the Reichstag. And only five days following ratification of the Concordat, the large Catholic Youth League was ordered dissolved. This was followed closely by the forced closure of Catholic schools.

Church-based opponents to the Nazis were outspoken, and their protests predated

---

*A concordat is a treaty between a government and a religious sect or group. In this case, the Vatican represented the interests of German Catholicism in its agreement with the German government.

Hitler's rise to power. As early as 1930, priests were taking positions against the Nazis, recognizing the impossibility of reconciling Catholic faith and Nazi ideology. A priest in Hesse, Father Weber, in a sermon of September 30, 1930, stated specifically that a true Catholic cannot also be a Nazi. He also forbade attendance by Nazis at church services, funerals, and other church functions, and declared that no Catholic Nazi would be allowed to take any of the sacraments.[3]

Such a strong position would clearly have had severe repercussions years later. But in 1930, when the Nazis were not yet in power, it was possible to criticize a political party. The *Gauleiter* of Hesse asked, however, for an explanation from Father Weber's bishop. The bishop of Mainz did reply, stating that not only did he support the position Father Weber had expressed but also that the priest had acted on instructions from the bishop's own office. In his reply, the bishop wrote:

> Hitler, to be sure, has written in his book *Mein Kampf,* some words of acknowledgment about the Christian religion and Catholic institutions, but that does not deceive us about the fact that the cultural policies of National Socialism are in contradiction to Catholic Christianity.... Can a Catholic be a member of the Hitler Party? Can a Catholic rector permit members of this party to attend Church funerals and other church services in group formation? Can a Catholic who professes the principles of this party be admitted to the holy sacraments? We must answer these questions in the negative.[4]

In 1933, a Catholic anti–Nazi organization, *Rhätin,* was formed in Bavaria. The group published its own newspaper, *Der Gerade Weg* (The Straight Path), in which Nazi theories were condemned. These sorts of activities were regarded by the Nazi regime as what it labeled "political Catholicism." The Volksgerichtshof (People's Court), established specifically to deal with cases of treason and related crimes, heard many such cases, especially after a directive of July 20, 1935, from Secretary of State Max Schlegelberger was sent to all state prosecutors. It specified that the judiciary, cooperating with the Gestapo, should act to put down all attempts on the part of "political Catholicism" to undermine the state. The Nazi regime encouraged complete agreement with its programs, and in the case of the clergy, supported those who did not question the state or, better yet, enthusiastically endorsed the Nazi regime. Support from the pulpit was coveted by the Nazis. They referred to it as "positive Christianity."

The regime viewed members of the clergy as potential threats and wanted to prevent them from becoming too political in their statements. That did not eliminate the problem, but it did provide the state with the means for punishing outspoken critics, using the law. One of the earliest of the so-called political Catholics was Michael von Faulhaber, cardinal archbishop of Bavaria. He had been archbishop of Munich since 1917 and was 64 when the Nazis came to power. As chaplain-general in the Bavarian army during the First World War, Faulhaber had been the first Catholic bishop to be awarded the Iron Cross.

In 1933, Faulhaber defied the Nazis openly through his sermons, referring to the Jews as God's Chosen People. He pointedly insisted that no race has the right to hate any other race and went so far as to point out that even Christ had not been a German. This was a bold stance and was also against the law. The Nazi *Staatsgesetzbuch* (code of law) number 130 provided for penalties for priests who preached "against the interests of the State."

Copies of Faulhaber's outspoken sermons were made and distributed in many other churches. The government forbade duplication of his sermons, and printers in Munich were threatened with fines and other punishments if they cooperated with the bishop. Even so, copies of the sermons continued to be distributed widely.

Faulhaber's protests were not limited to his sermons. He also wrote letters directly to Nazi officials critical of their antichurch policies. In 1938 he wrote several letters to the Bavarian minister of education, protesting the closure of 41 church-run schools, and another protesting closure of the Catholic Young Men's and Young Women's Associations earlier that year.

Faulhaber defied Hitler's ideal of nationalism, stating that real nationalism started with conversion to Christianity. He also stated that the only real leader of mankind could be God. He disputed the claim made by Baldur von Schirach, head of the Hitler Youth, that "Who serves Hitler, who serves Germany, serves God."[5]

In 1938 the Nazis attempted to intimidate Faulhaber into silence by organizing a mob and attacking his home. They broke all of the windows and tried to set it on fire, chanting "Away with Faulhaber, the friend of the Jews, who offers his hand in friendship to Moscow" and "Take him to Dachau!" Faulhaber was not afraid of the Nazis, and their attacks did not intimidate him. By November 1940, he was actively protesting state euthanasia policies and wrote to the Reich minister of justice, accusing the regime of violating the Concordat as well as God's divine law. There was no answer to his letter. Realizing that they could not silence Faulhaber, the Nazis by 1940 had chosen to ignore him as much as possible.

In spite of the outspoken stance adopted by Faulhaber and other members of the clergy, the Nazis took further steps to reduce the influence of the church. A November 4, 1936, decree ordered removal of all crucifixes from schools in the Oldenburg area, describing them as "symbols of superstition." Because of widespread protest, however, the order was canceled on November 25.

The anti–Catholic policies of the Nazi state went far beyond mere suppression of religion. Hermann Göring decreed in 1935 that the *Hitler Gruß* (the stiff-armed Nazi salute) should also be considered as "the only salute to Jesus Christ." In some schools, students were forbidden to make the sign of the cross.

State policy actually approved of paganism as an alternative to Christianity. In a nationalistic fervor, a 1935 announcement was made by ardent Nazis at Kiel University: "We Germans are heathens and want no more Jewish religion in our Germany. We no longer believe in the Holy Ghost. We believe in the Holy Blood."[6]

Nazis with these sentiments organized into the Deutsche Glaubensbewegung (German Faith Movement), whose members called themselves *Gottgläubige* (God believers). They were enemies of the Christian churches, which they referred to as "Germany's religious Versailles." Making little secret of how they felt about Christianity, the sect published in its journal *Sigrune* the following description of Jesus: "Jesus was a cowardly Jewish lout who had certain adventures during his years of indiscretion. He uprooted his disciples from blood and soil and, at the wedding at Cana, loutishly flared up at his own mother. At the very end he insulted the majesty of death in an obscene manner."[7]

While the official Nazi posture was that the German Faith Movement was a spontaneous and independent trend, it constituted the Nazi state's official neopagan sect. By 1939 the movement claimed that five percent of the German population, or more than 3.4 million Germans, had joined.[8]

Priests in Germany protested the state-endorsed declarations of paganism in the nation. Priests and bishops spoke from their pulpits against state policies affecting the right to worship, including so-called "protective arrests" of priests without trial and even without specific charges.

Many priests and nuns were sent to concentration camps simply because they were members of the church. Hitler Youth bands often marched past churches during services, chanting and intimidating churchgoers. Crucifixes were removed from churches and used by Hitler Youth for target practice. Priests were beaten and threatened with arrest for refusing to betray information gained in the confessional.

Abuses increased as the Nazis consolidated their power. Church leaders became increasingly alarmed, and in August 1935, a bishops' conference in Fulda featured discussion of persecution by the Nazis. This conference produced a pastoral letter* protesting interference by the state in church matters and the Nazi "war of annihilation" against Christianity.

One of the most activist and courageous of German bishops was Cardinal Clemens August von Galen, bishop of Münster. He was an imposing figure with a solid reputation as a fighter, and his fiery sermons earned him the reputation, "The Lion of Münster." A member of a Westphalian noble family with unlimited self-confidence, Galen made an impression on everyone who met him. In 1933, Galen took the oath to Hitler as required under terms of the Concordat, and he was not considered a threat. As a conservative and staunch anti–Communist, he originally embraced the Nazi government but was soon to realize his error.

By 1934, Galen was expressing disagreement with Nazi racial doctrine. And within two years, he was an outspoken critic, especially of Nazi propaganda publications. In a September 1936 sermon given in the town of Xanten, Galen directly accused the Nazis: "Obedience which places souls in servitude is the most base form of slavery.... It is worse than murder, for it is the subjection of all human personality. It is an assault on God himself.... There are fresh graves in German soil in which lie the ashes of those whom Catholic people regard as martyrs for the faith."[9]

In addition to speaking directly from his pulpit, Galen registered his protests through a series of pastoral letters, which were distributed widely and read in other congregations. He remained an outspoken critic of Hitler and the Gestapo many years after most public opposition voices had been stifled.

Galen's critical sermons led to debate at the highest levels. Many Nazi leaders wanted to arrest and execute Galen, but Hitler overruled them, recognizing the bishop's popularity as an obstacle. The Gestapo wrote an extensive report on Galen, and Hermann

---

*This is a letter issued within the church and intended to be read to all congregations or a letter of protest directed to church leaders.

Göring wanted to have him arrested. Galen, upon learning of these steps, wrote to the government claiming that he had done nothing but exercise his rights of citizenship and stating that he believed it was his duty to criticize. The threat of action against Galen did appear to have an effect. After his three sermons of 1941, he did not speak out as boldly again. He survived the war and died in 1946.

Not all Catholics were so fortunate. One example was Father Bernhard Lichtenberg, dean of the Berlin Cathedral of St. Hedwig. He was a dedicated pacifist who came to the attention of the Nazis for stating, "I have only one Führer, Jesus Christ." He was very public in his protests against mistreatment of the Jews in Hitler's regime. During church services in October 1941, he offered prayers for the Jews and prepared an announcement which was read during services by the priests in his diocese, which led to his arrest. In part, the announcement read:

> An inflammatory pamphlet anonymously attacking the Jews is being disseminated among the houses of Berlin. It declares that any German who, because of allegedly false sentimentality, aids the Jews in any way, is guilty of betraying the people. Do not allow yourself to be misled by this un-Christian attitude, but act according to the strict commandment of Jesus Christ: Thou shalt love thy neighbor as thyself.[10]

Lichtenberg was arrested on October 23, 1941, and charged with praying for the Jews and for concentration camp inmates and other "enemies of the state." He was given a two-year sentence but suddenly died while in *Schutzhaft* (protective custody) on the way to Dachau.

Another critic was Father Rupert Mayer, a Jesuit priest and outspoken anti–Nazi. He had won the Iron Cross during the First World War and had lost one leg from his wounds. He bluntly preached that it was impossible to be a good Christian and a Nazi at the same time. He was placed under a preaching ban on May 28, 1937, which he ignored. On June 5, he was arrested. The court called him a "menace to the state" and released him on condition that he not preach any further. Mayer was arrested twice during 1939, and toward the end of that year, he was sent to Sachsenhausen concentration camp. Near starvation, he was released in ill health, and suffering from his treatment while under arrest, he died in 1945.

The Nazi war against individual Catholics and against Christianity as a whole upset Pope Pius XI, especially since the Vatican had signed the Concordat with the German government. In protest, he wrote an encyclical* entitled *Brennender Sorge Mit* (With Burning Sorrow), and on March 14, 1937, he ordered it read from all Catholic pulpits in Germany. This paper charged the Nazi government with breaching the Concordat and condemned Nazi racial policies as well as treatment of Christians in Germany. The language was strong and specific. It accused the Nazi government of "sowing the tares of suspicion, discord, hatred, calumny, of secret and open fundamental hostility to Christ and his church." In 1937, Hitler was sensitive to the opinions of the international community, and the Vatican's criticisms were alarming and, for Hitler, ill-timed.

---

*Like a pastoral letter, an encyclical is intended for reading to all congregations. It is written by the pope or a bishop and usually concerns a matter of great seriousness or importance.

The Nazis, alarmed and embarrassed at the circulation of the encyclical, with its strong and direct criticisms, ordered the Gestapo to launch an immediate investigation to find out how the document had found its way to German pulpits without having been intercepted. The Gestapo had failed to uncover the underground route by which it had been smuggled into the country. The question on the minds of the Nazi leaders was, who was responsible for allowing the encyclical to be read in churches? The Gestapo was unable to provide an explanation.

Catholic opposition was not restricted to the clergy. One of the most significant developments in the German opposition was an effort led by a respected Catholic civilian, Dr. Josef Müller. Working with military and civilian opposition leaders, Müller was able to use connections to the Vatican to open up diplomatic discussions with the British government.

Coordination between diverse opposition groups began in late 1939, with the outbreak of the Second World War. Their original intention was to determine whether the Allied powers would entertain peace negotiations with Germans if Hitler were removed from power. The opposition needed an emissary to communicate these ideas, but the outbreak of war had made travel overseas impossible for most people. And the opposition did not have any official standing, so diplomatic contacts would be difficult to establish in any way.

The opposition selected Dr. Müller because he knew people in the Vatican, and many members of the opposition believed that the Vatican would be a likely place from which to establish discreet contact. In addition, Eugenio Pacelli, the newly elected Pope Pius XII, had extensive background in diplomatic circles and was known as an expert on German affairs, which made him an excellent diplomatic source. In 1917, Pacelli, while serving as nuncio (top-ranked Vatican diplomatic envoy) in Munich, had tried to get the German government to open peace discussions with the Allies. He spent the 1920s as nuncio in Berlin, and in 1933, as Papal Secretary of State, he had signed the Concordat with Germany as official spokesman for Pope Pius XI and the Vatican.

The opposition recognized Müller's background and the pope's concerns about events in Germany as valuable to their cause. They needed a representative who was respected within the Catholic church, so they recruited Dr. Müller. He was 41, a citizen of Munich, and a personal friend of Cardinal Faulhaber, with whom he had been actively involved in the Catholic resistance.

Hans Oster asked Müller to visit him at Abwehr headquarters in Berlin. Oster told Müller that he knew of his activities with the Catholic church. The shocked Müller was then informed that the Abwehr itself was involved in resistance activities, working directly with General Beck. Oster went on to state that he wanted Müller to establish a channel of communication with the Vatican in behalf of the resistance. The plan was for Müller to be drafted for military duty and assigned to the Abwehr. That would provide him the freedom to travel outside of Germany, which Müller could not do as a civilian because the Gestapo was aware of his anti–Nazi activities on behalf of the Catholic church. Within a short time, Müller was activated as a first lieutenant and was assigned to the Abwehr office in Munich.

In October 1939, Müller traveled to Rome to establish contact with the British government through the Vatican. Müller had two important friends living in Rome at the time: Monsignor Kaas, once a leader of the Catholic Center party in Germany and now an adviser to the pope, and Father Robert Lieber, a Jesuit and the pope's personal secretary.

Müller asked Father Lieber to meet with Pius XII and speak for him. Lieber approached the pontiff, who agreed to a meeting at once, saying, "The German opposition must be heard in Britain." At that meeting, the pope instructed Father Lieber to inform Müller that contact would be established on behalf of the opposition with the British government at the highest levels. The intention was to reestablish peace with a planned replacement government in Germany. The one contingency, of course, was Hitler's removal from power.

Pius XII also dictated arrangements for Müller's future visits to the Vatican. He was to contact Father Lieber, who would convey all questions, responses, and written documents directly to the pope, who would pass them on directly to Sir Francis d'Arcy Osborne, British minister to the Vatican. Osborne would then communicate directly with the British foreign secretary, Lord Edward Frederick Halifax.

These arrangements were later approved by Halifax, after the pope assured him that Müller spoke for the German opposition and could be trusted. The pope insisted on these measures because he wanted to ensure that there would be no face-to-face meetings between himself and Müller, so that both could state honestly that they had never met personally to discuss these sensitive matters.

Müller also asked Lieber to warn the pope that Hitler's government had a copy of the Vatican diplomatic code, which had been supplied to the Nazis by Mussolini and his spies within the walls of the Vatican. Müller had this information by virtue of his official cover as an officer in the Abwehr.

Müller made numerous trips in 1939 and 1940 to convey information back and forth. At first, he had reason to be optimistic. Osborne, the British minister to the Vatican, was quite receptive to discussions with the opposition but adamantly insisted that approval rested on removal of the Nazi government. Considering this proposed arrangement as significant, Müller quickly communicated the information to his allies in the resistance. The group approached the Army High Command and encouraged them to move against Hitler, using the army to stage a coup. They presented a report called the X Report,* so named because Müller was referred to in the document as "Mr. X" as a means of protecting his identity.

The report contained a summary of Britain's response and conditions. These included a requirement that the Nazi government must be removed and replaced with a democratic one and a guarantee from the new government that there would be no German attack in the West while negotiations were underway. (The report was drafted after the start of war, but before the German assaults on Holland, Belgium, and France.) England was prepared to guarantee in return that some provisions of the Versailles Treaty would be modified, including those dealing with Germany's eastern borders.

Military response to the X Report was not favorable. The commander in chief of the armed forces, Field Marshal Walther von Brauchitsch, was approached by his chief of staff, General Franz Halder, and shown the report spelling out Müller's negotiations

---

*In 1944, when the Gestapo got a copy of the report, they opened their own file concerning Catholic contacts with the Vatican. They gave the operation a title of their own: the Black Chapel, a reference to the color worn by priests.

in Rome and the English response. Brauchitsch told Halder: "You should not have shown me this. What is happening here is sheer treason. Under no circumstances can we be involved in this. We are at war. In peacetime you can talk about contacts with a foreign power, but in wartime soldiers cannot do that."[11]

Brauchitsch then demanded to know where Halder had obtained the report, saying he would arrest the offender. Halder answered, "If anyone is to be arrested, you had better arrest me." Brauchitsch, while refusing to become an active participant in the opposition, decided instead to maintain a discreet silence.

Perhaps because of the complex lines of communication from the opposition to the British, negotiations never went anywhere. The British did not trust the Germans, even with endorsement from the Vatican. With the intelligence provided to the Vatican through Müller, the pope was able to forewarn the British of German military intentions against France. The opposition offered to remove the Nazis before the French campaign began in return for guarantees for peace negotiations. On January 16, 1940, the British War Cabinet considered the offer and rejected it, saying that the Nazis would have to be removed before any ironclad guarantees would be given.

On February 17, 1940, the British government responded with a formal position statement to Osborne, which summarized their concerns:

> If His Majesty's Government were convinced that the intermediaries who approached His Holiness represented principals in Germany who had both the intention and the power to perform what they promised, His Majesty's Government would be willing to consider with the French Government any enquiries that those principals might make. But His Majesty's Government could not broach this question with the French Government on the basis of ideas emanating from undisclosed sources and so vague in character as those which have been conveyed to you.[12]

The opposition leaders were frustrated by British mistrust. Army leaders could not be convinced to launch an armed coup without British guarantees for peace terms, and the British would not provide such guarantees until Hitler had been removed from power and replaced with an acceptable democratic regime. This standoff was the first of many that would be repeated until the end of the Second World War. Extensive diplomatic contacts, made through several countries, always came to the same impasse.

On Müller's numerous trips to Rome, he also carried reports documenting Nazi actions against the Catholic church in Germany. These were compiled in Munich by Father Johann Neuhausler and given to Müller. The Vatican published a summary of these reports in 1940 in a document called "The Persecution of the Catholic Church in the Third Reich: Facts and Figures." Müller's efforts were the first of numerous diplomatic contacts between Allied countries and the opposition. Those efforts were not successful, but Müller kept the Vatican aware of Nazi oppression of the Catholic church in Germany. His negotiations with the Vatican led to his arrest in April 1943. He was kept on a near-starvation diet and was ill-treated for two years but survived to be liberated by the U.S. Army on May 4, 1945.

The majority of Germany's 45 million Protestants of the early 1930s were members of 28 Lutheran and Reformed churches. The largest sect was the Church of the Old Prussian Union, which claimed 18 million members.[13]

These churches were evangelical* in nature. Their fundamentalist policies restricted women to what was called the three K's—*Kirche, Kinder, Küche* (church, children, kitchen). As German evangelicals, the faithful were nationalistic. They believed that the German Volk was a spiritual experience and a divine revelation. The majority of churches were Lutheran, and Martin Luther's extreme anti–Semitism continued to form the basis of belief for many devout Protestants in the 1930s. While the Catholic church was organized under one international ruling body, Protestant churches were considerably more independent. This made it easier for the Nazi government to silence opposition, and it took advantage of the segmentation in the Protestant churches.

In addition to the structural differences between the two primary Christian groups, the Nazis were aided by a rift between Protestant sects that developed early in the Nazi regime and was never resolved. One group was determined to resist any state effort to regulate the Protestant church; another believed that a unified and state-sponsored Protestant organization was the only way to remain effective within Nazi Germany and to be allowed to continue operating effectively.

The problems began when several Nazi Protestants took steps to make the church organization a part of the Nazi government. To achieve this, they joined forces with the German Christians' Faith Movement in 1932. This organization was founded by Pastor Joachim Hossenfelder and two of the Kaiser's sons, Prince Eitel Friedrich and Prince August Wilhelm.

Members of the German Christians' Faith Movement professed the desire to create a type of "Nazified Protestanism" and attempted to draw comparisons between the cross of Christ and the swastika of the Nazis. Godlessness, according to the dogma of these German Christians, was expressed by Communism. They equated Germanism with Christianity, claiming that God had called upon the "pure" German race to undertake a holy mission. Hitler had been sent to Germany by God as part of that mission. By 1933 the regime was determined to unite all Protestants in Germany under a single state church; the German Christians' Faith Movement was, naturally, the most likely group to lead the cause.

In July 1933, the movement completed a new constitution for what it called the Reich church, which was recognized by the Reichstag on July 14. Debate broke out at once over nomination of the Reich bishop, with Hitler supporting Ludwig Müller, an army chaplain and dedicated Nazi. Under intimidation by the Gestapo, the other candidate, Pastor Friedrich von Bodelschwingh, withdrew from the race, and Müller won the synod† election unopposed. One-third of all Prussian synods refused to go along with Müller's election, but Hitler responded by simply abolishing all synods by decree.

The true purpose in attempting to unite the Protestant Churches in Germany under

---

The vast majority of Germans in the 1930s and 1940s were members of Evangelical Protestant churches. In many of those sects, religious and nationalistic concepts were tied so closely together that for some, Nazism and Christianity were not difficult to reconcile.

†*A synod is an advisory board or governing body of the church, with ruling powers similar to those of a judiciary.*

a state-controlled body was aptly described by Nazi philosopher Alfred Rosenberg, author of the 1930 book *The Myth of the Twentieth Century,* who drafted a 30-point program setting forth the objectives of the Reich church. These points included halting publication and distribution of the Bible, declaring *Mein Kampf* as the "greatest of all documents," which "embodies the purest and truest ethics," removing crucifixes, Bibles, and pictures of saints from church altars and replacing them with a copy of *Mein Kampf* and a sword, and replacing crosses on churches and chapels with the swastika.[14]

The German Christians' Faith Movement enthusiastically endorsed such views. At a mass meeting held in November 1933 at the Sports-Palast in Berlin, 20,000 attendees belonging to the sect approved several proposals offered by Dr. Reinhardt Krause, Berlin German Christian district leader. These proposals included abolishing the Old Testament in its entirety, expelling everyone with Jewish blood from the Evangelical community, and revising the New Testament so that the Christian philosophy of Jesus would conform "entirely with the demands of National Socialism." Krause referred to St. Paul as a "Jew rabbi," and when the vote on his proposals was taken, there was only one dissenting vote.

The Reich church had the approval and protection of the Nazi regime, but it was no match for the well-organized Protestant opposition. Unlike Catholic protests, which for the most part were undertaken individually and without any central organizing body, the Protestant opposition was well structured. In 1933 several Evangelical pastors formed the *Bekenntniskirche* (confessional church).

The Confessionals had the sole purpose of preventing state interference in church matters; this desire was far stronger than a specific disagreement with the Nazi ideology. They wanted to maintain their independence and were determined to prevent the Nazis from dictating policy to the Protestant church. The Confessional church became the center of religious resistance in Germany. Unfortunately, it, too, was split by internal disagreement. The Confessionals eventually claimed 5,000 members but never reconciled the interests of moderates and conservatives.

One of the most notable members of the Confessional church was Martin Niemöller, pastor of Dahlem. Niemöller had commanded a U-boat during the First World War and had become a Protestant pastor in the 1920s. He looked the part of a Prussian military officer and had a harsh, staccato voice with a clipped accent. He was contradictory and controversial, having been an ardent Nazi himself in 1924. In his book, *From U-Boat to Pulpit,* he had criticized the Weimar Republic and praised the Nazi rise to power as a "national revival."

Niemöller was conservative and less conciliatory than the more moderate Confessionals. His original praise of the Nazi movement did not last long. He reversed his stance as the Nazi program for the churches developed. In September 1933, he founded the Pfarrernotbund (Pastors Emergency League) as a means of combating government attempts to unify Protestant churches under a single state-approved entity. Over 1,300 pastors joined the union as soon as it was formed, and within three months, it had more than 6,000 members, or about one-third of all pastors in Germany.

Niemöller proclaimed, "We appeal to all pastors to anchor themselves on Holy Scripture and the beliefs of the Reformation, and to protest against every attack on their beliefs." He subscribed to the idea of creating a *Freikirche* (free church), to break away from society and live in the wilderness, where pure Christianity would be defended from the encroachment of the Nazi state.

The Reich bishop, Ludwig Müller, warned that any pastors not going along with the official Nazi line would be disciplined, and on January 26, 1934, he forced Niemöller to retire. Refusing to recognize the Reich bishop's authority, Niemöller became an early organizer of the Confessionals, and several meetings of its leaders were held in his home. At its synod in May 1934, the Confessional church declared itself the only official and legitimate Protestant church in Germany and established its own church governing body.

The Confessional church committed itself from this point forward to active opposition. In subsequent synods, held in October 1934 and in March 1935, the Confessionals elected their own leadership and issued a declaration condemning Nazi "racial mysticism" to be read from all Confessional church pulpits. It read: "We see our people threatened by a deadly danger. The danger consists in a new religion."

The statement was read in churches throughout Germany, leading to the arrest of over 700 pastors. Widespread protests led to release of most of those arrested within a few days. But at least 27 pastors were sent to Dachau, and 61 were forbidden from preaching any further.

After this incident, the government formed a new agency called the Department of State for Church Affairs. Müller, however, refused to resign and was left at his post without any influence or duties to perform. In his place, Hitler appointed a lawyer, Dr. Hans Kerrl, to the post of minister for church affairs. He, like Müller, was given the task of unifying the Protestant churches in Germany.

More conciliatory than Müller, Kerrl was able to consolidate a number of the more conservative churches, and even Niemöller's group cooperated when Kerrl included Confessional church representatives on a "Reich Church Committee." Although this committee was called an advisory body, it soon became apparent that the invitation was only a public relations ruse and that the committee held no real influence.

The Confessional church leadership presented a letter to Hitler in 1936, protesting anti–Christian practices and strongly denouncing anti–Semitism. The letter demanded an end to state interference in church business. In response, Minister of the Interior Frick had hundreds of Confessional church pastors rounded up and sent to concentration camps. Church investments, assets, and bank accounts were seized, and further collections were forbidden.*

Oppression of Confessional church pastors worsened. In June 1937, several pastors were arrested for refusing to hoist the swastika in their churches, while others had defied Nazi rules by publishing brochures and newsletters critical of the government.

Niemöller gave his last sermon in Nazi Germany to a crowded congregation on June 27, 1937, in his church at Dahlem. He stated during that sermon: "No more are we ready to keep silent at man's behest when God commands us to speak. For it is, and must remain, the case that we must obey God rather than man."[15]

---

*In response to widespread opposition from Evangelical churches, the regime cut state grants, which had been a primary revenue source prior to 1934. Only one-third of revenues came from grants by 1944, and income from church properties and investments was cut as well, as a consequence of Nazi seizure. The reduction of grants, seizure of property and assets, and prevention of church collections, broke down much of the resistance that originated in the Evangelical churches.

Niemöller was arrested on July 1, and sent to Moabit prison in Berlin. He was tried by a *Sondergericht* (Special Court) on March 2, 1938. He was fined 2,000 marks and sentenced to seven months in prison on charges of "abuse of the pulpit" and taking collections in his church in spite of a ban on collections. He was cleared on the more serious charge of conspiring against the state.

Niemöller was released because he had already spent more than seven months in prison before his case came to trial, but he was arrested again by the Gestapo on his way out of court and taken into "protective custody." He was sent first to Sachsenhausen and then to Dachau, where he was placed in solitary confinement. While not mistreated in prison, he had been silenced once and for all, and the opposition was forced to proceed without his voice. He spent the war years in prison.*

While Niemöller was preaching in defiance of the Nazi government, Evangelical bishops undertook a series of direct protests against state policies, including confronting Hitler in person. In January 1934, a committee of church leaders met with Hitler to present a list of grievances. They were not received warmly and were warned that their duty was to go along with the Nazi movement and stop protesting.

In March, Protestant bishops tried again to arrange an agreement between the churches and the government. This effort was led by Bishops Theophil Wurm of Württemberg and Hans Meiser of Bavaria, both of whom had been briefly arrested in 1933 for refusing to merge their provincial churches with the newly formed Reich church. The bishops complained that they had not been able to work out a satisfactory agreement with the Reich bishop, Ludwig Müller. They warned Hitler that any further pressure from the Nazis would force them into a "Loyal Opposition." Hitler had one of his famous temper tantrums when accosted by the bishops. He told them that the Evangelical churches had disintegrated in 1918 and had become dupes of the Roman Catholic church on one side, and the Marxists on the other. He screamed at the bishops, accusing them of being traitors and enemies of the state.

In August 1934, Bishops Wurm and Meiser formed a "Fighting Front" to resist a Nazi-organized synod to merge all Evangelical churches in Germany. The bishops continued to insist on independence. Wurm was arrested and accused of embezzling church funds and bankrolling Hitler's political enemies. He was released after four days. When Müller, the Reich bishop, asked him to retire, Wurm refused to go voluntarily, but he was removed from his position on October 9, 1934, and declared *Volks und Staatsfeindliche Elemente* (enemy of the State). He was again placed under arrest and confined to his home in Stuttgart.

About 7,000 citizens gathered at Bishop Wurm's home on October 21, 1934, angrily demanding his release. The Nazis gave in and released him from house arrest. On October 12, Bishop Meiser was arrested, an event that led to large, violent protests in several cities. Meiser was released and reinstated.

---

*True to his contradictory form, when the Second World War began, Niemöller applied for permission to join the navy, but at age 47 he was too old to be given a commission.

By February 1935, the two bishops were again active in their resistance to the Nazis. They helped organize demonstrations to protest paganism growing among German youth, especially among Hitler Youth bands. Over the coming years, both bishops were placed under house arrest several times and given repeated warnings for their activities against official policies.

In July 1940, Bishop Wurm protested to the Ministry of the Interior concerning the daily killings of over 40 mentally ill patients and epileptics at the Grafeneck Hospital. In 1941, Wurm tried to prevent the government from banning church publications, and he also began writing directly to Hitler to protest state interference in church matters. Beginning in 1942, Wurm and Meiser began mass conversions of Jews, arguing that once they were converted to Christianity, they could not legally be subjected to discrimination. In 1943, the bishops openly protested the treatment of Jews in concentration camps, which was officially still a "secret," though widely known. The Gestapo called on Wurm in 1944, without result, and on March 3 of that year, Wurm was given a "final" warning, following publication of his criticisms in the foreign press. Amazingly, both Wurm and Meiser survived the war.

The bishops were not the only ones who had thought of helping Jews through conversion to Christianity. In 1936, Pastors Heinrich Grüber and Martin Albertz founded the Bureau of Christians of Jewish Birth in Berlin. The purpose of this organization was to help Jews being persecuted under terms of the racially-based Nürnberg Laws. Grüber also worked discreetly to help many Jews emigrate with forged passports. He was arrested in 1940 and sent to Sachsenhausen and later to Dachau. He spent the remainder of the war in the camps, working courageously to help other prisoners survive.

Individual local pastors like Grüber, being relatively obscure, were in greater danger than high-profile church leaders like Wurm and Meiser. One example was Paul Schneider, pastor of a small town called Dickenschied.

Schneider was born in 1897 in the village of Pferdsfeld, the son of a country parson. He entered the church himself and attacked his job with spirit. Physically strong and robust, Schneider was at the same time a tender and caring person. He was often seen traveling around his parish on a motorcycle.

Schneider was absolutely opposed to the Nazis and believed that their philosophy was anti–Christian. He especially thought it distasteful to attract children as young as seven to join the Nazi-sponsored youth organizations and participate in military exercises. As early as October 1933, Schneider attracted attention to himself by criticizing the Nazis. At the time, he was pastor at Hochelheim, and he preached that the creation of a Nazi-led government would be a mistake. For the expression of this viewpoint, the local consistorial council asked Schneider to resign and leave the area, and his bishop also criticized him.

In February 1934, Schneider left and was reassigned to Dickenschied, located 120 miles away in a mainly Catholic region. The Evangelical congregation there numbered only 500. In spite of his banishment, Schneider continued to speak out, and by June 1934, he found himself in another confrontation with the Nazis.

While conducting funeral services for a member of the Hitler Youth who had died, Schneider was interrupted by the local group leader, who proclaimed that his dead comrade was now in a Hitler Youth brigade in heaven. Schneider contradicted this, reminding the young man that members of the Hitler Youth were not granted automatic entry to heaven by St. Peter.

Schneider was arrested and imprisoned for speaking out in such a manner, but was released after one week because of protests by his congregation. He was warned upon release not to make any more statements hostile to the government. He immediately wrote a letter protesting the warning. In 1935 he accelerated his criticisms and was in trouble constantly with the Nazi authorities. He protested the arrest of several hundred Confessional pastors in Prussia that year and took up collections to help the Jews being persecuted by the government. He was also accused of referring to Hitler as the devil's agent.

During the 1936 elections, when voters were asked to vote approval of Hitler's policies, Schneider drew attention to himself again. Since a "no" vote was not an option, Schneider simply didn't go to the polls. During the night, his house was painted with the words: "He did not vote for the Fatherland! Germans, what do you say to that?" Members of Schneider's congregation washed off the message the following day.

Schneider's anti–Nazi actions continued until, on May 31, 1937, he was arrested by the Gestapo and taken for questioning to Coblenz. He was given an order forbidding him to return to Dickenschied, which he tore up. He then boarded the next train for Dickenschied, where friends convinced him he should go instead to a small village in the Black Forest. Unhappy there, he corresponded with his parish council and was told that the Nazis had put an end to religious classes for children. There were no Sunday services some weeks, although neighboring pastors occasionally were able to hold services. No one was available to make visits to the sick, and frightened members of the congregation wanted Schneider to return.

On September 30, Schneider wrote to the Reich Chancellery and asked permission to return to his parish. Not waiting for a reply, he returned to Dickenschied on October 2. On the way to evening services the same day, he was arrested by the Gestapo.

Sent to Buchenwald, Schneider was kept in solitary confinement and periodically beaten and tortured. He was told that if he would promise to sign an agreement not to return to Dickenschied, he would be released. When asked if he preferred life in the concentration camp, he replied, "I do not prefer it, but if it is ordained that I must bear it, than I shall bear it also."

From his cell, Schneider could see the camp's main compound. He prayed loudly so that his resonant voice was heard across the entire compound. When SS guards shot or brutalized prisoners on the compound, Schneider would confront them by calling out from his cell: "I saw that, and I will accuse you of murder before God at your judgment."

Schneider was kept at Buchenwald for two years until, on July 18, 1939, he was taken to the prison hospital and given five injections, any one of which would have been lethal. His body was delivered to his home in a sealed coffin with orders that it was not to be opened. To the end, he continued to proclaim boldly against the Nazis, even when he was in their camps and being treated with the most extreme brutality. He exemplified the moral resistance to the Nazi philosophy and inspired others in the movement. Showing extraordinary personal courage, he died a true martyr to the cause.

About 5,000 German clergy were arrested and sent to concentration camps during Hitler's reign; about 2,000 of them died. Many non-clergy Germans among youth groups unwilling to be merged into the Hitler Youth were punished for their religious beliefs as well. Many other civilians also were arrested and sent to concentration camps for their religious beliefs. One sect particularly singled out was the Jehovah's Witnesses, whose opposition to military service automatically made all members enemies of the State. Virtually all of the German Jehovah's Witnesses, numbering about 6,000, were arrested and sent to concentration camps, where more than 2,000 perished.

The story of the church-led resistance is one of inconsistent outcome. While thousands went to prison, the response by the Nazi regime could not be predicted. Many of the most outspoken critics were warned but left unharmed through to the end of the war. The courage and defiance shown by the clergy helped many other Germans to survive the Nazi years and created a silent opposition among faithful and morally good people in hundreds of German congregations.

Chapter 5

POLITICAL OPPOSITION

It is certain today that every honest German is ashamed of his government.
Who among us has any conception of the dimensions of shame that will
befall us and our children when one day the veil has fallen from our eyes
and the most horrible of crimes — crimes that infinitely outdistance every
human measure — reach the light of day?

Hans Scholl, first leaflet of *The White Rose*, June 1942

Adolf Hitler was applauded when he was first appointed chancellor of Germany, as the first politician in many years able to create a political coalition in the Reichstag. Unfortunately, he achieved this by silencing his political enemies. Deputies unsympathetic to the Nazis were kept from assuming their legally gained seats, others were intimidated into silence or arrested and imprisoned without due process, and eventually all parties except the Nazi party were simply outlawed.

With emergency powers granted to him soon after assuming power, Hitler was able to take extraordinary measures, having identified a scapegoat in the form of the German Communist Party (KPD). From there, it was a relatively easy step to make the case that all opposition could pose a threat to Germany's internal security. On the night of February 27, 1933, the Reichstag building was set on fire. While there is no conclusive proof of Nazi complicity in this event, the incident was a great opportunity for Hitler, who immediately demanded that President Hindenburg approve a decree suspending civil liberties, allow the Reich government to take over all state power temporarily, and impose the death sentence for crimes as minor as disturbing the peace.

Hindenburg, well past his prime and easily tricked by Hitler, believed the explanation that the fire was the beginning of a Communist conspiracy to take over Germany. Hitler had all the power he needed to begin to silence his political opposition. As soon as the decree had been signed, Hitler's S.A. was on the streets, rounding up and arresting Communist party leaders. Members of the Social Democrats and other political parties soon became targets as well. It was soon clear to the newly outlawed opposition parties that any continued political activity would have to go underground to survive at all.

Hitler's gaining total power depended upon his silencing all opposition. The list of opposing political parties could be made up easily from a study of election results. The Center Party, Social Democrats, and Communists were virtually all of the serious political opposition the Nazis faced; together they represented a formidable group of opponents. Hitler took advantage of the fact that none of these groups had been able to form a coalition to keep him out of power.

Many of the Communist leaders, having been trained in the techniques of revolution, knew how to organize secret resistance cells and carry on political activities underground. Other political parties did not fare as well because they believed that it would be possible to continue to function within the government. For example, the Social Democrat party chairman, Otto Wels, predicted as the Nazis rose to power that the oppressive political climate created by Hitler would be short-lived in Germany. "Harsh rulers do not govern long," he declared.

Political parties driven underground by the Nazis turned to publication. A number of Germans, either in exile or working within German borders, continued their political activism by speaking out in print. Freedom of speech was repealed, but that did not prevent the presses from rolling. Germany was a society dependent upon the printed word for information. People were hungry for unbiased news, and all radio broadcasts were completely controlled by the State. A market for underground information grew and persisted from 1933 to 1945.

The Nazis especially targeted political writings and were quick to silence any and all opposition. One long-standing enemy of the Nazi movement was Ernst Niekisch. He founded *Der Widerstand* (The Resistance) in 1926, originally to publish protests against reparations. Niekisch labeled reparations as blackmail and called for a world revolution against capitalism. Well before Hitler's rise to power, Niekisch was labeled a "National-Bolshevist." In 1932 he took on the Nazis and criticized their policies and their leader. He published a pamphlet that year entitled, "Hitler, A German Disaster." He continued publishing until the end of 1934, when the Gestapo seized all copies they could find of *Der Widerstand*. Niekisch was not arrested until 1937, when he was given a life sentence. He was released from Brandenburg prison in 1945.

Other political writers were targeted as well. One of the first Social Democrat writers to be jailed after Hitler came to power was Julius Leber. Editor since the early 1920s of the *Luebecker Volksboten* (Luebeck People's Messenger), he became a member of the Reichstag in 1924. When the Nazis came to power in 1933, Leber was arrested as a political enemy and sent to the camps, where he was subjected to extreme brutality. Even in these conditions, he continued his writings, which included a thesis on the subject of the Weimar Republic.

Leber was released in 1937 and moved to Berlin. While he was not allowed to publish, he continued writing privately. He was arrested again in 1944 for his involvement in the July 1944 plot (in which a bomb was set that nearly killed Hitler), and he was executed on January 5, 1945.

Leber had chosen to remain in Germany, despite the Nazi authorities' scrutiny of him. But for many, the Nazi rise to power made it impossible to remain. During 1933, thousands of Social Democrats fled the country. No less than 3,000 left Germany, most going to Prague. From there, a number of newspapers were started up and smuggled into

Germany. These included the *Sozialistische Aktion* (Socialist Action) and *Neue Vorwärts* (New Progress). Publishers set up courier routes, slipping across the border into Germany in isolated areas.

Publishing news outside of the country and then smuggling it in had its advantages. Away from the watchful eye of the Nazis, political exiles could obtain foreign news and express it any way they wanted, without fear of capture. Their disadvantage was in being removed from their home and from the all-important domestic political scene of which they had been a part. A number of politicians, although they recognized the danger of continuing to speak out actively in Germany, chose to remain and publish their point of view under constant threat of discovery, arrest, and even execution.

One of these politicians was the most prominent Social Democrat in the Hamburg borough of Eilbek, Walter Schmedemann. He was arrested shortly after Hitler came to power and spent several weeks in prison. Upon release, he was warned not to participate in any political activities. Ignoring this warning, Schmedemann and his followers organized the "Eilbek Comrades" and produced a flyer of four pages, the purpose of which was to report uncensored political news. This paper, which reached a circulation of 5,000, was funded by the illegal sale of picture postcards. Using an extensive courier network, copies were smuggled to Czechoslovakia and Denmark, and even into the Oranienburg concentration camp.

Schmedemann was arrested in his third year of underground activity and sent to Fuhlsbüttel concentration camp for several months. Upon his release, he published and distributed a brochure describing what he had seen in the camp, including a complete listing of dates, crimes, and names of the Nazis responsible. In addition to sending the leaflets to large numbers of citizens, Schmedemann mailed copies to all leading Nazis in Hamburg. Schmedemann explained after the war that "At least they could not claim that they didn't know what was being done in the name of the Party."[1]

Schmedemann's activity was not an isolated case. Such political underground work was extensive. By July 1933, German prison camps held 26,789 political prisoners. Most of those were Social Democrats. In the year 1936, another 11,687 were arrested and charged with working for the Social Democrats, and in 1937, another 8,000 were taken in by the Gestapo.[2]

Publication was obviously a primary source of political opposition, and by 1937 the Gestapo was confiscating large volumes of illegally produced material — approximately 4,000 copies of underground publications each month. The arrests of political opponents were not merely for activities as overt as publishing newspapers or brochures, however. In Nazi Germany, even seemingly small acts of defiance were treated as crimes. It was considered a serious offense, for example, to tell a joke about the Nazis, and even laughing at such a joke could lead to arrest and imprisonment.*

The Social Democrat party had been one of the most powerful parties prior to the Nazi era. Perceived as a potential threat to singular political dominance, Social Democrats were purposefully removed from the civil service, police, teaching jobs, and the military.

---

*One may tell the mood of a country by the types of jokes it tells, even under threat of reprisal. During the Second World War, German beer quality declined, which caused much resentment. This was expressed by jokes such as this one: A disgusted beer drinker sent a sample of beer to a lab to be tested. The results came back: "Your horse has diabetes."

For the most part, the politically active members of this party advocated political solutions rather than any violent action against the Nazis. One exception to this was Bebo Wager, a leading Social Democrat involved with underground political groups in Augsburg. He advocated armed revolt but was unable to follow through because he was caught in a net of arrests in 1942. He was killed while being held in Stadelheim Prison in Munich in August, 1943; in his last letter to his wife, he wrote, "I will try to die bravely for my beliefs."

Another opposition group actively publishing during the early years of the Nazi regime was Roterstoßtrupp (Red Shock Troop).* Organized in bands called *Fünfer-Gruppen* (Groups of Five), they produced pamphlets up to 28 pages in length and enjoyed a circulation of 3,000 in the Berlin area, with new editions appearing as frequently as every 10 days. They also aided wives and children of political prisoners in concentration camps. They operated until November 1933, when their leader, Rudolf Küstermeier, was arrested.

Another well-organized group was Neu-Beginnen (Starting Anew). At the height of its activity, Neu-Beginnen was active throughout all of Europe. Small cells formed in towns and neighborhoods of cities, under the control of a central leadership. It had originated as early as 1929, when its founder, Walther Löwenheim (who used the pseudonym "Miles") became concerned about the dangers of a fascist revolution. Originally, his group called itself the "Leninist Organization," which they referred to with the abbreviation the "O."

The name "Neu-Beginnen" was taken from a 1933 pamphlet of the same name. Written by Löwenheim under the "Miles" pseudonym, it was issued by the Social Democrat party in exile through its publisher, Graphia. The pamphlet criticized the Nazis and proposed solutions that labor leaders might need to adopt to fight Nazism. It made a favorable impression on many in the labor movement. The publication was smuggled into Germany in large numbers. It and other underground pamphlets were given false bindings and false titles. For example, 5,000 copies of *Neu-Beginnen* found their way into Germany as "Schopenhauer on Religion."

The group hoped to influence the formation of a government after the hoped-for Nazi collapse. It published a news pamphlet called *Das Grüne Otto* (The Green Otto) to summarize foreign broadcast news and to reprint stories from overseas newspapers. Neu-Beginnen leaders spied on German arms transports and forwarded information to exiled Social Democrats, where the information was passed on to the Allies. Hundreds of members were arrested but because of the caution exercised in the secretive structure of the organization, most members knew the name of only a few other members. It continued to thrive until 1944.

Brochures and pamphlets were easy to use as political tools. They required little room, little time, and could be stockpiled without drawing attention to their authors. Duplicating machines were portable and widely used. Groups like Neu-Beginnen could publish regularly and move around, taking their equipment with them. It was less common for political opponents of the Nazis to publish books.

One exception to this was the *Brown Book of the Reichstag Fire*. It was printed in

---

The organization was originally called Reichsbanner Schwarz-Rot-Gold (Empire Banner Black-Red-Gold). Some former members broke away and formed Roterstoßtrupp.

one large volume and smuggled into Germany by the Vereinigte Kletterabteilung (United Scramblers), disguised with false bindings and covers (most frequently used was Johann Schiller's play, *Wallenstein*). More than 100 members of this group were killed or imprisoned by the Nazis.

For the most part, well-organized publication efforts were shut down by 1940. Those who had produced political publications underground had been arrested or frightened into silence by the efficiency of Nazi investigative forces. One example of underground work attracted international attention in 1943, however. That was the case of Hans and Sophie Scholl.

The Scholls were not members of the Communist party or of any other group that was a threat to the Nazi regime. They were young students in Munich, and their crime consisted of publishing and distributing several underground leaflets under the name of *Die Weiße Rose** (The White Rose). The publications the students produced, *Flugblätter der Weißen Rose* (Leaflets of the White Rose), protested Nazi policies but were by no means a call to insurrection. But publication of any dissent in the Third Reich was considered treason, and the penalty was death.

Hans Scholl, a 24-year-old student at the University of Munich, had joined the Hitler Youth at the age of 15. Although membership was virtually mandatory, Hans had joined with enthusiasm. He soon became disillusioned, however. He had attended the Nuremberg Party Rally and participated as a standard-bearer, but he complained that the speeches he had heard there contained no substance and were just a lot of meaningless political talk and empty promises.

Hans was also a member of the Bündische Jugend (Youth League), which was declared illegal under the Nazi regime. Refusing to give up his membership, Hans and several friends continued holding discussion meetings without the political indoctrination they saw in the Hitler Youth. In 1937 the group's activities were reported to the Gestapo; several youths were taken into custody and their books and phonograph records seized. Hans was held in jail for six weeks on the crime of "loose talk," and when he was released, the Gestapo began intercepting his mail and reading it. He was warned to go along with the Hitler Youth program or face dire consequences. He became entirely cynical about the Nazi movement but was one of the fortunate ones. Several of his comrades died in custody or were taken away, never to be heard from again.

Listening more to his own stubborn and rebellious nature than to the Gestapo, Hans helped form a group called "D. J. One-Eleven," which stood for "German Youth of the First of November." That was the date a comrade had died the previous year in a climbing accident. This group was strictly apolitical and was involved in nature hikes and innocent meetings, where intellectual discussions were held. The allure of formalizing their association lay largely in the fact that such groups were illegal in Nazi Germany.

Hans' rebellious activities were curtailed in 1937, when he was conscripted into the

---

This is the title of an adventure tale set in Mexico by an author named Traven. The name has no significance or relationship to the Scholl underground activity. Hans simply liked the name.

army. Released after the required two-year induction period, he entered the University of Munich and began premed studies. Within less than a year, the Second World War began, and Hans was redrafted and sent to France, where he served as a medic. While he was serving in the army, his father was arrested by the Gestapo for making remarks critical of Hitler. He was threatened but released the following morning. His father's brief but unsettling arrest as well as his own exposure to the ugly realities of war only added to Hans' personal cynicism about the Nazi movement.

While Hans was home on leave the weekend after his father's arrest, an anonymous flyer arrived at the house by mail. It was an 800-word criticism of the Third Reich based on the sermons delivered by the outspoken Nazi critic, Bishop Galen. Hans said he found it refreshing that someone had the courage to speak out against the wrongs of the Nazi regime.

Fired with youthful zest, Hans immediately bought a duplicating machine and other supplies and decided that he too would produce anti–Nazi literature. Several comrades in his medical unit who agreed with Hans' views joined with him in the venture. These included three men who, like Hans, were all 24 at the time: Christoph Probst, married with two children; Wilhelm Graf, who like Hans had once been arrested and jailed for belonging to an illegal youth organization; and Alexander Schmorell, a native of Russia and the son of a Munich doctor.

Schmorell spent many hours working with Hans and editing their first leaflet, which culminated in a thousand-word criticism of the Nazi regime. They quoted Goethe and Schiller as well as the ancient Greeks in challenging Germans to find the courage to engage in passive resistance. Then, entering the university before dawn, they placed the leaflets where students would easily find them. Many more copies were mailed to professionals in Munich, imitating the technique used by the author of the anonymous flyer that arrived at the Scholl household.

Sophie Scholl, Hans' sister, was a sensitive, intelligent 21-year-old student newly enrolled at the university. She had spent the previous six months as a conscript in the Reich Labor Service for Young Women. Discipline in the work camp was strict, and the girls spent long hours working in the fields or listening to Nazi indoctrination. The experience confirmed her as an ardent anti–Nazi, and she was looking forward to the relatively free and intellectual life of a university student. One evening Sophie found in Hans' room a copy of one of the illegal leaflets that contained a quotation from Schiller. Hans also had in his room a published copy of the work in which the same passage had been highlighted. When Sophie told Hans she knew he was the author of the pamphlet, he resisted at first, telling her it was best not to know about such matters. Eventually, though, Sophie insisted on working with him, and she was allowed to join the White Rose.

In June 1942, Hans and his friends were invited to dinner at the home of Frau Dr. Mertens, who wanted to introduce them to the brilliant professor and head of the philosophy and psychology departments at the University of Munich, Kurt Huber. The youths and the professor found they had much in common and shared the same dislike of the Nazi regime. From that evening onward, the professor worked with the zealous students, exerting a mature influence upon them and editing their future work.

Within a month, three more leaflets had been produced and distributed at the university and through the mail. They criticized *Mein Kampf* not only for its philosophy, but also for its writing style. They also criticized the treatment of the Jews, accusing the Nazi leadership of being an evil dictatorship. The leaflets called for work slowdowns and sabotage in armaments factories and warned of mounting German casualties on the Eastern Front. Readers were asked not to contribute money, clothing, or materials to the war effort. The leaflets proclaimed Hitler as the greatest liar in history.

The Gestapo was frustrated at the defiance of the White Rose. Within hours of the first leaflet's distribution, they had a copy. Numerous agents were placed on the university campus to catch those responsible, but without luck. Duplicating machines were so common that there was no way to trace the source. To the authorities, the leaflets seemed to appear suddenly, only to be snatched up immediately by students.

The White Rose activities were suspended in July 1942 when Scholl and his fellow medics were given one day's notice and shipped out to the Eastern Front. German casualties that summer exceeded 1.4 million, with an average of 3,300 wounded or killed every day. Medics were kept busy day and night. By that fall, as the German Sixth Army made its way toward Stalingrad and disaster, Scholl and his medical company were detached and returned to Germany.

In Munich, Hans registered for the fall semester at the university. While he had been away, copies of his four leaflets were distributed throughout Germany, primarily within the student community. The White Rose leaflets were well known and appreciated among the student population in numerous cities. Hans decided to expand his publication activities.

A friend who had been drafted offered Hans the use of his studio apartment in Munich. The timing was perfect. Hans and Sophie moved their duplicating machine and their other supplies to the studio in December, intending to use it as their headquarters to produce more leaflets and to distribute more copies than ever.

This new effort lacked the romantic references contained in previous leaflets and reflected Hans' sobering experiences of war. It was more blunt than the others and contained fewer references to the classics and more direct criticisms of the Nazis. By now, the name "The White Rose" had been abandoned and replaced by "Leaflet of the Resistance." The Scholls, working with their companions Probst and Schmorell and benefiting from Huber's editorial help, finished their fifth leaflet and made 3,000 copies.

Determined to spread their message throughout Germany, the group decided the leaflets should be transported in person. Sophie, carrying a suitcase stuffed with envelopes already addressed and containing leaflets, boarded a crowded train for Augsburg. Trains and train stations were full of policemen and Gestapo agents, and the group could not have picked a more dangerous method of distributing their material. But Sophie was lucky. She walked through the station to a mailbox, where she deposited the contents of the suitcase. Then, boarding a return train, she was back in Munich in time for dinner.

Hans had a similar experience. He traveled south to Austria and stopped at Salzburg, where 150 leaflets were mailed to that city's wealthiest and most influential citizens. Schmorell, meanwhile, went to Linz and Vienna, and finally to Frankfurt-am-Main, a 500-mile round trip on which 1,400 leaflets were delivered. Back home in Munich, the group went out at night and hand-delivered and posted hundreds more of the leaflets.

Emboldened by their success thus far, Hans Scholl and Alexander Schmorell made up stencils spelling out, "Down with Hitler" and "Freedom! Hitler the Mass Murderer."

Going to the town hall on the night of February 14, 1943, they painted over their stencil and left their message.

Additional stencils were left on at least 70 other buildings around the city. They also hand-painted additional slogans and political graffiti on buildings and walls, including government buildings, museums, libraries, and the university.

The group drafted a sixth leaflet which led to a disagreement between Hans Scholl and Kurt Huber. Huber wanted to insert the phrase "Stand by our glorious army," but Hans stubbornly refused, now calling himself a pacifist. Huber expressed his anger and, deeply offended at not having his advice taken, left the meeting. He could not know that it was the last time he would see the Scholls.

Early in the morning of February 18, Hans and Sophie walked to the university campus, each carrying satchels stuffed with the latest criticism of the regime. Arriving at the campus before anyone else, they left stacks of leaflets outside lecture halls and classrooms. Sophie, on a third-floor landing, reached into her satchel and threw a handful of leaflets over the banister and onto the courtyard below.

The scene was witnessed by Jacob Schmidt, a maintenance superintendent, who hurried off to report the incident to the Gestapo. He was back with them five minutes later. The Scholls were taken into custody at once and whisked off to Gestapo headquarters. Separated, they were interrogated through that day and the next two. The interrogation was rigorous and thorough, but the students were not mistreated. They both denied any involvement with the distribution of literature until confronted with the results of a search of their studio. That search had also turned up the names of their comrades. Sophie insisted that they were only friends and weren't involved in producing the leaflets. Hans tried to take all of the blame for himself. Finally, both Hans and Sophie Scholl signed confessions. On February 20, Probst was arrested; all three were charged with treason. Their trial was held on February 22, 1943, in the Munich Law Courts. During the trial, none of the students expressed any remorse. Sophie Scholl defiantly told the court, "You all really agree with what we have said and written, but you are afraid of saying so."

Hans Scholl asked the court for clemency for Probst, on the basis that he had a wife and small children. The court was not sympathetic. All three were found guilty and sentenced to death by decapitation. The sentences were carried out that day at Munich-Stadelheim prison, where the three went to their deaths with dignity.

Reaction among the student population of Munich was one of shock. Many began collections for the defense of students subsequently accused of being involved with the venture, and others began painting anti–Nazi slogans of their own around the city. The most popular of the new slogans was *Ihr Geist lebt weiter* (Their spirit lives on).

The Nazis were convinced that the wide distribution of the leaflets indicated that the White Rose had been organized by professionals. They appealed to the group's leaders to come forward and save the students' lives.

In April 1943, several others were placed on trial, including Professor Huber, Alexander Schmorell, and Wilhelm Graf. Huber addressed the court, stating, "During the past ten years the Party has destroyed every sense of moral obligation, as well as freedom in the next generation." At the end of the trial, Huber spoke again, saying, "I appeal for the return of freedom to the German people."

Huber and the two students were given death sentences, which were carried out on July 13. Arrests in other cities of accomplices or suspects totaled between 80 and 100 people. While the deaths of the White Rose group might seem to have been in vain, the story became one of the best publicized around the world. And its telling helped to discredit and embarrass the Nazi regime. Swiss and Swedish papers reported the executions at once, and in the United States, Eleanor Roosevelt referred to the Scholls as "good, splendid young people."

All of the members of the Scholl family were placed in *Sippenhaft* (Family Custody). The women were released after several months, but Hans and Sophie's father, already in trouble with the Gestapo, were held for two years and released near the end of the war.

The brutal suppression and punishment of the Scholls and their companions by the Nazis did great and long-lasting harm to the regime. It had an effect on already deteriorating morale in the Wehrmacht, notably on the Eastern Front. German prisoners of war, inspired by the Scholl story, drafted their own leaflets and speeches. Their Russian captors gladly assisted in duplicating these documents critical of the German government and air-dropped them on the German lines.

A less publicized case was that of Helmut Hübener, who lived in Hamburg. Like Hans Scholl, he had joined the Hitler Youth with great enthusiasm. An excellent student who displayed intelligence and charm, he had ambitions of joining the civil service after completing his education. He began listening to BBC broadcasts in 1941 when only 16 years old and came to realize that the Nazi regime was committing criminal acts.

Hübener immediately began writing leaflets and distributing copies around Hamburg. He produced more than 20 such leaflets between 1941 and 1942. For a boy of 16 (17 by the time of his arrest), his writing style and level of sophistication were extraordinary. Citing his obvious maturity, the court deemed he should be treated like an adult. He was sentenced to death and executed in October 1942.

Young people in Germany resisted the Nazis in a number of ways. Many defiantly refused to stop meeting with other members of youth groups that were outlawed by the Nazis, even after threats and intimidation by the Gestapo and pressure from the Hitler Youth. Some formed secret groups to continue meeting, in spite of the law. The largest group formed to resist among the young was *Edelweiss*, which originated from the Catholic Young Men's Associations after those groups were declared illegal. The organization was particularly strong in heavily Catholic areas, where large numbers of young men forced to belong to the Hitler Youth also secretly joined Edelweiss. Their main activity was discussion of events without the Nazi slant, confirmation of religious beliefs, and rejection of Nazi values.

Another version of anti–Nazi activity was that practiced by a group of rebellious teenagers who became known as the "swing kids." The name referred to their love of swing music, which was strictly banned by the Nazis as being "degenerate" and Negro-influenced.

The swing kids formed into gangs, usually in rougher industrial areas of the larger German cities, and often attacked and beat Hitler Youth members. Using gang names like Navajos, Pirates, and the Black Gang, their opposition was not ideological. It was resistance to the establishment and to the rule that membership in the Hitler Youth was compulsory beginning in 1936.

Youth opposition was so widespread that the State Security Department set up a special Youth Department to investigate antistate activities. And in the town of Neuwied in the Rhineland, a special youth concentration camp was opened, where offenders under the age of 20 were sent.

The Nazis arrested and silenced any citizens who disagreed with their policies, and the Communists were a special target. As one of the strongest political parties in Germany before 1934, Communists were the major opponents of the Nazis, and they were not above using the same strong-arm tactics in street fights or in campaigns for office. Hitler knew that between the Nazis and the Communists, only one party would be able to survive.

The German Communist Party itself declared its utter opposition to the Nazis and its commitment to armed overthrow of the regime. On April 1, 1933, the party's Executive Committee of the Comintern declared:

> The task of the Communists must be to make the masses understand that Hitler's regime is driving the country to disaster.... It is imperative to consolidate the Party and to strengthen the mass organizations of the proletariat, to prepare the masses for the crucial revolutionary battles, for the overthrow of capitalism, for the overthrow of the fascist dictatorship by armed revolt.[3]

Members of the Communist party and sympathizers to their cause claimed more casualties than any other political group. They were, indeed, opposites of the Nazis, and throughout the 1920s and early 1930s, the two groups clashed constantly in the streets and in the polls. According to the postwar East German government, 340,000 Communists were imprisoned within the first six months of the Nazi regime.[4]

Large numbers of Communists were arrested and sentenced to prison in mass trials throughout Germany in 1933 and 1934. Many were given sentences up to six years for crimes such as listening to foreign radio broadcasts or distributing information described as "seditious." Casualties among Reichstag Communist deputies were high. At least 57 legally elected deputies were executed or died in the camps.

The targeting of the German Communist Party enabled Hitler to get his Enabling Act, which allowed him to suspend civil rights while arresting and imprisoning large numbers of Communists. That did not silence the German Communists, however, it only drove them underground. The Berlin edition of the Party's primary newspaper, *Rote Fahne* (Red Flag), claimed an increase in circulation from 70,000 to 300,000 after the burning of the Reichstag building. Huge numbers of other underground Communist publications came into being during the same period.[5]

Forced underground, the German Communist party was ruthlessly suppressed throughout the 12 years of Nazi rule. Most Communist resistance groups used the *troika* (three-man) system. Cells of the underground contained only three people, trained to work together with absolute efficiency, with limited contact outside of the group itself.

One highly organized underground group was Rote Kapelle (Red Orchestra), formed in 1935 by Harro Schulze-Boysen. The group owned its own printing press and produced volumes of pamphlets and leaflets, as well as a newspaper, *Innere Front* (Internal Front). Schulze-Boysen had been a dedicated anti–Nazi as early as 1931, when he had organized a newspaper called *Der Gegner* (The Opponent). He had participated in numerous street fights with Nazi opponents and was jailed and beaten in 1933. Yet he was able to find employment in the "Research Office," the Luftwaffe intelligence service, because of his mother's personal friendship with Göring. And he was married to the daughter of Countess Eulenburg, also a friend of influential Nazi leaders.

Schulze-Boysen had friends and contacts in the several government ministries that were extremely valuable after Hitler attacked the Soviet Union. Although Communist opposition remained relatively dormant from 1937 through 1942, it became very active after the German invasion of the Soviet Union on June 22, 1941. For the following year, Rote Kapelle served as the Soviets' chief spy network in the Third Reich. They also continued to publish widely.

In addition to the *Innere Front*, the group also produced *21 Seiten Blatt* (21-Page Paper) and *Der Vortrupp* (The Front Line). They collected money to aid Jews escaping from Nazi arrest and planned the sabotage of armaments production. German intelligence estimates of the organization's effectiveness concluded that Rote Kapelle had cost at least 200,000 German lives on the Eastern Front, as the result of information they supplied to Russia.

In August 1942, Rote Kapelle was uncovered and destroyed by the Nazis. A Russian agent, caught while parachuting into Germany, revealed under interrogation several names of Rote Kapelle members. The organization's internal security was excellent, however, so that most members knew the names of only one or two others in the group.

As members were arrested and interrogated, names came to light. Only about 100 were actually caught in this way, however. While many more escaped discovery, the group was finished as an effective operation. Schulze-Boysen was among those captured. He was given a death sentence, which was carried out toward the end of 1942.

Although highly efficient, the Communists suffered a bad reputation in Germany. Their history was as violent as that of the Nazis, and they were notorious for not keeping their word. They were the one political group with enough power and organization to pose a serious threat to the Nazi regime, and the Nazis did all they could to prevent that from occurring.

In the concentration camps, the organizational skills the Communists had learned in their political training became valuable survival skills. They often were able to carry on an effective resistance even within the concentration camps. In Buchenwald, for example, they formed committees to collect arms and ammunition. They also organized slowdowns and outright strikes. As many as 8,000 inmates in Buchenwald were on strike at the same time; these strikes became a chronic problem for the SS guards, who could not overcome refusals to work in such large numbers. Communists also organized groups in Auschwitz, Neuengamme, Mauthausen, and Dachau. In Dachau, the Communist organization managed to smuggle two Catholic priests out so that they could reach the American lines and urge them to liberate the camp and rescue the inmates as quickly as possible.

Toward the end of the war, concentration camp guards, recognizing the extent of organization among the prisoners, feared entering barracks or trying to enforce camp rules. Under Communist leadership, many prisoners were able to acquire extra food, avoid or defer execution, or hide out within the camp itself.

Communist in-camp organizations even sheltered English and American airmen who, for various reasons, had been assigned to concentration camps rather than prisoner-of- war camps. They were fed and concealed within the camp until opportunities arose to help them escape, so they could make their way to outside resistance groups.

———————————

Unions were also a source of political resistance. Under the German political system before the Nazi regime, trade unions held considerable political power. Each classification of worker, every special interest group, and even religious organizations had their own trade unions, often with an impressive membership. Thus, workers organized in strong labor unions exerted influence on the entire German economy and political system. That all changed under Hitler.

The unions had worked throughout the late 1920s to improve conditions for workers. Benefits paid by employers on employees' behalf were on the rise. With 12 to 14 million workers having collective bargaining agreements, by the year 1927, accident and health insurance, retirement plans, paid holidays, wage contracts, and collective bargaining rights were common.

Union influence was not to last. Trade union headquarters were forcibly closed on May 2, 1933, and the majority of unions were dissolved. Their assets were confiscated by the State, and many union leaders were arrested and sent to concentration camps. On January 20, 1934, the Law Regulating National Labor (also called the Charter of Labor) was enacted by the Nazi government. The employer was declared the undisputed master, and workers were assigned the role of followers, without any voice or influence with management or its policies. Employers had to answer only to the State.

Workers were deprived under the new law of collective bargaining power. They no longer had the right to strike, to register grievances, to demand improved working conditions, or to negotiate for higher wages. In fact, wages were to be established by "labor trustees," who set rates according to the wishes of the employer. In the armaments industry, workers were paid mainly on a piecework basis, so the only way to earn more money was to work faster or to put in more hours.

On October 24, 1934, the Deutsche Arbeitsfront (German Labor Front) was created to represent German workers as a replacement for the unions. Workers often accepted this arrangement, because having a job was preferable to unemployment during the depression years. Author Richard Grunberger observed: "Restoration of the right to work seduced the workers into accepting the loss of trade-union rights of association and collective bargaining; to gain the ends of liberation through labor they accepted the means of servitude to the Labor Front."[6]

In fact, the German worker was no longer represented by anyone. The Labor Front's real job was to control German labor, not to work for its good. The law even specified that officials of the Labor Front were to be Nazi officials rather than former labor union leaders.

The average worker was heavily taxed and, to make matters worse, was also required to contribute to various Nazi charities. It was dangerous not to contribute, or to give too little. And although Hitler did, indeed, end the severe unemployment in Germany, it was at the cost of workers' rights.*

Beginning in February 1935, every worker was required to possess a workbook in which a record was kept of his or her skills and work history. If a worker wanted to quit a job, the employer could simply keep the workbook, making it impossible for the worker to obtain employment elsewhere. By June 1935, workers' rights, like the rights of everyone living under the regime, were eroded even further. In that month, all hiring and relocating went under the control of state employment offices.

On June 22, 1938, the right to obtain employment was taken under government control. A special decree by the Office of the Four-Year Plan introduced labor conscription, including the rule that every worker was to report for a job wherever the State assigned him. Failure to comply with this rule would result in fines and imprisonment.†

The absolute control the State exercised over the lives of workers extended far beyond the workplace. The Labor Front organized a program called *Kraft durch Freude* (Strength through Joy), which sponsored and organized discount vacations, recreational activities, clubs, and sporting events for workers. The Nazi ideal was total control of the worker, both during and after working hours. Hitler even mandated that every worker should own an affordable car, an idea which led to development of the Volkswagen (People's Car). The vehicle, designed by Austrian engineer Ferdinand Porsche, was to be sold to every German worker for 990 marks (just under $400). A car could not be manufactured at that price, so the Labor Front subsidized the cost by increasing the dues it collected from workers. The 990-mark price was collected from workers in advance through payroll deduction, as a type of lay-away purchase. Millions of marks were paid by workers toward cars, but not a single car was ever given to a worker during the Third Reich and no refunds were given either. The Volkswagen factory was diverted to production of goods for the army and the war effort.

In this work environment, without the right of protest and without the right to change jobs, workers began to resent their servitude. Since official channels for protest and negotiation did not exist, clandestine channels opened up in their place.

The widely circulated "People's Manifesto" was composed by workers and distributed in 1936. It called for an end to the Nazi regime, a return to the law, and restoration of democratic and civil rights.

One of the best-organized labor resistance organizations was the "Robby Group," formed in Berlin by Robert Uhrig. Uhrig had been arrested in 1934 for speaking out against the Nazis while employed at the Osram Electrical Works. After his release in 1938, he began organizing worker resistance cells in several electrical and engineering facilities.

---

*Deductions from wages were considered excessive enough that a popular cynical joke emerged in Germany: An entire factory was said to have gone under because the payroll clerk mistakenly paid out workers' deductions instead of their net pay.

†Many workers were far from upset with this new requirement. For the first time in their lives, they had real job security because the regulation specified that a worker could not be fired from his job without permission from the government.

He teamed up with Joseph (Beppo) Römer, a former Freikorps leader who was determined to one day kill Adolf Hitler. Together Uhrig and Römer published a monthly paper called *Informationsdienst* (Information Service), beginning in November 1941.

By 1941 the Robby Group was also supplying intelligence to the Soviet Union. This activity led to scrutiny by the Gestapo. Eventually, the group was infiltrated and destroyed, and in 1942 many members were arrested and executed.

The labor union underground was effective at setting up valuable contacts outside of Germany to provide assistance to people fleeing the Gestapo. The efforts of German labor unions established networks in Czechoslovakia, Holland, Belgium, Sweden, and the United States.

The key player in the labor union underground was Wilhelm Leuschner, deputy chairman of the large and influential Allgemeiner Deutscher Gewerkschaftsbund (General German Trade Union Alliance) before the Nazi rise to power. He had established ties between labor unions and Christian trade unions, whose leader was Jakob Kaiser. It was Leuschner who saw the need for resistance support from outside of Germany. He was an important organizer of the larger resistance movement among military and civilians between 1938 and 1944. Leuschner was executed for his role in the 1944 bomb plot.

The political genius of Adolf Hitler is apparent in the way he responded to opposition. His talent was demonstrated early in his career in the years of building the Nazi party. Few survive, however, to gain power on the level of dictatorship. Once in power, though, Hitler knew that it would be impossible to rule without the force of law; he also knew that principles of equity would not support his policies nor his views.

The Nazi regime was known from its inception as a regime that did not respect civil rights and used the law only as a means for suppressing others. Passing new legislation could not change these facts. An immoral regime that didn't respect the rights of citizens who dissented could not claim moral right convincingly. All it could do was silence its opponents or change the law to conform to its programs.

The task Hitler faced was twofold. He had to silence any political opposition, but he also had to operate within the law. He needed to create a legal community of his own design, devoid of fairness and flexible enough to allow his program to flourish. Hitler crushed political opposition by altering the justice system. He enacted laws in order to provide himself with the "legal" authority to do whatever he wanted, knowing that if he operated outside of the law, it would be politically disastrous.

Göring expressed the Nazi philosophy well when, on July 12, 1934, he announced, "The law and the will of the Führer are one." This idea was expanded upon in 1936 by Dr. Hans Frank, commissioner of justice and Reich law leader, who declared, "The National Socialist ideology is the foundation of all basic laws, especially as explained in the party programs and in the speeches of the Führer."

Nearly as soon as Hitler came into power, he clashed with the established legal system. The infamous Reichstag fire of February 1933, blamed on the Communists and called a conspiracy, led to the trial of several accused arsonists. The *Reichsgericht* (Supreme Court) found Marinus van der Lubbe guilty on the arson charge but voted to acquit three other defendants in the case. Hitler, upset that some defendants were acquitted, responded by establishing the Volksgerichtshof (People's Court) to try cases of treason, which was broadly defined by the regime. The People's Court consisted of two professional judges and five officers appointed for their understanding of Nazi dogma rather than the law. Since these officers held a majority, it was easy to out-vote the professional judges, should the need arise. There was no appeals process.

Death sentences were generously meted out and carried out swiftly, often on the day of the trial's conclusion. As opposition spread through Germany over the coming years, a lower court system called Sondergericht (Special Court) was established specifically to hear cases of political crimes.

The most infamous judge in the People's Court system was Roland Freisler. He was a dedicated Nazi who served as ministerial director in the Prussian Ministry of Justice in 1933 and became secretary of state in the Reich Ministry of Justice in 1934. Freisler became known for his shrill verbal abuses in court and for the harshness of his sentences. He served as judge for the White Rose trials and for the trials of the opposition members arrested in the July 1944 bomb plot.

The People's Court passed 16,560 death sentences, most of those after the Second World War began and especially when Germany's losses began mounting and opposition increased. In 1940 guilty verdicts with the death sentence were handed down in 4.8 percent of all cases. For the year 1944, death sentences were handed down in 47.4 percent of all cases.[7]

Activity in the People's Court is an accurate measure of German opposition. Because these courts heard treason cases and cases of political dissent, the increase in the volume of death sentences indicates the mood of opposition in Germany. Abuses in the justice system itself were common and known to the public. A primary complaint expressed by German citizens about the Nazis was their lack of respect for the law. For example, Hitler had reserved the right for himself to set aside criminal charges or findings. If trusted Nazis were accused in criminal cases, Hitler could dismiss the charges without challenge.

Lawyers and judges in the Third Reich had to demonstrate their loyalty to the state or face the consequences. Lawyers were regulated by the *Rechtswahrerbund* (honor court). Failing to exclaim "Heil Hitler" could result in reprimand, and not voting in Nazi plebiscites could lead to expulsion from the bar. Defense attorneys had little say in criminal trials and were in fact appointed by the court. Criminal trials became administrative proceedings rather than legal ones. A defense lawyer could be prosecuted for perjury if the court believed the defendant was lying.

Under terms of the Law for the Restoration of the Professional Civil Service (enacted on April 7, 1933), judges could be forced into retirement if there were any doubts that they were conducting themselves "in the interests of the National Socialist state."[8]

Trying to counteract injustices of the Nazi regime was Dr. Carl Sack, judge-advocate general of the German army. He used his considerable power to assist army opposition members who had been arrested by the Nazis. He became expert at delaying proceedings or allowing them simply to go unresolved. Sack often brought a psychiatrist into court to testify as an expert witness that a defendant was temporarily insane when an offense was committed. The result would be a short stay in an asylum rather than a trip to the guillotine. Sack was arrested for his role in the 1944 bomb plot, and on April 9, 1945, he was hanged at Flossenbürg concentration camp.

There was virtually no way for anyone opposed to the regime to receive a fair hearing in the Nazi court system. For most citizens, the abuses of the Gestapo were of more immediate concern. This organization was entirely above the law or, more to the point, it *was* the law. In 1935 the Prussian Supreme Court of Administration ruled that Gestapo actions were not under the jurisdiction of the courts and were not subject to review. And on February 10, 1936, the Gestapo's position was validated in law, officially placing the Gestapo outside of the court's administration. Two weeks later an additional law provided the Gestapo the right to arrest anyone it chose and place them in Schutzhaft (protective custody), which often meant placement in a concentration camp or a lunatic asylum. This provision was used widely against political prisoners.

Previous to that time, the Gestapo had often placed people under surveillance upon release from prison. Now, with the legal right to keep people in custody even after they had served their sentences, virtually anyone could be kept locked up indefinitely. Many judges, from a sense of compassion, were known to sentence criminals to longer than average sentences in order to keep them out of the concentration camps and in the relative safety of prison.

After the outbreak of war, convicts were rearrested routinely. The Ministry of Justice excused this policy on the basis that criminals might take advantage of the special dangers that came with war and pose a threat to the community.

With their exclusion from the rules of legal due process or the courts, the members of the Gestapo answered to no one. Whatever they deemed to be legal was legal under the Nazi regime. They had the right to rearrest an acquitted person on the way out of court and often did so, with the explanation that the court was "mistaken" in its judgment. They also had the right to execute or mistreat prisoners without recourse through the court system.

While the Gestapo clearly operated outside of the law, it was not exempt from its dissenters. The opposition reached into its higher offices. Arthur Nebe, chief of the Reich Criminal Office, was a valuable ally to the organized military and civilian resistance leadership. He had been with the Criminal Police long before the Nazi era and had distinguished himself for developing innovative procedures in crime detection. As a high-ranking Gestapo official, Nebe was able to provide the opposition with inside information on many occasions. He has been vilified, however, by many historians because as a member of the Gestapo, he was automatically assumed to be a criminal.

In his correspondence with other opposition members, Nazi slogans were often used as code-words. So reading letters to and from Nebe, one might conclude he was an ardent Nazi. For example, when correspondence included the popular Nazi phrase, "with complete confidence in the ultimate victory," it really meant that plans were still progressing for Hitler's removal from office.[9] Nebe was implicated in the July 1944 plot and was hanged in March 1945.

Chapter 6

THE *CIVILIAN* *OPPOSITION*

All my life, even in school, I fought against a spirit of narrowness and
force, of arrogance, intolerance, and pitiless, absolute logic which is a part
of the German equipment, and which found its embodiment in the
National Socialist state. And I did what I could to help vanquish this spirit,
with its terrible consequences.

Helmuth von Moltke, letter to his sons, January 1945

In 1938 it became clear to those opposed to Hitler that Germany was heading for a
Continental war. Hitler was determined to invade Czechoslovakia using military force,
even though his generals warned that French and English military power was much greater
than Germany's. The inevitability of war forced German opponents of Nazism in many
circles to join together in their common interest.

The initial threat of war began a six-year effort among civilians and military leaders. They began working together to achieve their goals: remove Hitler from power,
replace that power with a viable alternative, and install an acceptable government. This
was a formidable list. Operating without the benefit of open and public debate, the opposition was increasingly frustrated by the need for secrecy and the fear of discovery.

Hitler's determination to advance plans for the armed invasion of Czechoslovakia
and his instructions to military leaders to make plans for war made organized and coordinated resistance essential. The greatest fear among virtually all members of the opposition in 1938 was war. Both civilian and military leaders wanted to take whatever steps
were necessary to prevent war with England and France. Ludwig Beck, the primary military opposition leader, joined with a number of prominent politicians and government
officials in an opposition group that was to endure until 1944. This was an establishment
core of opposition comprising high-ranking military, political, and government officials.
The collective influence of the opposition leaders gave the group considerable authority
to speak on behalf of larger groups such as the German army, intelligence service, or the
diplomatic corps.

Just as General Beck was recognized as the military leader of the opposition, Carl
Goerdeler was to become his civilian equivalent. Goerdeler, born in 1884, was the son of

85

Carl Goerdeler was the recognized civilian leader of the resistance movement (Photo: National Archives).

a West Prussian district judge. He studied law and economics, having decided early on to pursue a career in civil service and politics.

Goerdeler had a keen, analytical mind but was inflexible and narrow in his point of view. He was known for his incredible energy and was possessed with extreme optimism. This optimism was with him right up to the day of his execution for his involvement with the resistance. He believed to the end that, by using rational arguments, he would be able to change the minds of his executioners at the last minute.

Goerdeler invariably took a great deal of time in studying a question, but once his mind was made up, nothing would change it. Highly moral and unyielding, he was honest and hard-working but intolerant of weakness and failure and puritanical to a fault. For example, he would not allow a divorced person to enter his home.

Goerdeler, at first a faithful and dutiful government employee, cooperated with the Nazi government. Although he came to despise the Nazi movement as undignified, emotional, and foolish, he never fully realized how ruthless its leaders were and how serious the Nazis were about carrying through their plans. To Goerdeler, with his respect for law and order and his intellectual, logical, and conservative character, Nazi violence and lawlessness was unfathomable. This was Goerdeler's blind spot. His failure to realize what the opposition was up against delayed his recognition of the urgency of the opposition's task.

Frustrated at the slow-moving and often entirely ineffective characteristics of parliamentary democracy, Goerdeler preferred rule by an oligarchy. His conservative idealism, plus a desire for efficiency, led him to dream of such a government, whose participants would be motivated not by power, but by principle.

Because he detested the ineffectiveness of the Weimar Republic, Goerdeler was not entirely opposed to the Nazis for the first few years of their rule. To the contrary, he held a purely political view of the Nazi movement and was at first an enthusiastic member of the government, willing to work to achieve social progress for Germany. He viewed Nazism at first as an immature ideology that could be controlled and allowed to mature politically.

In some aspects, Goerdeler was typical of many Germans. His respect for the rules sometimes obscured his personal feelings. For example, he first gained a national reputation when he refused in 1930 to allow the Nazis to fly the swastika at the town hall of Leipzig, where he was Lord Mayor.*

Once the swastika was declared the "official" state flag, Goerdeler quickly changed his position. He was later to explain that he had been doing his duty as a loyal German in his ardent early support of the Nazi government. It was, he claimed, a period during which the government was expected to mature. Instead, as he discovered, it worsened and the social and civil abuses of Hitler and his kind became obvious.

Goerdeler had a keen sense of right and wrong and would not tolerate Nazi abuses. While Lord Mayor of Leipzig, he personally intervened to prevent SA looting of Jewish shops. Considering the perils of taking a stand against Nazi abuses, this was an exceptional position to take, even for the Lord Mayor.

For the opposition, Goerdeler's immediate grasp of issues and politics was a valuable benefit. He had wide contacts in the political establishment, and his background in civil administration left its mark on the organization of the opposition. This was particularly true in its long-range planning for the future, a future which most opposition members would not live to see, a future that Goerdeler envisioned for a Germany living in peace and in harmony with its neighbors.

By 1936, though, Goerdeler finally realized that the Nazi movement was not a transition in the political life of the country. It was a regime that did not compromise and did not allow dissent. There was no "loyal opposition" in the eyes of the Nazis. By the following year, the inflexibility of Nazi policies ran into the inflexibility and stubbornness of Carl Goerdeler. The Nazi party demanded removal of a bust of composer Felix Mendelssohn from the front of Leipzig's concert hall, the *Gewandhaus*, because Mendelssohn had been Jewish. Goerdeler refused. In his absence, deputy mayor Rudolf Haack had the Mendelssohn bust removed. Goerdeler resigned in protest on April 1, 1937.

Still believing it might be possible to work within the political system, Goerdeler applied his blind logic in trying to convince government officials that Nazi policies were ill-advised. Stubbornly, even arrogantly, he believed that every human would respond to indisputable arguments grounded in logic, and it took him time to realize his error. For example, he thought that with the use of logic, he would be able to persuade Hitler to discontinue the war, if only Hitler would meet with him. Virtually everyone around Goerdeler realized that his attachment to logic prevented him from accepting the full truth.

Once he did realize his error, however, Goerdeler dedicated himself completely to the opposition of the Nazis and all they stood for. While engaged in opposition activities, Goerdeler was officially an adviser to Robert Bosch, an industrial entrepreneur. This position gave Goerdeler a cover for opposition activities, as well as an excuse to travel and widen his areas of influence.

In this unique position, Goerdeler was well connected in the civil administration of Germany, as well as in political and diplomatic circles. He also knew numbers of

---

*The Lord Mayor in a German city has considerably more local power than a mayor in another country. The position is a combination of modern democratic rule and the traditional powers of rule in a serfdom.

business owners, trade union leaders, clergymen, and financiers, and he kept in constant touch with opposition leaders in the military. Goerdeler was himself a rallying point and organizer for a number of diverse political, civilian, and military opposition groups. He first met General Beck early in 1937, and starting in the middle of 1938, the two were in close contact regularly.

Goerdeler was nearly 50 when Hitler came to power. A fellow leader of the opposition, Helmuth von Moltke, was only 27. Age was not the only difference between these two. Moltke was over six feet tall, strikingly handsome, and like Goerdeler, keenly intelligent. Goerdeler, however, was a staunch conservative rooted in logic and the practical, and Moltke was politically a liberal and idealist. Where Goerdeler was inflexible and puritanical, Moltke was tolerant and open-minded.

Moltke's parents were Christian Scientists, and although the younger Helmuth gave up active practice of this religion, it remained an influence on his character. He did not smoke and rarely drank, and he was entirely opposed to the Nazi attitude toward Jews. As an international attorney in Berlin, he specialized in private rights. He defended many Jews and other victims of the Nazi government and also traveled frequently to England and developed valuable contacts in the English government.

Moltke spoke English fluently and at a young age was a sophisticated and well-traveled man. When still in his early 20s, Moltke was forced to take over his father's financial affairs. The elder Moltke had invested poorly, and his creditors were demanding payment. Helmuth, at age 23, became manager of the family estate at Kreisau and within five years had repaid his father's debts.

Moltke and a number of like-minded aristocratic and liberal Germans met throughout the 1940s at the Moltke estate at Kreisau. They discussed the future of Germany and made plans for the government that would be installed after the Nazi collapse. Many of this group were pacifists and would not participate in assassination plans or discussions. They concentrated instead on debating the political and social plans of the future. The group was also in regular touch with Goerdeler and with General Beck. Because they met regularly at the Moltke estate, the group called themselves the Kreisau Circle.

The Kreisau Circle believed that in the future, Germany would be democratically ruled by a Christian and Socialist political state. They also believed that Europe would be united in the future and espoused the idea of "European nationalism" as an alternative to German nationalism. These young idealists and intellectuals saw Germany as the financial center of Europe and as the leader of a united continent, an idea that Goerdeler, while favoring a conservative form of government, also endorsed.

As war began to seem inevitable if Hitler remained in power, the scope of internal opposition expanded. Opposition leaders decided to establish contact with Great Britain, specifically to begin negotiating for recognition of a new government to be installed after Hitler's removal. Several contacts were made in London during the year 1938, after Hitler's plans for armed attack of Czechoslovakia became known to military leaders.

Attempting to negotiate agreements and support from other countries to prevent war involved great peril because the Nazi leadership of Germany would consider any contact an act of treason. That being the case, it is amazing that so many contacts were attempted. The opposition was intent on getting an agreement with Britain, in the belief that its commitment to stand up to Hitler's aggression could prevent a war. Or, in the event it did not, British support of the opposition was believed necessary for the success of any coup. The rationale was explained by opposition member Fabian von Schlabrendorff: "A tough stand against Hitler by the Western Powers would have strengthened our position immeasurably, and would have brought many still undecided or wavering generals and other key figures into our camp."[1]

During the period between his resignation in 1937 and the start of the Second World War, Carl Goerdeler traveled to Great Britain, Belgium, France, Holland, Canada, the United States, Switzerland, Italy, Yugoslavia, Rumania, Bulgaria, Algeria, Libya, Egypt, Palestine, Syria, and Turkey. Everywhere he went, he met with foreign statesmen and made his case against Nazi war aims and aggression. Goerdeler applied his sense of logic in making the case that war made no sense economically. His economic arguments were sensible but failed to rally international support against Hitler. He met personally with Anthony Eden, Winston Churchill, and Lord Halifax of England; Cordell Hull, Herbert Hoover, Henry Lewis Stimson, Henry Morgenthau, Jr., Owen Young, and Henry A. Wallace of the United States; and William Mackenzie King, prime minister of Canada. He also spoke with government representatives, industrialists, and diplomats in virtually every world power he visited. It was all to no avail.

The threat of war was acknowledged by most Germans, and even Hitler was concerned about the dangers of war. He knew better than anyone that the German army was too weak to withstand retaliation from Britain or France but was willing to bluff to get his way. Hitler perceived, quite correctly, that the British government would give him concessions just to avoid war for a year. He could use the time to continue strengthening Germany's army.

In order to verify his suspicions about British lack of will to go to war, Hitler sent his personal aide, Captain Fritz Wiedermann, to London in July 1938 to meet with Lord Halifax. Halifax explained that if Germany were to actually launch an armed attack on Czechoslovakia, the British government would be upset at the development. In August 1938, Wiedermann informed the British government that Hitler was determined to settle the question "by force in the immediate future."

It was apparent to well-connected opposition members like Goerdeler that war was imminent unless Hitler could be discouraged by threat of retaliation. But the British were unwilling to take a strong position, in spite of the military superiority they and the French enjoyed. Goerdeler turned to Germany's own diplomatic corps, hoping to finally convince Great Britain to listen to his warnings. He asked for help in swaying the British from Ulrich von Hassell, who was the German ambassador in Rome until Hitler dismissed him in 1937. Hassell joined with the opposition through contact with Goerdeler that same year. He associated with Goerdeler at the so-called Wednesday Club, a group that met weekly to discuss scientific, political, and cultural affairs. It was at these meetings that Hassell also met Ludwig Beck.

Hassell was from a family of aristocrats from Hanover whose professional careers included the civil service and education. Hassell, one of the last of the "old elite" in the tradition of the Bismarck era, disdained the Nazis and their goal of reshaping the world.

He was a conservative who had nothing but contempt for the Nazi movement. Many members of the opposition held onto a vision of a better future. Hassell held on to his own vision of a better past.

In a detailed diary, Hassell kept track of his activities with the underground. The diary, which survived the war, was a rich source of information, with details of meetings, dates, and participants. As a go-between, he coordinated many segments of the opposition; because of his connections as a diplomat, he was able to travel abroad frequently. Like Goerdeler, he used this advantage to make many contacts with foreign governments.

Hassell helped Goerdeler make further diplomatic contacts, including Ewald von Kleist-Schmenzin, a member of a wealthy family from Pomerania. An anti–Nazi since their rise to power, Kleist was arrested twice in 1933 for refusing to allow the swastika to be flown from the church steeple at his West Prussian estate and for declining to donate money to Nazi causes. He was on a "hit list" of June 30, 1934, the night of the Röhm Purge. But warned in time, he managed to escape, hiding out in a friend's apartment in Berlin until the danger passed. Kleist was respected as a conservative Christian who believed that the nations of Europe should live harmoniously with one another. He described Nazism as "lunacy" and Germany's "deadly enemy."

Kleist would be a perfect emissary for the resistance in General Beck's opinion. He asked Hans Oster to help. Oster prepared a false passport so that Kleist could travel to England discreetly. Just before Kleist's departure, General Beck told him: "Bring me certain proof that Britain will fight if Czechoslovakia is attacked and I will make an end of this regime."[2]

What Beck had in mind was a firm statement from the British government, vowing military response in the event of German aggression against Czechoslovakia. Although Beck had resigned his post as chief of staff in August 1938, he still had many friends among the army leadership, and he was well respected. He believed strongly that if he could organize enough armed resistance, a coup d'état would be possible.

Kleist did not realize that the British policy had already been decided. Prime Minister Neville Chamberlain was determined to buy peace from Hitler, in the belief that if Germany were allowed to take some territory without armed interference, peace would be assured.

When Kleist arrived in London in April 1938, he discussed the opposition's concerns with Ian Colvin, a friend and influential journalist in London. He told Colvin that Hitler, who had recently completed the takeover of Austria, had his eyes on Czechoslovakia next and that nothing short of world domination would satisfy the Führer's ambitions. It was imperative, Kleist explained, that the British government be informed of the dangers they faced unless Hitler could be stopped now. In May, Colvin conveyed this information to Sir George Ogilvie-Forbes, counselor in the British embassy, who in turn by mid–May communicated this message to Robert Vansittart, permanent undersecretary of state for foreign affairs.

By July, Colvin received word from an intermediary of "one of the three highest generals in the German High Command" that military action against Czechoslovakia would commence on September 28. He reported the information to his friend Lord Lloyd (George Ambrose), chairman of the British Council, in a letter of August 3. Lloyd had access both to Chamberlain and Foreign Secretary Lord Halifax. Lloyd also passed the Colvin letter on to Vansittart.

In the interest of aiding Kleist in his mission, Sir Nevile Henderson, British ambassador to Germany, provided Kleist with a diplomatic referral to be used in setting meetings in London. On August 16, Henderson recommended Kleist as an emissary of "the moderates in the German General Staff." On August 18, Kleist met with Vansittart in London. He emphasized that war between Germany and Czechoslovakia was imminent unless Great Britain took steps at once to sternly warn Hitler against the move. It was no longer the threat of war, but its certainty, that was compelling, Kleist insisted. He also warned that Hitler thought Britain and France would not be willing to intervene, though many German leaders, notably in the army, were alarmed at the prospect of an armed confrontation with Britain or France.

The British and French, militarily superior to Germany in 1938, could prevent war by pledging to intervene in the event of German aggression. Kleist urged that a speech by a prominent member of the British government, threatening retaliation in the event of German aggression, might convince Hitler that armed conflict would not be wise. On August 19, Vansittart detailed Kleist's recommendation in a report to Prime Minister Chamberlain. Chamberlain, though, dismissed Kleist's concerns out of hand. Writing to Foreign Secretary Lord Halifax, he concluded: "Kleist is violently anti–Hitler and extremely anxious to stir up his friends in Germany to make an attempt at his overthrow.... I think we must discount a good deal of what he says."[3]

On August 19, the day following his meeting with Vansittart, Kleist was received by Winston Churchill, at that time one of the few British politicians speaking out against the Nazis and against the British government's policy of appeasement. Churchill, impressed with the message and concerns expressed by Kleist, wrote an unofficial letter, the purpose of which was to discourage any German aggression against Czechoslovakia. The message read, "I am sure that the crossing of the frontier of Czechoslovakia by German armies or aviation in force will bring about a renewal of the world war."[4]

Unfortunately for the German opposition, Churchill had limited political power at this time and clearly could not influence British foreign policy. By the time Kleist returned to Germany, it was clear that his mission had failed. The Churchill letter, which had been sent via diplomatic pouch, did not identify anyone by name in order to protect Kleist. Admiral Canaris showed the letter to Hitler, hoping it would convince him to avoid war. But Hitler was not impressed by Churchill's guarded statement.

General Franz Halder, Beck's replacement as chief of staff, was as anxious as Beck to prevent an outbreak of war and agreed that steps should be taken to prevent that from happening. Upon learning that Kleist had failed to convince the British of the need for a commitment to peace, Halder took steps of his own. With Oster's cooperation, he sent his personal emissary, a retired lieutenant-colonel named Hans Böhm-Tettelbach, to London. Because of the absolute security and secrecy of Kleist's mission, Böhm-Tettelbach was unaware of it. He was not able to gain any appointments to meet with officials in the British government.

Böhm-Tettelbach did meet with a friend, an English businessman named Julian Piggot, who had important British military contacts. Piggot set up a meeting for Böhm-Tettelbach with a major in the British Military Intelligence Service. The major sent a report to Vansittart. The same issues were discussed as those presented by Kleist, with the same result. Prime Minister Chamberlain's mind was made up.

That same month, August 1938, Captain Victor von Koerber, a journalist who had retired from military service, made at least three attempts at communication with the government of Britain. His message was that while the overthrow of Hitler must come from within Germany, it required support from outside, specifically from Great Britain. The British military attaché argued against Koerber's points in his report summarizing his meetings with Koerber. He pointed out that if Britain announced its support and an attempted overthrow were to fail, it would adversely affect relations between Germany and Britain.

High-ranking German diplomats also tried to convince the British government of the urgency of the situation. Ernst von Weizsäcker, secretary of state in the German Foreign Ministry (and later ambassador to the Vatican), made contact with the British government on his own. Weizsäcker wanted to avoid a war, but he was not anti–Nazi and was not an active member of the resistance. He believed that a takeover of Czechoslovakia would be a positive policy for Germany but only if that could be done while also avoiding war. Weizsäcker was in contact with Beck, Halder, and Canaris during this period and decided to make his own attempt to sway the British to the cause of preventing war.

In late August 1938, Weizsäcker contacted Theodor Kordt, the acting chargé d'affaires in the German embassy in London. Weizsäcker asked him to confer with British government officials for the purpose of opening discussions to avoid war between the two countries. Kordt met with Sir Horace Wilson, an industrial adviser to the British government and confidant of Prime Minister Chamberlain. Wilson set up a secret meeting for Kordt with Foreign Secretary Lord Halifax. On September 7, Kordt and Halifax conferred at 10 Downing Street.

Kordt began by assuring Halifax that he spoke for many concerned military and political leaders in Germany, who "desire by all means to prevent war." Kordt also stated that if those leaders were to take decisive action, they first needed help from Great Britain. What the opposition had in mind was a statement from the British warning Hitler to leave Czechoslovakia alone or face the risk of retaliation from Czech allies, namely Britain and France.

Kordt's message was more specific than previous communications from Germany. Not just hinting at a coup, Kordt confidently promised that German army leaders would confront Hitler with a choice: removal from power or abandonment of plans for an armed attack against Czechoslovakia. Kordt told Halifax there was one condition: the British government must agree to also condemn Hitler's aggression. A war could be avoided if Britain took a stand now, Kordt explained. Halifax listened to Kordt carefully but responded by telling him that the prime minister had already decided to work with Hitler and to try to keep the peace and maintain friendly relations between the two countries. Furthermore, Halifax told Kordt, Chamberlain had already decided to go personally to Germany and meet with Hitler to work out an agreement. Halifax promised, however, that he would convey Kordt's message to the prime minister as soon as possible and that it would be treated with the greatest discretion.

Another idea hatched in the German Foreign Ministry during August 1938 involved Kordt's brother, Erich, who since spring 1938 had been working closely with Weizsäcker as head of the Ministerial Bureau of the Berlin Foreign Ministry. Hans Oster asked Erich

Kordt to try and influence General Brauchitsch, commander in chief of the army. The idea, Oster explained, was for Kordt to meet with Brauchitsch and brief him on the political situation outside of Germany. Weizsäcker agreed with Oster that Kordt should try to talk to General Brauchitsch.

Kordt managed to arrange a meeting at the War Ministry where Oster, using his contacts, had managed to ensure that Kordt's name was not entered in the visitor's book. He told Brauchitsch that Germany was completely isolated and that there was no doubt that Britain and France would launch an attack on Germany if the Czech invasion plan went forward. Oster had recommended that Kordt present his facts, supplemented with some documentation, and not offer an opinion. Kordt followed this advice and left Brauchitsch to draw his own conclusions. Brauchitsch did not respond, then or at any time, but allowed the entire matter to drop.

Meanwhile, additional diplomatic efforts were being made by Weizsäcker in Germany. On September 1, the League of Nations high commissioner for Danzig, Professor Carl Jacob Burckhardt, came through Berlin on his way to Berne, Switzerland. He visited with Weizsäcker, who told him of Kordt's ongoing efforts in London. Weizsäcker asked the commissioner to help with the peace effort. Burckhardt later wrote of Weizsäcker that he was "conspiring with a potential enemy for the purpose of preserving the peace — a double game of the utmost peril."[5]

However dangerous he thought Weizsäcker's efforts, Burckhardt was impressed with the urgency of his information. He drove the 550 miles to Berne without stop. Upon arrival in the Swiss capital, Burckhardt immediately met with Sir George Warner, the British minister, and also spoke by telephone to Lord Halifax's parliamentary secretary. Burckhardt passed on Weizsäcker's requests in both discussions. Several days later Burckhardt also explained the urgency of the German situation to Ralph Stevenson, a specialist for League of Nations issues in the foreign office. Stevenson wrote to Sir William Strang, head of the Central Department, on September 8. The letter included a recommendation that the only way to avoid war effectively would be for the prime minister to write to Hitler directly, warning him that there would definitely be a military response to a Czech invasion. Stevenson further suggested the letter be delivered by courier, taking great care that Hitler be provided with an accurate translation.

The next day, September 9, the British government, in a sudden change of position, wrote a warning message to Hitler; the language was specific and warned Hitler that Britain would intercede if there were any armed aggression against Czechoslovakia. The message was exactly what the resistance had asked for. Sir Nevile Henderson, the British ambassador in Germany, was instructed to deliver the message to Joachim von Ribbentrop, the German foreign minister. Henderson protested, however, that the message would only anger Hitler. He also explained that he had already expressed such concerns to Goebbels, Göring, and Ribbentrop on his own, emphasizing the probable involvement of the British in an armed conflict. Lord Halifax responded that as long as Henderson had already explained the British position, it would not be necessary to deliver the strongly worded additional warning. On the following day, September 10, the British government issued a press summary denying any intention to send a diplomatic message to the German government.

The organized resistance, which included political, military, and civilian leaders, debated during 1938 whether Hitler should be arrested and placed on trial, or assassinated. A number of young idealists, particularly those in the Kreisau Circle, were opposed to assassination on moral grounds. Many held that belief all the way until 1944; others came around after the start of the Second World War, finally admitting that there was no choice but to remove Hitler by violent means. The opposition's plots for a coordinated assassination effort included detailed plans for a replacement government. The proposed form of government, its leaders, policies, and positions concerning putting an end to the war, were subjects of intense debate over many years.

A number of lone assassins also made attempts on Hitler's life throughout his career as the leader of Germany. All national leaders, whether popular or despised, must expect assassination threats and even attempts; while such efforts against Hitler were not always based on political beliefs, they demonstrate the uncanny sense of survival that Hitler was able to draw upon, time and again. He was able to narrowly escape attempts on his life (both on the part of lone assassins and the organized resistance), seeming to possess a sixth sense when he was in danger.

The first known attempts on Hitler's life occurred even before he assumed power. In November 1921, he spoke at a beer hall rally in Munich, before a mixed crowd of supporters and opponents. As often happened in those years, a fight broke out. Beer steins were thrown back and forth, followed by chairs. Then fist fights broke out, and it turned into a general mêlée. Nazi thugs managed to move the fight outside while Hitler continued speaking.

When the police arrived in force, the fighting ceased. During the confusion, several shots were fired at Hitler, but all missed him. He continued speaking for another 20 minutes, causing yet more dissent. Finally, the police closed the hall and dispersed the crowd. Police reports stated that more than 150 smashed beer steins, broken chairs and tables, lengths of pipe, brass knuckles, and other weapons were found at the scene.

After the beer hall putsch in 1923, Hitler went into a period of relative obscurity. Many of his enemies thought they had seen the last of him, but in fact the incident, while landing him in jail for a time, also made him a national figure. He worked for several years rebuilding his party from nothing, gaining seats in the Reichstag and looking for opportunities to make his move.

In 1929 a disaffected soldier planted a bomb under a speaker's platform right before Hitler was scheduled to speak. He left to use the men's room, intending to set off the bomb upon his return. But he was locked in the men's room and was unable to escape until after Hitler had finished giving his speech.

When Hitler assumed the position of chancellor, another attempt was made to blow up his speaker's platform, this time by a more organized group. Kurt Lutter, a ship's carpenter and Communist, had met with a group of fellow Communists and hatched the plot for March 4, 1933, when Hitler was scheduled to speak at a rally in Königsberg. The night before, however, the police arrested the members of the group, which had been infiltrated by an informant. Because the police never found any explosives and no one in the group would confess, all were eventually released from custody.

In the years 1933 and 1934, police received word of assassination plots every week. Many were not taken seriously because they were too fantastic. Plans included poison being squirted from bunches of flowers, exploding fountain pens, and tunnels dug beneath government buildings. The more fanciful reports were dismissed, but the SS was kept busy investigating frequent serious threats.

The best-known plot of this time was the persistent rumor (true or not) that Ernst Röhm and the SA were planning to replace Hitler and take over the government. This rumor alarmed military leaders and President Hindenburg to the extent that when Hitler had Röhm murdered, they congratulated him for removing the danger.

Getting rid of Röhm and disbanding the SA did not end the threats to Hitler. In 1935 a right-wing political group calling itself the Radical Middle Class party developed an elaborate assassination plot. Headed by Dr. Helmuth Mylius and a retired naval officer, Hermann Ehrhardt, the group had a plan to infiltrate Hitler's SS security units. They got about 160 men into the SS and began accumulating information on Hitler's movements. Before they were able to execute a plan, however, the Gestapo discovered their intentions and arrested most of the group's members. Mylius himself avoided arrest with the help of some influential friends, including Field Marshal Erich von Manstein. He ended up going into the army.

During the year 1936, a Jewish medical student named David Frankfurter, originally from Yugoslavia, assassinated Wilhelm Gustloff, the leader of the Nazi party in Switzerland. Frankfurter, the SS learned, had wanted to kill Hitler but was unable to get close enough to him. The Gestapo was able to tie Frankfurter to a Paris-based group known as the *Alliance Israélite Universelle.*

In December of the same year, Helmut Hirsch, a German Jew living in Prague, arrived in Germany with the intention of setting off a bomb in the Nuremberg Stadium. He hoped to assassinate Julius Streicher or Hitler, determined to avenge the murder of his brother by the Nazis in 1934. His plan relied on a contact who was to cross into Germany from Poland to deliver a bomb.

Hirsch arrived in Stuttgart on December 20, unaware that his contact had been arrested by the Gestapo and had already given them the explosive as well as Hirsch's identity. It was a simple matter for the Gestapo to find Hirsch, who had checked into a hotel using his real name. On March 8, 1937, he was tried and found guilty of the assassination attempt. He was guillotined in Plotzensee Prison on June 4.

Another would-be assassin was Maurice Bavaud, a Catholic theology student from Switzerland. He was connected to a group of about ten other students led by Marcel Gerbohay, who was attending theology school in France. The students formed the *Compagnie du Mystère,* which had the declared purpose of destroying Communism.

Marcel Gerbohay, leader of the student group, exerted a great influence on Bavaud. Gerbohay had delusions that he would eventually become the leader of a new Russian empire, and he claimed to be a descendant of the Romanov dynasty. He convinced Bavaud that when Communism was destroyed, the Romanovs would again rule Russia in the person of Gerbohay. Bavaud, apparently believing this prophecy, became fixated on the idea that killing Hitler would somehow help Gerbohay's prophecy to come true. He read a French translation of *Mein Kampf,* studied German, and became determined to assassinate Hitler.

On October 9, 1938, Bavaud said goodbye to his family and set off from Brittany to begin pursuing Hitler across Germany. He first traveled to Baden-Baden, where he stayed with relatives. In the Swiss town of Basel, he bought a 6.35-mm. Schmeisser automatic pistol and then went by train to Berlin to find Hitler.

In Berlin, Bavaud discovered that Hitler was at his retreat in Berchtesgaden, 300 miles away. Bavaud arrived in the town of Berchtesgaden* on October 25 and there purchased ammunition for his pistol. After spending some time in the woods at target practice, he decided he would be able to kill Hitler from 25 feet away. Hitler, meanwhile, had left the area. During a conversation with fellow students, Bavaud mentioned that he would like to meet Hitler in person. His inquiries were overheard by a police captain, Karl Deckert. The policeman told Bavaud that a personal audience with Hitler could be arranged if Bavaud could produce a letter of introduction from an important foreign official.

Deckert advised Bavaud to go to Munich for the anniversary of the November 9, 1923, beer hall putsch, which Hitler attended every year without fail. So on October 31, 1938, Bavaud set off by train for Munich. He was able to get himself a ticket for a grandstand seat by posing as a Swiss reporter, with the intention of shooting Hitler as he passed during the planned parade. Authorities later discovered that Bavaud was the only foreigner given a ticket, and he was never asked for identification, even when he arrived to take his spot at the reviewing stand.

Bavaud purchased a program for the upcoming ceremonies, which detailed the entire parade route. He walked the route and concluded that the best spot from which to shoot Hitler was the reviewing stand, for which he had a ticket. On the morning of November 9, Bavaud dressed in a heavy coat, concealing his pistol in the pocket. He arrived early to ensure himself a front-row seat.

His plan was to run up to Hitler as he passed and shoot him from at close range. He soon discovered, however, that two rows of bodyguards stood shoulder to shoulder in front of the reviewing stand, to prevent anyone in the crowd from approaching the parade itself. When Hitler came by, Bavaud and everyone else stood to get a better view of the Führer. With his hand on the pistol grip, Bavaud saw that Hitler was marching down the street on the far side of the street and not in the middle, as he had expected. That put Hitler at a distance of more than 50 feet, too far for Bavaud to make his attempt. He was forced to abandon the plan and think of something else.

Bavaud's next step was to purchase expensive stationery and forge a letter of introduction. Using the name of the French foreign minister, Pierre Flandin, the letter of introduction stated that Bavaud had a second letter for Hitler's eyes only. He boarded a train back to Berchtesgaden in the mistaken belief that Hitler had returned there. He was informed that Hitler was still in Munich, so he took the next train back, arriving at about the same time that Hitler's private train was leaving that city for Berchtesgaden.

Bavaud had run out of money for train fares. He stowed away on a train bound for

*Hitler had discovered the Berchtesgaden area in the early 1920s and in 1928 rented a small country house in Salzberg, Haus Wachenfeld. He later purchased the home, and it became known as the "Berghof." In 1935, Hitler decided to remodel, and the project continued for the next 10 years. Citing security reasons, the Nazis began buying up land surrounding the Berchtesgaden retreat, often pressuring unwilling owners to sell. The original country house expanded to include apartments for visitors, SS barracks, garages, security gatehouses, additional guest quarters, homes for several Nazi dignitaries, a greenhouse, a mushroom plantation, and numerous roads. By 1945 the complex covered more than four square miles.

The main residence at Hitler's Berchtesgaden retreat (Photo: National Archives).

Paris. The stowaway was discovered by a conductor, who turned him over to the Gestapo because he was a foreigner with a gun. He was questioned thoroughly and told the Gestapo of his assassination plans. He was jailed and was later placed on trial and found guilty. He was beheaded on May 14, 1941.

One group intent on assassination in 1938 was led by Dr. Wilhelm Abegg, formerly state secretary in the Prussian Ministry. The group, calling itself "Committee A," recruited several Prussian ex-police officers who had been sent to concentration camps and subsequently ransomed out by Abegg. Their plan was to design a bomb small enough to be carried in a pocket. The assassins, disguised as Italian army couriers and dressed in that country's army uniforms, supposedly carrying important papers, were to try to kill Hitler and as many other high-ranking Nazi officials as possible. Each of 10 would-be assassins was assigned a target. The one assigned to Hitler was prepared to sacrifice himself along with his victim. But the group was unable to design a bomb small and compact enough for the job, and the plot never went beyond the planning stages.

In March 1939, Colonel F. Noel Mason-MacFarlane, a British military attaché stationed in Berlin, calmly suggested to the British Foreign Office that he should be allowed to kill Hitler. He recalled: "My residence in Berlin was barely 100 yards from the saluting base of all the big Führer reviews. All that was necessary was a good shot and a high-velocity rifle with telescopic sight and silencer. It could have been fired through my open

bathroom window from a spot on the landing some 30 feet back from the window."[6]
Mason-MacFarlane's plan was rejected in London, however.

Between 1939 and 1942, an ex-commander of the Freikorps group "*Oberland,*" Captain Josef (Beppo) Römer, watched Hitler's movements with great interest. Römer had vowed to assassinate Hitler. He received much of his information from a supporter, Lieutenant-Colonel Holm Erttel, Berlin city commandant. With the help of Gertrud von Heimerdinger, Römer was also well connected with the German Foreign Ministry.

Römer had been arrested on numerous occasions for his underground activities and connections, beginning in 1933. He was sent in 1934 to Dachau concentration camp. From that time through 1942, Römer was determined to assassinate Hitler and instigate a coup. During the time of his underground activities, Römer had been in contact with Robert Uhrig, head of the underground cell known as the "Robby Group." Römer and Uhrig eventually joined forces, hoping for a Communist victory over Nazism. Römer also was in touch with the Radical Middle Class party and its leader, Dr. Helmuth Mylius.

Römer was never able to devise a concrete plan for actually assassinating Hitler, but he was well known to the Gestapo. Römer was arrested for the last time on February 4, 1942, and was executed later that year on September 25.

Assassination was no easy matter, as Hitler was surrounded by security. The SS was diligent in protecting him. Parade routes and meeting halls were secured, guarded, and checked regularly, and inspections were undertaken several days before Hitler's arrival. Even with all of his precautions, however, Hitler could not completely protect himself from the exposure to possible danger from a determined and skilled assassin. One such individual was Johann Georg Elser, a 36-year-old from Württemberg. Hitler was known to always take part in the annual celebration of the beer hall putsch. He traveled every year to Munich to the old Bürgerbräukeller on Munich's Rosenheimer Straße for a parade and speech every November 9. The building, the name of which had been changed to the Löwenbräu, was the site of the annual celebration, which also provided Hitler the chance to meet again with the *Alten Kämpfer* (Old Fighters), those who were with him as early as 1923.

The certainty of Hitler's attendance on an exact date and in a specific place made it only natural that Elser would plan to make his move in Munich on November 9. As a matter of routine, the SS thoroughly inspected and guarded all sites in advance where Hitler was scheduled to speak. Several days before November 9, 1939, the Löwenbräu was placed under the usual diligent watch.

Elser, a skilled carpenter and electrician, had been held for a time in Dachau concentration camp because he had been a member of the Communist organization, the Red Front Fighters League. While a teenager, Elser had discovered his skill at cabinetmaking and watchmaking. He was exceptionally talented at both skills and worked at various jobs throughout his adult life, including custom furniture building. In December 1936, he began working in a munitions factory at Heidenheim.

Elser had decided to assassinate Hitler in the fall of 1938. He had even traveled to Munich that November and surveyed the beer hall and the parade route. Ironically, Elser, along with many others, followed the march down the streets of Munich in 1938 and had walked past the grandstand where Maurice Bavaud sat with his pistol in his coat pocket.

Like many lone assassins, Elser professed absolutely no interest in politics. In fact, he read newspapers only on occasion and had not even listened to Hitler's radio speeches. By 1938 he belonged to no organizations except the Woodworkers' Union. If Elser had any complaint against Hitler, it was regarding Nazi policies restricting workers' rights.

Elser was patient and methodical, willing to put time and thought into perfecting every aspect of his plan. His training in skilled watchmaking and cabinetry made him an exceptionally dangerous would-be assassin. By the fall of 1938, it was too late to plan the kind of detail Elser wanted to bring to the task, but he was willing to wait until November 1939. His brief trip to Munich confirmed for him that the beer hall would be the best place to plant an explosive device. People came and went without restriction, and Hitler was certain to be there to deliver a speech. Elser reasoned that if he placed a bomb in one of the huge support pillars near the back of the hall, Hitler and many other Nazi leaders would surely be killed. He decided he would plant an explosive in the center column, which was the main support for the roof. An explosion would bring tons of brick, masonry, wood and other debris crashing down on those on the main floor below.

Since security at his plant was too strict to enable him to steal enough explosives, Elser decided he needed to move to Munich. Although workers' movement between jobs was restricted, it was possible to quit if a worker had a fight with his supervisor. Elser instigated a fight, quit his job and on April 4 boarded a train for Munich. He walked into the large beer hall, noting that the inside doors leading to the large meeting room (called the festival hall) did not have locks. He measured the center column and sketched it in a notebook.

Elser then returned to Heidenheim, where he found work in a stone quarry. Security there was lax, and Elser managed to steal explosives from the storage bunker. During the summer of 1939, Elser made a number of trips during the night, taking small amounts of Donarit, an explosive which came in the form of ¼-inch thick tablets of ¾-inch diameter, and Gelantine, available in a small paper cartridge. He took small enough amounts that the thefts were not noticed. By the time he was done, Elser had 110 pounds of high explosives, 125 high-capacity detonators, and several coils of quick-burning fuse — all of which he stored under his bed.

In May, Elser was injured at work, giving him two months off which he used to devise the means for setting off the charge after it was planted. He decided to use an electrically charged spark, with a clock to close the circuit at a predetermined time. This was a quiet method compared to a hissing fuse or manually operated device, and Elser did not have to be present to detonate the bomb.

Elser left by train for Munich on August 5, carrying the heavy box with him that contained his explosives and other supplies. He later had a friend send along his tools and other supplies. He got into the habit of dining every night at the Löwenbräu beer hall, making friends with the staff and becoming such a familiar face that his comings and goings were not questioned. Then, finishing his meal at about 10 P.M., he walked into the darkened festival hall and went up the stairs to the gallery. Each night he followed the same routine, disappearing into the empty gallery and waiting for the building to close down at 11:30 P.M.

Once the staff had left and the building was locked up each night, Elser went to work. First he pried off the molding surrounding the rectangular middle section of the column. He then cut away the entire panel. He worked for three to four hours per night, ending each session by cleaning up the sawdust and replacing the outside molding so no one would detect his work. He then slept for a few hours, leaving the beer hall at 8 A.M., immediately after it opened. He told his inquisitive landlord that he was working at night on a secret invention and could not talk about it in any detail.

Once a section of the molding had been cut away, Elser cleared out a cavity in the column itself. This required chipping away at tight cement and stone. He lined the hollowed-out cavity with steel plate and cork, to protect his device and the timing mechanism in the event that someone tried to drive a nail into the column.

It was slow work, but Elser was patient and willing to take all the time he needed. He was discovered in the hall only once, when a waiter came in early in the morning to pick up an empty box stored in the gallery. When the waiter saw Elser, he hurried off to tell the owner. Elser calmly walked down the stairs, sat at a table, and began writing in his notebook. When asked why he was there so early, Elser answered that he was writing a letter. The owner told him to go into the garden, which Elser did. He ordered a coffee and sat in the garden, drank the coffee and paid for it, and then arose and walked away.

During the day, Elser worked in his room on the bomb's triggering device. The action involved two alarm clock works, so that in the event of failure, there was a backup system. By coordinating both clocks with a series of cog wheels and levers, Elser constructed a device he could pre-set up to six days. The complicated mechanism was flawless. The box containing the timing device was to be completely sealed except for two small holes, into which ignition wires were run. He muffled the ticking of the clocks by using an insulating material intended to protect machinery from extreme weather.

On the night of November 2, Elser began placing his explosives in the hollowed-out column. That night he placed fifty pounds of explosives plus detonators. Two days later he placed the rest of his explosives. He then double-checked his clock mechanism again, ensuring it was still working perfectly. That night, after the beer hall closed, Elser tried to fit his box into the column. It was too large, so he took it back to his room and planed it down. On Monday, November 6, he managed to place the box into the cavity. It was a perfect fit. He hooked up the detonators and at 6 A.M. set the timing device to go off in 63 hours and 20 minutes, at 9:20 P.M. on November 8. Elser had worked on his project for 35 nights, plus his planning time and work on the clock device. It was masterfully crafted and flawlessly designed.

The morning of November 6, Elser returned to his apartment and checked out, advising his landlord that he had perfected his invention. He then boarded a 10 A.M. train for Ulm, transferring to an express train for Stuttgart. Surprised to see him, relatives asked Elser what his plans were, and he told them he intended to cross the border into Switzerland. When they asked him why, he answered, "Because I must."

On November 7, Elser returned to Munich to inspect his bomb one last time. Arriving in Munich at 9 P.M., he went directly to the Löwenbräu and into the darkened festival hall. Using a knife blade, he pried open the cover and inspected the bomb. The primary clock was running and on time. Closing the box, he listened in the silence and could hear the ticking of his clock, but with a room full of celebrating, beer-drinking people, it was doubtful that the noise would be audible. At 6:30 the next morning, he left the beer hall and boarded a train for Konstanz, a German town on the Swiss border.

At 7:30 that evening, Elser's train was near Konstanz. By that time, the Löwenbräu was already packed to capacity with the Old Fighters and other Nazi faithful. All were awaiting the arrival of their leader, Adolf Hitler. The hall was a haze of cigar and cigarette smoke, and the empty beer steins far outnumbered the ever-arriving full ones. At exactly 8 P.M., the Führer entered the building, and everyone became silent, rising to their feet and saluting as Hitler walked through the room.

Also present were a number of Nazi dignitaries, including Himmler, Goebbels, Frank, Rosenberg, and Ribbentrop. Following a short introduction, Hitler began speaking at 8:10. Directly behind him was the center pillar which contained Elser's device, due to explode at 9:20. At about the time Hitler began speaking, Elser left the train and headed by foot for the Swiss border less than one mile away. He got to within 100 yards of the actual border, but was spotted by two guards listening to Hitler's speech on their radio. They stopped Elser and arrested him. When ordered to empty his pockets, Elser produced a small amount of money, a clock spring, a few cogs, technical drawings of detonators, a membership card in the now defunct Red Front Fighters League, and a postcard with a picture of the interior of the beer hall in which Hitler was still speaking. The guards immediately delivered Elser, along with his incriminating evidence, into the hands of the Gestapo.

Gestapo Criminal Inspector Otto Grethe was listening to Hitler's speech on the radio when Elser was brought to him. He later described the prisoner as appearing "harmless and inoffensive." He began his interrogation soon after 9 P.M., just before Hitler abruptly ended his speech and hurriedly left the building. The speech, which ran only 57 minutes rather than the customary 90, ended at 9:12 P.M. and was his shortest beer hall speech ever. It had also begun 20 minutes earlier than the scheduled time. Most of the Nazi leadership followed Hitler from the hall, leaving the hundreds of Old Fighters to continue drinking, celebrating, and singing.

At 9:20, waitress Maria Strobel was upset because Hitler and his group had left the hall without paying their tab. She was clearing the table when Elser's bomb exploded. The ceiling disintegrated, and a rain of wood, brick, dust, and masonry filled the hall. Strobel was hurled by the blast down the length of the festival hall and through the doors. She was stunned and bruised, but although she was closest to the center of the explosion, she was not seriously hurt.

Hitler's table was buried under more than six feet of timbers, brick, and rubble. Fallen ceiling beams and other debris killed eight people and injured another 63 badly enough that they could not walk from the hall on their own. At the moment of the explosion, Inspector Grethe was hearing Elser's explanation that he was not trying to cross the border illegally but had wanted only to visit a friend and had gotten lost. Within a few moments, a messenger delivered a telegram to Grethe advising him of the explosion. It was identical to hundreds of telegrams sent to border stations, placing them on alert for suspicious characters trying to leave the country.

Grethe had little trouble connecting Elser with the news, considering the items in Elser's pockets. Elser then confessed that he had placed the bomb in the beer hall, insisting he had worked alone and that his motive was to prevent another European war. Hitler, meanwhile, heard of the event while en route by train from Munich to Berlin. His early departure had been necessary because of an important meeting with military commanders in the capital early the next morning. Hitler said his survival was a miracle. He announced that the attempt on his life was no doubt the work of the British Secret Service.

It was the responsibility of the SS to secure all locations where the Führer was scheduled to speak, and the near assassination was an embarrassment to Heinrich Himmler, the SS chief. He was determined to confirm Hitler's speculation that, indeed, it was the work of the British. Since October, an SD agent working closely with Reinhard Heydrich had been working on an intelligence operation involving the British Secret Service. Himmler saw an opportunity to set up British operatives and blame them for the Munich bombing. The SD agent, Colonel Walther Schellenberg, was given orders directly by Himmler as soon as the train arrived in Berlin the following morning.

Schellenberg had been in touch since October with two British agents, Major S. Payne Stevens and Captain R. H. Best. Working under the false name Major Schämmel, supposedly a member of an opposition group containing a number of German generals, Schellenberg had told the British agents that his group was intent on removing Hitler from power. Considering that legitimate contacts from just such a group had already been made with the British government, the story seemed plausible. One purpose of Schellenberg's operation was to try to get information from the British agents about the real German underground movement. The SS suspected that such a movement existed, but at this point they knew little about it.

Best and Stevens had held a number of meetings with German security police agents posing as members of the resistance. The first face-to-face meeting was held October 21, and several additional messages were exchanged over wireless sets provided by the British agents. Now, under orders directly from Himmler, Schellenberg laid a trap for the officers. He passed word to the British officers that he wanted to meet with them on November 9 in Backhus, close to the Dutch border town of Venlo. Once there, the officers were kidnapped by a team of SS and taken to Germany.

This event came to be known as the Venlo Incident. From that point forward, the British were highly suspicious of all overtures from the German resistance. They suspected another trap and were cooler than ever to negotiating with representatives of the opposition. Best and Stevens were kept in various concentration camps until 1944, eventually ending up at Niederdorf camp in South Tyrol, where they were liberated by the American army on April 28, 1945.

Elser had also been returned to concentration camp. He was given special privileges, however, and was protected from the more common brutalities of camp life. Nazi authorities, doubting that Elser had worked alone, provided him with tools and instructed him to build a replica of his bomb, which was documented in a Gestapo-supervised film. Himmler took a personal interest in Elser, a fact that has led to much speculation about the entire chain of events. Some believe that Himmler masterminded the entire bombing, including plans to have the bomb explode after Hitler's departure, for the purpose of discrediting the British Secret Service.

Elser insisted during his many interrogations by the Gestapo that he had acted alone. Later, though, in Dachau, he told a different story to several people, including Pastor Martin Niemöller. He said that he had been approached while imprisoned in Dachau before the incident and promised he would be released on condition that he build and plant the bomb. The purpose, he was told, was to discredit Hitler's enemies by blaming them for the attempt. Elser said he was selected because of his skill in carpentry and electrical work. He was promised an easy escape to Switzerland, where a large sum of money would be waiting for him. Elser said he worked on the bomb in Dachau, where he was given extra food and cigarettes and treated well. He was also supplied with tools and given the use of a workshop where he constructed his bomb. Once the bomb was planted, however, Elser said he was arrested at the border instead of being allowed to cross.

Elser's story was that the Gestapo later coached him to testify against the two British agents and say that the British had hired him to build and plant the bomb. Best and Stevens were never placed on trial, however, so as the war's end neared, Elser died in an "Allied bombing raid," according to the official Gestapo reports. It is most likely that Himmler wanted to concoct a plot involving the British agents and hoped Elser would turn into a cooperative witness. Hitler criticized Himmler even in light of Elser's full confession, saying he had failed to find the "real" criminals behind the attempted assassination. Hitler was certain that the British Secret Service was behind the plot and that Elser was working for them.

Speculation has been rampant about the Elser incident. Elser may have begun telling the alternate story fed to him by the Gestapo, adding elaborations of his own. He no doubt believed that as long as there was a chance he was useful to the authorities, he would be kept alive. Perhaps Himmler hatched the entire plot as a propaganda move in order to frame the British Secret Service. Or it is possible that Elser acted alone, and Himmler later saw an opportunity to place blame after the fact. In any event, Elser was protected for the balance of his life in the camps, which itself is unusual. The full truth can never be known.

The Elser incident led to an overhaul of security measures. Security and police organizations were given new directives concerning Hitler's personal safety, including the Security Police and Security Service, the Gestapo, the regular police, criminal police, and the special SS police and security divisions. The SS produced a sixty-page manual called "Security Measures for the Protection of Leading Persons of State and Party," and a new agency was created specifically to coordinate these stepped-up security measures with all involved agencies.

After the Elser incident, Reinhard Heydrich, head of the Reichssicherheitshauptamt (Reich Central Security Office, or R.S.H.A.) announced that his organization's primary task was to take: "all measures for the prevention of assassination attempts against leading personalities of the Reich and of foreign states when they are on German soil."[7]

Hitler himself knew that his exposure to an assassin was a fact of life. All leaders, loved or hated, must accept this as inevitable. Hitler had expressed this reality with characteristic ego on August 22, 1939: "There will probably never again be a man with such authority or who has the confidence of the whole German people as I have. My existence is therefore a factor of great value. But I can be eliminated at any moment by a criminal or a lunatic."[8]

His great concern about his exposure to danger caused Hitler to take elaborate precautions. His erratic schedule and last-minute, unannounced changes in plans made any assassin's job difficult; he also took physical precautions. In public, Hitler wore a special cap that was reinforced with a steel band weighing 3½ pounds. He carried a pistol and surrounded himself with bodyguards, each carrying two 9-mm pistols with 50 rounds of ammunition. In his automobile and in escort cars, additional weaponry was readily

Hitler's high-security Mercedes-Benz contained every imaginable safety feature. This actual automobile is a popular exhibit in the Imperial Palace Antique and Classic Auto Collection in Las Vegas, Nevada. (Photo: Imperial Palace Antique and Classic Auto Collection, Las Vegas, Nevada).

available: pistols, six submachine guns, a light machine gun, and as much as 4,500 rounds of ammunition.[9]

Hitler rode in a reinforced armored car. Three such cars were commissioned and built in 1935. They were constructed with 4-mm steel bodies, 25-mm windshield and windows, and 20-chamber bulletproof tires. These early models could travel 106 miles per hour. An updated model in use until 1938 was built with three axles and with 30-mm windshields and 20-mm windows. The rear seat backs were reinforced with 8-mm steel plate. Eventually, the bulletproof tires used on all Hitler's touring sedans were removed, as they caused too much vibration. Hitler's personal driver, Erich Kempfa, was given perhaps the longest title any chauffeur has ever had, *Chef des Kraftfahrwesens beim Führer und Reichskanzler* (Chief of the Führer's and Reich Chancellor's Fleet of Cars).

In 1938, Hitler had a special Mercedes-Benz manufactured for him in that company's Stuttgart factory. It was a 770-K open touring sedan, built completely by hand at a cost of $250,000. It weighed five and one-half tons and had rubber bulletproof tires. The windows were 1½ inches thick and also bulletproof, and the floor was completely mineproof. Each door contained ¾-inch armor plate and weighed more than 900 pounds, and the rear of the car was an armored shield.

The engine was supercharged with eight cylinders, each fired by two spark plugs. The car could reach 50 miles per hour in 12.2 seconds and had a top speed of 120 mph.[10]

Security was also extended to other modes of transportation used by Hitler. By 1942 an improved model of Hitler's plane, a *Focke-Wulf* PW 200 Condor, was placed in service. It came with four machine guns and four 986-hp engines. The plane could remain in flight for up to 15 hours. Hitler's seat was equipped with a trap door through which he could drop with a parachute. In 1944 three additional, upgraded models of the plane were commissioned, with an improved ejector seat and a nonstop travel capacity of 6,000 kilometers. Hitler's seat was reinforced with 12-mm steel armor plating, and the windows were constructed of 50-mm bulletproof glass. These planes came with 10 large-caliber machine guns.

Since Hitler also traveled frequently by private train, security measures were upgraded with new rail cars put into service in 1937-39. All coaches on Hitler's private train were made entirely of welded steel, except for the windows, which were bulletproof. Each car exceeded 60 tons. Hitler's private train was named the *Führerhauptquartier* (Führer's Headquarters) and was code-named "*Amerika.*" The train consisted (in sequence) of two locomotives, an armored antiaircraft car with guns and a 26-man crew, a baggage car, the Führer's coach, a conference car and communications center, an escort car for bodyguards, a dining car, two sleeping cars for guests, a bath coach, a second dining car, two personnel coaches, a press car with communications center, another baggage car, and a second antiaircraft car with crew.

Chapter 7

PLANS FOR A COUP D'ÉTAT: 1938

It shows lack of caliber and understanding of his task, if a soldier in high position during times like these sees his duty only in the limited scope of his military tasks, without realizing the high responsibility he bears before the entire people. Extraordinary times call for extraordinary actions.

Ludwig Beck, memo to Field Marshal Walther von Brauchitsch, commander in chief of the army, July 16, 1938

The events of 1938 made the Second World War inevitable. That year was the last chance the opposition had to remove Hitler from power and avoid war altogether. The chance was lost.

At a conference that had begun at 4:15 P.M. on November 5, 1937, Adolf Hitler had informed his top military leaders that plans would proceed for the armed invasion of Czechoslovakia. The invasion plan was code-named "Operation Green." Hitler lectured to his generals that Germany needed *Lebensraum* (living space) and that the territories controlled by the Reich must be expanded. Reaction to the idea of a military adventure was negative among all the generals. Hermann Göring, always ready to agree with Hitler on everything, argued with the military leaders throughout the four-hour meeting. At the conclusion of the meeting, although professional opinion against the attack on Czechoslovakia was unanimous, none of the generals refused to support the plan.

Hitler's real motives went beyond the need for living space. Czechoslovakia was a creation of the compromises that grew out of the Versailles Treaty at the end of the First World War. Hitler viewed Czechoslovakia as a symbol of the flawed Versailles Treaty. The country was made up of the old kingdom of Bohemia, Slovakia, and a previously autonomous region populated by ethnic Russians called Subcarpathian Ruthenia.

Life in that young nation had not been trouble-free, however. Conflict among its ethnic minorities had developed shortly after its creation. The one million Hungarians, half million Ruthenians, and two million Sudeten Germans all believed they had been taken from their true home country, respectively Hungary, Russia, and Austria.* The

*The Sudeten Germans had never actually been a part of Germany. The area had at one time been (continued)

demands of the three smallest minorities were not the only problem faced by the Czech leadership.

A large number of the 10 million Slovaks in Czechoslovakia also desired autonomy. Discontent was the result of the artificial border adjustments that grew out of war settlements. None of the ethnic groups demanding freedom from the central Czech government complained of mistreatment or misrepresentation. No classes were excluded. All citizens had voting rights and civil rights and were well treated. Even so, the calls for autonomy were persistent throughout the short history of Czechoslovakia.

Hitler seized upon this dissatisfaction to further his own ambitions. A familiar pattern emerged: a crisis was created and confrontation followed. The situation was blown out of proportion to the point that nothing short of extraordinary measures could remedy the problem. Using a cry for Sudeten independence, Germany absorbed not only the originally contested regions, but the entire nation: Sudetens as well as Czechs, Slovaks, Hungarians, and Ruthenians.

The influence of Nazism in Czechoslovakia began in 1933, the year Hitler became chancellor of Germany. That year the Sudeten Deutsche Partei was formed, led by Konrad Henlein. By 1935 the German Foreign Office was providing Henlein 15,000 marks per month. In the 1935 election, 70 percent of Sudeten Germans voted for the party.[1]

At first, Henlein limited the party's activities to expressing grievances for the Sudeten minority. The German absorption of Austria, or what became known as the *Anschluß*,† emboldened Henlein, however. On April 23, 1938, the party issued Sudeten demands, which amounted to a call for complete autonomy from the Czech government. The demands, called the Carlsbad program, prepared the way for Hitler's planned attack. The eight demands were

> 1. Equality of Sudeten Germans and Czechs, with the Sudeten Germans no longer to be considered merely a minority
> 2. Recognition of the Sudeten Germans as a legal and corporate body
> 3. Determination of the Sudeten boundaries within the state
> 4. Full self-government for the Germans in this demarcated territory
> 5. Legal protection and guarantees for Germans living in Czechoslovakia outside this demarcated belt
> 6. Removal of injustices and discriminations against Germans in the matter of language, jobs, and the like inflicted since 1918 and reparations for them
> 7. State and civil employees and officials in German areas to be Germans
> 8. The Germans to have full liberty to profess German nationality and to proclaim allegiance to the ideology of Germany, that is, Nazidom.[2]

The demands were actually designed to create a pretext for German intervention because it was assumed the Czech government would reject the demands. Hitler was not truly interested in negotiating with the Czech government. Attempts by the Czech lead-

---

part of Austria. This detail was not important to Hitler, however, who also considered Austria to properly be a part of the German Reich. In March 1938, Austria had been annexed; now, Hitler insisted, Czechoslovakia must follow suit.

†Anschluss *means union, or joining.*

ership at working out a solution with German nationals within their border came to nothing, largely because Hitler, with help from Henlein, was intent on stirring up passion and support for Operation Green. As Henlein expressed it himself, "We must always demand so much that we can never be satisfied."

Most Germans feared that if Germany were to attack Czechoslovakia, France would retaliate and perhaps Britain as well. Czechoslovakia's treaty with France provided for mutual assistance if Germany attacked either country. That treaty was part of the Locarno Pact of 1925, a complex series of treaties and arbitration conventions. The participants in that pact were Britain, France, Germany, Italy, Belgium, Poland, and Czechoslovakia. A second treaty with Russia promised assistance in the event of an attack on Czechoslovakia, but only on condition that France acted to protect Czechoslovakia first.

Henlein, after publication of his Carlsbad program, visited London, where he posed as a moderate interested in working out a satisfactory agreement with the Czech government. In July 1938, Lord Halifax announced that Lord Walter Runciman was being sent to Prague to mediate the crisis. He arrived in Prague on August 3 and held a number of meetings aimed at working out agreement between the Czech government and the Sudeten Germans.

All attempts at compromising the proposals expressed in the Carlsbad program were flatly rejected by Henlein. Between German threats and British pressure, the Czech government finally agreed to all of the demands of the Carlsbad program. By that time, however, Hitler's ambitions were no longer limited to only the Sudeten regions. His plans included all of Czechoslovakia. He would be satisfied with nothing less than its complete destruction.

Hitler's aggressive stance toward Czechoslovakia galvanized military sources of resistance in Germany. War was widely believed among military leaders to be inevitable if Hitler proceeded. First discussions of a coup d'état took place as early as February 1938 between Fritz-Dietlof von der Schulenburg, vice president of the Berlin Police and an ardent anti–Nazi, and General Erwin von Witzleben, commander of Military District III (which included Berlin). Schulenburg asked the general to provide for intervention by the Wehrmacht in the event of a coup.

Witzleben agreed that from a military point of view, Hitler was leading the country down a dangerous and destructive path. He spoke with General Paul von Hase, commander of No. 50 Infantry Regiment stationed in Landsberg on Warthe. Hase agreed to a plan to deploy his regiment to move against the Gestapo and SS and, if necessary, against the government in Berlin. As they discussed details of this plan, the conspirators realized that a coup would require meticulous planning. They knew they did not have the resources available to accomplish their goals, so the idea was allowed to drop as quietly as it had come up.

Meanwhile, Operation Green moved forward. Military preparations were worked on by the General Staff through the winter and, by April 22, 1938, the strategic plan was ready. Hitler told his army, navy, and air force commanders that the invasion would begin no later than October 1, adding, "It is my unalterable decision to destroy Czechoslovakia by military action within a foreseeable time."[3]

Throughout the spring and summer, military experts voiced their fears, at least to one another, that if Britain and France were to retaliate, German military strength would be no match for them. The few generals who tried to reason with Hitler directly were subjected to a torrent of abuse. Apprehension was growing in many circles about the prospects for war. Resistance leaders continued their secret negotiations with the British government (see Chapter 6).

In August 1938, opposition members began serious plans for a coup d'état. By the end of August, several opposition members were working on a plan to remove Hitler from power. Even the generals charged with carrying out the invasion, Walther von Reichenau and Gerd von Rundstedt, expressed their belief to Brauchitsch that the war would be lost if France and Britain intervened. They asked Brauchitsch to convey their fears to Hitler directly.

On September 9, 1938, Brauchitsch met with Hitler to discuss Operation Green. General Franz Halder, Beck's replacement as chief of staff, also attended. Brauchitsch emphasized that if there was even the slightest chance of retaliation by Czechoslovakia's allies, the entire plan should be abandoned as too risky. Hitler responded with a characteristic tirade against faintheartedness and lack of confidence.

General Halder, who had assumed his post on August 27, 1938, was immediately involved with plans for a coup d'état. He was fully briefed by General Beck before he took the post and supported Beck's contention that Hitler must be stopped. Halder was a conservative, deeply religious man with a strong sense of responsibility and a growing sense of conflict. He took his military oath seriously, but he detested Hitler and the Nazi movement as immoral, reckless, and destructive for Germany.

Even prior to assuming his office as chief of staff, Halder had been introduced to State Secretary Weizsäcker and had been briefed on the Foreign Ministry's efforts at opening channels of discussion with London. Like many others at the time, Halder hoped that a strong statement of warning from Britain would forestall Hitler's ambitions toward Czechoslovakia. He and Weizsäcker kept in close touch, their communications channeled through Wilhelm Canaris and Hans Oster in the Abwehr.*

Halder knew Oster from their previous army service together. Oster had worked as one of Halder's staff officers when Halder had served as chief of staff in *Wehrkreis* (military district) VI in Münster. This association facilitated Halder's introduction to other resistance figures. Oster introduced Halder to Dr. Hjalmar Schacht, the ex-minister of economics who had managed Hitler's war economy.

Schacht had two years earlier sent an intermediary to General Beck to discuss the idea of removing Hitler from power. The discussion had ended in a standoff, with Beck willing to support a civilian-led coup and Schacht recognizing the need for military support. In September 1937, after suffering continual disagreements about economic policy with Hermann Göring, Schacht resigned from his post as minister of economics, to be replaced by Göring himself. At Hitler's request, Schacht remained in the cabinet as minister without portfolio. While Hitler was determined to go to war, Schacht became active

---

The Abwehr provided a perfect camouflage for such communications. Correspondence between the army and the Foreign Office was forbidden. It was perfectly legitimate, however, for the military intelligence unit to be in contact with both the army and the Foreign Ministry.

in the resistance, believing that war would be disastrous for Germany, not only militarily but politically as well.

Oster arranged a meeting between Halder as the military representative of the resistance and Schacht as the expert politician. Schacht recognized a civilian-led coup would succeed only with military support. Halder emphasized that a coup must not lead to civil war. It would require careful planning, including steps to neutralize the SS, the Gestapo, and any military units that might resist the overthrow.

Halder and Schacht agreed that the police should be used to arrest and hold Hitler, while army units ensured control over the SS and Gestapo forces. The idea of using the police to carry out arrests as part of a coup held a certain appeal for military members of the resistance, but uncertainty of support among the rank and file police forces made the scheme risky. Use of the military would be necessary, but for the military, becoming involved in purely political matters was troublesome. Exposing Hitler as a criminal would enable the military to take an active role.

Schacht and Oster put Halder in contact with Dr. Hans Gisevius, a counselor in the Ministry of the Interior. Gisevius had had an interesting and varied police career. Between 1933 and 1936, he had worked for the Gestapo, the Prussian Ministry of the Interior, and at the headquarters of the Criminal Police. His work kept him in touch with Oster and the Abwehr. Gisevius was later to play the role of go-between for the German resistance and the American OSS.*

Halder and Gisevius met at Halder's apartment in Berlin. Both expressed the belief that Hitler was a criminal who should be removed from office. Gisevius had come to realize the criminal nature of the Nazi regime from his inside experience. He could work with the opposition from within the Nazi system, where his access to information would be invaluable. Gisevius recommended that a coup should be instigated as a police action under law. The leaders of the Nazi regime should be indicted on criminal charges, he said. He cited practices of the Gestapo and SS and treatment of prisoners in concentration camps.

Halder was not so sure that criminal charges could be proved, and thus was concerned that military leaders would be placed in the position of abandoning their loyalty oaths. Gisevius responded that as part of the coup action, they would seize the files in Himmler's offices, providing ample proof of crimes. Halder still was not convinced.

To Gisevius, Halder seemed an unlikely candidate to lead a coup. He was, Gisevius recalled, pedantic and overly cautious. Halder was nervous about using the army directly in a coup, even in conjunction with the police. He favored a bombing attack on Hitler's train. That way Hitler's death could be blamed on an unnamed enemy power or political group. Halder favored waiting until hostilities broke out and Germany suffered a military setback, so that a purge would be more widely supported in military circles. He resisted any suggestions that the army should be openly involved in arresting Hitler on criminal charges. When Gisevius later reported his negative impressions of Halder to Oster, Oster was surprised and disappointed. But the next day, Halder had a change of mind. He notified Oster to cooperate fully with Gisevius in advancing a police-led coup.

Office of Strategic Services, the 12,000-member U.S. espionage organization founded during the Second World War, and precursor to the Central Intelligence Agency (CIA).

The groundwork was laid for Oster to lead Gisevius and Schacht in organizing a coup d'état, with Halder's promise of army support. They began at once to work out precise details for overthrowing Hitler. At the same time, they recognized the importance of trying to win over as much military support for their plans as possible, especially from formation commanders. The three also agreed that Halder must be kept apprised of all important foreign policy developments that would affect the timing of the coup. Oster took responsibility for maintaining this level of contact, with assistance from Schacht and Weizsäcker.

Now organized for action, the opposition had to contend with its own impatience. The action that would prompt the coup, they all agreed, would be actual orders issued by Hitler to begin an armed invasion of Czechoslovakia. Beck had known the exact timetable for Operation Green before resigning as chief of staff. It was scheduled to begin by October 1 at the very latest. Expecting that no changes would be made to that timetable, the resistance leaders agreed to set their coup tentatively for the morning of September 29. That would allow the 24 hours required to countermand an invasion order.

Timing was critical. They would have to act on short notice and without delay. To add to the tension, Gisevius was not at all convinced that General Halder had the will or decisiveness to act when the time came. Gisevius favored putting the plan into action at once, without waiting for the attack order. Schacht agreed, and as time went on and Hitler's announced deadline approached, both began pushing for execution of their plan as soon as possible rather than at the last minute.

Schacht and Gisevius visited Halder to determine whether he was still in agreement with the plans they had all made. They were dismayed to find that Halder was having second thoughts, confirming Gisevius' suspicions. Halder expressed the hope that Britain and France would give in to Hitler and allow him to annex the Sudeten region of Czechoslovakia without war. He also reiterated to Schacht and Gisevius, however, that he was prepared to put the coup into action if Hitler gave marching orders for Operation Green. Halder also gave his two visitors good news concerning the possibility of a last-minute attack order. Because of the need for preparations, Halder, as chief of staff, would have no less than three days' notice prior to an invasion. Prior notice gave opposition organizers an obvious advantage. Having the time to put everything in place meant the chances of succeeding were greatly improved.

The more advance notice of an invasion, the better. One of the officers who was helping work on plans for the coup d'état was General Karl-Heinrich von Stülpnagel, army deputy chief of staff. He was able to obtain assurances of even more lead time than the three days Halder had been promised. Stülpnagel contacted General Alfred Jodl, head of the OKW Operations Staff, and stated that when Operation Green was activated, he would need five days' notice. Jodl assured Stülpnagel that five days' notice would be given, subject to change up to two days prior to deadline in the event of unfavorable weather.

Schacht and Gisevius, not trusting in Halder's ability to see the plan through, appealed to Oster to solidify support for the coup among other military leaders. Oster agreed. He met with General Witzleben early in September 1938 to ask whether he would support a coup if that became necessary. The general agreed without hesitation. He had some questions, however, regarding the political implications of Hitler's planned invasion.

Witzleben's first concern was retaliation from Britain and France in the event of a German attack on Czechoslovakia. If the Czech campaign could be won through diplomacy, for instance, rather than armed aggression, Witzleben reasoned, there would be no reason to overthrow Hitler.

Oster suggested that Witzleben discuss his concerns with Schacht, the most politically knowledgeable member of the resistance. Soon after, Schacht and Witzleben met at Schacht's home at Gühlen. Witzleben brought along General Walter von Brockdorff-Ahlefeldt, commander of the Potsdam Division. Gisevius also attended. Schacht addressed Witzleben's concerns, assuring him that Britain and France were militarily superior and that an attack on Czechoslovakia would clearly lead to a wider war. Both generals became convinced that all steps should be taken to prevent war. They agreed to support the planned coup with or without Halder.

Now confident that adequate military support was available for the coup to succeed, resistance leaders proceeded with detailed plans for the preparation, execution, and follow-up of a coup d'état. Schacht began compiling a list of political appointees for a newly formed government. Brockdorff took on responsibility for coordination of military units during the coup. Gisevius worked out details for mobilizing the Berlin police to overpower or neutralize SS and Gestapo units in the capital city.

Gisevius gained the cooperation of Arthur Nebe, director of the Reich Criminal Police Office, in obtaining information on the location and strength of SS garrisons and Gestapo stations. Gisevius was provided with office space in Wehrkreis headquarters, in a room next to General Witzleben, who explained to his aide that Gisevius was a relative working on family matters.

Gisevius mapped out locations of SS strength throughout Germany, with information provided from both Nebe and Oster. He discovered that the criminal police and regular police were not routinely stationed in the same location as the Gestapo. This would make it difficult to neutralize all police forces at the same time and would require more detailed planning. He also needed to work out specific plans for seizing radio, telephone, and telegraph offices, and especially post office repeater stations, through which police telephone and teleprinter circuits were channeled. The plan also called for liberation of all concentration camps as quickly as possible. The task was huge. Orders would have to be issued to every Wehrkreis commander at the same time for the occupation of key sites, arrests, and the establishment of martial law. The state of emergency depended on fast, simultaneous action. There was no certainty that all commanders would promptly obey, so it would be necessary to arrange for dependable military units to be situated in the most critical places.

Halder had some control over the command structure of the army, and he used that control to position units advantageously for the planned coup d'état. He placed No. 1 Light Division, commanded by General Erich Hoepner, under Witzleben's command. The division was on maneuvers through September 23, when it would take up position at Plauen near the Czech border, poised for invasion. From there, Halder reasoned, the division could easily block access to the main road leading to Berlin. That would prevent SS units stationed at the Grafenwöhr training grounds to the south from moving through the area to Berlin to help resist coup forces in the capital. Halder also worked on plans to move other army units, led by sympathetic commanding generals, closer to

Berlin. These generals included General Fedor von Bock of the Eighth Army, General Wilhelm Adam of Army Group II, General Gerd von Rundstedt of the Second Army, and General Ludwig Beck of the First Army.

With the exception of Beck, these generals were not informed by Halder of the planned coup d'état. He reasoned that he could depend on their support once the plan had been launched, but that it was too dangerous to tell them in advance. Halder was certain of support from one additional leader, General Paul von Hase, commander of 50th Infantry Regiment. Witzleben had briefed Hase early in September of the plans, and Hase was ready to add his support.

———————

At this point, the resistance was confident about its chances for succeeding in a coup based on military support but was less certain about maintaining control. No one knew which groups would cooperate or exactly what might happen afterwards. As Halder explained the problem after the Second World War:

> The putsch, the assassination of Hitler, is only the negative side. Anyone interested in the fate of his people must look at the positive side. What was to happen afterwards? I was never given a glimpse of this positive side. The soldiers were asked to "clean the place up" like housemaids, but no one, neither Beck nor Goerdeler, told me what was then to be served up. Herein lies the overriding weakness of this entire resistance movement.[4]

Resistance leaders agreed that a short-lived military state of emergency would be necessary and that a provisional civil government should be declared with elections arranged as quickly as possible. Debate arose on the question of whether some of the Nazi leadership should be retained, at least temporarily. Some army officers, for example, suggested that Göring might serve as a valuable mediator during the transition following Hitler's removal.*

Gisevius had a different idea. He thought that retaining any top Nazis in the government was dangerous. Instead, he suggested explaining the coup as an SS-led putsch which the Wehrmacht had been forced to crush. In taking firm steps to reestablish order, Gisevius argued, the army could take the opportunity to get rid of the entire Nazi hierarchy and also reconcile its difficulties with the loyalty oath to Hitler.

Halder, keenly aware of the loyalty oath problem for himself as well as other generals, had avoided trying to elicit support from the commander in chief, Brauchitsch. He explained that "One can risk one's own neck but not that of someone else." In the minds of the resistance leaders, the coup would be possible without Brauchitsch's involvement. Brauchitsch continued to hold the position that he sympathized with opposition arguments but would not be disloyal to Hitler. The temporary military government planned by the resistance was to be headed by Brauchitsch. But Beck, remembering well his frus-

---

*With historical hindsight and awareness of history's judgment of Göring, this suggestion might seem ludicrous. However, these discussions took place well in advance of the events that led to his conviction for war crimes.

tration at the commander in chief's unwillingness to take a strong stand, favored advising Brauchitsch of the arrangements only after it was too late to turn back. The plan called for informing Brauchitsch of the coup after it had started, hoping that he would then endorse it. Questions remained whether Brauchitsch should be briefed immediately before Hitler's arrest or immediately after.

The success of the coup depended on fast action by troop commanders like Witzleben. The decisive action of strategically located units could make all the difference. Witzleben decided he would occupy the War Ministry if necessary and have other generals placed under arrest if they refused to support the coup.

General Brockdorff was responsible for coordinating army strength in Berlin. Early in September he toured the Berlin area. The general wanted to estimate the troop strength he would need to secure strategic sites. With Gisevius, he drove to the War Ministry, Göring's residence, the *Leibstandarte SS* barracks, the radio transmitter station at Königswusterhausen, and Sachsenhausen concentration camp.

Other issues remained to be resolved. Among these was the cooperation of the police in Berlin and elsewhere. Gisevius had contacts in the various police forces and the Gestapo, but no authority. Nebe had authority only within the criminal police but not with the regular police or the Gestapo. Gisevius and Nebe had the full support of the Berlin vice president of police, Fritz-Dietlof von der Schulenburg. The resistance desperately needed, however, to line up more cooperation at the top of the police hierarchy. By September 1938, Wolf Heinrich von Helldorf, police president, endorsed the planned coup. He had become anti–Nazi after the demise of General Blomberg earlier in 1938. Between them, Helldorf and Schulenburg assured that the Berlin police force would not interfere with military units during the coup.

Debate among the resistance leaders now began to focus on two issues — the type of government that should be installed after the coup and what to do with Hitler. All of the organizers agreed that a military state of emergency and provisional government would be necessary, but only for as short a time as possible. After that, decisions would have to be made about a legitimate replacement for the Nazi regime. Thus began a series of debates that were to last to 1944 about the future of Germany, forms of government, nominees for cabinet positions, and the long-term ideals for Germany and Europe.

The second point of debate centered on what to do with Hitler. Halder favored assassination, but in such a way that it could be blamed on unknown enemies. That way, military leaders would not be implicated and their adherence to the loyalty oath could remain unquestioned. He made the point that otherwise Hitler might become a martyr. If the coup failed, a continuing Nazi government could be strengthened by the memory of Hitler as fallen hero.

General Beck favored arresting Hitler and holding a trial so that he could be accused of criminal charges. Other resistance leaders opposed to an assassination plan put forward the idea of having a panel of doctors declare Hitler insane so that he could be confined to a mental hospital. The anti-assassination group, led by Beck, Goerdeler, and

Schacht, gained the label of "conservatives" within the resistance. In comparison, younger members of the resistance, mostly army officers, favored bold and final action, rejecting the conservatives' arrest plan as too dangerous. Leading this group was Major Friedrich Wilhelm Heinz.

Witzleben presented a plan of action during a meeting at Oster's home about September 20, 1938. Major Heinz and Carl Goerdeler also attended. Witzleben's plan was that as soon as the signal for the coup was given he would take a bodyguard of officers to the Chancellery and confront Hitler, demanding his resignation. At the same time, army units were to seize SS barracks and prevent any SS-led response.

The idea was approved, and Oster and Witzleben asked Major Heinz to recruit a raiding party as escort for General Witzleben. Heinz, favoring immediate elimination of Hitler, agreed but proceeded with plans of his own. He knew that Witzleben's group would not be allowed to simply walk into Hitler's office. They would have to fight their way in. Heinz intended to ensure that Hitler would be killed during the struggle. Even if they were able to get into Hitler's office without serious resistance, Heinz was resolved to provoke an incident so that he could shoot Hitler on the spot.

Heinz was able to recruit trusted fellow officers and have them transferred, with the help of Hans Oster and the Abwehr. Oster made the arrangements on the pretext of a "special training mission," not an uncommon practice for the intelligence organization. That way any suspicion by unit commanders about the movements of personnel was defused. Between 20 and 30 officers were gathered and housed in several Berlin apartments near the Chancellery, where they awaited orders to move. Heinz convinced Oster that his plan for killing Hitler during the raid was the only reasonable one, and Oster agreed. Oster asked Canaris to help, and Canaris asked Major Helmuth Groscurth, an Abwehr officer, to obtain necessary weapons and explosives. These were rounded up without trouble and delivered to members of the raiding party.

At this point, the coup d'état was completely ready. Military units were situated strategically to ensure adequate strength to prevent countermoves by the SS, Gestapo, or army units loyal to the Nazis. Proclamations announcing the state of emergency and martial law had been drafted and were ready to be read over radio and transmitted by wire as soon as the coup was underway. Orders were drafted to be delivered throughout the nation for seizure of key installations and arrests, and all precautions were ready. There was nothing left to do but wait.

Until September 15, the need for a coup d'état was clear. Hitler was going to give the order for Operation Green; Britain and France would retaliate. A German defeat would be certain. The mission was clear: remove Hitler from power in order to prevent war.

Events in the second half of September changed all of these assumptions. On September 12, Hitler delivered a fiery speech at the annual Nuremberg rally on the subject of Czech oppression of Sudeten Germans. Germany, Hitler promised, would take all necessary steps to protect Germans living under intolerable conditions. The tone of his speech was unmistakably threatening; war seemed imminent.

Prime Minister Neville Chamberlain represented the mood against war in Britain. He was to play a critical role in 1938 (Photo: National Archives).

French premier Édouard Daladier spoke with British prime minister Chamberlain on the night of September 13, suggesting that a strong and united approach to Hitler would be useful. Chamberlain, however, was determined to deal with Hitler by himself. Rather than condemning Hitler for his war soundings, as everyone expected, he took the initiative by offering to fly to Germany and meet with Hitler in person for the purpose of resolving the difficulties between Germany and Czechoslovakia. He advised his cabinet the following day of the decision.

Chamberlain represented the mood in Britain against war, and he believed that if Hitler were given what he demanded, war could be averted. The British prime minister made it clear that he was willing to appease Hitler and that the British were not in the mood for a fight.

Chamberlain's offer to go to Germany and meet with Hitler underscored the weakness of Britain's bargaining position. Clearly, the prime minister was willing to do anything, even go to Germany himself to beg for peace. His offer also confirmed Hitler's belief that Britain and France would not intervene to help Czechoslovakia. Response in Czechoslovakia was astonishment. Negotiations for settlement of the Sudetenland question were proceeding well, and the Czech government believed the issues were all but settled. The Czechs were certain that Chamberlain's announcement weakened their position considerably.

It also harmed the British negotiating position. This problem was clearly expressed by historian René Albrecht-Carrié:

> The spectacle of a British Prime Minister, the representative of the power and pride that were Britain's, a man of seventy, for the first time in his life resorting to airplane transportation, in order to plead with the Austrian upstart, was in itself a sensation of the first magnitude; it was a measure of the acuteness of the crisis, of Britain's devotion to the preservation of peace, and of the power commanded by Germany; perhaps one should add of the degree of recklessness and irresponsibility of that power.[5]

It is only possible to speculate how differently events might have proceeded if, instead of offering to visit with Hitler, Chamberlain had taken a strong stand and vowed to support Czechoslovakia in the event of a German invasion, especially if such a stand had been made together with the French government, as Daladier had suggested. Winston Churchill predicted at the time that the decision by Chamberlain to go to Germany was a costly and far-reaching mistake. He wrote, "It will be another example of the very small accidents upon which the fortunes of mankind turn."[6]

The meeting between Chamberlain and Hitler was quickly arranged for September 15 at Hitler's retreat at Berchtesgaden. Hitler as usual did almost all of the talking. He was uncompromising in his demands regarding the Sudetenland. The only way to protect the rights of Germans, Hitler argued, was through annexation.

Hitler proposed that if Britain would agree to annexation, the people living in the region would be granted the right to self-determination. Chamberlain asked that the residents of the Sudetenland be allowed to vote on the idea, suggesting a plebiscite in regions containing mixed populations. He also predicted that French prime minister Édouard Daladier would probably support the suggestion.*

Chamberlain said that he would need to consult with his government and with the French as well concerning the question of annexation but promised to return to Germany as soon as possible for further discussions. Chamberlain asked Hitler for an assurance that there would be no military action until they had a chance to speak again. Hitler agreed. Chamberlain remarked after the meeting on his impressions of Hitler: "In spite of the hardness and ruthlessness I thought I saw in his face, I got the impression that here was a man who could be relied upon when he had given his word."[7]

The unexpected announcement by Chamberlain of his willingness to talk to Hitler and the almost immediate meeting caused great confusion and doubt among the planners of the coup d'état. Suddenly, their plan, based upon the inevitability of war, was in doubt. The British, instead of adopting a strong position against Hitler, were now backing away from such a stance and expressing the willingness to give in to his demands.

Chamberlain was not the only one willing to appease Hitler and keep the peace at any price. Despite Daladier's original suggestion of combined resolve, the French prime minister had spoken to Chamberlain just before he left for his meeting with Hitler and advised him that France did not want another war. He suggested that Chamberlain "seek as good a bargain" as possible. Chamberlain was also responding to the desire to maintain peace among the British people. On September 7, well before his visit with Hitler, the London Times *endorsed ceding the Sudetenland to Germany to avoid war.*

Chamberlain met with Hitler on September 15, 1938, on his own initiative and in the mood to do whatever was necessary to avoid war (Photo: National Archives).

The sudden diplomatic turn of events caught the resistance leaders off guard. New questions arose. What should be done in the event that the invasion were delayed or postponed? What if Hitler achieved another bloodless victory, repeating his success in annexing Austria earlier the same year? For the moment, the coup planners continued their preparations, albeit with less assuredness than before.

Chamberlain was able to convince the British cabinet that annexation of the Sudetenland by Germany would be the best course. It would prevent war, he told them, while satisfying the demands of the predominantly German population in that region. The French cabinet, however, could not agree to the proposed solution and debated it hotly.

British and French government representatives entered into talks in London on September 18 and after some debate agreed to German annexation of the Sudetenland. The conclusion was that any territories containing more than 50 percent Sudeten Germans should be turned over to Germany to guarantee "the maintenance of peace and the safety of Czechoslovakia's vital interests."[8] Britain and France justified this course with assurances to the Czech government of "an international guarantee of the new boundaries ... against unprovoked aggression." On September 19, the British and French representatives in Prague jointly advised the Czech government of the decision. Up to this point, the Czechs had not been consulted.

A shocked Czech government response of September 20 predicted that acceptance of the proposal would place the Czech state "sooner or later under the complete domination of Germany." The Czechs wanted to appeal the decision and asked for hearings under terms of the German-Czech Treaty of Arbitration of 1925 (part of the Locarno Pact). They also protested that France had a treaty obligation to protect Czechoslovakia. Chamberlain called a cabinet meeting to discuss the Czech response and also discussed the problem by telephone with Prime Minister Daladier.

Winston Churchill issued a statement to the press on September 21 concerning the Czech crisis, stating that:

> The partition of Czechoslovakia under pressure from England and France amounts to the complete surrender of the Western Democracies to the Nazi threat of force. Such a collapse will bring peace or security neither to England nor to France. On the contrary, it will place these two nations in an ever weaker and more dangerous situation.... The belief that security can be obtained by throwing a small state to the wolves is a fatal delusion.[9]

The Czech leaders, realizing they were being abandoned by their allies, asked the French ambassador whether France would honor its treaty and come to the aid of Czechoslovakia if the latter were attacked by Germany. The French responded that the Czechs would have to accept the proposals or fight Germany on their own.

Czech leaders next called upon their other ally, Russia. The Russian minister responded that Russia would honor its treaty obligation. The treaty specified, however, that Russia would provide help on the condition that France first honored its agreement. Because France had refused to keep its promise, the Russian minister reported, Russia was not bound. Having no other choice, the Czech government agreed on September 22 to cede the Sudetenland to Germany.

On September 22, Chamberlain arrived in Godesberg, near Bonn, for a second meeting with Hitler. Chamberlain was optimistic, believing he had averted war and achieved an agreement satisfactory to all sides. In contrast to what had occurred during their previous discussion, Chamberlain began and talked for more than an hour. He explained to Hitler that his government had undergone extensive debate, but that he had been able to convince his cabinet, the French, and even the Czech government, to agree to Hitler's terms.

The meeting in Godesberg then took a nightmarish turn. To Chamberlain's dismay, Hitler's response was not cordial. He was no longer willing to accept the proposals discussed at their previous meeting. He rejected the agreement to allow a plebiscite in the Sudeten region. He also rejected the agreement to negotiate Czech-German frontier borders. He was impatient, he said, and would issue marching orders at once to destroy the entire state of Czechoslovakia. The only way to avoid that, Hitler warned, was movement of German troops into the Sudeten territories without any further delay. If that were not agreed upon, war would begin by October 1.

The next morning Chamberlain sent word that he wanted to negotiate further. Hitler was not interested in compromise or further discussion, however. He kept Chamberlain waiting the entire day. Finally, that evening, Hitler appeared, but with a new demand, expressed in a memorandum accompanied by a map of the territories in dispute. He now demanded the Czech evacuation of the Sudeten territories to begin on September 26, in less than three days, and to be completed by September 28. Chamberlain, shocked and offended, accused Hitler of presenting him with "nothing less than an ultimatum."

While this argument was underway, an aide entered the room with an urgent message for Hitler. After hearing the wire, he told the translator to read it to Chamberlain. It was the news that the Czech government had just announced a general mobilization of its armed forces. After an icy silence, Hitler said to Chamberlain, "Now, of course, the whole affair is settled. The Czechs will not dream of ceding any territory to Germany."[10]

A heated argument ensued, but the meeting broke up without any real agreements. Chamberlain headed back to Britain. Even after this experience, Chamberlain was committed to avoiding war. He attempted to convince his cabinet to agree to Hitler's latest demands. This time the cabinet refused. Duff Cooper, first lord of the Admiralty, was adamantly opposed and, to Chamberlain's surprise, so was Foreign Minister Lord Halifax. Even the French, who to this point had gone along with Chamberlain, rejected Hitler's Godesberg memorandum and ordered a partial mobilization. The Czech government condemned the memorandum, saying it would "deprive us of every safeguard for our national existence."

Within a few days, Britain mobilized its armed forces as well. France called up its army reserves, and Britain issued war footing alerts to its fleet. On September 26, the British government declared that if Hitler began armed aggression, France would honor her treaty with Czechoslovakia and Britain and Russia would join with France to oppose Germany. It seemed that war was imminent. British and French correspondents in Germany, fearing internment once hostilities broke out, made their way as quickly as possible for the French, Belgian, and Dutch borders.

Hitler was furious upon hearing that the British, French, and Czechs had all rejected his Godesberg memorandum. Hitler knew, however, that Germany's armed forces were no match for those of France and Britain. On September 27, he realized that there was little popular support for war. That evening, a parade of motorized troops through Berlin was greeted with stony silence by about 200 civilians, a far cry from the vast, frenzied crowds that had supported Hitler's defiance of Versailles in the recent past.

In England, France, Czechoslovakia, and even in Germany, people prepared for war. Children were evacuated from border areas, and trenches were dug. A continent wearied of war prepared for it once again. On September 27, Chamberlain broadcast to the British people this sentiment: "How horrible, fantastic, incredible it is that we should be digging trenches and trying on gas masks here because of a quarrel in a faraway country between people of whom we know nothing."[11]

Also on the twenty-seventh, Sir Horace Wilson, a close adviser to Neville Chamberlain, met with Hitler and advised him that Britain and France were serious in their resolve to retaliate in the event that Germany invaded Czechoslovakia. Hitler responded angrily: "If France and England strike, let them do so! It's a matter of complete indifference to me. Today is Tuesday; by next Monday we shall be at war."[12]

Soon after the meeting with Wilson, Hitler ordered seven divisions to travel from training areas to jumping-off positions on the Czech border and to ready themselves for an invasion to begin on September 30. A few hours after that order, an additional five German divisions were mobilized and placed on alert on the French border in the west. Hitler had available only about 12 divisions to resist the French in the event of an attack. A telegram later that day from the German military attaché in Paris estimated that by the sixth day of mobilization, France would have accumulated no fewer than 65 divisions.

Hitler believed he still had some room for bluff. He answered Chamberlain on the evening of September 27 that he was willing to negotiate with the Czechs. He offered to guarantee the integrity of the newly established Czech border once the Sudetenland was ceded. Hitler complained that it was up to the Czechs now to prevent war and accused them of provoking a crisis that would drag Britain and France into war. He appealed to Chamberlain to urge the Czech government to listen to reason.

Chamberlain was willing to come to Germany yet again to negotiate further with Hitler. He telegrammed Italian leader Mussolini to ask him to act as mediator. On September 28, Mussolini advised Hitler to seek conciliation.

The quickly developing war posture in Europe convinced the resistance members that they would be forced to initiate their coup d'état within a matter of hours. They were pleased that Britain had finally issued a stern warning to Hitler. Resistance military leaders and the raiding party were placed on alert.

The morning of September 28, General Halder called Brauchitsch in the commander in chief's headquarters. News of the British mobilization had made Brauchitsch so nervous that he now favored taking steps to stop Hitler. He advised Halder that he was now prepared to support the resistance and issue the order to begin a coup if that would avoid a conflict that Germany was certain to lose. Halder said he would wait for the telephone call from Brauchitsch that would initiate the coup.

Oster had obtained a floor plan of the Chancellery. Insiders sympathetic to the coup had arranged for the large double doors at the building's entrance to be left unlocked. By late afternoon, Brauchitsch was on the verge of issuing the order requested by Halder to begin the coup, but Brauchitsch wanted to make certain that Hitler had, in fact, decided to go to war. Brauchitsch went to the Chancellery to get confirmation for himself.

At mid-afternoon, before Brauchitsch had the chance to meet with Hitler, an announcement came over the radio that Mussolini had prevailed upon Hitler to host an international negotiation conference. Mussolini was to act as mediator between Hitler and the French and British leaders, Daladier and Chamberlain. The meeting was set up in Munich beginning the next day, September 29. Chamberlain announced the meeting the afternoon of the 28th in the House of Commons, declaring his intention to attend.

It appeared at the last minute that there remained a ray of hope for peace. Brauchitsch backed away from the coup, and the entire plan collapsed at the last minute.

The Munich conference opened early in the afternoon of September 29. The conference was brief and relatively cordial. At the opening of the meeting, Chamberlain and Daladier suggested that a Czech representative should be present. Hitler refused, and the matter was quickly dropped.

Chamberlain offered the concession that two Czech representatives, Dr. Vojtech Mastny, the Czech minister in Berlin, and Dr. Hubert Masarik of the Prague Foreign Office, should be allowed to wait in the next room. Hitler agreed, and the two Czechs were deposited in the room and left to wait. The conference proceeded, and an agreement was quickly reached, without Czech representation.

The agreement reached at this conference conformed to the Godesberg demands presented by Hitler, with a few minor revisions. The Czech government would be given 10 days, until October 10, to vacate the area to be annexed. An international commission would also be appointed to settle disputes of frontier borders between Czechoslovakia and the newly annexed Sudetenland. Britain and France guaranteed to protect Czechoslovakia against aggression. And an international commission would be established to oversee a plebiscite in areas containing both Sudeten German and Czech populations.

The Czech government's representatives, waiting in the adjoining room, were told the results after agreement had been reached. At 10 P.M. that evening, they were ushered to Sir Horace Wilson, who spoke for Neville Chamberlain. Wilson told the Czechs the outcome of the conference, including the decision that the indicated areas must be evacuated immediately. The Czech representatives protested but were told they had no choice but to agree to the terms.

On the morning of September 30, after the conference had concluded and the agreement was signed by England, France, and Germany, Chamberlain met privately with Hitler at the Führer's apartment in Munich. Chamberlain had prepared a declaration which he asked Hitler to sign. It read:

> We, the German Führer and Chancellor, and the British Prime Minister, have had a further meeting today and are agreed in recognizing that the question of Anglo-German relations is of the first importance for the two countries and for Europe. We regard the Agreement signed last night, and the Anglo-German Naval Agreement, as symbols of the desire of our two peoples, never to go to war with one another again. We are resolved that the method of consultation shall be the method adopted to deal with any

other questions that may concern our two countries, and we are determined
to continue our efforts to remove possible sources of difference, and thus
to contribute to assure the peace of Europe.[13]

Hitler read the declaration quickly and signed it. Chamberlain, flush with a sense
of success, arrived back in England the same day, where he made his famous announcement, while holding above his head the document he had asked Hitler to sign: "This is
the second time there has come back from Germany to Downing Street peace with honor.
I believe it is peace in our time."[14]*

Winston Churchill reacted to Chamberlain's triumphant announcement with a
statement of his own, delivered in the House of Commons on October 5:

> The British people should know that we have passed an awful milestone in
> our history, when the whole equilibrium of Europe has been deranged, and
> that the terrible words have been pronounced against the Western democ-
> racies: "Thou art weighed in the balance, and found wanting." And do not
> suppose that this is the end. This is only the beginning of the reckoning.
> This is only the first sip, the first foretaste of a bitter cup.[15]

Czechoslovakia, deserted by its allies and forced to accept a settlement reached at
a conference its representatives were not allowed to attend, was now utterly alone against
Hitler. Poland and Hungary, seeing that the Czechs had no allies, quickly grabbed Czech
territory in which their nationals lived. Poland seized 650 square miles around Teschen,
along with its population exceeding 200,000. Hungary took 7,500 square miles with Mag-
yar and Slovak populations of three-quarters of a million. Under official terms of the
Munich Pact, Germany was entitled to annex 11,000 square miles containing 2,800,000
Sudeten Germans and an additional 800,000 Czechs.[16]

Because Hitler had bullied Chamberlain into accepting his demands, Czechoslovakia's entire national infrastructure was torn apart. Rail lines, roads, and telephone and
telegraph communications were completely disrupted. Under terms of the agreement,
Czechs could leave the annexed area, but they could not take anything with them. Even
household goods had to be left. Farmers were allowed to leave annexed areas but could
not take cattle or equipment along. More than half of the Czech industrial and natural
resources, including coal, lignite, chemicals, cement, textiles, iron, steel, and electricity,
were turned over to Germany. Once among the most prosperous of European nations,
Czechoslovakia was impoverished within less than two weeks.

Hitler's victory was even more far-reaching than he knew. Resistance plans had
been premised on the theory that Britain and France would never allow Hitler to take
the Sudetenland without a fight. They had been proven wrong. For the moment, Hitler
seemed unstoppable. Without a shot being fired, Austria and Sudeten Czechoslovakia
had been annexed, adding 10 million to the population of Germany and expanding its
territories to make it the dominant force in central Europe. The credibility of the British

---

*Chamberlain was referring to Prime Minister Benjamin Disraeli who, in June 1878, attended the Berlin Con-
gress for discussions between Germany, Austria, Britain, Russia, France, Italy, and Turkey.

government was destroyed, encouraging Hitler and making further aggression inevitable. The opinion in Germany regarding the events of Munich is reflected in a riddle of the times: What is the difference between Chamberlain and Hitler? Answer: The one takes a weekend in the country, while the other takes a country in a weekend. The futility of appeasement was not lost on Carl Goerdeler, who recognized that Britain had only bought time rather than avoiding war. A few days after the signing of the Munich Pact, Goerdeler wrote to a friend in the United States: "The Munich Agreement was nothing but capitulation, pure and simple, by Britain and France before bluffing tricksters.... By refusing to take a risk, Chamberlain now has made war inevitable. Both the English and the French people now will have to defend their freedom by force of arms."[17]

Chamberlain's flawed thinking was obvious even to his own advisers. On October 6, British ambassador Sir Nevile Henderson wrote to Lord Halifax that "by keeping the peace, we have saved Hitler and his regime."[18]

By March 1939, Hitler had broken all of his promises regarding Czechoslovakia. No frontier negotiations, no plebiscite for citizens of the Sudetenland, and no orderly transition ever occurred. On March 15, 1939, Hitler paraded triumphantly through the streets of Prague. There was no response from Britain or France, in spite of their guarantee to protect the integrity of Czechoslovakia. The entire Czech nation, like Austria one year before, was taken without firing a shot.

Chapter 8

ON THE EVE OF WAR

The end of 1938 marked the watershed in Hitler's career, not least with the German people. He overestimated their will to power.... Hitler sensed [a] vacuum in German hearts. But he no longer sought to fill it. He would go forward with or without their enthusiasm. All he insisted on was their obedience. From 1939 he ceased to play the politician, the orator, the demagogue. He became a militarist, working from army headquarters, and by means of secret gangster-pacts. His methods of government began to approximate to Stalin's, losing their public dimension of approbation and leadership. He ceased to woo: he now sought only to force and terrorize.

Paul Johnson, *Modern Times*, 1983

The settlement of the Czech problem at Munich delayed the Second World War by a full year. It also prevented a coup d'état. After Munich, the momentum of the resistance was for the moment destroyed. Chamberlain's decision to meet with Hitler forced members of the resistance to cancel their plans and also convinced them they had been betrayed by Britain.

Opinions of Hitler after Munich were divided in Germany. Many, pointing to his bloodless victories, thought he was the supreme diplomat, a skilled politician, and a capable leader for the nation. His popularity soared. Others, in the minority opinion, recognized that Hitler's long-term aims still meant war. They considered him a dangerous, ambitious man and detested the Nazi regime and all it stood for.

After Munich, the resistance fell into disarray. Military leaders no longer believed a coup d'état was practical. Communication was impaired by the reassignment of the military leaders of the resistance, so that sympathizers were no longer stationed in the Berlin region. In November 1938, General Witzleben, whose support was critical for the successful overthrow of the Berlin government, was transferred to Frankfurt-am-Main in the west. He remained in touch with Goerdeler and Oster in Berlin but was no longer in any position to be an effective participant in a coup. Witzleben converted his newly appointed chief of staff, General Georg Sodenstern, to the cause. They worked together to devise an alternative plan for a coup, with the idea of waiting for an opportunity to put it into action. Their strategy involved the simultaneous arrests of regional Nazi leaders and taking over newspapers and radio transmission stations. Coordinating with Witzleben, State Secretary Weizsäcker in Berlin arranged for the appointment of resistance members in strategically critical posts throughout Germany. These Foreign Ministry civilian appointees served as liaisons for the resistance within the agencies. The result was a network of sympathetic people in both the civilian government and military commands.

Witzleben believed that a coup should occur well before a war began. Planning did not proceed with any particular speed because Witzleben thought he had at least one full year. As of the summer of 1939, resistance leaders agreed they should meet early in 1940 to firm up their plans. Later in 1939, when war did break out, Witzleben, still in Frankfurt-am-Main, was completely unprepared and realized he had missed the opportunity again.

In Berlin, the logical center for organizing a coup d'état, the resistance had been weakened. Resistance leaders considered Witzleben's military successor, General Curt Haase, to be undependable. Halder described Haase as being "incapable of conspiracy." Halder also found General Fritz Fromm, commander of the Reserve Army, unsympathetic to the resistance. During 1939, Halder himself became increasingly dispirited. He was convinced the opportunity had passed and nothing could be done to remove Hitler from power. He busied himself in his job as chief of staff, working on preparations Hitler had ordered for the attack on Poland.

In the year following Munich, intellectuals dominated resistance thinking. Discussion centered on what form of government should be installed once Hitler was removed. Discussions included forms of government, its leadership, and a new constitution.

First proposals for a constitution were drafted in 1937 by Professor Friedrich Alfred Schmid Noerr, who belonged to the opposition circle that included Oster, Heinz, and several others. The constitution was called the *Volksgemeinschaft* (Community of the People). It stated that nothing exceeded the interests of the Volk community except morality and that all people should coexist peacefully in the traditions of "European Christianity."* The constitution envisioned the German Reich defined as all contiguous lands inhabited by German people. Those areas were to be divided into *Gaue* (regions) which would be given broad self-governing power.

This constitutional draft included many of the romantic notions associated with the concept of "Volk," which also served as the nationalistic and ideological bases of Nazism. It expressed support for freedom of thought, but only to the extent that it was compatible with the interests of the Volk community. It defined members of the community as anyone containing at least one-quarter German origin in their blood. To others, the draft promised a guarantee of civil rights.

Carl Goerdeler was a key figure in the debate about the best form of government for Germany. Seeking consensus, he conferred for years, domestically and internationally, with many groups representing a broad political spectrum, with the intention of constructing a

---

*For many, the expression "European Christianity" was associated with a long history of anti–Semitism. Thus, any use of the expression in a political document condemned it for many as argumentative in intent.

new government that would include representation from all sides. He excluded only the Communists. Over time, Goerdeler exercised his skills to create broad support and unity. He gained support from Catholic leaders who had once belonged to the now-outlawed Center party. He also found support among labor and publishing leaders.

In 1939, Goerdeler acquired three prominent allies, Julius Leber, Wilhelm Leuschner, and Jakob Kaiser. Leber became an important ally. He had been a newspaper editor in Lübeck before Hitler's rise to power. Between 1933 and 1937, he had been imprisoned for his dissent from the Nazi view. No longer allowed to publish, Leber had become a coal merchant. His home became a center for meetings and discussions among the opposition. Wilhelm Leuschner, a manufacturer, was former minister of the interior in Hesse. Also a fierce enemy of Nazism, he too held opposition meetings at his home. Jakob Kaiser, formerly the chief of the Christian Trade Unions, was another important supporter. Goerdeler had him slated to organize reconstruction and labor matters in the new government. Of these three resistance leaders, only Kaiser would survive the war.

Goerdeler occupied himself throughout the prewar years building broad-based opposition to the regime. At the same time, he worked tirelessly on ideas for a new government, new constitution, and leadership cabinet. The Volksgemeinschaft, largely drafted by military leaders, was too nationalistic for many of the more moderate members of the opposition, and Goerdeler saw that a toned-down constitution would probably be pleasing to civilian opposition members. He favored establishing a constitutional monarchy developed along the model of the British government. Goerdeler expressed his preference for Prince Louis Ferdinand of Prussia, second son of the former crown prince, as nominee for the new monarchy. Other monarchists in the resistance preferred the elder son, Prince Wilhelm of Prussia, and they were able to convince Goerdeler that he would be a better choice.

While military leaders saw the idea of overthrowing the regime in terms of troop deployments, strategic concerns, and arrests, Goerdeler saw the entire matter as a huge administrative challenge. All aspects of the government would have to be reworked, reinvented, replaced. Rules, procedures, and controls would have to be devised.

Goerdeler was the most visionary of opposition leaders. He, more than his fellow resistance leaders, had a strong moral sense about what would be needed after Hitler. Goerdeler recommended that the first step should be reinstatement of laws ensuring civil rights and freedoms for every individual. He also insisted on immediate liberation of concentration camps. He pointed out to those looking at a coup from a purely military perspective that the camps included well-armed SS contingents which could be used as a counterforce. But more important was the need to rectify the injustices of the Third Reich as quickly as possible.

Goerdeler recognized that the parliamentary democracy of the Weimar Republic was a failure. To avoid repeating that mistake, he favored reestablishing a monarchy. That would ensure the continuity of the German state while still allowing a large degree of local control, in Goerdeler's view. He believed that the monarch would be able to remain above politics and parties, much along the model of the English government. This idea was debated in the resistance during 1938, while plans for the first coup d'état were proceeding. Goerdeler saw the monarch as commander in chief of German armed forces. First, though, a regent would be appointed to administer the government.

Goerdeler supported Ludwig Beck to act in this role. He had all of the important qualifications. As resistance member Fabian von Schlabrendorff observed: "Beck was the natural choice for this position, for he had all the prerequisites: integrity, dignity, objectivity, and age. The last qualification was important in Germany as a sign of firmly-rooted authority."[1]

The resistance leaders discussed Goerdeler's ideas as part of their planning for the 1938 coup, and the talks went on into 1939 and beyond. By 1939, Beck was accepted as the choice for regent. Goerdeler would serve as the new government's first chancellor. Leuschner was nominated as vice chancellor, and either Leber or the vice president of the Berlin police, Schulenburg, would be given the important post of minister of the interior. The Foreign Ministry was to be headed by an experienced career diplomat such as Ulrich von Hassell. On Goerdeler's suggestion, the remaining cabinet posts were to be given to representatives of interests across the political spectrum.

Goerdeler disagreed with the military leaders of the resistance on an important point: the fate of Hitler. The military believed assassination was necessary. Keeping Hitler alive would provide a rallying point for Nazis, inviting a desperate rescue attempt by the SS. The military position was that they could not afford the risks involved with simply taking Hitler prisoner. Goerdeler believed that it was essential for Germany to vindicate itself in the international community. The criminal nature of the Nazi regime could not be allowed to become associated with all of Germany, he argued. The only way to regain the respect of the world would be to place Hitler on trial for his crimes and fully document those crimes for history — not as German crimes, but as Nazi crimes ultimately brought to judgment by other Germans.

Another source of disagreement was between Goerdeler and the socialists, led by Johannes Popitz. Popitz aligned himself with the younger idealists of the Kreisau Circle, who argued for a state-controlled, planned economy. He was a respected politician, economist, and scientist, perhaps the most intellectual member of the opposition. He had served as Prussian minister of finance before Hitler's rise to power.

Popitz's political life had begun in 1918 with an appointment to the Finance Ministry. His career was interrupted briefly while he served as a professor at Berlin University. In 1932 he was promoted to the position of Prussian finance minister. Although opposed to Hitler and the Nazis, he remained in government with the hope of resisting from within the system.

Popitz became a leading thinker of the younger socialist and intellectual wing of the resistance, which was associated with the Kreisau Circle. Goerdeler, in contrast, was associated with the monarchists who were supported by the trade unions and the military. The Goerdeler group expressed a degree of mistrust of Popitz because of his long-term political career as well as his socialist views. To some in the resistance, he was viewed as part of the establishment.

Popitz was especially critical of the military wing of the movement. He believed these officers could not be relied upon to see through plans for a coup d'état. "They think only of their medals," was his opinion of the entire military. He favored working to divide Nazi loyalties to create an internal revolt. He approached Hermann Göring with hints of political opportunities. Popitz believed influencing Heinrich Himmler was the key to creating internal division among the Nazis.

The fact that Popitz, as a member of the government, was able to hold frank discussions with the likes of Göring and Himmler, helped save many lives. Popitz often approached the Nazi leaders to intercede on the behalf of others; his intervention sometimes resulted in the release of someone from prison or concentration camp, the delay of an execution order, or saving someone from the Gestapo.

The resistance contained various subgroups based on political and social beliefs. A group of conservative military and political leaders (Beck and Schacht) believed Hitler had to be assassinated and a military dictatorship established, at least for the short term. Goerdeler favored arresting Hitler and other top Nazis and having public criminal trials held. Younger intellectuals, primarily socialists and monarchists, avoided dealing with the immediate problems and focused instead on forms of government. Popitz used his connections with high-ranking Nazis in an attempt to moderate or compromise the regime.

Other members of the resistance had no influence in the government, but several believed their best course was to continue trying to establish contact in foreign governments, especially Great Britain. Efforts to gain support from the British government continued throughout 1939.

That summer attempts were made by the resistance to sway the British government toward taking a firm stand against Hitler. This was the message taken to London by Theodor and Erich Kordt, Helmuth von Moltke, and Rudolf Pechel, editor of the outspoken anti–Nazi newspaper *Deutsche Rundschau*. Fabian von Schlabrendorff, a lawyer in civilian life and a Wehrmacht reserve officer with Abwehr connections, visited with Lord Lloyd and Winston Churchill, without luck. Churchill was highly cynical by this time, later writing that the German resistance "had shown neither the will to act nor the courage to come into the open."[2]

Adam von Trott zu Solz also tried to make headway for the resistance. A Rhodes scholar and member of the Kreisau Circle, Trott was a world traveler and intellectual. His father had been Prussian minister of education. Trott's American grandmother was a granddaughter of John Jay, the first chief justice of the U.S. Supreme Court. Trott worked in the German Foreign Ministry, a career he had decided upon after working for a time in China. He met with Lord Astor, owner of the *Observer* and chair of the Royal Institute of International Affairs. Trott and Astor knew one another since Trott's days at Oxford.

The messages from the many envoys of the German resistance were the same: a strong position from the British government could prevent war, and a promise of cooperation would help the resistance to act. They also conveyed important political and military information. Most important among these messages were the warning that Hitler planned to invade Poland and the news that Germany and Russia were negotiating a nonaggression pact. The British reaction was nonchalant. The British position was that the nonaggression pact would never happen, and even if it did, it would not matter.

One visitor to London, Gerhard Schwerin von Schwanefeld, was able to elicit an interesting response from the British government following his July 1939 visit. He was well respected in Britain as a career officer and aristocrat and was described by British Naval Intelligence as a "very acceptable type of German with charming manners who speaks perfect English, was unobtrusive, receptive and a good mixer."

Schwerin recommended to Admiral J. H. Godfrey, director of Naval Intelligence, that the Royal Air Force hold bomber and fighter exercises over French air space as a show of force. He further recommended that the British fleet undertake exercises in the North Sea. He also stated that Churchill should be added to the British cabinet because he was the only Englishman Hitler feared.

The R.A.F. was ordered to hold air exercises and the British navy to undergo maneuvers in the North Sea. A heated debate in Parliament and a campaign in the press to add Churchill to the cabinet were to no avail, however. Chamberlain adamantly refused to include Churchill in his government. Unfortunately, none of the military exercises impressed Hitler, who continued to believe that neither Britain nor France had the will to fight. He said of them, "I saw my enemies at Munich, and they are little worms."[3]

Goerdeler also visited Churchill and Vansittart in London, still hoping to elicit a firm anti–Hitler stance to prevent war. Shortly after Hitler absorbed the entire Czech state, Goerdeler, Gisevius, and Schacht visited Ouchy, a town near Geneva, Switzerland, for a meeting with Dr. Reinhold Schairer, who served as liaison between the resistance and the British and French governments.

The group recognized that with Hitler's popularity at an all-time high in Germany, chances of a coup were slim. They also agreed that the army could be induced to move against Hitler only if officers believed that war was about to break out. Schacht had a separate meeting with a friend, Mantagu Norman, governor of the Bank of England and a close associate of Prime Minister Chamberlain. Schacht appealed to Norman to ask Chamberlain to send a warning to Hitler that any further aggression would lead to war.

Goerdeler also wrote memoranda to his contacts in London, Washington, Paris, and Rome. He pleaded for an alliance of world powers to stop Hitler, still hoping it was possible to stop the Nazi regime through diplomatic and political channels. Goerdeler wrote to the pope, hoping he would unite the entire world against Nazi policies. Goerdeler believed that such an outcome would influence Hitler. He hoped the pope would at least call for an embargo of raw materials so that Hitler's arms programs could not proceed. He asked the pope to call upon the people of Germany to rise up and defeat Hitler. Goerdeler also appealed to the leadership of several European nations to work for removal of some restrictions of the Versailles Treaty. He reasoned that if some of the damage done to Germany was reversed, Hitler would lose momentum. Goerdeler began through his memoranda to express an idea he would return to many times over the coming five years: a desire for the creation of a European federation of states based on the absolute banning of war for all time. Goerdeler also wrote several times to Göring, trying to explain why war did not make sense. He also communicated with generals of the Wehrmacht, including many unsympathetic to the resistance, to make his case.

During 1939 the resistance was in disarray. With momentum lost and supporters scattered, the state of readiness of September 1938 would be difficult to reconstruct.

Informal diplomatic efforts were unsuccessful. Individual members and small groups within the resistance began uncoordinated efforts to stop Hitler.

After the 1939 summer of diplomatic frustration, Adam Trott became involved in a plot hatched with Albrecht von Kessel, who was acquainted with Trott through mutual contacts in the Foreign Ministry. In late summer, 1939, they traveled to Dresden and approached General Alexander von Falkenhausen, an old family friend of Trott's from his time spent in China. They asked him to invite Hitler to inspect personally the newly built fortifications in Bohemia. They proposed that Falkenhausen isolate Hitler from his bodyguards in a bunker. There he would be given a choice: commit suicide or be killed on the spot. If Hitler refused the first option, Falkenhausen was to toss a grenade into the bunker. The general was astounded at the plan, saying, "So, this is what the Foreign Ministry comes up with these days!" Falkenhausen was sympathetic to the resistance but dismissed the plan as ludicrous.

Another plan was devised by General Kurt von Hammerstein-Equord. In 1939 he was called out of retirement and given command of Army Detachment A headquartered in Cologne. Hammerstein, who had long been a vocal opponent of Hitler, had pleaded with Hindenburg on January 26, 1933, not to appoint Hitler as chancellor.

Events had proven Hammerstein right in his apprehension about Hitler. Now, back in a command position, he was more than willing to help the resistance. When Rudolf Pechel asked for his support in the summer of 1939, Hammerstein told him, "Just give me some troops and I won't fail you."[4]

Hammerstein devised a plan to invite Hitler to visit his headquarters to inspect the western defenses that would be crucial in the event of an attack from France. Hammerstein would then arrest or kill Hitler during the visit. Hitler scheduled the visit but called it off at the last minute. Hammerstein was soon relieved of command and went back into retirement.

A last-ditch effort to reason with Hitler before the outbreak of war was undertaken by General Georg Thomas, chief of the Economics and Supply Group in OKW. Hans Oster convinced Thomas to document to Hitler the economic arguments against war. Thomas agreed that with Hitler determined to pursue his war policies, an economic argument might be the only way to prevent or delay the plan.

Thomas wrote a memo to Hitler and submitted it to chief of OKW Keitel in mid-August, 1939. The memo argued that an invasion of Poland could lead to a world war. That would be disastrous, given Germany's limited food and raw material resources.

Keitel met with Thomas and denied the danger of world war. The British, he said, were weak and frightened. The French were hopeless pacifists. And the United States was isolationist and wouldn't send any troops to fight in Europe. He reminded Thomas of Hitler's often stated belief that war itself would create the economic means by which to conduct war. Keitel refused to pass along the memorandum to Hitler.*

General Thomas, realizing that the order to invade Poland could be issued at any time, devised a plan with Schacht and Gisevius. At the point that Hitler issued invasion

---

*Keitel never presented Hitler with anything that would contradict the Führer's policies. Known to have never disagreed with Hitler on anything, even the smallest points, Keitel was referred to behind his back as "General Ja-Ja." Others showed their contempt by calling him "Lakaitel," a pun on the German word Lakai, which means "lackey" and has an effeminate connotation.

orders, but before the invasion actually began, the three, plus Admiral Canaris, would drive to army headquarters in Zossen and confront Hitler and Brauchitsch to demand that the invasion order be canceled. Since Schacht held a post in the government, it was likely they would be allowed through without being stopped.

The plan was called off on August 25 when Hitler delayed the invasion order at the last minute. Members of the resistance believed in error that war had been averted once again, and they let down their guard. When Hitler rescinded the delay the following day, Thomas, Schacht, and Gisevius were taken by surprise and did not act.

After Hitler's bloodless victory in Czechoslovakia, he turned his attention to the next target, Poland. One of the most punishing provisions of the Versailles Treaty, from the German point of view, was the creation of the Polish Corridor along the Vistula River. The purpose was to give landlocked Poland port access to the North Sea. On November 9, 1920, the German port city of Danzig was declared a "Free City" and made a protectorate of the League of Nations, as provided for in the Versailles Treaty. In practice, the city and the surrounding area went under Polish control.

Germany saw this as a theft of its territory. Control of the area had been a point of contention between Germany and Poland for many generations. The creation of the Danzig corridor cut East Prussia in half. The lands making up the corridor area had originally been taken from Poland by Prussia in 1772. On August 5 that year, Russia, Austria, and Prussia had agreed to a partition of Poland. Prussia seized the area known as Polish Prussia, with the exception of Danzig and Thorn. Poland lost one-third of its territory and one-half of its population as a result. On January 23, 1793, Prussia took Danzig, Thorn, and Great Poland, with populations of 1.1 million, in what was called the Second Partition. In 1795, in a Third Partition, Prussia also seized Warsaw and Mazovia and an additional one million in population. Over time, however, Poland had managed to regain much of its lost territory and, although Danzig and the surrounding area had remained under German control, the population of the corridor area was predominantly Polish.

The true history of the area did not interest Hitler. He had based his political career on the position that the Versailles Treaty was unjust, and he was determined to undo as many of its provisions as possible. On October 24, 1938, Hitler sent Foreign Minister Ribbentrop to meet with Polish ambassador Józef Lipski. During this meeting, Ribbentrop declared that it was time for Danzig to revert to Germany. He told the ambassador that Germany needed to build a highway and a two-way railroad to East Prussia across the corridor. Lipski indicated that he did not think there was much chance that the Polish government would return control of Danzig to Germany. Within a week of the meeting between Ribbentrop and Lipski, Germany had its reply. The Polish foreign minister, Józef Beck, instructed Lipski to advise the German government that its answer was no. Beck warned that "Any attempt to incorporate the Free City into the Reich, must inevitably lead to conflict."[5]

On November 24, 1938, Hitler issued a top secret directive to his military commands ordering preparations "to enable the Free State of Danzig to be occupied by German troops by surprise."[6] By March 1939, the Polish government began to realize that German pressure would not cease just because German demands had been rejected. After Hitler took control over all of Czechoslovakia on March 15, Poland was flanked by the German army on both the south and the north.

Hitler's demands became more insistent. If the Free City was not returned to German control, he warned, there would be war. Such threats were a repeat of the previous year's tactics against Czechoslovakia. The Poles, like the Czechs, had treaties. But, based on the events of 1938, Hitler had reason to doubt that Poland's allies would honor them.

On March 21, Ribbentrop met again with ambassador Lipski. He demanded a "satisfactory" answer to Germany's request to run a highway and rail line through the corridor. Lipski was also warned that Hitler was upset over alleged persecution of the German minority in Poland — a tactic reminiscent of messages to the Czechs the year before.

These were serious matters. The Polish government communicated at once with Britain and France. On March 28, Polish foreign minister Beck warned Germany that any attempt to alter the present status of the Free City would lead to war. And on March 31, Britain and France pledged their full support of Poland in the event of any German action.

Poland's history is one of changing borders. Situated between Germany and Russia, Poland has had a long history of border disputes. Between 1919 and 1920, Poland warred with Russia, resulting in Poland's extension of its eastern frontiers approximately 150 miles, to the border they had held in 1772. This meant that 4.5 million Ukranians and 1.5 million White Russians came under Polish control. (From 1919, Poland was also in conflict with Czechoslovakia over control of the area of Teschen.) When Hitler was granted his demands in 1938 by Britain and France, Poland seized the long-disputed area. That dispute, plus the Danzig question, meant that Poland's borders pleased neither Germany nor Russia.

Poland had entered a treaty with France on February 19, 1921, promising mutual assistance in the event of attack. This treaty was strengthened in 1925 by the Locarno Conference, in which another Franco-Polish treaty was signed. Now, with Hitler's aggression toward Poland, France reaffirmed its alliance with Poland and Britain added its unilateral guarantee as well.

The news that Britain and France had pledged to defend Poland against attack from Germany enraged Hitler. On April 3, 1939, he introduced a new plan code-named Case White, for the invasion of Poland. The goals of Case White were explained in the top secret directive mandating "the initiation of military preparations to remove, if necessary, any threat from this direction forever.... The aim will be to destroy Polish military strength.... The Free State of Danzig will be proclaimed a part of the Reich territory at the outbreak of hostilities, at the latest.[7]

Hitler had hoped to pressure Poland as he had pressured Czechoslovakia, but it now appeared that Britain and France would refuse to give in to his demands. This concern was reinforced on April 6 when Poland entered an agreement with Britain that converted their unilateral guarantee into a pact of mutual assistance, and on April 28, Britain ordered peacetime conscription.

While these steps clearly pointed to British resolve to limit Hitler's further expansion, Hitler also knew that even if Britain and France did respond, it would take them several months to organize military help for Poland. He intended to defeat the Poles in a matter of weeks, before any measures by the British could be mounted.

On May 23, 1939, Hitler convened a meeting with 14 of his top military advisers. He stated that no further expansion would be possible without war and that Germany must be prepared to fight for Lebensraum in Europe — the same argument he had made before the Czechoslovakian campaign. He also declared that defeating countries with non–Germanic populations would provide a cheap source of labor, foreshadowing the future policies Germany would enact in occupied countries.

Hitler predicted that Britain would fight to help Poland but declared that Britain would not be able to sustain war with Germany. As soon as her supplies were cut, Hitler predicted, Britain would surrender. Preventing food and fuel shipments was key to defeating Britain, whose defeat would be essential, he predicted. It would also be essential to eliminate any possibility of an alliance between Britain and France in the west and Russia in the east.

By 1939 three separate spheres of power had formed in Europe. The three were (a) Britain and France, (b) the Soviet Union, and (c) a rearmed Germany. Hitler needed to enter alliances of his own because he recognized that Poland would not give in as Czechoslovakia had the year before. On May 22, 1939, Hitler entered a military alliance with Mussolini that was known as the Rome-Berlin Axis, or the Pact of Steel. The pact gave Hitler a powerful ally in southern Europe, creating a situation which would demand the commitment of French and British military and naval strength.

In June 1939, Britain, France, and Russia began talks on creating a unified front to block further German aggression in Europe. The talks did not go well and became deadlocked over the summer. This opened the door for Hitler to open negotiations of his own with the Russian government. By the end of June, Germany had initiated its own feelers in Moscow. Initial talks centered on a trade agreement.

On August 3, Foreign Minister Ribbentrop of Germany sent a telegram to the German ambassador in Moscow, Friedrich Werner von der Schulenburg, with instructions to pursue negotiations with the Russian government aimed at creating an agreement between the two countries. Initial talks went well. On August 15, Ribbentrop offered to go to Moscow in person to arrive at a Russian-German agreement. Foreign Minister Vyacheslav M. Molotov of Russia invited Germany to enter into talks aimed at a nonaggression pact with Russia. When this idea was conveyed to Hitler, he accepted the invitation at once. Such a pact would meet perfectly with Hitler's goal: to neutralize one of the power spheres, enabling him to proceed with the invasion of Poland.

Ribbentrop, aware of Hitler's deadline of September 1 for the invasion of Poland, wanted to conclude a pact with Russia well before the end of August. The Russian government wanted to proceed in two phases: a trade agreement and a nonaggression pact. Details of the trade agreement were concluded on August 18, after which Ribbentrop applied all the pressure he could to hurry up negotiations on the second phase, the nonaggression pact. The Russians wanted to meet on August 26 or 27, but Hitler feared that would give him little time to prepare for an invasion of Poland on September 1. Having a signed pact in hand before starting the invasion would increase his confidence tremendously. Hitler wrote to Stalin directly, urging him to meet with Ribbentrop as soon as possible. Stalin replied that Ribbentrop would be welcome in Moscow on August 23.

The timing of events during the next ten days gave Hitler the conditions he needed to invade Poland and prevented the resistance from averting the Second World War:

August 21. Britain and France were shocked to hear the announcement on German radio that Germany and Russia were about to sign a nonaggression pact. Britain and France, aware that the balance of power was shifting against them, issued orders to escalate their military preparedness.

Hitler ordered increased troop deployment in areas bordering Polish territory. Clearly, he intended to invade as soon as the pact had been signed with Russia.

August 22. Britain declared its commitment to come to the aid of Poland in the event of attack, while also appealing to the German government to seek a peaceful settlement of its problems with Poland.

During a meeting with military commanders, Hitler announced that the order for the invasion of Poland would be issued on August 26, five days before the scheduled invasion date of September 1.

August 23. The German-Russian pact was signed in Moscow. Both countries agreed not to attack one another and to remain neutral in the event either country were attacked by a third country. The pact also defined each country's "spheres of interest," effectively yielding an agreement concerning future border alignments in Poland and the Baltic countries. Russia and Germany also agreed not to join in any alliance of other powers "which is directly or indirectly aimed at the other party."[8]

August 24. President Roosevelt of the United States wrote to Hitler and to King Victor Emmanuel III of Italy and suggested mediation of the Polish situation.

The British Parliament met in special session to grant emergency powers to the government. Chamberlain declared in the House of Commons that Britain would honor its commitment to Poland.

August 25. Britain signed a mutual assistance pact with Poland, and the Polish government called up its military reserves.

Hitler told the British ambassador that he must be granted his demands against Poland to avoid war.

Awaiting British response, Hitler delayed the September 1 invasion date.

Schacht, Gisevius, and Thomas met in Abwehr headquarters to initiate resistance plans in reaction to the scheduled invasion. As they discussed proceeding with their plan, Hans Oster arrived and informed the group that Hitler had changed his mind and that the invasion would be delayed. The group adjourned, believing that at the last minute Germany had again avoided war.

August 26. Premier Daladier of France urged Hitler to negotiate with Poland in the interest of peace. Instead, Hitler rescinded his cancellation of the invasion and ordered that it was to begin on the morning of September 1.

August 27. The resistance, believing there was still hope that Hitler would change his mind, tried once again to use economic arguments. General Thomas, with help from

Goerdeler and Schacht, quickly drafted a second memo for Hitler using the same economic arguments as before. He included a graph comparing Germany's economic capacity to that of potential enemies in the event of war. The clear disparity made a convincing argument. Thomas delivered this latest memo to Keitel, who forwarded it to Hitler. Hitler dismissed the warning. He responded that with a nonaggression pact with the Soviets, there was no longer a chance of world war. He also predicted that Britain and France would not fight.

August 28. Britain warned Germany that it would come to Poland's aid in the event of invasion and again appealed to Hitler to seek a peaceful solution. Britain ordered its fleets in the Baltic and Mediterranean to return home to be available for redeployment.

Military preparations throughout Europe increased, and Germany initiated a program of rationing at home.

August 29. Responding to pleas for negotiation of the crisis, Hitler demanded that a Polish representative arrive in Berlin within 24 hours.

August 30. Poland ordered a general mobilization of its armed forces.

August 31. Germany issued a 16-point proposal listing its demands on Poland. Communication with Poland was cut by Germany, however, before the demands could be sent. Hitler issued Directive No. 1, ordering the start of the invasion of Poland, to begin at 4:45 A.M. the following day, with the justification that Poland had rejected his proposals.

The Russian Supreme Soviet ratified the nonaggression pact with Germany.

September 1. Land and air forces launched an invasion of Poland without a declaration of war. Britain and France ordered full mobilization but offered to negotiate if German forces would withdraw from Polish territory. Italy announced its intention to remain neutral.

When the attack order was issued and the invasion began, resistance leaders were caught by surprise. Admiral Canaris knew they had lost their chance to stop the war. He told Gisevius, "This means the end of Germany."[9]

September 2. Italy called for a mediation conference. Britain refused to participate while German troops remained in Poland and demanded the withdrawal of German troops. Germany rejected the demand, blaming Britain for encouraging Poland and "provoking" the conflict.

September 3. Britain and France declared war on Germany. The Second World War had begun.

Chapter 9

THE OUTBREAK OF WAR

I fear that there will be war this autumn and that it will last for years.... We are completely incapable of preventing the catastrophe. We are inmates of a great prison. To rebel would be as suicidal as if prisoners were to rise against their heavily armed jailers.

Wilhelm Leuschner, letter to a friend, August 20, 1939

By September 5, 1939, less than one week after Germany's invasion, Poland was finished. The Polish Air Force had been destroyed completely in the first two days of the invasion. The out-gunned Polish army, at times attacking German tanks with cavalry unit charges in gestures of pointless courage, never stood a chance against the new German innovation, *blitzkrieg* (lightning war). German tank columns, coupled with ceaseless air support, moved swiftly across the Polish frontier. All 35 Polish divisions were encircled and destroyed within the first week. On September 17, the Russian army invaded Poland from the east, and the entire nation was divided up between Germany and Russia on borders based on their non-aggression pact, which specified prearranged "spheres of influence." By the end of the month, Poland no longer existed as an independent nation.

While Poland fell under the sword, resistance leaders took to the pen. During the month of September 1939, the resistance came alive again after a year of inactivity. The question of whether war would occur if Hitler followed his policies was no longer at issue. Germany was at war. The important step now was to try and gain support again from General Brauchitsch.

Discussion rather than action characterized the resistance at the beginning of the Second World War. High-ranking officers in the resistance excused their own inaction as they had in the past. Before the campaign against Czechoslovakia, they failed to act by using the argument that they should first wait until the order for an invasion had been given. In the year between the Czech campaign and the invasion of Poland, the same officers argued that without an actual war, there was no justification for overthrowing Hitler. If war did break out, they argued that would be the time to act.

For civilian resistance leaders, the delays were frustrating. Civilians could not lead

139

a coup without army support, and army leaders were uncomfortable in being asked to make political decisions. There was much discussion on both sides about identifying the "right psychological moment" for a coup d'état. No one, however, seemed to know exactly what that moment would be. The officers who now believed an attack on France would be the "right psychological moment" argued that the German army would quickly become bogged down in such a campaign, as had occurred in the First World War, providing the opportunity to plan Hitler's overthrow. This overlooked the new strategy of blitzkrieg that would later finish the French campaign in only six weeks. This meant not only that the resistance was left with no time to plan, but that Hitler's popularity at home remained high. The failure of Hitler's policies, on which the resistance depended, did not materialize. Instead, Hitler followed one stunning success with another.

Leaders like General Beck, galvanized by the actual outbreak of war, sounded the alarm in a flurry of written communications. Beck expressed his beliefs in September 1939 to the two top army leaders, Brauchitsch and Halder, in a memorandum he entitled "On the war situation after conclusion of the Polish campaign." He predicted that Britain and France would surely retaliate against Germany and that a war with Great Britain would be conducted as a world war because Britain's military strength included strongholds in India, Canada, Africa, and Australia. He also predicted that the United States would provide economic aid, if not full military support, to the Western allies.

With Poland defeated, Hitler next turned his attention to France. All of Hitler's western commanders, Leeb, Bock, and Rundstedt, protested the planned French offensive, writing to commander in chief Brauchitsch and chief of staff Halder. General Wilhelm von Leeb, commander of Army Group C in the west, wrote to Brauchitsch, on October 7, 1939. Leeb's memo, entitled "Memorandum on the prospects and effects of an attack on France and Britain violating the neutrality of Holland, Belgium and Luxemburg," concerned itself with war in the west, which he referred to as "this crazy offensive."

Leeb produced a second memo on October 31 in which he bluntly told Brauchitsch that German forces were inadequate for an offensive against the French. He suggested that with Poland defeated and the eastern front secure, Germany would be in a better position to await an attack from the west. Leeb observed that if Hitler were to propose peace now, it might be possible to adjust borders to retain Austria and the Sudetenland at the same time.

General Gerd von Rundstedt, commander of Army Group A, also wrote to Brauchitsch that German strength would prove no match for the combined power of the French and British forces and that the offensive would be long and costly. He observed that Britain and France had entered the war in spite of predictions that they would not. That miscalculation placed Germany in a vulnerable situation both militarily and politically. He recommended a defensive position on the western front.

General Fedor von Bock, commander of Army Group B, also delivered a memorandum to Brauchitsch. He objected to the planned violation of the neutrality of Holland, Belgium, and Luxemburg. At a meeting with Hitler on October 25 also attended by General Walther von Reichenau, commander of the Sixth Army in Bock's army group, Bock voiced his objections to the offensive. As usual, Hitler dismissed all objections.

General Reichenau also tried to dissuade Hitler. Upon hearing the details of the offensive in the west, he described the plan as "downright criminal." Reichenau argued that a defensive position would be better for Germany. Pointing out that an attack from the west would have to come through Belgium, he stated that it would be better if the Western powers violated that country's neutrality first. Hitler, disdainful of the idea of a defensive position under any conditions, was not impressed with the general's reasoning.

Protests were even more dire in the Foreign Ministry. Erich Kordt and Dr. Hasso von Etzdorf, a counselor in the Foreign Ministry, along with Helmuth Groscurth of the General Staff, wrote a memorandum entitled "The Threatening Calamity." It was distributed to several generals, including Halder and Brauchitsch. They predicted that invading France through neutral Belgium would invite world approbation. The combination of enemy troop strength and bad weather would doom the offensive, the United States would enter the war, and Italy would join with the Western allies against Hitler. Russia would be unchecked, and the result would be the absorption of all Germany by the Bolsheviks. They called for Hitler's overthrow, declaring: "Steps must be taken to stop the invasion order reaching the execution phase. This can only be done by an early overthrow of the Hitler government. Experience has shown that it will neither adjust its plans nor give way as a result of argument, protest or threat of resignation from the military leaders alone."[1]

The memo also argued that the loyalty oath to Hitler was not legitimate. A soldier was able to swear an oath only to his country, not to an individual. The need to complete a coup could no longer be delayed, they concluded. They outlined an action plan: end the war with a just peace for all sides, restore the rule of law, disband the Gestapo, and install an honest government and civil administration with democratic participation in the determination of political goals.

With expansion of the war looming, resistance leaders realized they had to renew their efforts. The movement had fallen apart and had to be reconstructed. In October 1939, Hans von Dohnanyi, a senior civil servant and retired public prosecutor working with Oster and Canaris in the Abwehr, took charge of the reorganization of the civilian and military resistance, getting both sides back in touch to discuss renewal of support for a coup d'état. Dohnanyi had a talent for detail and became the central organizer and planner for the resistance.

Although most of the military leaders were in agreement that the French campaign would be a disaster, they faced a dilemma. They found Nazism reprehensible, but Hitler had not yet suffered a battlefield defeat. His successes increased his popularity at home, and they feared that a coup attempt could lead to civil war. Several of the generals had predicted to Hitler that his campaigns would lead to immediate disaster; so far, events had proved them wrong, eroding their confidence. The two officers whose support was most critical to the resistance, Halder and Brauchitsch, were doubtful as supporters of a renewed effort. Brauchitsch steadfastly refused even to hear of ideas for overthrowing the government, arguing that if the people were truly against Hitler, they should express their feelings with a general strike.

Halder also wavered in his support. He would not commit himself to cooperating in a coup d'état — at least in discussions with civilian members of the resistance. He continued his attempts to influence Hitler to modify his plans, however. On October 27, 1939, both Halder and Brauchitsch met with Hitler and tried to change his mind about plans to begin a western offensive on November 12, but Hitler refused to entertain any dissent.

On October 29, Halder discussed his frustrations at a meeting with General Karl Stülpnagel. Stülpnagel proposed that Halder place Brauchitsch under arrest, take over as commander in chief, and initiate a coup on his own. Halder was dubious. In order to gauge potential support among other generals, Halder sent Stülpnagel on a tour of army frontline units, ostensibly to brief commanders concerning plans for the western offensive, but actually to assess field support for a military-led coup. Only Generals Witzleben and Leeb were supportive.

When Halder and Brauchitsch conducted an inspection tour of the western army groups on November 1 and 2, in anticipation of a November 12 offensive, they concluded that the German army was not yet prepared. None of the senior headquarters staff believed the offensive was ready. The invasion date was pushed back.

Brauchitsch continued to receive appeals and warnings, including a memo from Captain (Navy) Franz Liedig in December 1939. His memo, "Implications of the Russo-Finnish conflict on Germany's present situation," accused Hitler of opportunism and predicted complete disaster in the war. Liedig stated that this was the time to obtain a peace agreement with Britain and that was the only way to avoid Russian domination of all of Europe. He proposed in the memo that Germany and Britain needed to join forces to fight the real enemy, Russia.

Writing objections was not enough. Even General Halder realized this, and now that Germany was at war, he knew that Hitler had to be stopped. Before war had been declared, Halder had believed himself bound by the loyalty oath. Now, though, he was convinced that killing Hitler would be the only way to end the war short of disaster for Germany. He even began attending meetings with the Führer carrying a loaded pistol, with the intention of one day working up the nerve to assassinate him.[2]

In the first week of November 1939, Halder had authorized Major Groscurth to update the 1938 plan. Generals who were to take part included Hoepner, Falkenhausen, Witzleben, and Guderian. Under Groscurth's plan, the capital was to be surrounded and occupied. Key communications such as radio and telegraph stations would be seized. All Nazi leaders would be arrested and SS and Gestapo strongholds taken over. Oster had in his files lists of Nazis to be arrested when the coup began, leaders to be appointed in the provisional government, and identification of commanders ready to join in the coup. While such documents were necessary, keeping them was highly dangerous. If discovered, virtually everyone connected with the resistance would be exposed. Still, Oster knew that the meticulous planning required to organize a coup meant that the details had to be written down.

Resistance leaders, aware of Hitler's popularity, feared that the public might not support a coup d'état. Once an overthrow was accomplished, they did not want to find themselves still at war with Britain and France and also faced with civil war at home. General

Beck was to head up the provisional government. He was naturally concerned about the possibility of civil unrest after a coup. General Halder shared Beck's concerns; in a coup, there would be no second chances. Hoping to gain fast public support for the coup, Oster had worked for months with Dohnanyi to collect evidence about the crimes the Nazis were committing. They had ample documentation in Oster's safe at Army Headquarters in Zossen and were prepared to publish all of it when the time was right.

These shocking facts were meant not only to foster public support against the Nazi regime. They would also serve as the basis for criminal charges against Nazi leaders. Crimes included ordering the murders of political opponents, mistreatment of Jews in labor and concentration camps, and overriding the rule of law. Since passage of the Nürnberg Laws in 1935, the domestic abuses of the Nazi state, particularly against the Jews, had worsened. Now, with the defeat of Poland, the reign of terror was exported. Treatment of civilians in Poland was bestial. The SS timetable was put into motion within hours of each town's being occupied by the German army. Squads of *Einsatzgruppen* (replacement units)* followed the army, entered each town or village, and rounded up the Jews and shot them. In many instances, the Jewish population was herded into a synagogue or other building, which was then set on fire. The savagery of the SS operation in Poland was unprecedented, and resistance leaders intended to ensure that the Nazi leaders, who had devised the plan, would be brought to justice.

Beck agreed with Oster that the Nazis were criminals, but he was also responsible for keeping the peace during the transition. He began organizing labor support for the coup. Hoping to rally the workers of Germany behind a provisional government so there could be no hope of a Nazi resurgence, Beck met with Wilhelm Leuschner, whose contacts with trade unions and the labor underground were extensive. Beck told Leuschner that a show of labor support for a provisional government would be invaluable. Leuschner promised to organize a general strike which would coincide with the coup, so that everything in the Third Reich — manufacturing and armaments production as well as the government — would come to a complete halt at the same moment. Leuschner was in touch with several workers' underground groups, and he arranged communication links so that a general strike could be declared on short notice.

The resistance planned to launch its coup after the orders to invade France had been issued but before the offensive began. Dohnanyi took a lead in this effort. He wrote a series of proclamations that would be read over the radio once the coup had been initiated. These were redrafted by Beck and Oster. The proclamations declared that an invasion against France had been ordered, involving violations of Dutch and Belgian neutrality.†

The proclamation declared General Beck as new commander in chief of the army, stating he would call for new, free elections at the earliest possible moment. The resistance leaders would be careful not to blame matters on Hitler, but on his advisers. The proclamation would declare that Hitler, suffering from an illness, was withdrawing from

---

In spite of their military-sounding name, the Einsatzgruppen *served only one function: to kill civilians.*

†*Hitler's plan called for sweeping around the heavily defended frontier of France, moving swiftly through Holland and Belgium, and advancing rapidly across France from the north and east. It would be necessary to go through the neutral countries, but that did not concern Hitler. It was later to prove to be an ingenious plan.*

office temporarily in order to recover. The proclamation would also state that other top Nazis — Himmler, Göring, and Ribbentrop — were under arrest as part of the emergency reorganization.

Furthermore, charges were being prepared that Göring had been embezzling public funds and Himmler had imprisoned thousands of innocent people. The proclamation would declare that the Gestapo and the Ministry of Propaganda were immediately abolished and that the current emergency measures were necessary to thwart attempts by criminals in the Nazi party to seize power from Hitler.

Everyone in the resistance — military and civilian — agreed completely on one point: war was not in Germany's best interests and would only lead to suffering on all sides. There was a strong moral dimension as well. Morality was profoundly offended even in the early months of the war, when Nazi methods became known to the German public. Ulrich von Hassell noted in his diary on October 19, 1939:

> Among well-informed people of Berlin I noticed a good deal of despair.... There is a growing awareness of our impending disaster. The principal sentiments are: the conviction that the war cannot be won by military means; a realization of the highly dangerous economic situation; the feeling of being led by criminal adventurers; and the disgrace that has sullied the German name through the conduct of the war in Poland, namely, the brutal use of air power and the shocking bestialities of the SS, especially towards the Jews.[3]

The question of morality extended beyond military concerns. The true nature of the Nazi movement, especially as expressed by the leadership of the SS, was offensive as well. Even though it was dangerous to speak out, some members of the resistance put their objections on paper. Groscurth became an outspoken critic of SS actions. A decree issued by Heinrich Himmler on October 28, 1939, encouraged all men "of good blood," especially in the SS, to mate with women and produce good Aryan offspring, whether their own wives or someone else's wife, or single girls. The purpose, Himmler's decree stated, was to provide populations "of good blood" for conquered territories and to replace casualties lost in the war.

Himmler's decree was protested widely, especially in the Wehrmacht. Groscurth did not hide his contempt for Himmler. He sent a number of memoranda to General Halder complaining about the Himmler decree and protesting SS atrocities in Poland. Under pressure from Himmler, Halder was forced to relieve Groscurth of duty on February 20, 1940.

While the resistance moved ahead with renewed plans for a coup, diplomatic members of the resistance continued their efforts to gain alliances in foreign governments. In the early months of the Second World War, while the resistance was reorganizing, secret diplomatic contacts continued. In October 1939, Adam Trott zu Solz, the German Foreign Office counselor who had contacted the British government on behalf of the resistance the year before, traveled to the United States to address a conference sponsored by the Institute of Pacific Relations that was held in Virginia Beach.

While in the United States, Trott held several meetings with Paul Scheffer, a German emigrant and ex-editor of the German newspaper *Berliner Tageblatt*. Together Trott and Scheffer drafted a paper aimed at informing the American government of the goals of the German resistance. They explained German attitudes toward the Versailles Treaty, recommending ideas that could end the war to the satisfaction of the German citizen, while rectifying the injustices of the treaty. The memo also urged the Allied powers to clearly state their war aims, presenting a united front to Hitler.

On November 13, the paper was delivered by William T. Stone of the Washington Foreign Policy Association to the State Department in Washington, where it was reviewed by Assistant Secretary of State George S. Messersmith and Under-Secretary of State Sumner Welles. From there, it passed to Cordell Hull, secretary of state. The British ambassador in Washington, Lord Lothian, was also given a copy. Concerned for his safety, Trott had wanted the paper distributed discreetly, but at least 24 copies were made and given out in the U.S. capital.

Messersmith and Trott met on November 20 to discuss the issues the paper raised. Trott said he was concerned that some members of the British government favored compromise with Hitler and would settle for peace even if it meant granting Hitler an inordinate amount of power in Europe. The attitude in the Washington government was favorable toward Trott at first, but by December, it had turned suspicious. Messersmith told associates a few days after their meeting that he suspected any German who, in time of war, could come and go at will. The FBI began following Trott and opened a file entitled "Espionage Activities, Adam von Trott in US." The file noted him as a person who had made contact while visiting the U.S. with "certain persons here who are acting directly or indirectly for the present German government."[4]

While still in the United States, Trott wrote Lord Halifax in London to recommend that British aims should not be punitive toward Germany. In order to elicit support from as wide a cross-section of German citizens as possible, Trott cautioned, it was important for Britain to emphasize the desire for peace and not for punishment of Germany. Otherwise, Trott stated, anti–Nazis in Germany would be forced into the position of supporting their government in order to avoid a repeat of Versailles.

Trott sent another communication to Halifax in December 1939. He expressed the belief that the war should be viewed as a war of liberation from Nazism not only for non–Germans, but for the German people as well. Britain's fight was with the Nazi movement, not with the German people. On behalf of the resistance, he asked for assurances from Britain as part of their conditions for peace. These included a promise that Germany would not be divided, agreement by the Allies to work with a replacement government, and free trade and economic agreements.

Trott's trip to the United States ended early in 1940. Rather than gaining alliances in the U.S. government, he had only created suspicion. Alexander Kirk, American chargé d'affaires in Berlin, received instructions from the State Department that, in the event of any discussions with Trott, he was to report the essence of those discussions to

Washington. The outcome of Trott's efforts, as described by historian Hans Rothfels, "only resulted in supplying Washington with considerable insight into the internal situation in Germany. In every other respect Trott's efforts failed completely. Whatever may be thought of the practical value and feasibility of his proposals, the refusal to show even the most modest degree of sympathy with the German Resistance was very clear and represented a discouraging precedent."[5]

Trott's tireless efforts to gain the confidence of the British and American governments were ultimately in vain. Even with his credibility in question, Trott was to continue to take part in resistance activities in Germany. Over the coming years, he also remained in contact with governments outside of Germany, working tirelessly trying to gain foreign support for the resistance even though he was misunderstood and mistrusted by the Allied powers. Trott was implicated in the July 1944 bomb plot against Hitler and was executed in August 1944.

Resistance leaders were finally having some effect by the end of 1939. The British foreign minister, Lord Halifax, sent a message on November 15 to Theodor Kordt in Switzerland. He stated that peace was still possible and asked Kordt to meet with his adviser, Conwell Evans. The two met several times in Berne. The British had two conditions. First, the Nazi government had to be removed. Second, Poland must be evacuated of German troops as soon as a new government took over in Germany.

Kordt responded that such decisions would be up to General Beck upon assuming leadership of the country and that Germany would withdraw once it was determined that there would be no threat of aggression from Russia. The balance of power and the situation in the east was obviously too complex for Kordt to give guarantees to Britain. The resistance needed written assurances that Britain would not exploit the political upheaval that would follow a coup but would cooperate with the new government. The British government, suspicious of the entire resistance movement, was unwilling to provide any written commitment.

J. Lonsdale Bryans, a friend of Halifax, volunteered to act as mediator between Britain and the German resistance. On January 8, 1940, Halifax authorized Bryans to meet with Ulrich von Hassell in Arosa, Switzerland. Hassell suggested that a cooperative agreement should be reached before the opening of a western offensive. He explained that without a British commitment to cooperate with a replacement government in Germany, it was doubtful that the resistance would be able to remove the Nazi regime from power.

Hassell wrote out a statement he hoped would serve as a guideline for formulation of the British position and gave it to Bryans for delivery to Halifax. The paper included several points: the war must be stopped or all of Europe could end up under Communist control, Germany as a strong, independent nation was essential to the health of Europe as a whole and should be recognized for its importance, the Allied powers should agree to Germany's right to keep Austria and the Sudetenland, and the frontier with Poland should be revised to approximate the 1914 borders.

The British were extremely suspicious of this proposed draft, especially since it came from a German representative trying to convince the British to adopt those positions. Halifax, upon reading Hassell's draft, said, "It's a tricky business." Hassell's proposed settlement terms did not endear the resistance to the British government; to the contrary, Halifax said he doubted that any future contact with the German resistance would be worthwhile. He concluded, "I'm beginning to wonder today if there *are* any good Germans."[6]

Britain, under treaty obligations to Poland, saw no reason to agree to terms entirely favorable to Germany. Furthermore, the proposal included no commitment for the removal of Hitler as head of government. The Bryans initiative ran into the same stalemate that others had met: mutual distrust that resulted in no promises being made and further delays of any action.

Dr. Joseph Wirth, who had served as chancellor of Germany in the early 1920s, made a more successful contact with Britain on behalf of the resistance. In early 1940, Wirth, who then lived in Switzerland, wrote to Chamberlain to explain that the German resistance had considerable strength but would likely move against the Nazis only with assurances from Britain. Knowing that Britain would not exploit Germany after a successful coup d'état would be most reassuring, Wirth wrote. Two representatives from the British Foreign Office visited Wirth in Switzerland in February to convey the first proposed commitments from Chamberlain for support of the German resistance. These commitments, Wirth was told, would be valid only through the end of April 1940. First was an assurance from Chamberlain that "the British government will not, by attacking in the west, use to Germany's military disadvantage any passing crisis which might be connected with action by the German opposition."[7]

The British government also expressed willingness to work in cooperation with a new German government, provided that relations would be entered in good faith and with confidence in the goodwill of both sides. Ironically, after so many efforts to obtain assurances from Britain, there is no record that Wirth ever communicated this important offer of support to the leaders of the German resistance.

The resistance leaders were poised for a coup, their timing geared around Hitler's announced target to begin a western offensive on November 12, 1939. By November 4, General Halder had at last made up his mind to support a plan of assassination. A few days earlier he had advised Groscurth that not only Hitler, but Göring and Ribbentrop as well, should all meet with "fatal accidents." On November 4, Halder told General Thomas that killing Hitler was the only practical solution and that plans should proceed at once before the western offensive began. Halder repeated the same conclusions to his deputy, General Stülpnagel.

The following day, November 5, Brauchitsch met with Hitler, arguing against a winter offensive. The decision to proceed with or delay the western offensive needed to be made by that afternoon to allow seven days for military preparations and troop movements into staging areas. Hitler accused Brauchitsch of presenting only negative arguments, and he pointed out that if it rained on German troops, it would also rain on the enemy. Hitler raged that his army staff was full of cowards and said he suspected a conspiracy among his generals. He issued orders to continue preparations for a November 12 offensive.

When Brauchitsch told Halder that morning about Hitler's statement that he suspected a conspiracy, Halder feared resistance plans had been uncovered. In a panic, he

began destroying anything in the headquarters offices that could be incriminating, expecting the Gestapo to show up at any moment. By 3 P.M. Halder was convinced that the coup
d'état had to be canceled. Dohnanyi and Groscurth were able to save some of the papers
they would need if the coup did proceed. The Gestapo did not show up; Hitler had merely
been ranting as usual. It became obvious to resistance leaders that Halder could not be
depended upon. He had panicked too easily.

Everyone had agreed that the coup should take place once invasion orders had been
issued but before it was launched. The window of opportunity was open on November
5. At 5 P.M., Halder changed his mind once again. He met with Groscurth and asked him
to speak with Oster and Canaris that evening to proceed with coup plans.

Brauchitsch agreed with Halder that the offensive should be stopped. After Hitler's
earlier outburst, Brauchitsch told Halder that if someone else started an action against
Hitler, he would not stand in the way. It was the most encouraging sign the resistance
leaders had received from the commander in chief, and they decided to act.

On November 6, Oster met with Stülpnagel to assess troop strength in Berlin
required to neutralize SS and Gestapo strongholds. Gisevius drafted proclamations accusing the SS of engineering a putsch which the army had been called upon to crush.

Oster and Gisevius traveled by car around Germany over the coming days, visiting
field generals and showing them copies of the proposed proclamations. When Halder discovered this, he was extremely nervous about the chance of discovery. If the Gestapo
heard of the proclamations, everyone would be arrested. Halder quickly distanced himself from the resistance movement.

At the last minute, Hitler postponed the beginning of the invasion to November 19
because of weather conditions. This gave the resistance a one-week delay. Oster and Gisevius met with General Witzleben on November 8. The general expressed serious doubts
about counting on Halder or Brauchitsch to support a coup. Without the support of the
commander in chief and the chief of staff, Witzleben was dubious about the chances of
success. Most junior officers were fervent supporters of the Nazis. No one could predict
whose orders they would follow.

Gisevius agreed that Halder's support was essential. On November 10, he wrote a
memo to Halder arguing for immediate initiation of a coup. He gave the memo to
Groscurth for presentation to Halder. In the memo, Gisevius argued that conditions now
were most favorable for a coup. The army should place Hitler under protective arrest
and announce that the coup was necessary to prevent an SS overthrow of the government. When Groscurth gave Halder the memo on November 12, Halder said he was going
to tear it up without reading it. The next morning, however, Halder still had the memo
and told Groscurth that he agreed with everything in it. He also told Groscurth he had
shown it to Brauchitsch, who agreed with it but would not take action against Hitler.
Once again an opportunity passed because no one could convince Brauchitsch to join
with the resistance and support a coup.

During the months of October and November, 1939, the wavering of military support for a coup took its toll. It became evident to many in the resistance that support was

lacking and an organized coup might not happen. To some, including Erich Kordt, it became apparent that a concerted effort was unlikely. It would be necessary, he believed, for someone acting alone to assassinate Hitler. He approached Hans Oster in the first week of November and offered to sacrifice himself in order to accomplish that mission. In his capacity as assistant to Foreign Minister Weizsäcker, Kordt had regular access to Hitler. He accompanied Weizsäcker on his frequent meetings with the Führer at the Chancellery and was not searched or asked to produce identification. He was free to go into the Chancellery at will, making it possible for him to make an attempt on Hitler and take the guards by surprise. Oster told Kordt, "We have no one to throw the bomb which will liberate our generals from their scruples." Kordt answered, "All I need is the bomb," and Oster promised, "You will have the bomb by November 11."[8]

The planned date of the attempt was critical. At the time, the western offensive was scheduled to begin on November 12. With Oster's promise, Kordt began making regular visits to the Chancellery over the next few days, so the guards would become accustomed to seeing him there. Oster met with General Erwin Lahousen, chief of Abwehr Section II (Sabotage) to ask for explosives and detonators for an attempt on Hitler. Lahousen explained that all explosives were held in Group T (Technical) and none could be removed, even by the section chief, without a good reason. Lahousen said he needed time to think about the request.

In the meantime, an attempt on Hitler's life very nearly succeeded in Munich when Georg Elser planted a bomb in the hall where Hitler was to speak (see Chapter Six). The bomb exploded moments after Hitler left the building. The result was a tightening of security. That, plus the problem of actually getting the needed explosives, led to a cancellation of the Kordt bombing plan. After the Elser incident, measures controlling access to explosives were tightened, and General Lahousen was unable to help.

Kordt told Oster he was willing to make an attempt using a pistol, but Oster talked him out of it. There would be no guarantee of success with others present, and there was no chance that Kordt would be able to meet alone with Hitler.

In the first months of 1940, the resistance adopted a wait-and-see attitude, hoping that a western offensive would quickly become bogged down. Then they would act. They knew by April that the western offensive was scheduled to begin at any moment. That month, General Beck, with the support of Oster and Groscurth, proposed a new plan for a coup. Beck wanted to take control of all government departments by force and declare a temporary three-man directorate. The directorate would remain in power until elections could be called, and Beck's plan included appointment of a constitutional council. Popitz drafted the text of a Law for the Restoration of Orderly Conditions in Political and Judicial Life, to be declared as soon as the coup was completed.

The western offensive was launched on May 10. By June 25, France had fallen, along with her neutral neighbors, Luxemburg, Belgium, and Holland. Britain's army narrowly averted complete destruction at Dunkirk, where it was encircled and barely escaped to Britain in a massive evacuation by sea. By the end of June, Britain stood alone in the west as Hitler's last remaining foe. For the resistance, Hitler's unbroken string of successes made it difficult to justify an overthrow. Military victory makes a leader popular, and even though the resistance saw nothing but disaster in the future, hopes for a coup d'état seemed distant.

Without hope for a popular uprising, the resistance once again lost momentum and fell into despair. The hope for a coordinated effort against Hitler gave way, to be replaced by desperate schemes by individuals and small groups. Typical of these plots was one hatched by Fritz-Dietlof von der Schulenburg and Dr. Eugen Gerstenmaier. Schulenburg, a reserve officer, was ordered in May 1940 to report for duty. Giving up his post as vice president of the Berlin Police, he reported to his unit, No. 9 (Potsdam) Training Regiment. Dr. Gerstenmaier worked for the Information Division of the Foreign Ministry and was a personal friend of Schulenburg. Together they proposed that a company of officers would confront Hitler in Berlin and place him under arrest. Expecting to meet with a fight from Hitler's bodyguards, they were prepared to shoot Hitler on the spot. The unit was organized and several attempts were made to put their plan into effect, but they were unable to get close enough to Hitler.

When Paris fell, Hitler scheduled a victory parade in the French capital. Gerstenmaier and Schulenburg planned to assassinate Hitler as he stood in the reviewing stand during the parade, but the parade was postponed and finally called off altogether. The plan was eventually abandoned because of Hitler's erratic schedule and tight security.

With the defeat of France, there remained no country in western Europe with the power to stop Hitler. Britain's armed forces were ill-equipped and outnumbered. Their only defense was the thin waterway of the English Channel.

Hitler believed the war was over. The pope also concluded that Britain could not successfully resist Germany. Assuming negotiations would soon begin for a peace settlement, he sent a secret message to Hitler on June 28, 1940, offering to mediate between Germany and Britain.

Hitler never had the opportunity to take up the pope's offer. The British were through talking and were now led by a fighter. At the beginning of the short-lived French campaign, Winston Churchill had been appointed by the king to take over as prime minister and to create a war-footing government. Churchill had no doubt that Britain would be the next target, but unlike his predecessor Chamberlain, he was determined to fight. On June 4, 1940, Churchill had expressed Britain's determination in the House of Commons in his famous rallying speech:

> Even though large tracts of Europe and many old and famous States have fallen or may fall into the grip of the Gestapo and all the odious apparatus of Nazi rule, we shall not flag or fail. We shall go on to the end, we shall fight in France, we shall fight in the seas and oceans, we shall fight with growing confidence and growing strength in the air, we shall defend our island, whatever the cost may be, we shall fight on the beaches, we shall fight on the landing grounds, we shall fight in the fields and in the streets, we shall fight in the hills; we shall never surrender, and even if, which I do not

for a moment believe, this island or a large part of it were subjugated and starving, then our Empire beyond the seas, armed and guarded by the British Fleet, would carry on the struggle until, in God's good time, the New World, with all its power and might, steps forth to the rescue and the liberation of the Old.[9]

Hitler, not accustomed to defiance, was unsettled by Churchill's resolve to fight. Nonetheless, he believed that the British would be willing to negotiate in order to avoid an invasion. He also knew it was imperative to keep the United States neutral. In Washington, the German embassy was doing all it could to encourage the isolationists in Congress, hoping that by keeping the United States out of the war, Britain would be forced to negotiate. The embassy made a cash payment of $30,000 to an unnamed "well-known Republican Congressman"[10] to place a full-page ad in the New York Times, "Keep America Out of the War."[11]

The German embassy also paid the expenses of isolationist congressmen attending the Republican convention. Hans Thomsen, German chargé d'affaires in Washington, negotiated with an American literary agent to have five well-known American authors write books opposed to U.S. involvement in the war. Thomsen asked the Berlin government for $20,000 to fund advances for those projects, and the money was promptly sent. As part of the propaganda campaign to keep the United States out of the war, Hitler, in an interview with a Hearst correspondent, Karl von Wiegand, said he was interested in securing peace. He urged America to leave Europe to Europeans.[12]

During the month of June 1940, it seemed only a matter of time until Britain either gave in and negotiated with Germany or was invaded and quickly defeated like the rest of Europe. Suddenly, however, the British rallied under the leadership of Churchill and became determined to defeat the Nazi regime. The obvious disparity in military and air power made the British attitude audacious; Hitler was confounded by the stubborn refusal by the British to recognize the inevitable. When the king of Sweden contacted the British government and urged Churchill to make peace with Germany, Churchill replied: "Before any such requests or proposals could even be considered, it would be necessary that effective guarantees by deeds, not words, should be forthcoming from Germany which would ensure the restoration of the free and independent life of Czechoslovakia, Poland, Norway, Denmark, Holland, Belgium and above all, France."[13]

Neither Hitler nor his naval commander, Admiral Erich Raeder, were enthusiastic about transporting the German army across the English Channel. Raeder advised Hitler that the risks of such an invasion were high and that it would succeed only after Britain's air force had been destroyed. He told Hitler that the invasion should be undertaken "only as a last resort to force Britain to sue for peace."[14]

Winston Churchill also understood Britain's advantage in the role of island defender. Of the planned German invasion, he wrote: "Sea power, when properly understood, is a wonderful thing. The passage of an army across salt water in the face of superior fleets and flotillas is an almost impossible feat.... Every complication which modern apparatus had added to armies made their voyage more cumbersome and perilous, and the difficulties of their maintenance when landed probably insurmountable."[15]

On July 16, 1940, Hitler issued a top secret directive ordering his military commanders to begin preparations for the invasion of England. Planning for this invasion, code-named "Sea Lion," was to be completed by August 15. Hitler, like his chief naval adviser, worried about the risks and would have preferred to have Britain ask him for favorable terms. On July 19, Hitler spoke in the Reichstag, his pipeline to the international press, where he made a last appeal for a negotiated end to the war:

> In this hour I feel it to be my duty before my own conscience to appeal once more to reason and common sense in Great Britain as much as elsewhere. I consider myself in a position to make this appeal since I am not the vanquished begging favors, but the victor speaking in the name of reason. I can see no reason why this war must go on.[16]

Operation Sea Lion hinged on the destruction of the Royal Air Force and gaining mastery on the seas. Hermann Göring confidently promised Hitler that Britain's entire southern defense system would be destroyed within four days by his Luftwaffe and that the Royal Air Force would be wiped out in two to four weeks. Ignoring the problem of Britain's naval power, Göring even boasted that the Luftwaffe could force Britain's capitulation all on its own.

The Luftwaffe's offensive began on August 15. Three German air fleets attacked Britain from launching points in northern France, Holland, and Norway. At the beginning of the battle of Britain, Germany had air forces of 963 fighters, 998 bombers, and 316 dive bombers, for a total of 2,277 planes. Britain's defenses consisted of fewer than 800 fighter planes. From the first day, however, the British response surprised the overconfident Luftwaffe. Although German forces held a three-to-one superiority, British fighters were winning in the skies.

The British had the advantage of a relatively new invention, radar (radio detection and ranging). Radar stations enabled the British defenders to identify approaching German squadrons well before their arrival and to send up fighter planes to meet them. Radar not only provided notification that the Germans were coming, it also told the British their numbers, distance, and bearing.

Göring made two serious strategic errors. First, he lost the element of surprise by failing to continue targeting British radar stations. It would have been a simple matter because those stations were easy to spot. Some stations were taken out of commission by bombing but were quickly repaired. Because the Luftwaffe leadership ignored the importance of British radar, the defenders held a clear strategic advantage.

Second, on September 7, Göring abandoned the original plan of destroying the Royal Air Force and began massive night bombing attacks on London. He was frustrated to discover that it was not as easy to beat the Royal Air Force as he had predicted; he decided he could break the British resolve by bombing civilians instead. Enough bombing, Göring believed, and the British government would gladly agree to peace terms.

Göring could not know that his sudden change of tactics came at a point when Britain was losing the battle from attrition. Winston Churchill later wrote that within a matter of weeks, the R.A.F. would have been unable to continue defending Britain against the superior numbers of German planes. The bombing of London and other cities in Britain continued for 57 consecutive nights, until November 3. On average, two hundred bombers per day pounded the civilian populations. But throughout this time, Britain continued taking a toll on German bomber squadrons, and their losses mounted. Germany never recovered its air power.

The failure of the Luftwaffe to destroy the Royal Air Force made a channel crossing too risky, and Hitler abandoned plans for invading and occupying Britain. He decided that keeping the British in check would suffice. Hitler turned his attention eastward, to Russia.

Chapter 10

THE WAR
TURNS EASTWARD

The Führer's "intuition," now military as well as political, had once again triumphed over the cautious professionalism of his experts. The effect was disastrous all over the world. The military prestige of the Allies sank to a hitherto unprecedented level and that of Germany was correspondingly exalted. Moreover, the infallibility of the Führer's judgment was now seemingly established beyond all doubt or error. The believers became the more fanatical; the doubters wavered and rallied to their pledged allegiance; those few who still genuinely opposed retired in bewildered despair at the persistent disasters which doomed the realization of their hopes.

John W. Wheeler-Bennett, *The Nemesis of Power*

For centuries, German military strategists acknowledged that a two-front war in Europe could not be won. Hitler had repeatedly promised his generals that before beginning an attack to the east, the west would be neutralized and defeated. In late 1940, Hitler convinced himself that the western continent was defeated, Britain was contained, and he was free now to turn eastward.

Hitler claimed "destiny" and the need for living space as his motive. But in fact, he recognized that Russia's own ambitions in the Balkan states were a direct threat to his war plans and could see that in order to maintain control over needed resources in the Balkans, it would be necessary for Germany to invade Russia. Hitler was determined to attack to the east out of need for war materiel. Russia held vast resources Hitler needed to fuel a war economy. He also insisted that Germany needed to defeat Russia for new territory. In *Mein Kampf*, Hitler wrote: "When we speak of new territory in Europe today we must think principally of Russia and her border vassal states. Destiny itself seems to point the way to us here…. This colossal empire in the East is ripe for dissolution, and the end of Jewish domination in Russia will also be the end of Russia as a state."[1]

The war in eastern Europe provided Hitler with the opportunity to put into practice his most barbaric plans. The crimes committed against civilian populations in Poland and Russia took place openly. Military leaders were aware of atrocities as they occurred in their regions, and the SS was given the authority to act independent of army com-

155

manders within the same command areas. The command structure of the SS was parallel to that of the army. The SS agenda took precedence even over military requirements,
and the army had no command jurisdiction over the SS or its activities. This situation
frustrated army leaders used to a tradition of unquestioned and universal authority during military campaigns, a prerequisite for order in the minds of most military experts.

Army generals were forced to accept the parallel authority they shared with the SS.
Plans for the treatment of civilian populations had been announced before the invasion of
Russia, and at that time none of the top military commanders protested. It was only later,
when the tide of war turned against Germany, that active army resistance again came alive.

Soon after the defeat of Poland, Hitler began laying plans for further eastward conquests. He instructed his generals to treat conquered Polish territory "as an assembly area
for future Germany operations."[2] On July 31, 1940, Hitler instructed army leaders to proceed with plans for an invasion of Russia. General Halder had the task of implementing
Hitler's plans. Hitler outlined a two-speared drive, one each to Moscow and Kiev, followed by a third operation to take the rich Baku oil fields. Hitler estimated the Russian
campaign would require 120 divisions.

Relations between Germany and Russia rapidly deteriorated in late 1940, with both
sides engaged in numerous violations of the nonaggression pact. For example, German
troop movements in conquered eastern territories were a constant source of concern to
the Russians. And Russia had obvious designs on the Balkans, notably Rumania. Disagreements reached the crisis point, and on August 28, 1940, Hitler ordered panzer,
motorized, and airborne infantry divisions to prepare for a surprise invasion of Rumania's oil fields, reasoning that when he launched an attack on Russia, protecting the oil
fields would be a top priority. On September 20, Hitler issued a top secret military directive for this purpose. The directive spelled out the strategy for using Rumania as a southern flank for an invasion of Russia. Hitler ordered preparations to send "military missions" to Rumania "to guide friendly Rumania in organizing and instructing her forces"
but also "to prepare for deployment from Rumanian bases of German and Rumanian
forces in case a war with Soviet Russia is forced upon us."[3]

By this time, Hitler was not considering a mere contingency. In December 1940, he
issued top secret orders for the military to begin preparations for the invasion of Russia
the following year. The invasion, with a 1,500-mile front from the Arctic Ocean to the
Black Sea, would be the largest operation in military history and was code-named Operation Barbarossa.*

Hitler's orders for Barbarossa spelled out a fast-moving invasion plan: "The German Armed Forces must be prepared *to crush Soviet Russia in a quick campaign* even
before the conclusion of the war against England."[4] The plan identified Finland in the
north and Rumania in the south as staging areas and as the northern and southern flanks
of the attack.

---

*The operation was named for Frederick Barbarossa, German king and Holy Roman emperor (ca. 1123–1190).
Frederick's dream was to restore the Roman Empire.

In preparation for Operation Barbarossa, Hitler moved to secure his flank in the south. By February 1941, Hitler had deployed 680,000 troops into Rumania in cooperation with that country's government. Rumania shared a 300-mile border with the Ukraine between Poland and the Black Sea. Hitler managed to gain Bulgaria as an ally early in February. Yugoslavia also agreed to join with the Axis powers, but while government representatives were meeting with Ribbentrop in Vienna to sign the agreement, Yugoslav army and air force officers in Belgrade overthrew the Yugoslav government. Although the new Yugoslav government was willing to sign a nonaggression pact with Germany, the instability of the situation troubled Hitler. He was also unaccustomed to being defied. He decided to invade and destroy that small country.*

Hitler ordered the capital of Belgrade to be destroyed by Luftwaffe bombing. By April 13, the Yugoslav army was unable to continue resisting, and a surrender was arranged at Sarajevo. Later the same month, Hitler's forces also accepted the surrender of the Greek army; they had taken Crete as well. Hitler's southern flank was secure.

During the planning of Operation Barbarossa in March 1941, Hitler announced a controversial decision that came to be known as the "Commissar Order." He instructed the generals:

> The war against Russia will be such that it cannot be conducted in a knightly fashion. The struggle is one of ideologies and racial differences and will have to be conducted with unprecedented, unmerciful and unrelenting harshness. All officers will have to rid themselves of obsolete ideologies.... I insist absolutely that my orders be executed without contradiction. The commissars are the bearers of ideologies directly opposed to National Socialism. Therefore the commissars will be liquidated.[4]

The Commissar Order was significant for the resistance. As Halder later recalled, all of the generals were outraged at the illegal order. Several protested to Field Marshal Brauchitsch† in person. Brauchitsch was moved to resist the order.§ The generals were then placed in the position of planning an invasion in which secured territories would be turned over to the SS for "special tasks." Although scores of commanders denied at Nuremberg that they knew what was going on behind their own front lines, planning of

---

*This sudden development required a delay in Barbarossa of about four weeks. Because Hitler recognized the need to destroy Russia's fighting power before winter began, his decision to delay in order to attack Yugoslavia may have been the most costly of his career. All of Hitler's generals later blamed the decision to invade Yugoslavia for the failure of the Russian campaign. When, later that year, the Russian winter came earlier than expected, the four-week delay in the start of the battle proved to be critical, eventually ending in complete disaster.

†Brauchitsch was among several generals promoted by Hitler to the rank of field marshal on July 19, 1940.

§At the Nuremberg Trials after the war, Brauchitsch testified that he did not take a stand against the order because it would not have changed Hitler's mind. Instead, he ordered field commanders that "discipline in the Army was to be strictly observed along the lines and regulations that applied in the past."[5]

this massive military operation was extensive. It called for the extermination of people in entire regions. Generals were instructed to cooperate with SS execution squads working within their command areas.

Many soldiers protested Nazi policies on the eastern front in various ways. One, Captain Axel von dem Bussche-Streithorst, joined the resistance as a result of his experiences. While stationed in the Ukraine with his reserve army unit, Bussche witnessed the mass execution of about 5,000 Jews in one day. The SS forced the Jews to strip and lie down in a large pit, where they were each shot in the neck. The orderly manner in which the soldiers conducted the operation convinced Bussche that it was not an isolated incident. He was devastated by the experience and was haunted by guilt, later stating that he wished he had stripped and lain down with the Jews to die with them in protest. He volunteered in 1944 to kill Hitler in a suicide attack.

Occasionally, generals on the eastern front were able to find ways to defy the order successfully. Fabian von Schlabrendorff, on General Henning von Tresckow's staff on the eastern front and an active member of the resistance, recalled the first instance in which the order was tested:

> During the briefing Hitler again told his generals that the SS would follow in the wake of the advancing German armies and would establish in the occupied Russian territories a regime of blood and terror similar to that in Poland. Again, this declaration was met with silence by the generals.... Shortly after the hostilities against Russia had begun, the first Russian commissar was taken prisoner. Colonel Baron von Gersdorff, who belonged to our side, informed Tresckow, who without hesitation decided to let the man live. This incident illustrates that, risky though it was, Hitler's orders occasionally could be, and were, successfully defied.[6]

A clearly stated policy of genocide defined the Russian campaign. As army units moved eastward, they were followed closely by execution squads, whose job it was to round up political leaders, Jews, and other "enemies" of Nazism and to kill them. Plans were also laid for the mass starvation of large numbers of Russian civilians. On May 2, 1941, a memorandum produced during a meeting of German state secretaries estimated that as a consequence of the invasion of Russia, "many millions of persons will be starved to death if we take out of the country the things necessary for us."[7]

Hermann Göring had been placed in charge of economic planning in the conquered Russian areas. On May 23, 1941, he issued a directive ordering that surplus food stocks in the southern industrial areas were not to be given to the inhabitants but to the German troops or were to be sent back home to Germany.

Numerous warnings to the Russian government of Hitler's planned invasion were ignored in Moscow. As early as January 1941, a U.S. attaché in Berlin, Sam E. Woods, reported to the State Department that Hitler was planning a spring invasion of Russia. Secretary of State Cordell Hull believed at first that Woods had been given false information by a German agent. He was finally convinced, however, that the information was accurate. He ordered Undersecretary of State Sumner Welles to report the information to the Russian ambassador, Constantine Oumansky. Welles met with the ambassador on March 20 and later wrote: "Mr. Oumansky turned very white. He was silent for a moment and then merely said: 'I fully realize the gravity of the message you have given me. My government will be grateful for your confidence and I will inform it immediately of our conversation.'"[8]

The Russian government, however, disbelieved the information it had received from the United States instead of expressing gratitude. The Russians were further forewarned by Winston Churchill, who had information from intelligence sources concerning the pending invasion. Churchill asked the British ambassador in Moscow, Sir Stafford Cripps, to deliver a report to Stalin. By the end of April, Cripps reported to the Russian government that the Germans were planning to launch their invasion on June 22.

The Russians refused to believe outside sources warning of German intentions. On June 14, eight days before the invasion began, Molotov met with the German ambassador, Schulenburg, and showed him the text of a Tass statement to be published the following morning. The statement blamed the British ambassador, Cripps, for "widespread rumors of 'an impending war between the U.S.S.R. and Germany' in the English and foreign press … a clumsy propaganda maneuver of the forces arrayed against the Soviet Union and Germany…. In the opinion of Soviet circles the rumors of the intentions of Germany … are completely without foundation."[9]

Although Russian diplomats had heard rumors at the highest level, the Russians refused to believe that Germany would attack, and Hitler was able to achieve complete surprise at the June 22 start of the invasion. Hitler himself established new military headquarters near Rastenburg in East Prussia, headquarters that were called *Wolfsschanze* (Wolf's Lair).*

The selection of June 22 as the launch date for the invasion was significant. It was on that date in 1812 that Napoleon crossed the Niemen to begin his march on Moscow. It was also exactly one year since the French surrender at Compiègne. All along the front, German units achieved surprise, capturing all bridges intact. The Luftwaffe was able to destroy Russian planes still on their airfields, and the army surrounded and took prisoner entire Russian armies. General Halder, elated that the plan was proceeding so well, predicted that the Russian campaign would be over in a matter of weeks.

As the war extended eastward, military leaders sympathetic to the resistance remained in the west. Field Marshal Witzleben,† still determined to take direct action against Hitler if and when the opportunity arose, was commander in chief west, with his headquarters located near Paris, in Saint-Germain.

Witzleben recruited staff officers to the cause of the resistance and had several aides

---

*The name was befitting. Hitler's nickname was "the Wolf" and his name, Adolf, was derived from the words Adel Wolf, meaning "noble wolf."

†Witzleben was among several generals promoted by Hitler to the rank of field marshal on July 19, 1940.

ready to act. These officers included Major Hans-Alexander von Voss and Captain Ulrich Wilhelm Schwerin von Schwanefeld. Witzleben also convinced staff officers outside of his command but in the area to join with the resistance. Captain Alfred von Waldersee, operations officer for the commandant of Paris, committed himself to the resistance and was prepared to take part in an arrest or assassination plan. In January 1941, Goerdeler visited Waldersee in Paris. Waldersee promised Goerdeler that if Hitler came to Paris, he would be assassinated as soon as he arrived.

The conspirators surrounding Witzleben believed their opportunity was coming. In May 1941, a parade of German military strength was to be held in Paris. Hitler and Brauchitsch were scheduled to attend. Resolved to take action, Witzleben's group devised a plan. Two officers would shoot Hitler at the reviewing stand. If for any reason that plan failed, Witzleben's aide Captain Schwerin would throw a bomb at the Führer. But Hitler, busy with his preparations for the offensive against Russia, decided at the last minute not to attend.

———————————

Ulrich von Hassell continued to hope that peace with Britain could be arranged. He made contact with Federico Stallforth, a businessman from New York doing business in Germany. Stallforth had made previous contacts in the Berlin government and had met with Göring the year before. Göring had drafted a peace proposal for Stallforth to present to the Allies that included several conditions: the British Empire would be left intact except for some German colonial claims; political independence would be returned to France, Belgium, and Holland (Germany would retain control over Alsace-Lorraine and Luxemburg); and Germany was to be granted a promise of freedom to act in the east.

Britain and the United States had flatly rejected Göring's proposals. In May 1941, Stallforth visited Berlin once again and met with high-ranking army officers at a luncheon. He reported that the Allies refused to deal with Hitler and that the Nazi government would have to be replaced before any serious peace terms could be discussed.

The following day an unidentified officer approached Stallforth on behalf of the resistance and asked if leaders of the German army would be acceptable as negotiating partners with the Allies if power were seized from the current regime. The officer presented Stallforth with two conditions. First, Germany must not be betrayed by the Allies as they had been at the end of the First World War (a reference to guarantees given as part of Wilson's Fourteen Points and later withdrawn without notification). Second, the army must be allowed to remain in control in Germany to prevent civil unrest, meaning that disarmament could not occur instantly. The officer told Stallforth that a replacement government would be willing to cede all territories except Austria.

Stallforth advised that the resistance would have to act quickly or public resentment against Germany would grow to the point that it would be too late. He emphasized that all action would have to originate from within Germany because the American public was isolationist and the U.S. government was sensitive to the appearance of any American involvement.

Shortly after the German invasion of Russia, Churchill and Roosevelt met in Newfoundland and drafted the Atlantic Charter on August 14, 1941.* While this was primar-ily a declaration of goals for ending the war, it also stipulated in Point 8 that Germany would have to be disarmed. To the German resistance, this recalled the punitive tone of the Versailles Treaty. This caused considerable alarm, especially among resistance mem-bers who feared a Communist domination of all of Europe.

Hassell stated that Point 8 of the Atlantic Charter "destroys every reasonable chance for peace."[10] Even so, Hassell still hoped as late as the fall of 1941 that a negotiated peace was possible. On August 18, Professor Carl Burckhardt was in Berlin on his way to Britain on business for the International Red Cross. Burckhardt met with Hassell in Munich, and the two discussed prospects for arriving at a peace agreement with Britain.†

In October 1941, Federico Stallforth was again in Berlin. He reported to Hassell that the U.S. government could not speak for Britain but that "the 'proposition' had been well received."[11] This line of contact was disrupted by the Japanese attack on Pearl Harbor on December 7, 1941, and was not resumed.

Resistance intellectuals gathered their forces from 1941 forward. Carl Goerdeler worked tirelessly, devising ideas for a new German post–Nazi government. During the period of 1941 to 1942, he drafted these ideas into a document called "The Aim." Goerdeler favored the formation of a ruling elite to avoid the problems experienced in the Weimar Republic years. A consensus builder, Goerdeler asked for advice from a divergent array of people. He consulted with Jakob Kaiser and Wilhelm Leuschner and with a group known as the Freiburg Circle: Professors Constantin von Dietze, Alfred Lampe, and Ger-hard Ritter.

"The Aim" emphasized the value of self-government, which Goerdeler hoped to achieve through an elaborate system of decentralization. It favored establishing *Gemein-den* (parishes) and *Bezirke* (districts) that would govern themselves with very little con-trol from the central government and direct election of candidates rather than election by party list.

Goerdeler also sought ideas from members of the Kreisau Circle: Adam Trott, Hel-muth von Moltke, and a young idealist and landowner, Count Peter Yorck von Warten-burg. Yorck had met Moltke when both were attached to the Wehrmacht as economic advisers at the outbreak of war. Like Moltke, Yorck believed it was more important to work for the spiritual and social rehabilitation of Germany in the future than for the immedi-ate removal of Hitler. The Kreisau Circle drafted its own plan, which advocated a planned economy and much greater central control. The Kreisau Circle by this time consisted not only of intellectuals and socialists, but had expanded to include high-ranking church

---

*The Atlantic Charter was a declaration by Britain and the United States defining peace aims. It included state-ments declaring the right to self-determination for all nations, access to raw materials, freedom of the seas, inter-national security, and worldwide reduction of armaments.

†Toward the end of January 1942, Burckhardt saw Hassell again on his return trip. He reported the British posi-tion: peace was impossible as long as Hitler remained in power. He also told Hassell that the British were highly skeptical about the ability of the resistance to succeed with a coup d'état.

officials, attorneys and judges, military officers, and members of the Foreign Office. There was no one leader of the Kreisau Circle, although Moltke is credited with its leadership because many of its meetings were still held at his estate.

The Circle grew to such proportions that the membership found few issues they could all agree upon. The need to replace the Nazi government was the single thread of agreement that kept the group together. While some favored capitalist democracy in the extreme, others were for the expropriation of private property and big industry, all to be state-owned and state-run (even though these Circle members considered themselves socialists, not Communists). The Kreisau Circle as a group favored government by a benevolent elite. The desire for an authoritarian government is expressed repeatedly throughout the Kreisau documents. The predominant voice in the Circle was that of conservative intellectuals and aristocrats. Historians Jeremy Noakes and Geoffrey Pridham described the Kreisau Circle in these terms: "It provided the intellectual inspiration for the German opposition, but its proposals were highly utopian and implied a return to the universal society of the Middle Ages with its rejection of modern industrial society."[12]

Even the Kreisau Circle intellectuals were not to be spared the wrath of the Nazi regime. After the failed July 1944 bomb plot, the intellectuals and theorists were rounded up along with those who took a direct part in the planning of Hitler's assassination. The Nazis made no distinction between planting a bomb and discussing replacement governments. Both actions were treason, and both were punished with a death sentence.

The rapid advances into Russia during the summer of 1941 were stalled by the end of the year. At the end of the summer, conditions had pointed toward a likelihood of a short war with Germany the victor. General Halder's prediction for a short campaign seemed right. Army Group Center was within 200 miles of Moscow, and Army Group North was advancing rapidly on Leningrad. The entire operation was proceeding well beyond Hitler's expectations.

As the summer ended, however, German units began to encounter surprising strength from the Russian military. Original estimates had put Russian army strength at 200 divisions, but 360 were identified by August 1941. As the German army eliminated Russian divisions, they were promptly replaced with fresh troops. The German front, spread over a vast area, contained no depth. Sustaining supply lines and replacements for the front became increasingly difficult, and for the first time, the Germans had to contend with squadrons of Russian air force fighters that harassed the front lines.

The conduct of the war on the eastern front became dominated by the materiel and economic demands of war itself. By the autumn of 1941, the Russian army had concentrated its strength east of Smolensk in defense of Moscow. Moscow was the major Russian transportation and communications center of the country and produced a significant share of armaments as well. Capturing the Russian capital would present a psychological victory as well as a tactical one.

However, Hitler also needed to gain control of the vast oil fields in the Caucasus and the industrial and food production capacity of the Ukraine. On August 21, therefore, he ordered the advance on Moscow broken off. The German army was diverted south to Stalingrad.

General Halder described Hitler's interference as "unbearable" and met at once with Field Marshal Brauchitsch, complaining that it was the job of the High Command and the General Staff to control battlefield priorities. He believed that Hitler's decision to intervene was "inadmissible." Halder suggested that he and Brauchitsch should both resign in protest.

Brauchitsch spoke to Hitler to urge him to proceed with established plans and was reinforced in his arguments by General Guderian and Field Marshal Bock. On September 5, Hitler agreed to resume the assault on Moscow. Tank regiments had to be redirected and did not return until October 2, when the offensive on Moscow was resumed. By October 20, in a spectacular thrust, the German army advanced to within 40 miles of the capital and foreign embassies were evacuated in the belief that Moscow's fall was imminent. But the fall rains began, and roads turned to quagmires. Hitler's supply transport and tanks stopped. The success of the Wehrmacht had depended in every campaign on blitzkrieg. German troops were ill-prepared for the conditions near the Russian capital, which produced a sudden halt in the German advance that was reminiscent of Napoleon's experiences in the same place during the winter of 1812. On November 3, temperatures fell below freezing and the German soldiers, without winter clothing, began suffering from frostbite. Their machinery also refused to work in subzero temperatures.

Resistance activity previously centered in the west spread to the eastern front under the leadership of General Henning von Tresckow. He was 40 when first posted to the eastern front to serve as chief of staff to Field Marshal Fedor von Bock, commander in chief of Army Group Center. Tresckow's post became the hub of efforts to resist Hitler and his policies, in spite of Field Marshal Bock's intolerance of any disobedience or disloyalty to Hitler. Army Group Center was strategically important both militarily and for the resistance. As the sector squarely facing Moscow, it took the brunt of the Russian counteroffensive. Because of its importance to the extended front line, chances were good that Hitler would visit, providing the resistance an opportunity to strike against him.

Tresckow was resolutely opposed to Hitler. Born in 1901 in Magdeburg to a family with 300 years of military tradition, Tresckow had fought in the First World War. He left the army in 1922 to pursue a career as a stockbroker and banker. Even though he was the descendent of a military family, Tresckow was not a typical Prussian officer. He wore his uniform only when absolutely required and disliked the regimentation of army life.

When Tresckow was posted to the eastern front, he arranged for the assignment of Fabian von Schlabrendorff, a trusted friend, as his aide-de-camp. Knowing that Field Marshal Bock could not be recruited, Tresckow needed a trusted A.D.C. to work with him on resistance activities. Schlabrendorff's wife was Tresckow's cousin, and Schlabrendorff also had valuable political connections and experience. Schlabrendorff made frequent trips to Berlin and other army headquarters on behalf of Tresckow, enabling him to coordinate resistance activities throughout Europe.

Tresckow did not like Hitler and did not share Bock's military ideal of blind loyalty. Tresckow confronted Bock with the reality of the war situation, that they would not be able to take Moscow. A disaster was certain, and it was Hitler's fault. Bock's reaction to Tresckow's statements was recalled by Schlabrendorff: "Before Tresckow could finish, Bock interrupted him. Trembling with rage, he sprang to his feet and stormed from the room, shouting, 'I shall not tolerate any attack upon the Führer. I shall stand before the Führer and defend him against anyone who dares to attack him.' After that outburst we wrote off any efforts to win over Bock as a total failure."[13]

Even without the cooperation of Field Marshal Bock, Tresckow and Schlabrendorff managed to arrange for assignments of officers sympathetic to the resistance. Major Hans von Hardenberg and Lieutenant Heinrich von Lehndorff were brought into headquarters as aides to Bock, but they were sympathetic to Tresckow and the resistance. They were followed by Colonel Rudolph von Gersdorff, Major Ulrich von Oertzen, and Colonel Hans-Alexander von Voss (previously a major and a member of Witzleben's staff in the west).

This group of officers worked together on three levels at once. First, they had military duties that had to be performed full-time at the headquarters of a massive front. They planned resistance activities aimed at removing Hitler, and they worked tirelessly to thwart SS atrocities against civilians taking place throughout occupied territories.

The officers were ready and willing to act. Hitler scheduled a visit to Army Group Center, located at Borisov. As was typical of Hitler's plans, the visit was rescheduled several times. Security was tight as usual. Although headquarters was less than three miles from the airstrip where Hitler's plane landed, he refused to use a car provided by Bock. Several days before the visit, Hitler had ordered a long motorcade sent ahead, so that he could be escorted to headquarters by his own guards and in his own vehicles. He was surrounded by too many SS guards for Tresckow's group to act.

Shortly after it became evident that the German army had lost the initiative at Moscow, Hitler dismissed Bock and replaced him with Field Marshal Günther von Kluge. The new commander in chief was not a Nazi and was sympathetic with the resistance. He was, however, an indecisive and weak-willed man.*

On December 6, 1941, the Russian army defending Moscow unleashed 100 divisions against the German army over a 200-mile front. Over the coming months, Hitler began firing and replacing generals who were unable to halt the Russian counteroffensive. The German army never regained its initiative.

Brauchitsch asked Hitler to accept his resignation on December 7. Then, following an inspection of the front on December 15, he repeated his request on the seventeenth. Hitler accepted on the nineteenth, deciding to take over as commander in chief of the army on his own. He told Halder of the decision and asked him if he would like to remain as chief of staff. Halder replied that he would remain.

The campaign turned into a disaster. At the end of six months of winter, German casualties exceeded one million men. Blaming his military leaders for the failure, Hitler dismissed about 40 corps and divisional commanders during the winter of 1941-42.

Behind his back, Kluge was referred to by other officers as der kluge Hans *("Clever Hans"). The reference was to a famous performing horse who tapped out answers to simple math problems with his front hoof on subtle clues given by his trainer.*

When Germany's ally Japan attacked the U.S. fleet at Pearl Harbor on December 7, Hitler was elated, believing the United States would be distracted with war in the Pacific. On December 11, Hitler also declared war on the United States. He underestimated U.S. willingness to fight and capacity to wage war, however. Bringing America into the war, with its powerful material capacity, was a fateful miscalculation. Now Hitler had several powerful enemies, and Germany would be unable to withstand the combined forces of the Allied powers.

As the war became global, Hitler tightened the reins of power both in Germany and in occupied territories. He decided to take full personal control over the armed forces; he also devised new policies and regulations to punish his enemies, real and perceived. These actions shocked and dismayed not only the organized resistance, but the average German citizen as well.

First was the infamous *Nacht-und-Nebel-Erlass* (night and fog decree), issued on December 12, 1941, the day following his declaration of war on the United States. The decree stated that for the more serious enemies of the Reich, a "lasting deterrent can be achieved only by the death penalty or by taking measures that will leave the family and the population uncertain as to the fate of the offender."[14]

Under this decree, thousands of people disappeared without a trace. They were never to be heard from again and were assigned to the elaborate system of labor and concentration camps without possibility of release, nameless and existing by number alone. If the imprisoned person's family made inquiries, officials were unable to tell them anything. Under the "night and fog" rule, the individual was arrested and officially ceased to exist.

The decree made any form of outspoken resistance extremely dangerous. The terror that accompanied the idea of disappearing entirely was enough to keep many people silent who might otherwise have expressed dissent.

The control Hitler achieved with his "night and fog" decree came during the same week he took over personal command of the armed forces. Convinced that the setbacks on the eastern front were the fault of weak generals, Hitler was certain he could turn the situation around. At the same time, he was determined to crush all opposition in Germany and in the occupied territories.

On April 26, 1942, Hitler promulgated a law giving himself unrestricted control over life and death of all Germans. The law read in part:

> The Führer must be in a position to force with all means at his disposal every German, if necessary ... to fulfill his duties. In case of violation of these duties, the Führer is entitled after conscientious examination, regardless of so-called well-deserved rights, to mete out due punishment and to remove the offender from his post, rank and position without introducing prescribed procedures.[15]

The resistance was forced to operate in this environment of extreme personal danger. Years before, its leaders had hoped for battlefield reversals. Now such reversals were plentiful, but although losses were occurring on a massive scale, there was to be no stop-ping the Russian counteroffensive. Until the war turned against Germany, Hitler had too much civilian support for a coup d'état to succeed. The resistance had been forced to wait until the war grew to catastrophic proportions. In the meantime, Hitler tightened his grip on the civilian population by removing all civil rights. This, plus the losses on the eastern front, had the effect of widening the resistance and reinforcing the resolve of those German officers and politicians who had previously held doubts.

In 1942 the activities of the Kreisau Circle expanded. In the spring and autumn, they organized meetings at the Moltke estate involving up to 40 members. This group was involved primarily with planning for a replacement government and social system after the war. They did not take an active part in the planning of a coup d'état. The Kreisau Circle favored passive resistance, and for some members the idea of assassina-tion or any other type of violence was unacceptable. Helmuth von Moltke especially held strong feelings in this area as part of his Christian religious beliefs. He believed Nazism would decline of its own accord. He emphasized the importance of looking far ahead to address the problems that would be faced by Germany and by Europe after the war. He expressed his concerns in a letter to a British friend, Lionel Curtis, in 1942:

> An active part of the German people are beginning to realize, not that they
> have been led astray, not that bad times await them, not that the war may
> end in defeat, but that what is happening is sin and that they are personally
> responsible for each terrible deed that has been committed.... We can only
> expect our people to overthrow this regime of terror and frightfulness if we
> are able to point to a goal beyond the paralyzing and hopeless immediate
> future.... The real question which will face postwar Europe is how the pic-
> ture of man can be restored in the hearts of our fellow-citizens.[16]

Years later, during a BBC broadcast called "Germans of the Resistance," aired July 15, 1962, Moltke's widow expressed her late husband's philosophy and his place in the resistance. She said that Moltke had "looked at National Socialism as a poison which not only existed in Germany, but which you can find all over the world in human beings. And he felt the only way to really get rid of the poison was to let National Socialism defeat itself."[17]

Moltke and the Kreisau Circle did not limit their activities to theoretical discus-sions. They also made and maintained contact with leaders of resistance groups in occu-pied countries. Contact was especially close between the Kreisau Circle and Dutch and Norwegian resistance leaders. The purpose of these contacts was to coordinate long-range planning for social and political order in postwar Europe. Kreisau Circle members also used their diplomatic, military, and legal connections to alleviate suffering in occupied countries, often intervening on behalf of those who had been arrested and imprisoned.

Moltke and other members of the Kreisau Circle played an instrumental role in maintaining contacts in Germany and abroad, saving many lives and keeping diplomatic channels to the Allies open. They also provided other members of the German resistance with a sense that long-range planning was taking place and that some thought was being given to matters that would come up after the war. The Kreisau Circle also led in efforts to establish diplomatic support with foreign governments. Resistance contact with foreign governments accelerated with the pace and scope of the war.

Adam Trott worked with other Kreisau Circle members to produce a report for the British government, which Trott delivered in April 1942 to Dr. W. A. Visser't Hooft, secretary-general of the Ecumenical Council of Churches. Trott asked him to deliver the document to Sir Stafford Cripps, British lord privy seal. The report predicted that all countries involved in fighting the war would suffer economically unless the war could be ended quickly. The report suggested that overthrowing the Nazi regime was the only way to end the war, short of a Russian victory over Germany. The report summarized the goals of the resistance and repeated the need for assurances from the Allies of cooperation with a new government in Germany. The report was delivered to Cripps, who forwarded it to Prime Minister Winston Churchill. Churchill was not sympathetic and the initiative ended.

In May 1942, the resistance again tried to maintain contact with Allied governments, this time through neutral countries. In Stockholm, Sweden, Dr. George Bell, who was the bishop of Chichester, received two visitors from the German resistance during the month of May, Dr. Hans Schönfeld and Dietrich Bonhoeffer. Bell, a church leader as well as political activist, was in Stockholm at the behest of the British Ministry of Information for the purpose of creating and maintaining diplomatic contacts in neutral countries for the Allied powers.

Bell had arrived in Sweden on May 13. On May 28, he met with Schönfeld, who had worked with Trott on the April memo. Schönfeld's credentials were impeccable. He was research director for the World Council of Churches and was a member of the Foreign Affairs Department of the German Evangelical Church. Oster and Dohnanyi had asked him on behalf of the resistance to meet with Bell. Schönfeld was in a difficult position, however, because his superior in the German Evangelical Church was Bishop Heckel, a Nazi supporter.

Schönfeld advised Bell that over the previous six months the resistance had become organized and well prepared. Its goal was to eliminate the entire Nazi presence from Germany, including the organizations associated with the Nazis, especially the SS and Gestapo. Although Schönfeld was attempting to represent the entire resistance, he had been exposed primarily to the idealistic wing of the resistance found in the Kreisau Circle. His primary message concerned the resistance goal of restructuring European social life after the war. He told Bell: "The basic principles of national and social life within this federation of free European peoples should be oriented or reoriented according to the fundamental articles of Christian faith and life."[18]

Schönfeld asked Bell to convey the message to the British government that the resistance existed and was serious. The resistance needed to know whether Britain would encourage and support them and whether the Allies would negotiate with a resistance-led military government after the coup. Without such assurances, Schönfeld explained, it was unlikely that a coup d'état could be launched.

The two met a second time the following day. Bell asked Schönfeld to prepare a memorandum stating his position, and he promised to deliver it to the British government upon his return. Bell then left for Sigtuna, 30 miles north of Stockholm. There he received his second visitor, long-time friend Dietrich Bonhoeffer.

Bonhoeffer's meeting with Bell had also been arranged by Oster and Dohnanyi through the Abwehr. Bonhoeffer knew Bell from time he had spent as pastor of the German Church in London. Bonhoeffer was a Protestant pastor prominent in the Confessional church. Although still in his 30s, Bonhoeffer had accomplished much in his life. He was a world traveler, university professor, and pastor and had lived in Barcelona, London, and New York throughout the 1920s. Bonhoeffer was a prolific writer, and his books had been banned by the Nazis. He had been placed under a preaching and publishing ban shortly after the Nazi rise to power. Although offered permanent asylum in the United States, he refused, stating: "I must live through this period of our national history with the Christian people of Germany. I will have no right to participate in the reconstruction of Christian life in Germany after the war if I do not share the trials of this time with my people."[19]

Through both his religious affiliations and through contacts with military and civilian circles, Bonhoeffer had been involved with the resistance for many years. In 1935 the Confessional church had picked him to organize a theological college. Because the college's political teachings were anti–Nazi, the Gestapo closed it down in 1937. Nonetheless, Bonhoeffer remained fearless and outspoken. He referred to Hitler as the Anti-Christ.

Schönfeld had presented the Kreisau Circle idealism to Bell, but Bonhoeffer diverged from this position. To end the moral wrongs of the Nazi regime, Bonhoeffer favored removing Hitler by any means possible, even if that meant Germany's losing the war. He also believed that all Germans had to share in the guilt for the crimes committed by the Nazis. At a conference of church leaders in 1941, Bonhoeffer had said: "I pray for the defeat of my Fatherland. Only through a defeat can we atone for the terrible crimes which we have committed against Europe and the world."[20]

Bonhoeffer offered Bell more complete information about the resistance than Schönfeld had. He described its military and civilian leaders, their character, and the scope of support throughout Germany. At Bell's request, he named the primary leaders of the resistance. Bell told Bonhoeffer it would help the credibility of the resistance if he were able to provide the British government concrete evidence that the resistance was active and credible. Bonhoeffer assured him of resistance support in every government ministry in Germany, without exception.

Bonhoeffer took a different stance from earlier resistance diplomatic missions. Previous resistance contacts with the British had asked to retain German conquests and sought assurances that some of the Versailles provisions would be abandoned. That had left the British cold. Now, however, Bonhoeffer brought a different message. He told Bell it would be necessary for the Allies to occupy Berlin to help resistance leaders establish a replacement government while maintaining order. The resistance was willing, Bonhoeffer reported, to consult with the British as to what form of government would be instituted.

Bell was impressed with Bonhoeffer's message, and he knew that resistance leaders wanted to arrive at a solution in cooperation with the British government. As their meeting continued, Schönfeld arrived with the memorandum Bell had requested. Bell assured them that when he returned to London on June 11, he would present the resistance message to the British government but cautioned them that he could not promise a favorable response.

Bell met with Anthony Eden, British secretary of state, and included Schönfeld's memorandum with his own report. The message, according to Bell, was that the German resistance was willing to promise the withdrawal of all military forces from occupied countries and to pay reparations for damages. Germany would also renounce its treaty with Japan. In return, the resistance wanted the Allies to cooperate with a replacement government to arrive at peace terms. The resistance asked that the Allied powers make a public statement of their support.

Eden told Bell that it would be impossible to make public statements or give assurances without the full cooperation of the American and Russian governments. Eden was skeptical of the strength of the resistance movement in Germany. Bell assured Eden that the resistance was sincere, but Eden concluded the matter on July 17, saying it would not serve Britain's national interests to make any replies to Bell's contacts.

The resistance next turned to the United States, communicating its message through the chief of the Associated Press Berlin office, Louis P. Lochner. The year before, Lochner, when introduced discreetly to leaders of the resistance, had promised to inform President Roosevelt about their efforts. When Germany declared war on the United States in December 1941, however, Lochner, like other correspondents, was interned. He was not allowed to leave the country until June 1942. Upon his return to the United States, Lochner asked for a meeting with the president to inform him of the activities of the German resistance, but his request was denied.

The United States government was not ignorant of the existence of a resistance movement in Germany. Through emissaries like Adam Trott the previous year, the United States had gathered a considerable amount of information on underground activities in Germany. The problem was one of timing. Historian Hans Rothfels has observed that the refusal to grant Lochner an audience with the president or even to receive his information

> was not accidental but was dictated by official policy. The underlying attitude not only excluded every form of encouragement or advice for which the men of the German opposition were asking ... from the point of view of Washington the mere recognition of the fact that the oppositional elements existed in Germany ... [was] felt to be "most embarrassing."[21]

The United States actually wanted to establish and maintain contact with the resistance, but only on an unofficial basis. In November 1942, the OSS sent Allen Dulles to Berne, Switzerland, to establish contact with German resistance leaders as a means for aiding the United States in its conduct of the war. Dulles, later director of the CIA, had the specific mission of determining the degree of anti–Nazi activity in Germany. Dulles was able to make contact with several well-informed members of the resistance, whom he referred to collectively as the "Breakers" in coded messages to Washington. His most important contact was Hans Gisevius, who was able to travel frequently to Switzerland in his official Abwehr position. From early 1943 through July 1944, Dulles and Gisevius kept in touch regularly, Gisevius feeding reliable information to Dulles concerning the internal situation in Germany.

Chapter 11

THE TURNING POINT

> When half of Europe lay at his feet and all need of restraint was removed, Hitler abandoned himself entirely to megalomania. He became convinced of his own infallibility.... Ironically, failure sprang from the same capacity which brought him success, his power of self-dramatization.... The sin which Hitler committed was that which the ancient Greeks called *hybris*, the sin of overweening pride, of believing himself to be more than a man. No man was ever more surely destroyed by the image he had created than Adolf Hitler.
>
> Alan Bullock, *Hitler, A Study in Tyranny*

Franklin D. Roosevelt and Winston Churchill met at Casablanca in January 1943 to discuss issues of war policy. Stalin had been invited but declined to attend. Stalin was suspicious of his allies and their intentions, fearing that they might negotiate separately with Germany and perhaps even join forces with the Nazi regime against Russia. The British and American leaders had been under pressure from Stalin since Germany had launched its invasion of Russia. He was demanding that the Allies increase war materiel shipments and assign top priority to the opening of a second European front against Germany. This pressure led Roosevelt and Churchill to agree to the announcement of a new war policy that would reassure Stalin: they would accept nothing less than unconditional surrender from Germany.

To the resistance, this unyielding policy declaration was a crushing blow. The Allied powers refused to acknowledge a German resistance movement and now refused to negotiate any terms whatsoever. It was now clear that if Hitler were assassinated, any replacement government would be forced, under the Allied announcement, to accept surrender without any assurances of terms for peace. This, coupled with the previously announced Allied policy of the Atlantic Charter demanding the disarmament of Germany, destroyed hope in the resistance for a cooperative effort at removing Hitler.

The Allies held onto their policy of unconditional surrender until the end of the war. As late as October 1944, President Roosevelt continued to proclaim the policy, stating during a speech:

> As for Germany, that tragic nation which has sown the wind and is now reaping the whirlwind, we and our allies are entirely agreed that we shall not

bargain with the Nazi conspirators, or leave them a shred of control, open or secret, of the instrument of government. We shall not leave them a single element of military power, or of potential military power.[1]

In 1943 it was unclear even to heads of the Allied military why their political leaders were imposing such terms. Captain Harry C. Butcher of General Eisenhower's staff noted, "No surrender was ever made without some conditions." Butcher further observed that "our psychological experts believe we would be wiser if we created a mood of acceptance of surrender in the German army."[2]

The Allied position concerning Germany was severe from the point of view of the resistance. Still, conditions at the eastern front were grim, and General Tresckow at Army Group Center continued resisting Hitler's policies. Working with other officers in Army Group Center, Tresckow did all he could to prevent the murder of Russian prisoners and civilians. False reports of shootings were sent to headquarters, and those reports were never verified. By mid-1942, the Commissar Order was abandoned as ineffective. Virtually all intelligence reports indicated that the practice of executing civilians had only served to increase the resolve and morale of the Red Army.

The Berlin resistance leaders increasingly placed their hopes on Tresckow. The chances were far better for a coup originating in the east than in the west. There were no armored divisions in France and few in Germany. The army's military power was concentrated on the Russian front, and the war there was going poorly. Chances that more commanders would support the coup increased as the war deteriorated. When Field Marshal Bock was replaced by Kluge, Tresckow continued his resistance.

Tresckow arranged for a visit between Field Marshal Kluge and Carl Goerdeler. Goerdeler traveled to Army Group Center's headquarters in late 1942 near the town of Smolensk. Goerdeler, after meeting with Kluge, believed he had succeeded in convincing Kluge that Hitler must be overthrown. Kluge had been swayed by Goerdeler's arguments and agreed to join with the resistance. But as soon as Goerdeler was gone, Kluge wavered, a pattern he was to repeat.

With the war concentrated in the east, members of the resistance were forced to coordinate their efforts over a vast territory. They believed it would be necessary to launch the coup on the eastern front, but it would also be essential to seize vital installations in Berlin and other major cities around Germany and in occupied countries. In 1942 their planning centered on the idea of a two-step coup d'état. First, Hitler would be assassinated during a visit to the headquarters of Army Group Center. Second, the Reserve Army would be ordered to occupy communications centers and neutralize SS and Gestapo barracks.

The Reserve Army was a force of recruits and cadets, the walking wounded, and elderly soldiers. While not suitable for frontline service, these units were well armed and adequate for the purposes the resistance had in mind — the temporary occupation and protection of key strategic sites.

The Third Reich had imported millions of civilian prisoners from occupied countries to work in factories within Germany. This was a large force of people, and Hitler feared an uprising. So the Reserve Army had been ordered to prepare military plans for dealing with such problems within Germany's own borders, code-named Operation Valkyrie.*

General Fromm, commander of the Reserve Army, had rebuffed the resistance, but his deputy commander, General Friedrich Olbricht, was actively involved in resistance planning. The resistance had an established base in the Reserve Army, and Operation Valkyrie gave its leaders an opportunity for meeting together to make plans and even for deploying units within Germany that could be used for a coup. Managing the Reserve Army was no easy matter. The numbers and locations of units were changing constantly, as men were transferred to front lines as replacements and new members added. Units were constantly on the move. The resistance needed to judge Reserve Army strength compared with the strength of SS barracks in a given area, but the constantly changing situation made this impossible.

The resistance was counting specifically on units placed in and near Berlin. These units would be called into action to occupy strategic buildings and facilities and to take over SS and Gestapo strongholds. The plan was to claim that the SS had attempted to engineer a coup and was responsible for assassinating Hitler. The Reserve Army, it would be explained, had launched Operation Valkyrie in order to put down that plan. That would justify taking over SS and Gestapo barracks and even arresting the remaining Nazi leaders. They would be accused of participating in the planned coup. This idea was more palatable to army leaders than an outright admission that they were involved in a political move to overthrow the government.

The plan would explain actions in the capital, where emphasis would be placed on the seizure and control of vital installations and control over the SS and Gestapo. The resistance would use the local criminal police to supplement Reserve Army units. Outside of Berlin, the resistance would have to depend on infantry, tank, artillery and cavalry training schools. There was no way to judge the combined strength of these units. Even if current estimates were available, they could change without notice because of the volatile situation on the eastern front. There was also the uncertainty of how each individual commander would respond when the coup was launched. As Fabian von Schlabrendorff explained:

> We had to take into account the attitude of local commanders and influence them without making them confidants. We also had to reckon with the fact that the German officer could not do anything he wanted to with his troops. National Socialism had so thoroughly permeated all facets of German life, including the army, that some way had to be found to convincingly explain our acts to the troops.[3]

Olbricht met with Tresckow in Berlin in November 1942. Olbricht said that with eight weeks for preparations, he would be able to devise a plan for coordinating troop movements in Berlin, Vienna, Cologne, and Munich. With the limited telephone and

*In German mythology, Valkyrie was a maiden of the gods whose task was to hover above fields of battle and select soldiers who would die, then lead the worthy to Valhalla.

telegraph technology of 1942, contacting numerous outposts at a moment's notice was a particular problem for the resistance. Simultaneous action would be necessary to ensure success of the coup. Contacting Reserve Army and regular army leaders would not be a simple matter of placing a telephone call or sending a teleprint, either. Orders would be questioned, clarification would be demanded, and confusion had to be expected. Olbricht had to devise a plan in which specific steps were mandated far in advance and would be known to commanders. Upon receiving orders to proceed, each unit would already know what was expected. That was the only way the coup would succeed.

The resistance plan to appropriate the Reserve Army through Operation Valkyrie was a brilliant course of action. Commanders knew they would be given the order to seize and protect key sites if and when an internal emergency came about. The Valkyrie code word was the signal for units to immediately occupy and protect all government buildings and communications installations. It also established emergency military control over civilian authority. The resistance could activate the Valkyrie orders to move against key sites and then arrest Nazi leaders.

Resistance leaders devised plans in anticipation of problems expected to arise. One problem was that the Valkyrie order was supposed to be issued by General Fromm, commander of the Reserve Army. Since Fromm was not a member of the resistance, Olbricht was to issue the order using Fromm's name. Resistance leaders assumed that once the coup was launched, Fromm would see the wisdom of cooperating with them.

Following the initial proclamation issued under Fromm's name, a second one would then be issued, signed by Field Marshal Witzleben, announcing his emergency appointment as commander in chief of the armed forces (a position Hitler had assumed for himself). Since it would be necessary for someone to assume this important position, resistance leaders hoped that Witzleben's esteem among other generals would garner support needed to move quickly against the SS and Gestapo. They could then use the regular army to support the coup under Witzleben's leadership.

The resistance leaders set about to update their original plans that had been derailed in 1938 with Chamberlain's visit to Munich. This task was undertaken by Hans Gisevius, who was given an office in the War Ministry, also referred to as the "Bendlerstraße" because of the street where it was located. Here Gisevius had convenient access to Olbricht. His top priority was to update locations for all SS and Gestapo units throughout Germany. Because these locations were supposed to be secret, Gisevius could not ask too many questions without arousing suspicion. He finally figured out a way to locate virtually all of the new SS locations. Whenever an SS barracks was established, it was invariably accompanied with a new brothel nearby. Gisevius asked a friend in the Berlin vice squad to supply him a list of known brothels in Germany. From this list, it was a simple matter to locate the nearby SS barracks, and Gisevius was able to update his list completely.

———————————

Resistance determination to act was strengthened by the deteriorating military situation. In November 1942 in North Africa, the battle for El Alamein was lost to Allied forces and Hitler's plans for domination of the Mediterranean were dashed. Field Marshal

Erwin Rommel's original army of 96,000 suffered 59,000 killed, wounded, and captured. Then, in January 1943, the German army suffered its worst defeat at Stalingrad. General Friedrich Paulus, commanding the Sixth Army, was presented an ultimatum of surrender by the Red Army on January 8. Hitler refused to allow Paulus to make a strategic retreat and ordered a fight to the last man.

By February 2 the Sixth Army was surrounded and out of supplies. Two months before, it had numbered 285,000; Paulus surrendered its surviving 91,000, most of them wounded or suffering frostbite. They were marched eastward to captivity in Russia. Only 5,000 of these men would survive to return eventually to Germany. The loss at Stalingrad, magnified by Hitler's refusal to allow retreat of the encircled army, was one of the greatest catastrophes in military history. Paulus, from captivity in Russia, became one of the leaders of an organization called the National Committee of Free Germany. By way of radio broadcasts, a disillusioned Paulus voluntarily urged army officers to overthrow or assassinate Hitler.

By the beginning of 1943, it was clear to all of the army leadership that Germany had lost the war. The only person who seemed not to recognize this was Adolf Hitler. The resistance now realized that, even lacking promises from the Allied powers, Hitler's removal was necessary. The longer he remained in power, the more lives would be lost. Continuing the war made no sense. The resistance had to put its plans into action at the earliest opportunity.

––––––––

Assassination plans were developed by resistance circles at the eastern front. The conspirators met on March 7, 1943, at Army Group Center headquarters in Smolensk to discuss specific dates for the coup. This gathering was set by Canaris under the guise of a meeting of Wehrmacht intelligence officers. He arrived from Berlin accompanied by Oster and Dohnanyi. They discussed all aspects of the plan with Tresckow and Schlabrendorff: method of assassination, organization in Berlin and other strategic centers, the seizure of installations, and communications between Smolensk and Berlin. Canaris brought along a copy of the complete plans of Hitler's plane, showing where reinforced armor plating had been installed, anticipating the possibility that it might be possible to plant a bomb to explode during flight. The conspirators were ready to act.

With preparations complete in the major cities of the Third Reich, only one obstacle remained: the actual removal of Adolf Hitler. They decided to invite Hitler to Smolensk for a military inspection and meeting. Tresckow accepted responsibility for the actual assassination of Hitler but was not content with one plan. He wanted as many contingency plans as possible, it being likely that security would be too tight to actually plant a prepared bomb in Hitler's car or plane.

One of the only times it was certain that Hitler would remain in one place for any length of time was during a meal. So the Tresckow group came up with a plan to shoot him while he was taking lunch in the officer's mess at Army Group Center headquarters. Captain Walter Schmidt-Salzmann and Colonel Berndt von Kleist volunteered for the attempt, along with ten additional officers from No. III Battalion. The idea had to be given up, however, as Field Marshal Kluge refused to allow it. He said that the idea of killing a man while he was eating was unacceptable. The conspirators had to compromise with Kluge, who was allowing them to proceed with their plans even though he wavered back and forth in his own support. They had to abandon the plan for a frontal attack on Hitler and wait for the opportunity to plant their explosive charge.

Tresckow settled on the idea of planting a bomb. That was more certain than a bullet, where the chances for failure were high, and using a bomb would also mean none of the conspirators needed to be present at the critical moment. He arranged with fellow conspirator Colonel Rudolf von Gersdorff, intelligence officer for Army Group Center, to obtain explosives to be used in the bomb. The charge had to be small and quiet, but provide the greatest possible explosive power. Gersdorff checked the sabotage section supply depot maintained by the Abwehr. He explained that he was working on plans for anti-partisan action on the eastern front and needed to equip Russian volunteers working with German forces. Gersdorff decided to use a British-made plastic explosive called "Plastic C" that was held in the depot. Its only limitation was that it would not be effective at temperatures below freezing or above 104° F (40° C).

In an initial test, less than one pound of the explosive blew a turret off a Russian tank, hurling it more than 60 feet. Gersdorff gathered a supply of the explosive sufficient to construct a small bomb. Then, with Tresckow and Schlabrendorff, he conducted several tests and became familiar with the explosive's potential.

The group also had to decide which fuses and casings to use in their bomb. A silent fuse was essential, and many types of British-made fuses were available. They decided upon an acid-activated spring fuse. A spring was held back until the acid ate through a wire. The spring was then released and the firing pin driven into the detonator, resulting in a spark and an explosion. The various time delays were based on temperatures of 65° F (18° C). At the freezing point, the group's tests showed, time to ignition was doubled.

For a casing, they selected a mine uncovered by Abwehr agents, a British mine known as the "clam." It consisted of a black casing with four recesses with magnets, so that it would stick to anything made of metal. The device measured less than six inches by three inches, and a single clam could penetrate a one-inch steel plate or destroy a railroad tie.

They decided to place the device in Hitler's automobile. Four of the clams were prepared, filled with the plastic explosive previously tested. In an enclosed area such as an automobile, the concussion and explosion would surely be fatal. As a secondary plan, the conspirators would place the explosive in Hitler's airplane. The explosive power, if not fatal, would cause the plane to crash.

Hitler agreed to visit Army Group Center on March 13, 1943. Aware that it would be difficult to approach a well-guarded auto or plane with a bomb, Tresckow and Schlabrendorff decided to disguise the device. Tresckow noticed that when two of the clams were placed together, they were about the size and shape of a bottle of Cointreau, a brandy that comes in a square bottle. He and Schlabrendorff prepared four clams and arranged them in two sets, back to back, holding the double bomb together with tape. A fuse was inserted, and the entire package was wrapped and tied to look like two bottles of Cointreau.

On the morning of March 13, Schlabrendorff took the two-bomb package and locked it in his quarters. Before Hitler's plane landed, an escort of Me.109 fighter planes accompanied the three *Focke-Wulf* Condors of Hitler's entourage. It required three planes for the entourage of stenographers, guards, photographers, Hitler's personal cook, his physician, other staff members and his personal automobile that accompanied him.

Tresckow had arranged for a second plan, which was to shoot Hitler upon his arrival. It was to be put into action if the opportunity arose. Colonel Georg Boeselager, commander of Cavalry Regiment Center, had volunteered for this frontal assault. Several squads of volunteers were placed along the route it was assumed Hitler would take from the airstrip to Kluge's headquarters. Under this plan, which was called the Boeselager Plan, the squads were placed as guards and equipped with submachine guns. As Hitler's car arrived at the edge of the forest where headquarters was located, he would leave the car and travel the final section on foot. Hitler had arranged to use his own car, which was built for protection. He had also arranged for a motorcycle escort as well as a contingent of SS guards who were heavily armed. Security was so complete that any direct attack on Hitler would have resulted in a firefight, and it was uncertain whether Hitler would be hit. Making matters even more difficult, the route was changed at the last minute, so that most of Boeselager's volunteers were not in position.

A brief war conference was followed by lunch, after which Hitler prepared to leave for Wolfsschanze, his headquarters in Rastenburg, East Prussia. Schlabrendorff went to his quarters and brought out the bomb. On a signal from Tresckow, he pressed on the outside of the package where the fuse was located, breaking the vial of acid. He handed the package to Colonel Heinz Brandt, chief of staff to General Adolf Heusinger, chief of operations of the army and deputy chief of the General Staff. Brandt, unaware of what the package actually contained, had agreed to deliver the present to General Helmuth Stieff, a friend of Tresckow's who was stationed at Rastenburg.

Tresckow and Schlabrendorff had set up the bomb using a 30-minute fuse, which meant the plane should explode in midair about 200 miles from Smolensk, somewhere near the city of Minsk. As the plane taxied and departed, Tresckow placed a telephone call to Berlin and announced that the operation had begun.

Above Minsk, Hitler was engaged in discussion with chief of armed forces operational staff General Alfred Jodl during the return trip to Rastenburg. The acid ate away the wire, and the firing pin sprang forward into the detonator. The event went unnoticed. Hitler continued his discussion, and pilot Major Hans Bauer flew onward toward Rastenburg. The conspirators assumed that when the explosion occurred, one of the fighter escort pilots would radio a report of the crash. No such report was made.

Two hours after Hitler's departure, Tresckow received word that the entourage had landed without incident at Rastenburg. Schlabrendorff immediately called Berlin and delivered the urgent message that the plan was to be stopped. Tresckow phoned Wolfsschanze and spoke with Brandt. As casually as possible, Tresckow told him he had been given the wrong package. He asked Brandt to hold onto it until the following day, when Schlabrendorff would arrive and exchange packages. Brandt agreed. General Stieff was not involved with the resistance as of this time, or it would have been a simple matter to let Brandt deliver the package. Tresckow and Schlabrendorff had not told Stieff of their plans, however, and not knowing why the bomb had not exploded, both feared that it might still go off at any time.

The next morning Schlabrendorff flew to Hitler's headquarters and located Brandt. He retrieved the bomb and went at once to a railway station at Korschen, boarding a special military train for Berlin. He went to his reserved sleeping compartment, locked the door, and carefully unwrapped the bomb. As Schlabrendorff dismantled the device, the problem was revealed. Everything had worked as expected, but the detonator had not ignited. Either it was a dud, or the bomb had been placed in the unheated luggage compartment. The low temperature might have affected the operation of the device. Schlabrendorff packed away the defused bomb for later disposal. He traveled on to Berlin, where he gave a personal account of events to Oster and Dohnanyi.

A week after the failed Smolensk attempt, another opportunity arose. On March 21, 1943, at the *Zeughaus*, an armory and war museum in Berlin, Hitler was to deliver a speech at the annual ceremony to honor German soldiers killed in battle, Heldengedenktag (Heroes Memorial Day). The ceremony would conclude with an exhibit of weapons captured from the Red Army. Those weapons would be supplied by Army Group Center under the sponsorship of the Intelligence Service, of which Gersdorff was a member.

The Führer had always shown great interest in new weapons, so it was virtually certain that he would spend considerable time at the exhibit. Colonel Gersdorff was assigned for duty at the exhibit by General Tresckow. He was to answer any questions Hitler might ask about the weapons on display. Gersdorff told Tresckow he wanted to volunteer to assassinate Hitler at the Zeughaus. He would plant a bomb in the speaker's podium if possible. His backup plan would be a suicide mission. He had lost his wife in January 1942, and he felt that without her, he had little reason to value his own life. He would attend the exhibit with bombs in both pockets of his greatcoat. When Hitler approached, Gersdorff would activate the bombs, wrap his arms around Hitler, and kill them both.

Hitler attended the ceremony each year, accompanied by Himmler and other Nazi dignitaries. In past years, after an orchestra played a tribute, Hitler gave a speech and an honor guard moved several flags outside, where a wreath was placed on the memorial, followed by a parade. Then Hitler went to the exhibition hall to view the current year's collection of new weapons, a process which normally took 10 to 15 minutes.

Schlabrendorff gave Gersdorff the two British clams left over from the attempt the week before. Gersdorff wanted to plant the bombs in the speaker's podium but would need to know precisely when Hitler would speak. The exact time was not announced, and even if it were known, Hitler often changed his schedule at the last minute. Gersdorff pressed Hitler's aide, General Rudolf Schmundt, for the time of the Führer's speech, and Schmundt revealed that Hitler was scheduled to speak at 1 P.M. He appealed to Gersdorff not to give the information to anyone else, as it was considered highly secret. He also said that approximately a half hour was allotted for Hitler to review the captured weapons exhibit.

On the afternoon of the twentieth, Gersdorff inspected the building and grounds and discovered that hundreds of police, SS, and Gestapo armed guards patrolled the area. Planting a bomb would be difficult, and the risk was high that it would be discovered. In the open, the explosion would not have as much force as it would inside the exhibition hall. Upon seeing how tight security was at the armory, Gersdorff resolved to carry out his suicide plan instead. The shortest quiet fuse available had a 10-minute delay; the German variety was shorter but emitted a loud hiss, unacceptable for even a few seconds. As awkward a situation as it was to work with a 10-minute fuse, Gersdorff thought it would work. He placed one bomb in each pocket, determined to activate one when the right moment arrived. He reasoned that the explosion of the first bomb would also set off the second bomb, creating enough force to ensure Hitler's death.

As the ceremonies began on March 21, Gersdorff waited by the entrance to the exhibition. High-ranking Nazis attended, including Himmler, Göring, and Goebbels. More than 300 soldiers who had received wounds at the eastern front were there to hear Hitler's speech. The Führer spoke for approximately 12 minutes, an exceptionally short speech for Hitler. The highly optimistic theme was "the danger has now been averted." When the speech was done, Hitler made his way toward the exhibition hall. Gersdorff was ready.

Gersdorff would have preferred setting the bomb before Hitler approached, but it was impossible to know beforehand how long the speech was going to take. Hitler was notoriously unpredictable. As the Führer approached, Gersdorff and other officers at the entrance saluted. Gersdorff pressed the metal tubing of his bomb in the left pocket of his greatcoat, releasing the acid. The bomb would explode in 10 minutes.

Gersdorff knew he had to stay as close to Hitler as possible so that as the time approached, he would be close enough to make a grab for Hitler. The bomb's timing mechanism would be affected by temperature, so Gersdorff would have to estimate. In previous years, Hitler had taken some time to review the weapons displays. This year, however, he did not slow down as he entered the hall, but instead picked up his pace. Gersdorff struggled to keep up, trying to interest Hitler in one exhibit after another, to no avail. Within two minutes, Hitler had gotten through the entire hall. As he left the building, he was nearly at a run, and his entourage was barely able to keep up with him. Gersdorff went at once to a bathroom, where he defused the bomb.*

Resistance contacts in the Abwehr arranged for a shipment of explosives to Wolfsschanze, where they were stored for another attempt on Hitler's life. General Helmuth Stieff of the headquarters staff, who had been recruited to the resistance, received the explosives shipment. He hid the explosives under a watch tower in the headquarters area. Shortly after this was accomplished, the explosives blew up for reasons unknown. The incident caused great alarm among Hitler's security staff. Colonel Werner Schrader was

---

*Several other officers later tried to assassinate Hitler with suicide attacks. Captain Axel von dem Bussche-Streithorst, a highly decorated officer, volunteered to take his own life with a bombing attempt on Hitler after witnessing SS atrocities on the eastern front. He was scheduled to take part in a uniform demonstration in January 1944, which Hitler rescheduled endlessly. Bussche never had the opportunity to follow through with his plan. Then Lieutenant Ewald Heinrich von Kleist (son of political leader Ewald von Kleist-Schmenzin) volunteered to take Bussche's place, but again the opportunity did not present itself. Finally, Colonel Eberhard von Breitenbuch, aide to Army Group Center Commander Busch, attended a briefing conference at Berchtesgaden on March 11, 1944. Resistance leaders asked Breitenbuch to carry a bomb in his coat. Being unfamiliar with the explosive, Breitenbuch declined but volunteered to kill Hitler with his pistol. When he arrived at the conference, security guards prevented him from entering, explaining that on this occasion, no aides were allowed to attend.

ordered to conduct a thorough investigation. A member of the resistance, Schrader did not reach any conclusions about the origin of the explosives. General Stieff managed to obtain another supply of the same Plastic C explosive from Army Group Center. He stored it until it was used in a final attempt on Hitler the following July.

Stieff's primary contact in the resistance was Schlabrendorff, who served as go-between from his post in the eastern front to conspirators in Berlin and now with Stieff in Wolfsschanze. Schlabrendorff was able to travel more freely than most officers, ostensibly on Wehrmacht business. Army Group Center bore the brunt of the Russian counteroffensive, and emphasis was placed on this part of the front. Schlabrendorff had legitimate reasons for meeting with resistance leaders in the Reserve Army in Berlin and to travel to Wolfsschanze headquarters as well.

Because it was too dangerous to use the telephone system, the resistance counted on Schlabrendorff to convey messages between resistance centers. With General Stieff now working with the resistance, Schlabrendorff thought it might be possible to plant a bomb within the grounds of Wolfsschanze. He visited Hitler's headquarters twice during the summer of 1943, where he met with Colonel Dietrich von Bose, who was also involved with the resistance.

Bose briefed Schlabrendorff on Hitler's regular daily schedule. Hitler began the day at 10 A.M., eating breakfast in his room. He then reviewed excerpts of news from the foreign press prepared for him by Ribbentrop. At 11 A.M. Hitler met with his adjutant and reviewed administrative and personnel matters. At noon each day, military briefings began; they were usually held in the situation room, a reinforced concrete bunker. Chiefs of staff of the various services reported on the situation at the front. By 2 P.M., Hitler broke for lunch, after which he took a nap. He arose again between 6 P.M. and 7 P.M., eating dinner at 8. He then held audiences lasting into the night, retiring at 4 A.M. Because the Führer was constantly surrounded by security guards, Bose advised Schlabrendorff that there was no hope of shooting Hitler at close range. Schlabrendorff decided that the best method available was the use of explosives. It had a degree of certainty and could be accomplished without direct contact.

Schlabrendorff and Stieff devised an assassination plan using the explosives Stieff had stored. Since Hitler was keenly interested in weaponry and uniforms, they decided to modify Gersdorff's plan to detonate a bomb during a demonstration. An officer willing to sacrifice his own life would model a new type of uniform at one of Hitler's briefing sessions. The officer would activate a bomb hidden within the uniform, throw his arms around Hitler, and accomplish the deed. There was no shortage of volunteers for this mission. Several officers were prepared to sacrifice their lives, and a review of a new type of uniform was set up. The date was moved several times during the summer and fall of 1943, with Hitler canceling the review each time at the last minute.

Schlabrendorff and Tresckow also decided to arrange another assassination attempt at Army Group Center's headquarters. Several officers agreed to fire at Hitler from close range with their pistols in a collective attempt on his life, but Hitler declined to visit the headquarters. The chances for luring Hitler to Army Group Center faded as military conditions in the east continued to deteriorate.

For years the resistance had operated without detection by the Gestapo. That all changed in April 1943 with the arrests of several prominent members of the resistance. An exporter named Wilhelm Schmidhuber had been arrested in October 1942 while trying to smuggle foreign currency into Germany. He knew of the Abwehr connection to the resistance and gave damaging information to his Gestapo interrogators.

With this information, the Gestapo in April 1943 arrested Hans Dohnanyi and his brother-in-law, Dietrich Bonhoeffer. Since Dohnanyi was Oster's assistant in the Abwehr, suspicion was cast on Oster, who was placed under house arrest. In June, Oster was released to "leadership reserve" and was later banned from contact with the Abwehr. Oster and his associates, including General Beck, were under active surveillance by the Gestapo. Oster, who had been the organizational leader of the resistance, was forced to distance himself from his fellow resistance members for their own protection.

From their interrogations, the Gestapo learned of Bonhoeffer's meeting in Sweden with Dr. Bell and Josef Müller's contacts with the Vatican. Müller was arrested. Hans Gisevius, following an initial interrogation, escaped to Switzerland before the Gestapo was able to arrest him. The resistance was severely impeded by these developments.

A new leader of the resistance emerged in the summer of 1943 to fill the loss of Oster and Tresckow. Colonel Claus Schenk von Stauffenberg was appointed as Olbricht's chief of staff in the Reserve Army, on Tresckow's recommendation. This position gave him considerable influence and power in Berlin.

Stauffenberg was a cousin of Peter Yorck, a prominent member of the Kreisau Circle and Moltke's friend. An aristocrat from an old Swabian family, Stauffenberg was a gifted intellectual and an avid reader of history; he spoke English fluently and was recognized by his military superiors as an organizational genius. He had been transferred to General Staff positions in the Army High Command in the early years of the war, in recognition of his exceptional talent for strategic planning. Assigned to Field Marshal Erwin Rommel's Afrika Corps, he was severely injured in Tunis on April 7, 1942, losing his left eye, his right hand, and two fingers of his left hand. After he recovered, he was reassigned to the Wehrmacht General Staff.

Tresckow and Stauffenberg had been acquainted since the summer of 1941, when Stauffenberg told Tresckow of his disdain for the Nazis. He had told Tresckow of his efforts to convince General Manstein to refuse Hitler's ludicrous orders concerning the battle of Stalingrad. Stauffenberg had asked Manstein to join with the other two army group commanders to demand that Hitler give up his control of the military.

Olbricht arranged a meeting between Stauffenberg and prominent members of the resistance. Schlabrendorff wrote of that meeting that Stauffenberg "seemed to have been born for the part," and he described his qualities for the role of leader: "His calm courage, his circumspection, clarity of mind, tenacity and persistence, as well as his professional knowledge and ability made him a natural 'general manager' of the resistance."[4]

Tresckow advised Stauffenberg he would need an energetic and talented aide, and he recommended Major Ulrich von Oertzen, who had been a staff officer with Tresckow at Army Group Center. Oertzen was soon appointed to the position. Oertzen and Stauffenberg became an excellent team, breathing new life into the resistance. Both men understood planning and organization and worked over many months to formulate detailed plans addressing every contingency of a coup d'état.

As Stauffenberg worked out new detailed plans for a coup, Goerdeler pursued his own course of action. In March 1943, Goerdeler produced a lengthy paper entitled "Situation and Possibilities," regarding conditions in Germany and likely solutions to be planned for after the war. Goerdeler circulated copies to several members of the resistance. Confident that he could sway anyone, even Hitler, Goerdeler was barely dissuaded from meeting with the Führer to present his arguments. He was ready to ask Hitler to resign for the good of Germany. Historian Hans Rothfels observed that Carl Goerdeler was optimistic and self-assured to a fault: "Goerdeler all too readily indulged in idealistic simplifications and excessive optimism. Often enough his fellow conspirators had cause to complain of these characteristics. But nobody could or can deny that they were rooted in the optimism of a faith which took spiritual rather than material forces into account."[5]

Goerdeler also continued to make contact with the Allied governments. He tried to set up an appointment with the American minister in Stockholm, Herschel V. Johnson, but received no answer. Goerdeler did develop contact with the Wallenberg family, Swedish bankers who were well connected with the British government. Jakob Wallenberg urged that a coup d'état proceed even without assurances of cooperation from the Allies. He argued that without that first step, there would be no meaningful commitment from Britain. Goerdeler was unable to see beyond the injustices of the Versailles Treaty and continued to try to negotiate for favorable terms of peace with territorial concessions, even though the situation for Germany was growing ever more desperate. In late 1943, he even communicated through Jakob Wallenberg that in its bombing raids, the R.A.F. should be instructed to avoid bombing Berlin, Leipzig, and Stuttgart "as the oppositional movement has its centers there and the interruption of communications would make the putsch more difficult."[6]

Other members of the resistance continued to make contacts with Allied governments as well. Adam Trott met with Allen Dulles in Switzerland. Helmuth von Moltke also continued his unofficial diplomatic efforts through Professor Hans Wilbrandt, a personal friend, and Professor Alexander Rüstow, who had contacts in the U.S. Secret Service. Moltke, under the guise of a mission for the Abwehr, traveled to Istanbul to meet there with the two professors. Moltke proposed that a high-ranking member of the German general staff travel to Britain to enter an agreement with the Allies to grant free passage for Allied troops in the west, while German forces continued to fight at the eastern front. Moltke also proposed that the Allies withdraw demands for unconditional surrender if the leaders of the resistance would allow the occupation of Germany by the Allies. The Allies were uncomfortable, however, with the proposal to allow Germany to continue its fight with Russia, who was now their ally. Russia was pressuring the other Allied powers to open a second front. If the Russian government discovered that American or British agents were holding discussions with Germans, they would be alarmed and suspicious. With these problems in mind, the American representatives did not respond to Moltke's overture. As 1943 expired, so did Moltke's chances for further diplomatic efforts. Events of the following month would make any initiatives on his part impossible.

Chapter 12

THE FORCES GATHER

A wave of fear and horror swept through Germany when the fall of
Stalingrad became known. The police were ordered to arrest anyone heard
complaining about the conduct of the war, or about rising prices. Hitler
still had an iron grip on Germany. Even the mildest protests were regarded
as treason, and the prisons were full.

Robert Payne, *The Life and Death of Adolf Hitler*

The German defeat at Stalingrad destroyed more than the fighting power of the
Wehrmacht. It also ended the myth of German invincibility and destiny to rule the world.
The people, having believed in Hitler's military genius before that defeat, were now forced
to accept their own vulnerability. Hitler's deteriorating mental state and the irrational
demands he made of his generals gave rise to dissent within the military and, for the first
time, among the civilian population as well.

No one was more aware of Hitler's true mental condition than the head of the SS
and Gestapo, Heinrich Himmler, who had reason to believe that Hitler's term of office
would be limited, even if the war could be prolonged. He had obtained a copy of an
extremely confidential medical report on the Führer, diagnosing advanced syphilis. The
report claimed that it was only a matter of time before Hitler would succumb to paraly-
sis and insanity.[1]

Himmler was an ambitious opportunist. He had been trying to initiate secret negotiations with the Allies for more than two years, even contacting the same people being
visited by members of the resistance. Whereas the resistance had been trying to gain support for a replacement government, Himmler wanted to open negotiations with himself
as Germany's new leader.

A realist, Himmler saw that the war was lost. He also knew that his own future would
be in question if the Allied powers defeated Germany on the battlefield. Motivated by
self-preservation, Himmler became a defacto double agent for the resistance. As head of
the security and police agencies in Nazi Germany, it was his job to root out insurgency.
The Gestapo was known for its efficiency and investigative talents, yet Himmler himself
acted to shield those most effective in the resistance movement and even made contact
directly with resistance leaders.

Himmler's contacts with the Allies and with the resistance were facilitated through

Carl Langbehn, a lawyer whose daughter attended the same school as Himmler's daughter. Langbehn worked closely with Ulrich von Hassell in the diplomatic service. Langbehn was also friendly with Johannes Popitz, ex–Prussian minister of finance and an influential political member of the resistance. Langbehn arranged a meeting between Popitz and Himmler on August 26, 1943. Popitz told Himmler the only way to save Germany was through a negotiated peace, but that the Allies would never negotiate with Hitler. He appealed to Himmler's ego by pointing out that someone with power and prestige would have to take over the reins of government. Himmler, obviously interested in the ideas Popitz was expressing, set up a second meeting with him.

Himmler asked Langbehn to make inquiries discreetly during his travels to Switzerland. Langbehn was to determine whether the Allies would negotiate peace directly with Himmler in the event Hitler were removed from power. Langbehn, believing that the Allies would respond favorably to Himmler's interest, went at once to Switzerland to pursue contact, but the Gestapo intercepted a radio message from Langbehn concerning his contacts with the Allies. When he returned to Germany, he was placed under arrest. Himmler distanced himself from the matter and ended his contact with Popitz.

Himmler was in a sensitive position. He had to maintain the appearance that he was working to protect Hitler from danger while attempting to maintain some possibility for seizing power should Hitler's reign end suddenly. As a result, it became almost a corollary that the most innocuous and innocent people in the resistance movement were the most likely to be arrested during this period. The Gestapo was extremely active but, under Himmler's controlling hand, not effective in getting to the key people in the resistance.

Historians Roger Manvell and Heinrich Fraenkel describe the relationship between Himmler and the forces of the resistance:

> The attitude of Himmler and of the Gestapo to the resistance was not the simple one of discovery, arrest, interrogation, trial and punishment. The Gestapo were engaged in the endless process of gathering evidence of the network of conspiracy that they knew to exist, and they seemed quite prepared to risk the Führer's life by leaving at large the men and women they suspected; the theory was that they tended to provide more useful evidence while they were at liberty than they did under interrogation, which was in its way a tribute to their courage.[2]

Typical of Gestapo practice under Himmler during this period was what happened to members of the Solf Circle, a small group of aristocratic, educated Germans. They met at the home of Hanna Solf, widow of Dr. Wilhelm Solf, German ambassador to Tokyo before his death in 1936. At a meeting on September 10, 1943, which came to be known as the "Solf Tea Party," several people expressed their concern about the course of the war and Nazi repression. One of the attendees was a Gestapo agent posing as a Swiss citizen who used the name Dr. Paul Reckzeh. With the intelligence gathered from Reckzeh, Himmler learned much of the extent of the resistance and communication between various resistance groups.[3]

Through his Abwehr contacts, Helmuth von Moltke learned of Gestapo infiltration at the September 10 meeting and warned everyone who had attended. Moltke was promptly arrested by the Gestapo for having put out the warning. The Gestapo arrested all the attendees and others associated with them as "dangerous" enemies of the state.

With the threat of Communism in mind, the resistance worked tirelessly to convince the Western powers that a negotiated settlement was in everyone's interests. They hoped to work out a plan for a western cease-fire while fighting continued on the eastern front. Some resistance members even proposed that Germany join with the Allies so they could together fight the Russians.

Plans from the Beck-Goerdeler group included one brought to Dulles in Switzerland by Gisevius on behalf of the resistance.* Gisevius met with Dulles in April 1944 to advise the American government that Beck and Goerdeler were prepared to instigate a coup d'état in Germany. In his report to Washington, Dulles explained the conditions the resistance was requesting: "Such action would be contingent upon assurances from Britain and the United States that, once the Nazis had been overthrown, negotiations would then be carried out solely with the Western powers and under no circumstances with the U.S.S.R.... The group expressed its anxiety to keep central Europe from coming under Soviet domination."[4]

Dulles advised his superiors that he had told the conspirators the United States would never agree to any terms without first consulting its allies, including the Russians. Even so, Gisevius and Eduard Waetjen approached Dulles again the following month with an extended offer, indicating the growing desperation with which the resistance wanted assurances from the Allies. Dulles said in his report:

> The group was reported ready to help Allied units get into Germany if the Allies agreed that the *Wehrmacht* should continue to hold the eastern front. They proposed in detail: [1] three Allied airborne divisions should land in the Berlin region with the assistance of the local army commanders, [2] major amphibious landings should be undertaken at or near Bremen and Hamburg, [3] landings in France should follow, although Rommel cannot be counted on for cooperation, [4] reliable German units in the area of Munich would isolate Hitler and other high Nazis in Obersalzburg. The opposition group is reported to feel that Germany has lost the war and that the only chance of avoiding Communism in Germany is to facilitate occupation of as large a section of Europe as possible by American and British forces before collapse of the eastern front.[5]

Resistance efforts to deal with Britain and the United States to the exclusion of Russia did nothing to endear the Allies to the anti–Hitler cause. When Dulles sent his report

---

*Gisevius was by this time unable to travel freely. His association with Dohnanyi and Bonhoeffer the year before brought him to Gestapo attention. He managed to escape into Switzerland but maintained contact with the resistance through the German consulate general in Zurich, Dr. Eduard Waetjen.

to Washington, copies were given to the British and Soviet embassies. The British and American governments steadfastly refused to entertain any proposals coming from the German resistance, keeping their promise to Stalin that there would be no separate negotiations. Unconditional surrender was the only course the Allies left open.

Some members of the resistance, accepting the fact that the Western Allies would not negotiate, attempted to open talks with the Russian government. They believed that it would be possible to work with Russia and that some postwar political compromises were even possible. The resistance obviously contained some individuals who were willing to consider a Communist government in Germany. Others, like Hassell, tried to reason that a strong, united postwar Germany was in the interests of the Allies, including the Russians. Considering the course of the war and especially the crimes committed on the eastern front, Hassell's opinion was extremely unrealistic. He wrote: "We must bring off this one remaining achievement of making either the Russians or the Anglo-Americans understand that an intact Germany lies in their interests. It is true that a sound European center is in the interests of both East and West. I myself prefer the western game, but would also accept an understanding with Russia."[6]

The Western Allies refused to acknowledge officially that an opposition movement existed in Germany. The official position was that all of Germany was the enemy. The Goerdeler draft was embarrassing to other resistance leaders, who were more pragmatic and knew that the Western Allies were not willing to negotiate under any circumstances. In fact, Roosevelt had made his position quite clear all along: he considered all Germans to be the same as far as the war was concerned. When he was approached at the beginning of 1944 through channels with an offer of negotiation from the resistance, Roosevelt said he would never negotiate with "these East German Junkers." This view was largely responsible for the development of the demand for unconditional surrender. The United States and Britain adopted this hard line in order to placate Stalin and his fears that his allies might negotiate separately with Germany at his expense.

Ironically, Stalin himself was willing to entertain overtures from the German resistance, stating, "It would be absurd to equate the Hitler clique with the German people, with the German state."[7] He recognized that there was a strong Communist underground in Germany that persisted throughout the Hitler regime. The Communists never united with the military and civilian resistance, however, although contact had been established.

Most members of the resistance were opposed to including the Communists in a postwar government because they were too extreme to work in cooperation with other groups. Any form of contact, furthermore, was dangerous. It was widely known that Communist cells were infiltrated by the Gestapo. Even Goerdeler, who constantly sought consensus, specifically excluded the Communists. Only one prominent member of the resistance, Colonel Stauffenberg, believed that a coalition with the Russians would be possible. He spoke to fellow resistance members about joining with Russia in a massive move to liberate Germany from Hitler's oppression. But the older, politically more experienced members of the opposition advised that compromise with the Communists was impossible, and the matter was never pursued.

Adam Trott, who was free to travel in his position with the German Foreign Ministry, continued his contact with the Allies. Trott met with British government representatives in Sweden throughout 1943 and 1944. He also traveled to Switzerland in January and again in April 1944 to meet with Allen Dulles. He argued that the Allied demand for unconditional surrender was unrealistic and that it was preventing the resistance from seeing through its coup d'état. Dulles shared Trott's frustration and wrote: "Both Washington and London were fully advised beforehand of all the conspirators were attempting to do, but it sometimes seemed that those who determined policy in America and England were making the military tasks as difficult as possible by uniting all Germans to resist to the bitter end."[8]

On his second visit to Switzerland in April, Trott told Dulles:

> Constructive thoughts and plans for post-war reconstruction of Germany are coming steadily from the Russian side, while the democratic countries make no proposals whatever concerning the future of central Europe. Socialist leaders in Germany stress the necessity of filling this vacuum as quickly as possible. If it is allowed to continue, German labor leaders fear that, in spite of their military victory, the democracies will lose the peace and that the present dictatorship in central Europe will merely be exchanged for a new one.[9]

Trott arranged meetings in Stockholm at least three times in 1944, in March, June, and July, using the cover of his legitimate diplomatic credentials, although at this late phase in the war, such extensive and frequent international travel was unusual. On his June 21 visit to Sweden, Trott met with David McEwan, a British diplomat and member of the Secret Service. McEwan confided to Trott that the Allies were planning a stepped-up bombing program intended to destroy Germany's industrial centers. He added that the plan might be dropped if the resistance would help the Allies end the war more quickly. This information added to pressure on the resistance to put their coup plans into action. With an eye toward Germany's future, the destruction of the country's industrial areas would be a severe blow in the recovery years. McEwan asked Trott to prepare a written memorandum describing conditions in Germany and the extent of the resistance movement. Trott did so without including names of resistance leaders. He asked, however, that in the event of Hitler's removal, the Allies respond by negotiating peace terms with a new German government. He wrote that it was unreasonable to expect the resistance "to shoulder the burden and blame of Hitler's defeat unless they can hope to offer the people some improvement or advantage in their situation compared to what would follow Hitler's own defeat. Accepting unconditional surrender now, they would feel unable later on to counteract the mass slogan of having 'stabbed in the back' our fighting forces."[10]

Also in June, Trott was in Stockholm, where he spoke with John Scott, correspondent in Sweden for the American magazines *Time* and *Life*. He told Scott that by demanding unconditional surrender, the Allies were helping the Nazis and preventing a successful coup. Unless the demand were withdrawn, Trott explained, Germany was left with no choice but to continue fighting. That would inevitably lead to the Russian domination of Germany and central Europe. Trott expressed the belief that the only way to avoid these dangers would be by promising Germany it would be allowed to maintain a degree of sovereignty after Hitler's removal.

Otto John, another long-standing resistance member, was also active during this period, making Allied contacts in Madrid. John had been involved with the resistance since before the war. He was legal adviser to the German airline Lufthansa, a position that allowed him freedom to travel. He was in close contact with the Abwehr and, under cover of his position with the airline, had worked as an Abwehr agent in neutral countries.

Since November 1943, John had been in touch with Allied intelligence contacts in Madrid in an attempt to establish a link between the resistance and General Eisenhower's headquarters in Britain. Stauffenberg wanted to be able to set up a meeting with Eisenhower as soon as the coup was completed, believing that after Hitler's removal, the Allies would be willing to negotiate peace terms. John reported that Sir Ronald Campbell, British ambassador to Portugal, confided to him that the Allies might negotiate with a new government following a successful coup. John advised resistance leaders by February 1944 that he had succeeded in establishing a link to Eisenhower through the U.S. Embassy in Madrid.

While it is certain that John established a link through these diplomatic channels, it is doubtful that the Western Allies would have negotiated separately from their Russian ally. The United States and Britain were consistent in their refusals to entertain such initiatives and continued to insist on unconditional surrender. If the resistance had succeeded in removing Hitler, there is little doubt that this policy would have continued regardless of Germany's internal political situation. The resistance also appears to have assumed that General Eisenhower had the power and authority to negotiate a political settlement as a representative of the American and British governments, which was clearly not the case.

John remained in Madrid awaiting developments until July 1944. He returned to Germany in the week of July 20, only to quietly escape again a few days later. His contacts with Allied governments might have proven invaluable if the coup had succeeded and a new government had been established, if only to arrange the details of surrender. Beyond that, it is unlikely that the replacement German government would have been able to obtain any advantage through its diplomatic contacts.

John informed resistance leaders in February 1944 that the British and Americans were in full preparation for an invasion of Europe, which was to occur in June. A second front would hasten the end of the war and, most resistance members reasoned, enable the Western Allies to overrun as much of Europe as possible as an alternative to Russian domination. They also reasoned that if the invasion were launched and failed, the Western Allies would be more willing to negotiate. Stauffenberg thought the invasion had a 50-50 chance for success.

Stauffenberg knew that in order for the coup d'état to succeed, the resistance would also need to control communications throughout the Third Reich for as long as possible after Hitler's assassination. In the hours of confusion following the Führer's death, the plan could succeed or fail depending on which side controlled communications, both between strategic and command centers and between government centers and the people. The chances for success were enhanced by the cooperation of General Erich Fellgiebel, chief of the Wehrmacht-Nachrichten-Verbindungen, or WNV (Army Communications). Fellgiebel had total control and authority over army communications. The chief signals officer, Colonel Kurt Hahn, and his chief of staff WNV, General Fritz Thiele, were both members of the resistance as well.

With the majority of German troops fighting on the eastern front, Hitler abandoned his historically erratic movements and settled in at his isolated Wolfsschanze headquarters near Rastenburg, which was located in Prussia only 60 miles from the front lines. His static location provided the resistance with an opportunity to develop plans. Killing Hitler at his isolated headquarters would make it possible for Fellgiebel to delay communications from Nazi leaders to the outside for several hours. That would give the conspirators in Berlin and other locations more time to seize strategic sites and arrest SS, Gestapo, and Nazi political leaders.

At the isolated Wolfsschanze headquarters, several methods of communication were available: telephone, teleprinter, Morse and voice radio, and land or air courier. Radio communications were the most efficient and, short of outright force, could not be entirely shut down at Wolfsschanze. There were a large number of sets, including radios on Hitler's special trains sided there with cars designed and equipped especially for teleprinter and telephone communications. Additional radio sets were located at the nearby Rastenburg airfield, at the Reich Press Office within the headquarters grounds, in Martin Bormann's offices, and at the headquarters offices of Göring, Himmler, and Ribbentrop. A main headquarters radio station was also located at Heiligenlinde, about 12 miles from Rastenburg. Hitler's headquarters compound and its support services were geographically isolated but were not a small complex. The operations of the entire Third Reich, including communications with every major city and all front lines, operated from the area.

The plan to delay and minimize communications was ambitious, even with the centralization that Wolfsschanze provided. If the conspirators were to assassinate Hitler in other locations, such as Berchtesgaden or Berlin, they knew that radio, telephone, and teleprinter communications would be impossible to control. Even at Wolfsschanze, it would be unrealistic to expect to be able to shut down all communications from Hitler's headquarters for more than a few hours. The best the resistance could hope for was a period of confusion.

Fellgiebel intended to use that confusion to the advantage of the resistance. Although he did not have the authority to shut down communications completely — the top Nazis with offices at the headquarters, Himmler, Bormann, and Ribbentrop, had their own communications set-ups and operated independently of the Wehrmacht chain of command — Fellgiebel commanded four critical repeater stations at Rastenburg, Angerburg, Allenstein, and Lötzen, which passed on all headquarters communications. Fellgiebel would hold up long-distance radio traffic from Wolfsschanze, enabling the resistance to communicate while curtailing and delaying the Nazis from doing so. He even hoped to convince the SS that sending word of the assassination to other areas would have a detrimental effect. Silence from the SS would support the resistance claim that Valkyrie had been launched to counteract an attempted SS coup. By the time the SS, Gestapo, and Nazi leadership recovered and organized themselves, the resistance hoped to have firm control over military commands.

Working with his aides Hahn and Thiele, Fellgiebel had arranged postings of sympathetic officers in many Signals Service stations. Hahn had been recruiting officers to the cause since the spring of 1943 with considerable success.

Signals sections were in a state of constant readiness for a coup from October 1943 to July 1944. But as thoroughly as the Fellgiebel group planned, there was no contingency plan for a failed assassination attempt. If the attempt were made and failed, the resistance had no choice but to proceed. There was no mechanism or code to abort the coup d'état if, in fact, Hitler survived the attempt on his life. The signal that Fellgiebel was to give as part of the plan would lead to the Valkyrie order. Once events were set in motion, there could be no turning back.

Planning the coup d'état was complicated because of the vast area involved. The Third Reich covered the entire area of Western Europe, and Berlin, the capital, was only one important center. In the west, control of Paris was equally important. Conditions in and around Paris were relatively calm, whereas German cities were being bombed daily, and the war raged on the eastern front. More than in any other center, the resistance had strong and widespread support in Paris.

The military governor of France, General Karl-Heinrich von Stülpnagel, had been a member of the resistance since the original coup plans of 1938. He had early on pledged his support to Beck and Halder in their various plans for overthrowing the Nazi regime. In 1944, Stülpnagel was as strong a supporter of the resistance as ever and had a strong ally in the commandant of Paris, General Hans von Boineburg-Lengsfeld. Boineburg had been a ready supporter since 1942, when he had commanded the 23d Panzer Division and had offered to put them at the disposal of Field Marshal Witzleben. He had been working on coup preparations for nearly one year with Colonel Karl von Unger, his chief of staff in Paris. Boineburg and Unger worked out detailed plans for an uprising against the extensive SS, SD, and Gestapo strongholds in Paris.

On January 1, 1944, Field Marshal Erwin Rommel was appointed commander in chief of Army Group B, headquartered in La Roche-Guyon, France, and in April, General Hans Speidel was appointed his chief of staff. Speidel, a member of the resistance, did all he could to win over the field marshal to the cause. Rommel's support was considered most desirable because the field marshal was widely respected in the army and was a popular hero among the German civilian population as well. Now that the resistance was trying to recruit him, Rommel admitted that the war was lost. When the Allied invasion of France began on July 6, Rommel finally agreed to join with the conspiracy.

Rommel was considered essential to the resistance because his commander in the west was Field Marshal Kluge, who had previously commanded Army Group Center on the eastern front. The resistance knew from the year before, when Tresckow and Schlabrendorff tried to recruit Kluge, that he was weak-willed and vacillating. With Rommel part of the conspiracy, resistance leaders believed they could work around Kluge.

Even so, Field Marshal Kluge sent a message to General Beck in July through Colonel Cäsar von Hofacker.* In the message, Kluge promised he would fully support a coup,

---

Hofacker, the only Luftwaffe officer involved with the resistance, was Stauffenberg's cousin.

including the use of troops under his command, but only after Hitler was dead. That was the critical factor that would end up determining whether the coup could succeed. With Hitler's death, the resistance expected events to happen quickly. Rommel would enter peace negotiations with Generals Eisenhower and Montgomery. Stülpnagel would propose withdrawing German forces to the Siegfried Line while Allied troops occupied the west. The eastern front would be stabilized while negotiations went on, and a cease-fire would be arranged as quickly as possible. So went the resistance version of how events would unfold.

As Stauffenberg became acknowledged as the driving force of the resistance, friction grew between him and Carl Goerdeler. Their discord grew from three causes. First was their age difference. In 1944, Goerdeler was 60 and Stauffenberg was 36. Stauffenberg criticized Goerdeler's resistance leadership as a "revolution of grey-beards."

Their problems went far beyond age, however. A second cause for resentment between the two was the desire for leadership status in the resistance movement. Goerdeler had been working for many years against the Nazi regime, and he viewed Stauffenberg as a brash newcomer, impatient to create results and politically inexperienced. Stauffenberg thought of Goerdeler as an administrator, more interested in writing memos than in taking action. Stauffenberg was a determined individual with a dynamic personality, strikingly handsome and a natural leader. Both men could be accused of arrogance and ego, traits which affected their relationship with one another, but also made them the strong personalities demanded for leadership in the resistance.

The third source of conflict was political. Stauffenberg was determined never to let Germany return to the parliamentary deadlock of the past, whereas Goerdeler believed such a political system could be modified to work well. Goerdeler, because of his maturity and years of experience, believed that he should be designated to make major political decisions in the resistance, including the planning for Germany's political future. Stauffenberg, he thought, should restrict his activities only to military matters, including planning for the coup d'état. Goerdeler wrote months later while in prison that Stauffenberg "wanted to play politics. I had many a row with him but greatly esteemed him. He wanted to steer a dubious course with the left socialists and the communists and gave me a bad time with his overwhelming egotism."[11] The two would probably have come to open disagreement were it not for General Beck's diplomacy. Beck, in ill health and retired both from the military and an active day-to-day role in the resistance, became peacemaker between the growing factions led by Goerdeler and Stauffenberg. The disagreement between these two leaders intensified as the military situation became more desperate in 1944.

Stauffenberg began withholding information from Goerdeler concerning assassination plans, largely because Goerdeler's carelessness and indiscretion were known throughout resistance circles. Historians Roger Manvell and Heinrich Fraenkel described Goerdeler as

> the perpetual gadfly of the conspiracy, admired but often disliked. He was out of political sympathy with many of his fellows and regarded by most of

them as dangerously indiscreet at a time when members of the civilian wing
were only too well aware that the Gestapo was playing an uncertain game,
cat-and-mouse, with the men and women its agents knew to be engaged in
interesting forms of treasonable activity.[12]

Even at this late date, Goerdeler tried to make a case for convincing Hitler to resign;
failing that, he thought that arresting the Führer would be preferable to assassination.
Stauffenberg would not trust Goerdeler with sensitive information. Goerdeler retaliated
by making political decisions and not advising Stauffenberg. Although the two met frequently, they distrusted one another.

Even with their disagreements, Stauffenberg and Goerdeler worked together on
political plans. A temporary government would have to be devised, assuming a sudden
removal of Hitler and the Nazi regime. Over a period of nearly two years, resistance leaders devised a temporary leadership and cabinet. In most versions of the planned government, General Beck was to be appointed head of state, with Goerdeler as chancellor
and Leuschner as vice chancellor. Hassell was slated to serve as foreign minister and
Leber as minister of the interior.

Stauffenberg was involved in political planning and intended to play a role in the
new government. He was, however, primarily concerned with the assassination of Hitler
and organization of the coup d'état. As various plans were devised and abandoned,
Stauffenberg concluded that he would have to assassinate Hitler personally. He was in a
position to get close to Hitler to a greater degree than anyone else in the resistance, so
he had the best opportunity. As chief of staff of the Reserve Army, his duties included
frequent attendance at military conferences. He was required to report to Hitler on reserve
movements and availability of manpower for replacements at the front.

Stauffenberg's wounds restricted his dexterity. He practiced breaking the capsule
of a time-fuse with a pair of pliers, using the three fingers of his left hand. Because of his
war wounds, he believed he would never be suspected of planning an attempt on Hitler's
life. He had been prepared since December 1943 to carry a powerful explosive charge in
his briefcase to a meeting with Hitler. He had been scheduled to represent General
Olbricht at a meeting at Wolfsschanze that month, but the meeting had been canceled
by Hitler at the last minute.

The resistance no longer had the luxury of time. Three critical situations brought
pressure to bear to take action at the earliest opportunity. First, the war was being lost.
Every realistic person in the military and in the government realized this and, with the
rapid shrinking of the eastern front, it looked as though the Russian armies were likely
to reach Berlin before the Allies.

A second situation concerned the Nazi policy of genocide. Resistance leaders knew
that Hitler was giving top priority to the SS and the death camps, and the rate and
efficiency of mass murder was accelerating on a scale previously unimagined. Hitler even
ordered that rail deliveries of ammunition, clothing, and medical supplies were to be held
up when shipments of human cargo were scheduled at the same time. Those trains slated
for the concentration camps were of higher priority than those heading for the front.

Third, the resistance saw that the Gestapo was closing in on them. Various forms of widespread resistance had been underway for nearly six years without a breach in security. In June and July, 1944, however, that began to change. Resistance leaders knew that under the strain of Gestapo interrogation, someone would eventually break and begin listing names.

When the Allied invasion of France began on June 6, 1944, Hitler had taken a sleeping pill and left orders that he was not to be disturbed. Supported by more than 10,000 planes and 4,000 ships, a massive first wave of American, British, and Allied troops landed on a 60-mile front in Normandy. For several hours, frantic bulletins from the front for reinforcements were held up. No one wanted to disturb the Führer; crucial panzer divisions were held in reserve and not moved to the front. When informed of the invasion, Hitler believed it to be a diversion, insisting that the real attack would come elsewhere. He continued to insist this was true for several weeks.

Field Marshal Rommel had predicted that when the long-awaited invasion came, it would be decided on the beaches of France. If German troops were unable to stop the attack at its start, Rommel argued to Hitler, then they would never be able to repel the Allies later. Now, with Hitler's stubborn refusal to use his reserves properly, Rommel finally threw his support with the forces of the resistance.

The news from all fronts was grim. The Allies held complete command of the skies everywhere, and the German navy, its U-boats neutralized by Allied detection technology, was unable to mount any initiative. What strength Germany still had was defending the eastern front. By July 20, the Western Allies had clearly established themselves, and the plan of destroying the invasion on the beaches had clearly failed. In the east, the Red Army launched a massive offensive, smashing through the center where Hitler had concentrated most of his remaining strength. On July 4, Russian forces crossed Poland's eastern border and all German reserves were thrown into the defense of Germany's eastern frontiers, leaving none for the fight in France.

With the shattering defeats Germany suffered in June, the resistance could see that the end was near. The sooner they acted, the more lives would be saved. There was no longer a choice. As July 1944 approached, the resistance leaders knew that their time had come.

In the first week of June 1944, Stauffenberg was promoted to full colonel and given the position of chief of staff to General Fromm, commander of the Reserve Army.* The promotion was General Fromm's idea. With increased demands being made upon the Reserve Army, he needed Stauffenberg's organizational skills.

As soon as his promotion went through, Stauffenberg approached Fromm about joining with the resistance. Fromm agreed there was a need for a change in leadership. He did not offer to help, but neither did he express alarm at Stauffenberg's involvement.

*The Reserve Army was responsible for providing replacement units to the front and for behind-the-lines military organization, such as the formation of straggler battalions. Accordingly, Fromm was required to brief Hitler frequently. The level of reporting led to Stauffenberg's promotion. Fromm depended on him to prepare and present reports to the Führer.

Fromm, who detested Hitler's chief of staff, Field Marshal Wilhelm Keitel, told Stauffenberg, "For God's sake don't forget that fellow Keitel when you make your putsch."[13]

Stauffenberg's promotion gave the resistance a great advantage. The new position provided him regular access to Hitler because he would be called upon to take part in Hitler's military briefings. Stauffenberg took on the primary responsibility for Hitler's assassination. He also held onto the responsibility for organizing and managing the coup d'état itself, a nearly impossible dual role.

In this critical period, one leading member of the resistance, Julius Leber, became careless. In June 1944, he made contact with leading Communist functionaries and set up a meeting for June 22. The purpose was to try and bring the Communist political underground into some form of coalition with the rest of the political, military, and civilian forces. The meeting took place at the Berlin home of Dr. Rudolf Schmid, and Leber was accompanied by his friend Adolf Reichwein, who was a Social Democrat. They met with two Communist representatives, Franz Jacob and Anton Saefkow. A fifth attendee, Hermann Rambow, was unknown to Leber. He was a Gestapo infiltrator.

During the meeting, Leber described the resistance in broad terms without naming names. He stated that a number of military leaders were involved and that they were planning to overthrow the Nazi regime, but he declined to give a likely date for the action. The Communists were interested in hearing more. Leber promised to bring some of the resistance military leaders with him to a second meeting, and one was set up for July 4.

When Reichwein attended the July 4 meeting, he and all other attendees were arrested as they arrived. Leber had not attended, but he too was arrested the following day. In that first week of July, Communist and Social Democrat cells were broken up and mass arrests were made around Berlin as those arrested provided names to their Gestapo interrogators. Leber was questioned and tortured for four days and nights, but did not betray anyone else in the resistance. He signed a confession and was subsequently sentenced to death. Stauffenberg and other resistance leaders were understandably concerned, not only for the well-being of their friend, but for the safety of everyone connected with the resistance. Even though Leber had not betrayed them, he was in Gestapo custody.

This incident escalated the pressure on Stauffenberg to act quickly to implement a workable plan for destroying the Nazi regime. He and General Stieff met with General Fellgiebel and agreed to use a bomb in their assassination plan. Stieff gave Stauffenberg explosives which he had hidden away for this purpose.

The Normandy invasion begun by the Allies on June 6 was a huge success, and the advance of British and American armies was hampered only by the inability of supply lines to keep up with the rapidly expanding front. As the British and American armies expanded their hold, no one believed it would be possible for Germany to win the war. Resistance leaders anxiously hoped to succeed in their coup before the invading armies reached Berlin. Some resistance members thought that with the Allied landing, an attempted coup was no longer necessary; others disagreed. Shortly after the Allied landings at Normandy, Stauffenberg sent a message to Tresckow asking his opinion about how to proceed. Tresckow wrote back:

> The assassination must be attempted, at any cost. Even should that fail, the
> attempt to seize power in the capital must be undertaken. We must prove

to the world and to future generations that the men of the German resistance movement dared to take the decisive step and to hazard their lives upon it. Compared with this, nothing else matters.[14]

Stauffenberg also consulted with Beck, who said that although the "great moment" had been lost, it was their moral duty to proceed with the coup d'état.

With other resistance leaders confirming Stauffenberg's decision to proceed, he sought opportunities to put his plan into action. On June 7, the day after the Normandy invasion, Stauffenberg, in his new role as Fromm's chief of staff, attended his first conference with Hitler, at Berchtesgaden. He was again summoned to Berchtesgaden nearly a month later for a July 6 conference. This time Stauffenberg took with him a bomb similar to the one Tresckow and Schlabrendorff had planted on Hitler's plane the year before. At the two-hour conference, Hitler announced his decision to form 15 new "blocking divisions" to halt the Russian advance on the eastern front. Himmler was at the meeting along with several others. It is not certain whether Stauffenberg intended to set the bomb but lacked the opportunity or was merely becoming accustomed to having the device in his possession while meeting with Hitler.

Stauffenberg also carried the bomb to a third Berchtesgaden conference on July 11. He was accompanied by his trusted aide, Captain Friedrich Karl Klausing. Klausing's orders were to remain in front of the building and to keep the car ready for a fast departure to the airport. Stauffenberg planned to set the fuse and excuse himself from the meeting on some pretext, leaving his briefcase with the bomb in the conference room. When he arrived, he immediately telephoned Olbricht in Berlin and advised him that all was ready but reported that Himmler was not present. Olbricht advised Stauffenberg to wait until another opportunity because resistance leaders had agreed that Hitler and Himmler should be assassinated together, to prevent Himmler from seizing the opportunity to take over power for himself after Hitler's death.

The following day resistance leaders met and decided that missing an opportunity had been a mistake. They agreed that the bomb should be set whether Himmler was present or not. With some members under arrest and many others being watched by the Gestapo, resistance leaders knew they would have to act soon or risk the ever-increasing chances of being caught.

The sense that something was about to happen was strong. Hans Gisevius slipped back into Germany on July 12, not wanting to miss the great moment of the coup, even at the risk of arrest. That evening, during a meeting at the home of Theodore and Elizabeth Strünck, Gisevius and Stauffenberg met for the first time. The Strünck home had become a regular meeting place for resistance members. It was a basement apartment and had not been damaged in the regular Allied bombing raids.

At this meeting, Gisevius was at first apprehensive that his own status in the resistance would be usurped by Stauffenberg, the relative newcomer. Stauffenberg spoke at length on the political and military situation. Gisevius first thought Stauffenberg was a boorish aristocrat, and the two disagreed on many points. Gisevius saw, however, that

Colonel Stauffenberg (far left) and other officers greet the Führer at the Wolfsschanze headquarters on July 15, 1944 (Photo: National Archives).

Stauffenberg was "a man who would go to the limit." He admired his courage and recognized that he was accepting extraordinary responsibility.

On July 14, the Führer insisted on moving his operations headquarters back to Wolfsschanze, even though it was dangerously close to the eastern front. Stauffenberg was ordered to attend a conference at Wolfsschanze on July 15. He went by plane with his commander, General Fromm, and with his aide, Klausing, landing at Rastenburg Airport at 9:35 A.M.

As soon as Stauffenberg arrived, he telephoned Olbricht in Berlin and told him they had arrived safely. That was a coded signal for Olbricht to issue the Valkyrie order. Olbricht issued the order at 11 A.M., and troops were mobilized and started moving into Berlin. He then waited in his office in the War Ministry, waiting for further word from Stauffenberg. As soon as he heard, he intended to issue the proclamations and remaining Valkyrie orders announcing the state of emergency. Goerdeler and Gisevius waited for news at General Beck's home in Lichterfelde.

The briefing conference started at 1:10 P.M. Midway in the conference, Stauffenberg excused himself to make a telephone call and left the room. He again called Olbricht and told him that he was about to set the bomb in the conference room. Hitler cut the conference short, however, and it broke up at 1:40. When Stauffenberg returned, the conference had ended and Hitler was gone.

In Berlin, Olbricht and others were convinced that the coup d'état was on. Troops were on full alert and moving into the capital. Goerdeler had been told to be available to assume office as the new chancellor. Nebe, having been notified by the police president, Wolf von Helldorf, that the coup was on, notified criminal police officers and assigned them to arrest key Nazi officials, notably Goebbels, who was at his home in Berlin that day. As early as 11 A.M., after first hearing from Stauffenberg, Olbricht had also alerted the Guard Battalion at the army school on Berlin's outskirts.

At Wolfsschanze, Stauffenberg frantically called Olbricht and told him to cancel the alert. Troop movements had been underway since 11 A.M. Olbricht began telephoning mobilized units to tell them to stand down. He thanked the Guard Battalion commander for participating in the "training exercise."

In the confusion, Olbricht forgot to call Beck's home, so the three conspirators were still in the dark beyond 2 P.M., when Gisevius telephoned his friend Helldorf, president of the Berlin police. Helldorf said to Gisevius, "You know, of course, that the celebration did not take place." At 3 P.M., Olbricht and one of his staff officers, Major Fritz Harnack, and Stauffenberg's aide Major Oertzen went around by car to each of several units that had been placed on alert earlier in the day to ensure that they had canceled the alert as ordered.

When Fromm returned to Berlin, he was furious at Olbricht for issuing the Valkyrie order, warning him to never again issue orders in his name without authorization. Stauffenberg and Olbricht knew that they would not be able to cover any future false alarms. The organizers in the War Ministry discovered from their false alarm that some aspects of their planning were flawed and resolved to do better at the next opportunity. Next time, once the order was issued, there would be no turning back.

Chapter 13

$\mathcal{V}$ALKYRIE

The fact that someone has full legal authority to act in the way he does gives no answer to the question whether the law gives him power to act arbitrarily or whether the law prescribes unequivocally how he has to act. It may well be that Hitler has obtained his unlimited power in a strictly constitutional manner and that whatever he does is therefore legal in the juridical sense. But who would suggest for that reason that the Rule of Law still prevails in Germany?

F. A. Hayek, "The Rule of Law," in *Private Life and Public Order*

Stauffenberg was ordered to attend a July 20, 1944, conference at Wolfsschanze. In preparation, he held a two-hour meeting on July 19 at Reserve Army headquarters in Berlin to set up plans for a coup d'état the following day. Over 30 officers of the military resistance attended, and Field Marshal Erwin von Witzleben and General Erich Hoepner were contacted and asked to travel to Berlin on the twentieth to be available for the coup.

Commanders of sympathetic battalions and training schools were placed on alert. Plans called for Witzleben to become commander in chief of the armed forces and Hoepner to be the new minister of war and commander of the Reserve Army. Dozens of other key people were also put on the ready to assume strategic positions. Critical to plans in the capital were General Paul von Hase, commandant of Berlin, and the president of the Berlin Police, Wolf von Helldorf. The resistance was depending on them to maintain control during first few hours of the coup d'état.*

Stauffenberg ordered his driver, Corporal Karl Schweizer, to pick up a briefcase at the offices of Colonel Fritz von der Lancken and deliver it to Stauffenberg's apartment. The briefcase contained two packages tied with string, each one a bomb. The bombs were made from the British-manufactured plastic explosive favored by the resistance and each weighed about two pounds with a silent fuse.

The British chemical time fuse worked quietly, unlike the German variety, which made a hissing sound. A wire held back a striker spring. When a vial of acid was broken,

---

Overlooked in the detailed planning was the need to contact some important commanders. General Otto Hitzfeld and his aide, Colonel Wolfgang Müller, were both members of the resistance. They would be away from their commands the following day, however, having not been told that it was the day of the coup. Their Döbernitz Infantry School was slated to take over the Broadcast House, where the public radio aired.

the acid began eating through the wire. The thickness of the wire determined how long this process would take. When the wire broke, the striker spring was released, thrusting the detonator into the explosive and creating a spark, leading to an explosion.

Stauffenberg selected the thinnest wire available, so that the acid would eat through it in ten minutes. Stauffenberg had limited dexterity. His right hand had been lost when he was injured, and he had only three fingers on his left hand. He had practiced cutting the acid capsule with a small pair of pliers he kept in his briefcase. Stauffenberg carefully wrapped one bomb in a shirt and placed it in his briefcase with the papers needed for the meeting at Wolfsschanze. The second, backup bomb was placed in another briefcase, to be carried by Stauffenberg's aide, Lieutenant Werner von Haeften.

On the morning of July 20, 1944, Stauffenberg arose early and with his aide Haeften arrived at Rangsdorf airport at 6 A.M. for a 7 A.M. flight to the town of Rastenburg, 350 miles to the northeast. A car was waiting to take them the nine miles to Wolfsschanze when the flight arrived at 10:15, and Stauffenberg ordered the pilot to be ready for departure in the early afternoon.

10:30 A.M. Wolfsschanze. The headquarters complex was spread out over 625 acres deep in the Prussian forest, surrounded by arrays of electrified fencing, minefields, observation towers, searchlights, ditches, and barbed wire. The entire area was patrolled by guards with dogs, and the constant construction going on in the area required the presence of dozens of conscripted workers. The buildings of Wolfsschanze were camouflaged in defense against air raids. The headquarters area had its own railway station, where Hitler's special security trains were available to him at all times. Keitel, Göring, Jodl, and Hitler's personal physician, Dr. Theo Morell, all had their own headquarters offices within the compound.

Hitler's bunker and the conference room, called the *Lagebaracke* (conference barracks), were housed within a special area within the inner compound that was surrounded by its own electrified high-wire defenses and sentries. General Alfred Jodl, chief of the armed forces operational staff whose offices were at Wolfsschanze, described the headquarters as "a cross between a monastery and a concentration camp."[1]

Stauffenberg and Haeften had to clear a checkpoint at the airport and two additional checkpoints in the outer security zones, each manned by armed SS guards who demanded special passes valid for that day's meeting only. Although security measures were exhaustive, there was no procedure to check briefcases brought into the inner compound. Stauffenberg and Haeften went through all checkpoints without challenge.

11:00 A.M. The War Ministry, Berlin. The headquarters of the War Ministry was to be the command center of the coup. General Olbricht and his fellow conspirators waited there on the morning of July 20. They established a direct link between the War Ministry and army headquarters at Zossen, 20 miles to the south, where Quartermaster General Eduard Wagner, was awaiting word. He was ready to order his troops to move at a moment's notice to seize vital installations.

Olbricht was set to call General Beck and Field Marshal Witzleben as soon as he heard from Wolfsschanze that the Valkyrie (Walküre) plan had been launched. They were to come to the War Ministry as soon as they were informed. The leaders hoped that General Fromm, Olbricht's superior, would go along with the coup once it was launched. If he did not, Olbricht would place him under arrest. In either event, orders had been drafted

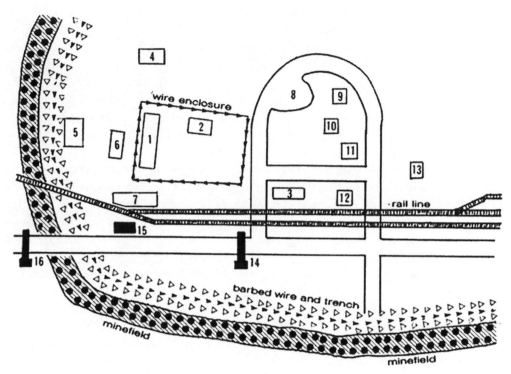

Wolfsschanze, July 20, 1944

[1] conference room   [2] Hitler's quarters   [3] kitchen   [4] air-raid shelter   [5] visitor quarters   [6] sentry post   [7] railroad station   [8] parking area   [9] Dr. Morell's quarters   [10] Fellgiebel's office   [11] Keitel's office   [12] Jodl's office   [13] Göring's office   [14] checkpoint 1   [15] sentry station   [16] checkpoint 2

for Reserve Army troop movements, under Fromm's name. They would be issued whether Fromm cooperated or not.

11:00 A.M. to 12:30 P.M. Wolfsschanze. It was turning into an exceptionally hot day. Stauffenberg ate breakfast outdoors with headquarters commandant Captain Leonhard von Möllendorff. Hitler wanted to form new divisions to prevent the Russian advance through Poland, and a meeting to work out details of the new divisions was set between Stauffenberg, General Walther Buhle, and Hitler's chief of staff, Field Marshal Wilhelm Keitel. The new *Volksgrenadier* divisions were to be manned by older members of the Reserve Army.

Stauffenberg's young aide Haeften waited nervously in a sitting room near the meeting room at Keitel's quarters. He had the briefcase containing the second bomb with him. He knew that before going into the conference with Hitler, Stauffenberg would need his help in preparing the bomb.

Keitel's orderly, Sergeant-Major Werner Vogel, noticed that Haeften passed much of the time pacing nervously. Stauffenberg's meeting with Buhle and Keitel went on longer than expected. At about 12:15, Hitler's valet, Heinz Linge, telephoned Keitel to inform him that the Führer had moved the main conference up from 1:00 P.M. to 12:30 because Mussolini was scheduled to meet with Hitler at 2:30 and Hitler wanted to ensure that the military briefing would be completed before that time. Keitel urged Stauffenberg to wind up his presentation because of the schedule change.

Keitel stated that the meeting would take place in the conference hut. Stauffenberg had hoped that the meeting would be in the underground concrete bunker, where the concussion from his bomb would ensure Hitler's death. With the meeting scheduled for the less confined conference hut, Stauffenberg was not certain that the single bomb would be enough. Much of the energy from the explosion would escape through the room's wood frame and windows. He realized at once that it would be better to use both bombs to be certain of Hitler's death.

For Stauffenberg, the immediate problem became gaining a moment of privacy to break the capsule of acid on the bomb. As the group of officers was about to depart for the conference, Stauffenberg told Keitel he needed to freshen up and change his shirt and asked where he might have a moment of privacy. Keitel had his adjutant, Major Ernst John von Freyend, escort Stauffenberg, now joined by his aide Haeften, to an anteroom. Keitel urged Stauffenberg to hurry, as they were already late.

Stauffenberg opened his briefcase and used the small pair of pliers to break the acid capsule. The time was 12:32. Before they could set the second bomb, Keitel's orderly, Vogel, appeared at the door to report that Keitel was insisting Colonel Stauffenberg come at once. He waited by the door for Stauffenberg to finish and proceed to the conference. Stauffenberg closed his briefcase and went from the room. There would now be no opportunity to add the second bomb.

The acid began eating through the thin wire of the bomb. As Stauffenberg joined the other officers and began the three-minute walk to the conference building, John von Freyend offered to carry his briefcase, but Stauffenberg declined. As they neared the building, however, Stauffenberg allowed John von Freyend to take the briefcase. He asked him, "Could you please put me as near as possible to the Führer so that I catch everything I need for my briefing afterwards."[2]

John von Freyend, aware that Stauffenberg had suffered a partial hearing loss along with his other wounds, agreed. The bomb was set to explode in seven minutes.

12:30 P.M. Paris. In the French capital, 550 miles to the west of Berlin, General Karl-Heinrich von Stülpnagel, military governor of France, was the senior officer involved with the resistance. With Field Marshal Rommel out of commission after suffering his wounds, Stülpnagel was in a position similar to Olbricht's. His commander was Field Marshal Kluge, who the year before had commanded Army Group Center on the eastern front. When Tresckow had tried to organize an assassination plot in 1943, Kluge had refused to take part but did not stand in the way either. His position was the same now. He would not endorse the activities of the resistance, although he did not prevent or report its actions.

Stülpnagel had established a command post for himself for the coup at Rommel's former headquarters offices, located at La Roche-Guyon. This day he took lunch with fellow officers at the Hotel Raphael as he did every day. To his lunch companions, the usually cheerful and talkative Stülpnagel seemed quiet and nervous.

12:30 P.M. Wolfsschanze. The meeting began on time. As he entered the outer rooms, Stauffenberg stopped at the switchboard and told the operator, Sergeant-Major Arthur Adam, that he was expecting an urgent call from Berlin, with updated information he would need for his presentation to Hitler. He asked the operator to let him know when the call came in. All of the officers placed their caps and belts on a rack in the outer office.

It was 12:35 when Stauffenberg entered the room. John von Freyend placed the brief-case beneath the map table, leaning against the inside of the large table supports. The room measured 15 by 32 feet. On this stifling hot day, all of the windows were wide open, so that much of the explosion's force could escape to the outside. Hitler was seated on a stool at the center of the room, his back to the door, at a huge oak table 18 feet long and 5 feet wide. The table was covered with situation maps and surrounded by 23 men from all branches of the armed services.

General Adolf Heusinger, chief of operations, was making the first presentation, a dismal report concerning the deterioration at Lembeck on the eastern front. Fresh replace-ments were needed urgently, Heusinger was saying. Keitel interrupted to announce Stauffenberg's arrival. Hitler nodded at Stauffenberg and shook hands, and the presen-tation continued.

At approximately 12:37, two minutes after his arrival, Stauffenberg whispered to Keitel that he needed to make an important telephone call before starting his presenta-tion. Keitel nodded. Stauffenberg moved his briefcase closer to Hitler beneath the large table, near Colonel Heinz Brandt, Heusinger's chief of staff.*

Stauffenberg slipped from the conference room while General Heusinger contin-ued his presentation. He quickly made his way to the signals bunker about 200 yards to the east to wait out the remaining time. He left his belt and cap in the conference build-ing's outer room. Haeften and Fellgiebel were standing outside Fellgiebel's building, and in the parking area nearby, their driver, Lieutenant Erich Kretz, waited with the car.

In the conference hut, Heusinger continued with his presentation. When Stauf-fenberg left, Colonel Brandt moved closer to the table so that he could see the maps. His foot nudged Stauffenberg's briefcase, so he moved it to the far side of the large table sup-port. The heavy support shielded Hitler from the briefcase and its bomb, now about six feet away. At about the same time, Keitel became irritated that Stauffenberg had not returned because he was scheduled to speak next. Keitel sent out General Walther Buhle to find him. Buhle inquired with the operator in the outer office, who told him that Stauffenberg had left the building. Buhle returned and conveyed this information to Kei-tel who, confused at Stauffenberg's ill-timed disappearance, was not sure what to say or do.

It was now 12:42. Heusinger spoke on: "The situation in the East Prussian sector is increasingly critical. The Russians are drawing closer. A major Russian striking force to the west of the Duna is wheeling around toward the north. If we don't withdraw our army groups around Lake Peipus, a catastrophe —"[3]

Hitler was leaning on his elbow staring at the map as the explosion ripped through the room. The powerful blast destroyed the ceiling and created a large hole in the floor. One end of the room disintegrated completely. Everyone present was thrown from their feet, some hurled through the open windows to the outside. At first, those outside the conference building thought a mortar shell had scored a direct hit. Those who did not

---

*Brandt was the officer on Hitler's plane who had transported Tresckow's bomb disguised as Cointreau the year before in Smolensk.

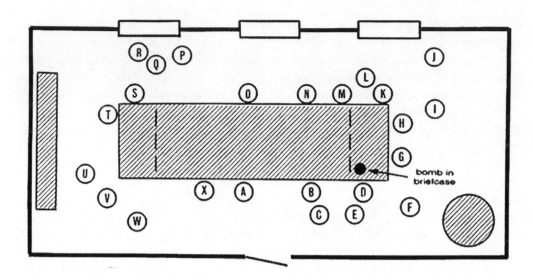

bomb in
briefcase

Conference Room, July 20, 1944

^A Hitler   ^B General Adolf Heusinger, chief of operations of the army and deputy chief of the General Staff   ^C General Günther Korten, chief of General Staff of the Luftwaffe   ^D Colonel Heinz Brandt, Heusinger's chief of staff   ^E General Karl Bodenschatz, Göring's Luftwaffe liaison officer ^F Colonel Heinz Waizenegger, adjutant to Keitel   ^G General Rudolf Schmundt, chief adjutant, armed forces   ^H Colonel Heinrich Borgmann, general staff adjutant to Hitler   ^I General Walther Buhle, chief of Army Staff at Armed Forces High Command   ^J Rear Admiral Karl von Puttkamer, naval adjutant to Hitler   ^K Heinrich Berger, stenographer   ^L Captain (Navy) Heinz Assman, admiralty staff officer   ^M Major Ernst John von Freyend, adjutant to Keitel   ^N General Walther Scherff, special commissioner appointed by Hitler as writer of military history   ^O Rear Admiral Hans-Erich Voss, representative for commander in chief of the navy.   ^P SS Captain Otto Günsche, adjutant to Hitler ^Q Colonel Nicolaus von Below, Luftwaffe adjutant to Hitler   ^R Hermann Fegelein, SS group leader representing the Waffen SS   ^S Heinz Buchhotz, stenographer   ^T Major Herbert Büchs, adjutant to Jodl   ^U Dr. Franz von Sonnleithner, ministerial counselor, Foreign Office representative in headquarters   ^V General Walter Warlimont, deputy chief, Armed Forces Operational Staff   ^W General Alfred Jodl, chief of Armed Forces Operational Staff   ^X Field Marshal Wilhelm Keitel, chief of the Armed Forces High Command

see the blast thought an animal had stepped on a mine surrounding the compound, a not uncommon occurrence. Some of the security guards believed one of the conscripted workers had planted the bomb.

Hitler was hurled to the left and to the floor. His eardrums were pierced by the concussion, a hand was bruised, and one elbow was bleeding. His legs were pocked with wood splinters. He was not seriously injured, however, and was able to continue with his day's schedule. The fact of his survival seemed to place Hitler in exceptionally good spirits. For the next several hours, he repeatedly told those around him, "I am invulnerable, I am immortal!"

Not everyone in the room was so lucky. Colonel Brandt, who had moved Stauffenberg's briefcase to the right side of the table support, lost a leg and an eye and was sent to Rastenburg hospital, where he died two days later. His action in moving the briefcase saved Hitler but cost him his own life. Also badly injured was Luftwaffe General

Stauffenberg's bomb demolished the conference room. Four officers were killed in the blast. Hitler, however, escaped without serious injury (Photo: National Archives).

Korten, who was impaled in the midsection by a large shaft of wood splintered from the table. He too died later from this wound. The stenographer Heinrich Berger lost both legs and died the same day. And General Schmundt, Hitler's adjutant, died three months later as the result of infections in thigh wounds received in the blast.

As the explosion occurred, Stauffenberg, Haeften, and Fellgiebel all jumped, startled at the strength of the blast. Recovering at once, Stauffenberg and Haeften walked briskly to their car and ordered the driver to proceed to the airport. Kretz told Stauffenberg he had forgotten his cap and belt, but Stauffenberg snapped that it didn't matter and ordered him to drive as quickly as possible. As the car departed, men were running toward the conference building, helping the wounded and shouting for medical assistance for the more seriously wounded.

To Stauffenberg, it appeared that no one could have survived the tremendous blast. As Stauffenberg departed, Fellgiebel knew he had an important task to perform: calling Berlin to advise them that the bomb had gone off, a message that was to set the coup d'état in motion. At that moment, however, Fellgiebel was shocked to see Hitler, dazed but on his feet, obviously not seriously injured, staggering from the conference building on Keitel's arm.

In their planning, the conspirators had not worked out a code for the situation they now faced. The bomb had exploded, but Hitler was alive. Stauffenberg had left quickly, obviously certain that Hitler had been killed in the blast, and Fellgiebel had no way of letting him know the bomb had not done its job. Resistance leaders had not discussed what course of action to take after the explosion in the event of Hitler's survival: to proceed with the plan or to abandon it altogether.

Stauffenberg's car approached the first checkpoint. Having heard the blast, the sentries should have closed down at once and allowed no one through. Stauffenberg asserted that he was on urgent business and had to leave on Hitler's personal orders. The bluff worked. The gate was lifted, and the car proceeded. The sentry noted in his log, "12:44. Col. Stauffenberg passed through."

At the second checkpoint, the gate had been closed and obstacles positioned in the road. The guards refused to let the car through, so Stauffenberg entered the guardhouse and telephoned the office of Captain Leonhard von Möllendorff, headquarters commandant, with whom he had eaten breakfast that morning. He told Möllendorff, "I'm in a hurry. General Fromm is waiting for me at the airfield." The commandant spoke with the guards and ordered them to let the car pass. The gate was lifted and the road obstacles removed.

On the trip to the airport, the driver, Lieutenant Erich Kretz watched in his rear view mirror as Haeften dismantled the second bomb and threw it out the window into the woods as the car sped toward Rastenburg airport. The guards at the airport checkpoint, not yet notified of the explosion, did not challenge the car. Stauffenberg and Haeften were in the air by 1:15.

As Stauffenberg's plane took off for Berlin, Hitler emerged from his bunker with a clean uniform, his wounds dressed. Even though several people in the room had been mortally wounded, Hitler was in exceptionally good spirits. One of his aides later recalled that Hitler "had the lively, almost cheerful expression of a man who had been expecting something terrible to happen, and now luckily survived it."[4]

1:15 P.M. War Ministry, Berlin. General Fritz Thiele, Fellgiebel's chief of staff, was in Berlin awaiting word. He and the other conspirators at the War Ministry had been told that the conference with Hitler was scheduled for 1 P.M., and they were unaware that the time had been moved to 12:30. Thiele received a call from Fellgiebel at 1:15.*[5]

The message was confusing and cryptic. He told Thiele, "Something fearful has happened. The Führer is still alive." Fellgiebel was unable to provide specifics. Any telephone line could be tapped by the Gestapo, so words had to be picked carefully. As a consequence, he could say little else. Fellgiebel hoped to convey the point that Stauffenberg had placed the bomb, but it had failed to kill Hitler. Nonetheless, he assumed that the conspirators in Berlin would immediately launch the Valkyrie orders and begin seizing power. The plan had to go forward, or everyone in the resistance would be in danger.

Thiele reported the message to Olbricht at once. Both were confused. What was the "fearful" thing that had occurred? Had the attempt never been made? Had Stauffenberg been discovered and arrested? Had Hitler survived the blast? There was no clear indication of whether Fellgiebel's signal was to proceed or to do nothing.

---

*The timing of the phone call is agreed upon by Fitzgibbons in The Shirt of Nessus, Hoffmann in The History of the German Resistance, and Prittie in Germans Against Hitler. It is disputed, however, by Manvell and Fraenkel in The Men Who Tried to Kill Hitler, in which Fellgiebel's call is reported to have gone through at about 3:30 P.M.

Olbricht's agreed-upon task was to launch Valkyrie as soon as word came from Fellgiebel. Olbricht was to notify district commanders that the SS was attempting to seize power and order them to arrest all SS, Gestapo, and Nazi leaders. He was also to contact resistance leaders in Paris, Vienna, and other major centers and order local troops to seize communications centers and deploy reliable troops. He was also to notify Beck and Witzleben to come to the War Ministry to assume their respective government and military roles.

Olbricht knew that Stauffenberg would rush back to Berlin as soon as his task at Wolfsschanze was complete. Uncertain of the meaning in Fellgiebel's message, Olbricht decided to wait for Stauffenberg to return, which meant a delay of several hours.

1:15 P.M. Paris. Berlin and Paris were the two most strategic centers. Once Valkyrie was launched, a coded telephone message from army headquarters in Zossen near Berlin would be placed to resistance members in Paris. Colonel Eberhard Finckh, quartermaster-general on Field Marshal Kluge's staff, awaited the call knowing that when it arrived, simultaneous Valkyrie actions were to begin across the Third Reich.

Finckh received a call in the late morning. An unidentified caller said "exercise" and then hung up. That was the first of two signals, intended to alert Paris contacts that the plan was underway. Finckh assumed that the same coded telephone call had been made to the most important resistance leader in France, General Stülpnagel. No such notification had been given from Berlin, however. Stülpnagel heard nothing.

1:15 P.M. Wolfsschanze. General Fellgiebel's task was to do all he could to block communications. He contacted his accomplices at the major radio receiving stations, as planned, and told them to hold up communications traffic from Wolfsschanze as long as possible. He was aided in his task by none other than Hitler himself, whose first order after recovering from the explosion was that communications at Wolfsschanze were to be shut down. Of the attempt on his life, Hitler said, "No one must know of it."[6]

Colonel Nicolaus von Below, Hitler's air force adjutant, carried out the order, having all signals personnel unplug their terminals and move their chairs back one yard from the equipment. This ensured that the blackout order was obeyed without exception. Even communications in progress were cut without explanation.

Hitler and his security teams first suspected the bomb had been planted by one of the dozens of conscripted workers in the area. Hitler ordered a thorough search of all buildings in the inner compound, fearing that more bombs might be found.

Before imposing the blackout, Hitler authorized telephone calls to the major Nazi leaders. Hitler wanted a thorough investigation to begin at once, and he wanted Himmler to head it up. Himmler was working at his headquarters near Lake Maursee about 15 miles away. A signals officer, Colonel Ludolf Sander, telephoned Himmler and told him he was wanted at Wolfsschanze at once but provided him with no explanation. Sander also called Göring's headquarters and demanded to speak with Göring in person. After an argument, Göring came on the line, and Sander asked him to come to Wolfsschanze immediately. Sander then reached Goebbels at his residence in Berlin and advised him that an attempt had been made on Hitler's life. Goebbels was shaken by the news.

Himmler arrived at Wolfsschanze within a half hour and took charge of the investigation. He suspended the communications blackout while he called Berlin headquarters to order a team of his top criminal investigators to Wolfsschanze at once by air. As soon as that order was given, communications were again sealed off.

After 1:30 P.M., senior officers were allowed to use the telephones to call out, although no incoming calls were accepted. Fellgiebel took advantage of the relaxed rules to telephone Colonel Hahn in nearby Mauerwald Camp and repeat the message he had given earlier to Thiele. When Hahn asked Fellgiebel what to do, Fellgiebel told him to block everything. As a result, incoming communications were held up effectively for several hours. Hahn immediately called Thiele in Berlin and gave the coded message, "The signals equipment has left." This let Thiele know that Valkyrie was to proceed with all speed.

Before 2 P.M., Hitler summoned signal officer Sander and asked him how soon arrangements could be made for a broadcast. Hitler wanted to announce the attempt and tell the German people that he had survived. Sander replied that he could make all necessary preparations by 6 P.M. Although all of the necessary equipment was on hand, it would take some time to arrange it so that Hitler's broadcast would be simultaneous over all stations in the Reich.

2:00 P.M. War Ministry, Berlin. Olbricht's chief of staff, Colonel Albrecht Mertz von Quirnheim, was eager to get things started. He had pressured Olbricht to issue orders, but Olbricht was uncertain and confused by the Fellgiebel message. Thiele and Olbricht went to lunch and would not return to the War Ministry until 3:30. At 2 P.M., Mertz acted on his own, issuing some preliminary orders without Olbricht's knowledge.

Goebbels was also confused. He had no concrete information concerning Hitler's condition. The phone call he had received earlier provided only the news that an attempt had been made on Hitler. Now, an hour later, Goebbels had no way of knowing whether Hitler was alive or dead. He tried several times to reach Wolfsschanze by telephone, only to discover that calls were blocked. He had no choice but to wait.

2:00 P.M. Wolfsschanze. Activity at Wolfsschanze concentrated on treating the wounded and on piecing together the facts. Fearing that more bombs might be on the premises, Hitler ordered a detailed search of his quarters. Assessing the conference room, Himmler's investigators realized that the 18-inch hole in the floor of the conference room had blown downward, revealing that the blast originated in the room and not beneath it.

The telephone operator in the conference building, Sergeant-Major Adam, suspected that Stauffenberg must be the one who planted the bomb. Adam had seen Stauffenberg depart in a hurry without his belt and cap. He reported his suspicion to Martin Bormann, one of the highest-ranking Nazis in the compound. Bormann took Adam to Hitler and had him repeat the information. As a result of Adam's report, Hitler rewarded him with a promotion, 20,000 marks, and a house in Berlin.

Assuming Stauffenberg was still in the headquarters area, all checkpoints were ordered not to let anyone through. A search for the colonel was begun, but the word soon came that Stauffenberg had left shortly after the explosion, more than an hour before. Himmler speculated that Stauffenberg had taken a 10-minute flight to the front lines to the east, with the idea of seeking asylum from the Russian government. But an inquiry at the airport revealed that Stauffenberg had headed west.

The day's schedule was resumed. As the on-site investigation and questioning of witnesses continued, Hitler and his entourage walked to the rail station to meet Mussolini, whose train arrived at 2:30 P.M. Hitler greeted his friend with an animated retelling of the explosion. When he showed Mussolini the destroyed building, Mussolini was properly impressed that anyone had survived the devastation.

2:00 P.M. Paris. Since the "exercise" call an hour before, Colonel Finckh had been trying to continue his normal routine, awaiting the second part of the coded message from Berlin. Shortly after 2 P.M., the call came through. Finckh identified himself. The anonymous caller said "finished" and then hung up. That was the signal Finckh was expecting. The Valkyrie plan was on.

Finckh assumed again, wrongly, that General Stülpnagel had also been alerted. Finckh called for his car and ordered the driver to take him to the Western Command general staff headquarters near Paris. His task was to report to General Günther Blumentritt, chief of staff to Field Marshal Kluge. The conspirators hoped that Blumentritt would support them after being told the action was in response to an attempted takeover by the Gestapo. The conspirators needed the support of Kluge and Blumentritt in the west. Only they could order the armed forces under their command to obey a cease-fire.

Once the coup was completed, the resistance planned to begin negotiations with the Western Allies, and that would require cooperation from Kluge and from his chief of staff, Blumentritt.

3:00 P.M. Wolfsschanze. The communications blackout had been in effect for two hours. No incoming calls were allowed through, and only the most senior officers (including Fellgiebel) had been allowed to make calls to the outside. Himmler's security police had taken over supervision of communications. At 3 P.M., Himmler lifted the blackout.

3:30 P.M. War Ministry, Berlin. General Fritz Thiele telephoned Wolfsschanze and, with the blackout lifted, got through at once. He inquired about the attempt on Hitler. He was told only that there had been an attempt on the Führer's life, but that was all the information provided. The telephone operators at the headquarters were under orders to release no further information. When Thiele reported to Olbricht that no further word was being released, Olbricht decided he would have to issue the Valkyrie orders even without complete information. The first teleprinter orders began to go out from the War Ministry at 3:50.

3:30 P.M. Rangsdorf Airport. Stauffenberg and Haeften's plane landed outside of Berlin. The car they expected to be waiting for them was nowhere to be seen.* Stauffenberg told Haeften to telephone the War Ministry for a report on the progress of the coup. They had been in the air for nearly three hours, and Stauffenberg was eager to find out how matters were progressing. Haeften was briefed by Colonel Mertz von Quirnheim. Stauffenberg was shocked when Haeften repeated the message to him that orders were just now going out. Stauffenberg took the telephone to hear the news for himself.

4:00 P.M. War Ministry, Berlin. Orders were finally being issued in a sudden frenzy of activity. General Hase, commandant of Berlin, received telephoned orders to move on vital installations. Hase ordered the Grossdeutschland Guard Battalion to secure assigned buildings. Teleprinter orders went out to army and reserve army commanders around Germany.

The plan had been to issue the orders in General Fromm's name and only then to

---

*Stauffenberg's driver, Karl Schweizer, was waiting at Rastenburg Airport, where the plane was scheduled to land. The connection was not made. Schweizer might have been too early or too late. There is also the possibility that Stauffenberg and Haeften landed at another airport, either Gatow or Templehof. Some have speculated that this was done in the fear that the SS would be waiting to arrest the two. It is most likely that signals were crossed, however, and the plane did land at Rastenburg or that the driver was given the wrong instructions.

inform Fromm. The first part was now done. Olbricht knew he would have to go to General Fromm's office and advise him that the Valkyrie orders had been launched. Fromm would not be pleased, and Olbricht hesitated. Mertz pressured Olbricht, reminding him that orders had already been sent out. Olbricht went to Fromm's office and informed him that Hitler was dead.

He added formally, "I propose in the circumstances to issue to all Reserve Army commanders the codeword Valkyrie arranged for the eventuality of internal unrest, and so transfer all executive powers to the armed forces."[6]

Fromm asked Olbricht who had given him the news. Olbricht answered that Fellgiebel told him personally that he had seen Hitler's dead body. Olbricht expected Fromm to agree to the plan. Instead, however, he picked up his telephone and placed a call to Keitel at Wolfsschanze. To Olbricht's surprise, Fromm got through immediately, and Keitel came on the line.

"What has happened at General Headquarters? There are the wildest rumors here in Berlin." Fromm said.

Keitel responded: "What do they say has happened? Everything is normal here."

"I have just had a report that the Führer has been assassinated."[7]

"Nonsense," Keitel answered. "It is quite true an attempt has been made on his life. Fortunately, it failed. The Führer is alive and only slightly injured. Where, by the way, is your chief of staff, Colonel Stauffenberg?"

"Stauffenberg is not back yet," Fromm replied.[8]

The conversation ended, and Fromm told Olbricht that Valkyrie was unnecessary. Olbricht left Fromm's office unsure of what to do next. The Valkyrie orders had already been issued under Fromm's name, and Olbricht wanted to be sure that by the time Fromm found out, it would be too late to cancel the alert. He retreated to his own office, aware that Fromm would eventually have to be told.

Meanwhile, Mertz had gathered together the senior officers in the building to announce that Hitler was dead, that Field Marshal Witzleben had assumed command of the armed forces, and that General Beck was temporarily acting as civilian head of state. He concluded the gathering with an order to Major Fritz Harnack of the Reserve Army Operations Section to issue "Valkyrie Stage 2" orders to all military districts, training schools, and replacement units.

4:00 P.M. Paris. Colonel Finckh arrived at General Blumentritt's office in the Western Command headquarters. He reported that there had been a Gestapo-led putsch in Berlin, that Hitler was dead, and that Beck and Goerdeler were forming a provisional government. Blumentritt was stunned. He thought a moment and then expressed relief that Beck and Goerdeler had taken over. He asked Finckh where he had gotten his information, and Finckh, wanting to protect his resistance contacts in Zossen, replied that he had been given the news by Stülpnagel, military governor of France.

Blumentritt called Kluge's headquarters at La Roche-Guyon and asked for his commander. Kluge's chief of staff, General Speidel, told Blumentritt that Kluge was at the front and was not expected back until later that evening. Blumentritt said, "Things are happening in Berlin," but was unwilling to say too much on the telephone. Speidel had several questions, but Blumentritt declined to hold further discussions by telephone, offering instead to drive to La Roche-Guyon and report to Kluge in person.

4:30 P.M. War Ministry, Berlin. Stauffenberg was shocked and dismayed when told by telephone at the airport that the first orders had just gone out. He rushed to the War Ministry as soon as he was able to arrange a car. He arrived at about 4:30 and reported to Olbricht that Hitler was dead. Stauffenberg claimed: "I saw the whole thing from outside. I was standing outside the hut with General Fellgiebel. There was an explosion inside the hut and then I saw a large number of medical personnel come running up and cars being brought along. The explosion was as if the hut had been hit by a six-inch shell. It is hardly possible that anyone could be alive."[9]

Stauffenberg took over, finally putting the wheels of the coup in motion. He telephoned Hofacker in Paris to let him know the coup was on. Hofacker told Stauffenberg he would inform General Stülpnagel at once. Up until that point, Stülpnagel had heard nothing, even though Finckh had been informed hours before.

Stauffenberg ordered Berlin police president Helldorf to come to the War Ministry immediately. Helldorf was charged with the task of neutralizing the SS in Berlin. He was not given estimates of SS strength, however, or the correct location of their barracks. Helldorf, who had been waiting patiently all day for a telephone call, arrived at the War Ministry soon after Stauffenberg's call. He was surprised to see that there were no armed guards around the building. Even inside, there was little sign of extraordinary activity.

Helldorf, who had an impressive force at his disposal to carry out orders from the resistance, could not understand why he had not been notified earlier. He believed that seizing the radio broadcasting station should have been a top priority so that the conspirators could get their word out over the radio, while preventing any contrary broadcasts from the Nazis. Instead, the leaders at the War Ministry seemed to lack a sense of direction.

Helldorf was led into a meeting with Olbricht and Stauffenberg. Beck and Gisevius were there too. Olbricht ordered Helldorf to place the police forces at the disposal of the army. General Beck interrupted Olbricht: "One moment. We must in all loyalty tell the chief of police that according to certain reports from headquarters, Hitler may not be dead. We must decide clearly how —"

"Keitel's lying! Keitel's lying!" Olbricht shouted, with Stauffenberg adding confirmation.[10]

Helldorf realized at once that there were conflicting versions of what had happened. He saw the danger of relinquishing control of the Berlin police if, in fact, Hitler was still alive. Beck continued: "It doesn't matter whether Keitel is lying. What matters is that Helldorf ought to know that the other side has claimed the assassination has failed, and we must also be prepared for a similar announcement on the radio. What are we to say then?"[11]

Stauffenberg repeated his claim that he had personally witnessed the explosion. It was impossible, Stauffenberg insisted, that anyone inside had survived.* Helldorf returned to police headquarters to await orders.

---

*Whether or not Hitler was alive, the Nazis were planning a broadcast, and the conspirators knew it. Yet, even with their extremely detailed planning, no one thought it a high priority to ensure the takeover and control of the Berlin broadcasting centers. At the very least, the resistance could have ordered the telephones in the War Ministry disabled so no one could communicate with Wolfsschanze. Goebbels even commented on this failure later, saying, "To think that these revolutionaries weren't even smart enough to cut the telephone wires. My little daughter would have thought of that."[12]

The gaps in planning were only part of the problem. The resistance had lost several crucial hours' initiative. They now made an additional mistake. Getting word to the more than 20 military commands throughout the Third Reich was imperative. Orders specified, however, that the teleprint announcements were to be sent as "top secret" communications. That meant each had to be typed and sent individually and dispatched. The typists had to proceed slowly since the messages went out as they were being typed. A careless error might scramble the entire message. A more efficient choice would have been to send the message with a lower classification using the round-robin system: each district would receive the message and pass it on to the next district. It took two clerks more than three hours to send the first message to all of the addresses.

The first order began going out at 4:30 P.M. under Field Marshal Witzleben's name with the title supreme commander of the Wehrmacht. It read:

> The Führer Adolf Hitler is dead. An irresponsible gang of Party leaders, far behind the front, has tried to exploit this situation to stab the hard-pressed army in the back and seize power for its own ends.[13]

The order also proclaimed a state of emergency and stated that Witzleben was assuming temporary authority over the armed forces. Regional commanders were to assume executive powers immediately.

A second message was authorized for immediate dispatch, even though the teleprinters were backed up already. It was prepared under Fromm's name without his knowledge and signed in Fromm's behalf by Stauffenberg. As the Valkyrie plan specified, orders included the immediate deployment of troops to protect government buildings and important installations in each Wehrkreis, especially radio stations, repeater stations, and telephone and telegraph offices. Commanders were also ordered to arrest immediately all Nazi officials and government leaders, especially senior SS and Gestapo officers. The concentration camps were also to be occupied and all guards placed under arrest. Finally, new political representatives were appointed in each Wehrkreis, who were responsible for dealing with any political problems arising during the military emergency. Because of the slow pace of transmission, this message would not begin going out until 6 P.M.

4:30 P.M. Paris. When Hofacker received the telephone call from Stauffenberg with news of Hitler's death, he promised he would advise Stülpnagel right away. Hofacker reported the details of his telephone conversation to Stülpnagel, who enthusiastically summoned his staff and repeated the news. Present were the chief signals officer, General Eugen Oberhäusser; the chief of staff, Colonel Hans-Ottfried von Linstow; the chief of military administration, Dr. Elmar Michel; and the commandant of Paris, General Hans von Boineburg-Langsfeld.

The officers shook hands all around. Hofacker, now the shadow ambassador to France according to the cabinet appointees, was especially happy. He was young for the post but felt ready to assume his new responsibilities.

Stülpnagel had to remind his entourage that they still had a long evening's work ahead of them. He made sure that they all knew their duties. He asked Boineburg, as commandant of Paris, to arrange for the arrest of the large contingent of SS and SD in Paris. Stülpnagel also authorized his officers to permit their men to shoot anyone who resisted.

A large map had been prepared detailing the homes or apartments of SS, SD, and Gestapo officials, and each officer had his assignments for the arrests. Now sobered by a reminder that they still had to gain control, the young officers clicked their heels, saluted, and left immediately and fanned out around the French capital to carry out their orders.

Stülpnagel then telephoned General Beck in Berlin. They spoke briefly, and Stülpnagel told Beck that action was being taken in Paris. Stülpnagel pledged his full support and commitment to the coup.

4:45 P.M. War Ministry, Berlin. Although Stauffenberg was moving the coup along, Olbricht knew that Fromm still had to be dealt with. At 4:45, he informed Stauffenberg that Fromm was refusing to cooperate with the coup. Fromm was also unaware, Olbricht said, that the Valkyrie orders had already begun going out under Fromm's name. Stauffenberg and Olbricht decided to go to Fromm's office together and confront the situation.

Stauffenberg was blunt. Hitler was dead, and Fromm had no choice but to agree to issue the Valkyrie order. Fromm replied that Keitel had contradicted Stauffenberg's version of events. "Field Marshal Keitel is lying as usual," Stauffenberg said. "I myself saw Hitler being carried out dead."[14]

Olbricht then advised Fromm for the first time that the Valkyrie order had already been issued. Fromm was aghast at this news. He began screaming and pounding the desk with his fist, accusing Olbricht and Stauffenberg of insubordination and treason. He threatened them with a death penalty. He demanded to know who had issued the order, and Olbricht said it was his chief of staff, Mertz.

Fromm called for Mertz, who arrived in Fromm's office and confirmed that the Valkyrie order had been sent out. Fromm declared that Olbricht, Stauffenberg, and Mertz were all under arrest. He suggested that Stauffenberg shoot himself immediately. Stauffenberg refused. Olbricht said to Fromm, "It is we who are arresting you." Fromm jumped from his desk and lunged at Stauffenberg and Olbricht. By this time, a number of other officers, hearing the loud argument, appeared in Fromm's office. Kleist and Haeften drew their pistols and forced Fromm to back up.

Stauffenberg gave Fromm five minutes to consider whether or not to join with the conspirators. Everyone left, and Olbricht returned in five minutes to hear Fromm's decision. Fromm refused to have any part in the coup d'état, so Olbricht ordered Fromm and his aide, Captain Heinz-Ludwig Bertram, placed under arrest. They were forced into Bertram's office, where the telephone was disconnected and a guard was placed at both exits.

A short time later General Erich Hoepner visited Fromm in his confinement. Hoepner, who had been expelled from the army by Hitler the year before,* sympathized with Fromm and his situation and promised he would not be harmed. Hoepner also stated that he was the new commander of the Reserve Army and Witzleben was now in command of the armed forces.

5:00 P.M. Wolfsschanze. Fromm's telephone call to Keitel started the speculation at Hitler's headquarters that the assassination attempt was part of a larger conspiracy. By

---

Hoepner had defied Hitler's no-withdrawal order on the eastern front. As a consequence, he was thrown out of the army and forbidden to wear the uniform.

5 P.M., teleprint messages were circulating and calls were coming in to Wolfsschanze from all around the Third Reich. Commanders were asking confirmation of Hitler's death and asking for verification of the Valkyrie orders they were receiving.

Calls from Wolfsschanze placed to Fromm at the War Ministry were not being put through, adding to the suspicion. Hitler had remained calm and exceptionally quiet throughout the afternoon, even as the evidence mounted that Stauffenberg's attempt was part of a larger conspiracy. He continued meeting with the visiting Mussolini and his own trusted circle, including Admiral Karl Dönitz, Field Marshal Keitel, Göring, and Ribbentrop. The meeting quickly deteriorated into a confrontation among the top Nazis. Dönitz and Ribbentrop blamed the army for the military reversals currently being suffered. Keitel protested the accusation loudly. Göring called Ribbentrop a "dirty little champagne salesman" and threatened to strike him with his baton. Dönitz chimed in, blaming Göring for the failures of the Luftwaffe.

Suddenly Hitler, who had seemed oblivious to the loud brawl going on around him, took center stage. Historian John Wheeler-Bennett describes that Hitler's quiet mood gave way to the outburst of hatred and revenge and fury which had been simmering since the moment of the explosion. He leapt to his feet and paced the room in a screaming, raging frenzy; foam flecked his lips and gathered at the corners of his mouth. He was "a man possessed with a passion for rancorous vengeance. He would root out all these traitors and utterly destroy them — their women and children with them…. Not one should escape him — not one![15]

Chapter 14

THE COLLAPSE

> The failure of the resistance movement was largely due to the fact that it
> was too little and too late. Its chances of success would have been much
> greater if it had taken advantage of the earlier crises in the regime instead
> of waiting for a time of war ... but apart from a small group of leaders
> there were no large German groups ready to hazard a mass uprising against
> the terrorist police state. In part this was the very result of the terror
> system ... political martyrdom in Germany produced little or no effect
> because no one ever learned of the act of martyrdom. The inspiring effect
> of courageous resistance was, therefore, nullified by the rigid suppression
> of all news pertaining to such resistance.
>
> Koppel S. Pinson, *Modern Germany*

About 5 P.M., a communications war began between the conspirators in the War Ministry and the Nazi leaders in Wolfsschanze. For the commanders of the various Wehrkreise (military districts), the contradictory orders and messages continuing throughout the evening hours created confusion and doubt.

With all their detailed planning, the resistance overlooked the advantage they gave to the Nazi leadership by using the teleprinter to send out orders. Teleprinter communications to military command posts also went automatically into Hitler's headquarters at Wolfsschanze. That would not have been a problem had the attempt on Hitler's life succeeded. But now, the Nazi leadership knew precisely what had been sent from the War Ministry and how to countermand virtually everything the conspirators were communicating.[1]

5:00 P.M. Berlin city commandant's office. General Paul von Hase was working at a disadvantage. The plan had been to notify him the day before the coup, so that the extensive troop movements he would have to organize could be readied in advance. In the capital, he needed to coordinate taking simultaneous control over many buildings spread out over the city. To help in this task, the Berlin police were to be placed under his command, in cooperation with the police president, Wolf von Helldorf.

Everything had gone wrong. Hase was not notified until late in the afternoon of July 20, allowing no time for advance planning. He had been advised on the morning of the twentieth that something was going to happen at about 12 noon, but no word came from the War Ministry until after 4 P.M. The conspirators were frozen into inaction because of incomplete information and were afraid to take decisive action because of the false alarm of July 15, when Olbricht had ordered Valkyrie too early and was reprimanded by General Fromm.

As evening fell, Hase finally received precise orders from Stauffenberg. He was directed to assume plenary powers and mobilize the all-important Grossdeutschland Guard Battalion. Hase went into action. He reinforced the Guard Battalion with Armored School units, the Spandau garrison, and Army Schools of Pyrotecnics and Ordnance.

One of the first people Hase summoned to his office was Major Otto Ernst Remer, commander of the Grossdeutschland Guard Battalion. At the age of 32, he had already been in the army for 12 years. Remer had proven his bravery in combat and was a highly decorated officer, having been awarded the Knight's Cross with Oak Leaves and several other battlefield medals. Remer had not been included in coup plans, but the conspirators needed troops under his command as the primary forces to support the coup.

Now the conspirators would discover whether Remer would follow their orders like a good military man. Hase ordered Remer to seal off traffic in Berlin and surround key government buildings and several SS barracks.

Hase ordered commanders from other units to report to him. He ordered troops to seize Reich agencies and communications centers, including newspaper offices. Hase held some units in reserve to respond in case any fighting broke out in the capital.

5:30 P.M. Guard Battalion headquarters, Moabit. Remer drove back to his headquarters in the Berlin suburb of Moabit. He gathered his officers together, assigning each a section of Berlin to cordon off. Within an hour all of Berlin's traffic corridors were under control.

Remer was troubled by the unusual turn of events. He recalled a conversation earlier that day with an officer in his command, Lieutenant Hans Hagen, a liaison officer between Remer's headquarters and the Ministry of Propaganda. Hagen told Remer that at 2:45 that day, he had seen an open Mercedes traveling down the Friedrichstrasse carrying Field Marshal Walther von Brauchitsch in full uniform. It seemed suspicious because Brauchitsch had been fired and had retired more than three years before. Hagen was mistaken in his identification of the officer, but the information led Remer to believe that something unusual was going on.

Remer's suspicions were also aroused by the fact that Hase had given him oral orders. For such important actions, it seemed that orders should be given in written form. Worried, Remer again spoke with Lieutenant Hagen. Hagen suggested that Remer release him to find Goebbels to verify Hitler's death. Remer sent Hagen off to search for Goebbels.

5:30 P.M. London. The BBC in London intercepted a German News Bureau Home Service announcement at 5:42 P.M. What they heard was the release issued by Keitel, Hitler's chief of staff at Wolfsschanze, transmitting news to military districts and to radio stations. The bulletins said that an attempt had been made on Hitler's life, but he was unharmed. The announcement was repeated regularly throughout the evening. The broadcast was picked up in the Far East, the Netherlands radio service, and North Africa. Within an hour, the announcement had been picked up and translated into Portuguese, Arabic, and Turkish, as well as English, and the news traveled in broadcasts throughout the world. The resistance had failed to prevent the Nazi leadership from sending out its version of events, not only in Germany but around the entire Third Reich and the outside world.

At Wolfsschanze, Hitler, having realized that the attempt on his life involved many more people than just Stauffenberg, knew that communications could make the difference between success and failure of a coup. Keitel's announcement would need to be followed by a message from the Führer himself. He contacted Dr. Joseph Goebbels, with instructions for the minister to prepare an announcement for Hitler to read on the radio as soon as possible.

5:30 P.M. Joseph Goebbels' home, Berlin. Dr. Joseph Goebbels was at his private residence at 20 Hermann Göring Straße when he received a telephone call from the Führer. Hitler informed him that an uprising was underway in Berlin and ordered that an official announcement be prepared and broadcast at once.

As Goebbels worked on the radio announcement, Lieutenant Hagen arrived and insisted on seeing the minister. When he told his story of a Brauchitsch-led coup, Goebbels was incredulous. He assured Hagen that Hitler was alive. "I was talking to him only a couple of minutes ago. It is true there has been an attempt on his life, but by a miracle he escaped. The orders you refer to make no sense at all."

Goebbels advised, "Go and ask your commander to come and see me." He then calmly asked, "Is Remer a safe man?"

"I could vouch for him with my life, Herr Minister." Hagen replied.[2] Hagen departed to find Remer, while Goebbels returned to his work on the announcement.

6:00 P.M. War Ministry, Berlin. By 6 P.M., three separate visitors to the War Ministry challenged the conspirators' authority, marking the beginning of collapse. Stauffenberg planned to use the forces of the Armored School at Krampnitz as reinforcements for Remer's Guard Battalion. The resistance had slated several important tasks for the school's three battalions. Various companies were needed to execute the Valkyrie orders, with the main body slated to protect the War Ministry. Some units were to stand by as a mobile reserve to put down any resistance. The Armored School was a crucial force, necessary to the resistance.

The school's commandant, Colonel Wolfgang Gläsemer, did not simply follow the Valkyrie orders he received, however. He was troubled by them and reported in person to the War Ministry, where he demanded from Olbricht an explanation of what was going on. Olbricht said that Hitler was dead and that the Reserve Army was taking control to prevent an SS-led coup d'état. Gläsemer recognized at once, however, that it was Olbricht who was involved in a coup. Confronting Olbricht, he refused to take part in any action. He called the coup a "stab in the back" that would lead to a military defeat for Germany. Olbricht placed Gläsemer under arrest but allowed Gläsemer's adjutant to leave. Gläsemer gave the adjutant orders to carry back that the tanks under his command were not to be moved. Gläsemer was later released himself, after lying to Olbricht that he had changed his mind and would cooperate.

A second challenge arrived in the person of SS-Oberführer Humbert Achamer-Pifrader, who had arrest orders for Stauffenberg. Unknown to the conspirators in the War Ministry, the SS in Berlin and throughout Germany had been placed on alert three hours before. SS communications, which were independent of army and civilian communications systems, were fully operational, and SS units had been on call since early afternoon. Achamer-Pifrader was taken by Colonel Fritz Jäger to see Stauffenberg, whom he tried to question about the day's events at Wolfsschanze. Stauffenberg ordered Colonel Jäger to place the SS officer under arrest.

The third challenge came within moments. General Joachim von Kortzfleisch, district commander of the Berlin area, was summoned to headquarters by Olbricht to receive orders. Like Gläsemer, Kortzfleisch demanded to know exactly what was happening. Upon his arrival, Kortzfleisch demanded to speak with General Fromm but was taken instead to Hoepner. Kortzfleisch refused to acknowledge Hoepner's authority. Olbricht and Beck tried to calm the general, who kept insisting, "The Führer is not dead! The Führer is not dead."[3]

Kortzfleisch then tried to leave, but the conspirators blocked his exit. He ran down a corridor, the conspirators shouting behind him, "Watch out at the exit!" Kleist, stationed near the door, drew his pistol. Kortzfleisch was led back at gunpoint and confined to a room with a sentry at the door. He protested, loudly proclaiming his oath to Hitler.

6:00 P.M. Paris. From his headquarters in Paris, General Stülpnagel telephoned General Boineburg-Lengsfeld, city commandant of Paris. Boineburg reported he was planning to arrest SS and SD leaders shortly after dark. Stülpnagel urged him to act sooner, but Boineburg explained, "This way, we won't have to gratify the Parisians with the spectacle of Germans arresting their fellow countrymen. Besides, it will be better to move against the SS and the SD when they're concentrated in their barracks — we can just throw out our nets and haul them in."[4] Stülpnagel agreed.

After completing his discussion with Boineburg, Stülpnagel received a call from General Beck in Berlin. He asked, "Stülpnagel, are you aware of what has happened in the last few hours?"

"Yes."

"In that case, I must ask you if you are still with us."

Stülpnagel did not hesitate. "Herr General, this is the very thing I've been waiting for."

"We're committed now," Beck said. "But we have no exact news yet. Are you with us, come what may?"

Stülpnagel assured Beck that he was and that orders had already been issued for the arrest of all SS and Gestapo in Paris. He assured Beck, "The troops here as well as their commanders are absolutely reliable."[5]

Beck was relieved at Stülpnagel's assurances and asked whether Field Marshal Kluge would be as cooperative. Stülpnagel suggested that Beck speak to Kluge personally and had the call transferred to La Roche-Guyon. As the transfer was completed, Stülpnagel received a message from Kluge's chief of staff Speidel. Kluge wanted Stülpnagel and Colonel Cäsar von Hofacker of his staff to report to him at La Roche-Guyon at 8 P.M.

6:45 P.M. Joseph Goebbels' home, Berlin. Hitler called again, angry that no radio announcement had yet been broadcast. Goebbels promised to finish it up and have it on the air at once. At 6:45, he telephoned the brief announcement to the Deutschlandsender station, where it was broadcast immediately. The text of the announcement read:

> Today an attempt was made on the Führer's life with explosives.... The Führer himself suffered no injuries beyond light burns and bruises. He resumed his work immediately....[6]

The announcement, quoting Goebbels, was convincing and was broadcast through-out Europe. Word went out quickly to the commanders in the streets of Berlin, and the doubts and suspicions concerning their orders were confirmed.

6:45 P.M. Paris. Field Marshal Kluge had just returned to La Roche-Guyon from his inspection tour to the western front when Beck's call arrived at about 6:45. Beck briefed Kluge on actions underway in Berlin. "Kluge, start the revolt now and join our action openly," Beck pleaded. As Beck was speaking, an aide placed a transcript of the Goebbels radio announcement in front of Kluge. He read it to himself as Beck spoke.

"What is the real position at the Führer's headquarters?" Kluge asked, without telling Beck he had the text of the radio announcement in front of him.

Beck admitted there was some confusion and different versions of events were going around. He argued, "I am asking you the only thing that matters. Do you approve of what we have started here, and are you prepared to take orders from me?" Kluge did not reply, so Beck tried again. "I ask you once more. Will you unreservedly put yourself under my orders?"

Kluge told Beck, "I must first of all discuss it with my officers. I will call you back in half an hour."[7]

6:45 P.M. War Ministry, Berlin. The radio announcement was heard in Reserve Army headquarters, and morale fell at once. Stauffenberg immediately sent a teleprint message to all army commanders, denying that Hitler survived the attack. The message read:

> Broadcast communiqué not correct. The Führer is dead. Measures ordered
> to be carried out with utmost dispatch.
>
> C-in-C Replacement Army and
C-in-C Home Forces[8]

The teleprint went out at once. It was too late, however, to counteract the effects of the Goebbels announcement. The damage was done. Some officers abandoned the cause entirely, left the building, and made their way home. Others remained, but their confidence was shaken.

7:00 P.M. Joseph Goebbels' home, Berlin. When Goebbels' aide, Rudolf Semmler, came to the minister to announce that a major had arrived to arrest him on orders from General Hase, commandant of Berlin, Goebbels reached into his desk and removed a loaded revolver, placing it out of sight but within easy reach.

Major Martin Korff of the Pyrotechnical School had orders to arrest Goebbels. His 300 men surrounded the building as he entered. Once inside the apartment of the famous Dr. Goebbels, the nervous major explained his assignment to the minister. Goebbels disdainfully told the major it was treason. He ordered him to return and tell his superior officers that Hitler was alive.

At this point, Major Remer arrived with the news that the attack on Hitler had been orchestrated by officers in Berlin, including some in the city commandant's office. Coming to Goebbels' home was a dangerous move because Remer's orders did not include the freedom to question one of the individuals accused of organizing the alleged uprising.

Goebbels asked Remer if he were a dedicated National Socialist, and without hesitation, Remer said he was. He told Goebbels he only wanted to know whether Hitler was alive or dead, and Goebbels assured him that the Führer lived. The minister then put through a priority call to Wolfsschanze and quickly got Hitler on the line. Goebbels briefly explained the situation and handed the telephone to Major Remer. Hitler asked Remer if he recognized his voice, and Remer, who had met Hitler during the presentation of one of his medals, said he did. Hitler said he had been the victim of a criminal plot but was unhurt. He placed Remer under his direct command until Himmler arrived in Berlin to assume command of the Reserve Army. Hitler also gave him an immediate promotion to colonel and said that the safety of Berlin was now in Remer's hands.

Remer, sober with the importance of his task, left to gather up the scattered troops of his Guard Battalion. He ordered all units to Goebbels' home, where many were left as a guard for the rest of the night. Korff also placed his squads from the Pyrotechnical School under Remer's command. A contingent of the Guard Battalion was ordered to move to the War Ministry and surround the building.

Colonel Friedrich Jäger arrived as Guard Battalion troops were positioning themselves around the Goebbels home. Jäger had received orders from the War Ministry to assume command of two raiding parties of the Wehrmacht Patrol Service. He was to join forces with the squads from the Pyrotechnical Schools and arrest Goebbels. When he arrived, Jäger discovered that Korff's troops were now under Remer's command. Lacking the troop strength to defy Remer's Guard Battalion, he did not try to follow through on his orders and the strong protective cordon now around Goebbels' home remained intact.

7:00 P.M. Other cities. In the majority of military districts, teleprint orders from Berlin arrived at about the same time the Goebbels radio broadcast was made. The contradictory information created enough doubt that no real momentum was achieved in any of the provinces. As a matter of practice, whenever there was doubt concerning orders, commanders called neighboring districts to compare information. By 7 P.M., most districts knew that their neighbors were operating on a wait-and-see basis. As the evening progressed, any initial actions were quickly and quietly reversed. The failure of the coup d'état became apparent as, during the evening, telephone contact with Field Marshal Keitel in Wolfsschanze confirmed the suspicion that the Berlin group had no authority to issue orders.

The series of events in most cities was identical. The teleprint orders from the War Ministry were received shortly after the broadcast announcing the failure of the attempt on Hitler. It took some time to decode the teleprint message, and several commanders were away from their headquarters. By the time a decoded series of orders was placed in a commander's hands, the failure of the coup was already known. The four-hour delay in putting the entire action in effect meant that the important decision makers were already at home for the evening.

In Vienna, SS and Gestapo leaders were placed under arrest, but military commanders were dubious. They gave their prisoners sandwiches and wine. A telephone conversation with Stauffenberg was followed by a call to Keitel, who countermanded the teleprint orders. In late evening, commanders apologized to their prisoners and released them.

In some districts, the Nazi political leaders and the military leaders were friends.

In Hamburg, Gauleiter Karl Kaufmann and District Commander General Wilhelm Wetzel were amused at the volume of contradictory orders coming through all evening. They spent the evening together, joking about whose turn it was to arrest the other. The tension at a meeting between the high-ranking military and Nazi leaders was relieved when the chief of staff, General Friedrich Wilhelm Prüter, offered everyone a glass of sherry.

In Dresden the district office was closed for the day when teleprint orders to arrest Gestapo officers arrived. The duty officer, ignoring the proper procedure for top secret military orders, called the local Gestapo office and asked what should be done. The Gestapo advised taking no action.

In Königsberg, Salzberg, Danzig, Poznan, and Cracow, commanding officers were away on inspection tours or other business, and no action was taken pending their return. In Munich, considered one of the most important centers for fast action, air raids the day before had partially knocked out communications stations, and the teleprint orders were never received.

No actions were taken in most other cities. In some areas, such as Kassel, initial alerts were announced but canceled almost immediately. The radio announcement had its effect, and Keitel was spending as much time on the telephone from Wolfsschanze as Stauffenberg was from Berlin. In Wiesbaden, the teleprints arrived hours after the collapse of the revolt.

One exception was Nuremberg, where Berlin's orders were put into effect as soon as they were received. At 7 P.M., however, Keitel telephoned and ordered that all alerts be canceled and SS and Gestapo detainees be released. Keitel's orders were followed. The Nuremberg commander, chief of staff, and personnel officer were all relieved of their posts after July 20.

Prague presented a special situation. The Czech capital was in a virtual state of siege, with frequent partisan assaults and a hostile civilian population. The Valkyrie orders received at 4:45 were taken in all seriousness. The district commander, General Ferdinand Schaal, understood better than most the threat of a civilian or worker uprising. Schaal telephoned Stauffenberg and promised to put the orders into effect. Troops were dispatched to protect signals installations, and Schaal also spoke to Hoepner to confirm his orders. Later in the evening, however, Schaal received a telephone call from Wolfsschanze and was ordered not to respond in any way to orders coming from the War Ministry. Troops were recalled, and all alerts were canceled. Throughout the Third Reich, nervous commanders moved as quickly as possible to demonstrate their loyalty to the regime. Realizing the coup had failed, no one wanted to be discovered on the wrong side when the retaliations began.

8:00 P.M. Paris. The hour was approaching for the meeting Kluge had set up with Stülpnagel, Hofacker, and other officers. At 8 P.M., Kluge received a teleprint message from Berlin that was identical to the message being sent to cities throughout Europe. It was Witzleben's announcement of the change in command over the army which read in part:

> The Führer Adolf Hitler is dead. An irresponsible gang of Party leaders, far behind the front, has tried to exploit this situation to stab the hard-pressed army in the back and seize power for its own ends.[9]

The teleprint also ordered Kluge to assume command over SS and Gestapo in the west and report directly to the new commander in chief, Field Marshal Witzleben. Kluge trusted Witzleben and considered his word dependable. Kluge then received a second teleprint message, this one from Keitel at Wolfsschanze. This message read:

> The Führer is alive! In perfect health! *Reichsführer-SS* [Himmler] C-in-C Replacement Army. Only his orders valid. Orders from General Fromm, Field Marshal Witzleben and General Hoepner not to be executed![10]

Kluge placed an urgent telephone call to Wolfsschanze but was told that the senior officers were all in conference. Kluge next telephoned General Stieff in Mauerwald Camp, near Wolfsschanze. Stieff told Kluge that Hitler was alive and well.

8:30 P.M. War Ministry, Berlin. On the surface, the seizure of broadcasting and transmitter stations in and around Berlin was proceeding successfully. Throughout the region, SS guards at broadcasting stations were replaced with guards from units of the Reserve Army or local Wehrmacht battalions. What the conspirators had not counted on, however, was the possibility that troops occupying these stations would allow broadcasting to continue.

At the strategically important Broadcasting House, Major Friedrich Jakob of the Infantry School at Döberitz was given orders to occupy the facility and had done so before 5:00 P.M. SS sentries were replaced with his men, and other SS troops were confined to their barracks while Jakob set up squads of guards and machine gun crews around the building. Jakob ordered the superintendent to cease broadcasting immediately. The superintendent agreed and told Jakob that everything was disconnected. Jakob, who had received no technical training in communications and had no experts with him, believed what he was told. In fact, however, broadcasting never stopped. Jakob was not told that the studios and switching rooms had been moved to an adjoining building because of air raids.

Even though General Hase, the city commandant, had 20 signals officers whose task was to ensure control over facilities like Broadcasting House, when the signals officers reported to Hase's office, they found a muddle of conflicting reports and indecision. They were not issued clear orders. In Broadcasting House and other locations, control over the facilities drifted back into the hands of the SS.

At the War Ministry, Remer's troops moved in and surrounded the building. They were met with additional troops and tank battalions under Witzleben's command. The scene outside the building degenerated into confusion, no one knowing exactly what units had been ordered there nor whose orders had real authority. The situation remained peaceful only because commanders did not want to issue orders for German soldiers to begin firing on one another.

The radio broadcasts, now controlled by the Nazis, were having their intended effect. The Goebbels message was repeated at regular intervals. Commanders who had been willing to go along with the coup now doubted that it could succeed and began withdrawing troops.

Inside the War Ministry, Stauffenberg and Olbricht directed their efforts at reassuring commanders. The telephones rang incessantly. Stauffenberg still insisted that Hitler was dead and was constantly saying into the telephone, "All is going according to plan. What the radio says in false."

8:30 P.M. Paris. When General Stülpnagel and Colonel Hofacker arrived at Field Marshal Kluge's headquarters at La Roche-Guyon, he received them coldly. The field marshal had gathered all of the top officers of his command to confer on the situation in Berlin. In addition to Stülpnagel and Hofacker, Generals Speidel and Blumentritt and Field Marshal Hugo Sperrle were present. Colonel Hofacker spoke in support of his cousin Stauffenberg and other members of the resistance, in the hope of convincing Kluge to join with them. He pleaded:

> Field Marshal, what is happening in Berlin is not decisive. Far more impor-
> tant are the decisions made here in France. I appeal to you, sir, for the sake
> of our country's future, to act as Field Marshal Rommel would have acted
> in your place, according to what he told me when I last saw him privately
> on July 9. I beg you, sir, to cut loose from Hitler and to lead the liberation
> in the west yourself.[11]

Kluge was not moved. He arose from the conference, finally speaking: "Well, gentlemen, it has misfired."

Stülpnagel responded, "But I thought, Herr Field Marshal, that you knew all about [the resistance]."

Kluge responded, "Certainly not, I had no idea."[12]

Stülpnagel walked out to the balcony and contemplated whether to tell Kluge that under his authority as military governor of France, he had already ordered drastic measures in Paris. As Stülpnagel considered what to say, Kluge asked the assembled officers to join him for dinner. As they dined, everyone remained silent except Kluge, who cheerfully reminisced about his days on the eastern front. Finally, Stülpnagel asked Kluge to speak with him privately. Kluge agreed, and the two officers walked to the next room.

The remaining officers sat at the dinner table in silence. A moment later, Kluge reentered, angrily announcing that Stülpnagel had ordered arrests in Paris, calling the act an "unprecedented act of insubordination." He screamed at Blumentritt: "Telephone right away. The order must be countermanded, or I shall not be answerable for the consequences." Blumentritt made the telephone call and reported back that the action had already started and could not be pulled back. Stülpnagel reentered the room, and Kluge went into a rage. "Why didn't you consult me?" he demanded.[13]

Kluge then regained his composure. Acting as though the incident had not happened, he asked the officers to rejoin him at the dinner table. He completed his meal while the others sat in silence.

8:30 P.M. War Ministry, Berlin. Field Marshal Witzleben arrived at the War Ministry in full uniform, ready to assume his new role as commander in chief of the armed forces and join in a radio broadcast with Beck. When he met with Beck and Stauffenberg and was briefed on the situation, he realized immediately that the day was lost. He protested to Beck that "One must have a ninety percent probability that a putsch will turn out well."

Beck answered, "Nonsense. Fifty-one percent is enough."[14]*

According to the original plan, one of the first essential steps was to have been a radio broadcast by Beck and Witzleben, each reading their proclamation (see the Appendix) announcing the state of emergency, Hitler's death, and the formation of a new government whose first role was suppression of the SS and Gestapo-led putsch. But no one had thought to make arrangements to set up the War Ministry for broadcasting. And, at this hour, no one in the headquarters knew whether forces loyal to the resistance controlled the broadcasting stations.

Witzleben, appalled at the delays and lack of planning, warned Beck that the conspiracy lacked troop strength to secure the capital. He left the building in disgust and went to army headquarters in Zossen. There, General Eduard Wagner, who had been one of the most enthusiastic members of the military resistance, was so deeply disappointed at the failure of the coup that he was no longer answering his telephone. Witzleben spoke with Wagner only briefly and then returned to his home 30 miles outside of Berlin.

As Witzleben was leaving the War Ministry, General Fromm was transferred from detention in his office to his quarters one floor below. Three members of Fromm's staff asked to see the general, and they were admitted to his quarters unsupervised. Fromm briefed them on the situation, told them about a rear exit, and ordered them to escape and return with help. The three officers left, undetected by the sentry outside the room.

9:00 P.M. Joseph Goebbels' home, Berlin. Through the evening, control slipped from the conspirators. Joseph Goebbels home became the Berlin center of Nazi organization. Himmler was sent there from Wolfsschanze. Upon his arrival, Himmler coolly went about gathering the forces of his secret police and bodyguards. He ordered cordons of guards placed around Gestapo, SS, and SD headquarters and then sent out high-ranking officials to gather intelligence. He and Obergruppenführer Ernst Kaltenbrunner, head of the SD, methodically tracked down commanders of all units in the area, ensuring that their loyalties were with the regime and not with the conspirators in the War Ministry. Himmler and Kaltenbrunner began compiling a list of names of people to be arrested and questioned.

10:30 P.M. Paris. As the situation in Berlin deteriorated rapidly, the resistance in Paris met with almost total success. The well-organized forces loyal to Stülpnagel had assembled in the early evening at a central location and fanned out to begin their arrests. By 10:30, at least 1,200 SS and Gestapo officials were held in the military prison at Fresnes on the outskirts of Paris, with not a single shot having been fired.

Although naval and Luftwaffe commanders in Paris soon received instructions from Keitel to ignore all orders from Witzleben, Luftwaffe security troop efforts to halt the arrests of SS leaders proved futile. The resistance plan was executed without a hitch.

10:30 to 11:30 P.M. War Ministry Berlin. Stauffenberg and Olbricht were on the telephone all evening, trying to hold together their deteriorating coup d'état. The stream of telephone calls had not slowed, but one by one, military commanders in outlying provinces abandoned the plan. The constant rebroadcast of the Goebbels announcement destroyed the limited momentum the resistance had been able to mount.

---

*Beck was paraphrasing General Otto von Lossow, one of the triumvirate of Bavarian rulers in 1923, at the time of Hitler's famous attempted beer hall putsch. Lossow, under pressure to support Hitler's plan, said "I am ready to take part in any putsch which has fifty-one percent probability of success."[15]

Outside the building, Remer's Guard Battalion had prevailed, and resistance forces inside could see it was only a matter of time before they would be overpowered by the Guard Battalion. Olbricht assembled the officers on the premises and told them an assault on the building was inevitable. He ordered the building prepared for a defensive stand. Several officers objected, including Colonel Franz Herber of Olbricht's own staff. Herber, a loyal Nazi, had been highly suspicious of the entire matter. He now demanded to know why it was necessary to guard the building. The purpose of the Reserve Army, Herber said, was to supply reinforcements at the front lines. Why, he asked, were they now in a situation of defending themselves against other German troops?

Olbricht's reply was evasive: "Gentlemen, for a long while we have been observing the developing situation with great anxiety. Undoubtedly it has been heading for catastrophe. Measures had to be taken to anticipate this. Those measures are now in the process of being carried out. I ask you to support me."[16]

Herber, aided by Colonel Bolko von der Heyde and other Nazi supporters, had earlier managed to sneak in a cache of small arms and automatic weapons from a nearby arsenal and had hidden them on the second floor of the building. Unpersuaded, Herber and his group left the briefing and went down to the second floor to arm themselves. They returned armed to Olbricht's office and held him at gunpoint.

Meanwhile, Olbricht's secretary left the outer office to find Stauffenberg and Haeften to notify them that armed soldiers were in Olbricht's office. The officers went to Olbricht's outer office but were quickly forced to retreat when met by gunfire. Stauffenberg was hit in the upper left arm. For the following ten minutes, the two sides battled in the corridors of the building. The Nazi contingent won, rounding up the resistance conspirators, including Stauffenberg, Haeften, Olbricht, Beck, and Hoepner, and placing them under guard.

11:00 to 12:00 P.M. Paris. The long, awkward dinner at Kluge's headquarters was finished in silence. As the officers left the dinner table, Kluge walked outside with General Stülpnagel and suggested he order the release of the SS and Gestapo leaders. Stülpnagel answered that events had gone too far to turn back. Kluge told Stülpnagel to consider himself relieved of his command and suggested that Stülpnagel change into civilian clothes and go into hiding before the Gestapo recovered and came looking for him, but Stülpnagel refused.

When Stülpnagel returned to his office in central Paris, he received a report from Colonel Hans-Ottfried von Linstow that Berlin was in complete chaos and the conspiracy was falling apart. Linstow said he had just finished speaking by telephone to Stauffenberg. During the telephone call, Linstow said, Stauffenberg had told him that the Nazis were surrounding the War Ministry and would soon be inside to place him under arrest. Stülpnagel and Linstow agreed that their best course of action at this point was to cut all communications between Paris and Berlin. That would prevent anyone from giving orders to release the SS and Gestapo in the French capital.

After Stülpnagel left Kluge's headquarters, Kluge was contacted by Admiral Theodor Krancke, commander in chief of the Western Naval Group. Krancke, a loyal Nazi, reported on the widespread arrests in Paris. Krancke had alerted all naval units around Paris to be ready to take to the streets to fight Stülpnagel's forces if necessary.

11:30 P.M. to 12:30 A.M. War Ministry, Berlin. Freed by Colonel Herber and his fellow Nazis, General Fromm returned to his office carrying his revolver to confront the leaders of the conspiracy. He placed them under arrest and ordered them to lay down their weapons. Beck requested to be exempted from the command, asking to keep his pistol for "private purposes." Fromm coldly agreed, telling Beck to be sure to keep the pistol aimed at himself. Beck placed his gun to his temple and pulled the trigger. The bullet grazed his forehead, dazing him. He sank to a chair, bleeding and in great pain. Fromm ordered two officers to take Beck's gun, but he asked to be given a second chance. Fromm agreed. Beck shot himself again, but only increased the pain and the bleeding. He slumped in his chair.

Fromm turned to the other officers: Stauffenberg, Haeften, Olbricht, Mertz, Hoepner, and several others. He announced, "In the name of the Führer, a summary court-martial called by myself, has reached the following verdict: Colonel of the General Staff Mertz von Quirnheim, General Olbricht, the Colonel — I cannot bring myself to name him — and Lieutenant von Haeften are condemned to death."[17]

He gave them a few minutes to write letters to their families. Hoepner asked Fromm to delay his execution on grounds that he believed he would be able to justify his actions to a court. Fromm agreed and ordered Hoepner removed and sent to Moabit prison. Stauffenberg, pale from the loss of blood from the wound to his arm, addressed Fromm. He claimed full responsibility for the failed coup, saying everyone else had merely been following his orders.

Fromm left the prisoners to make hasty arrangements for a firing squad. He quickly rounded up ten men from Remer's Guard Battalion for the job and set them up in a courtyard lit by the headlights from an army truck.*

Olbricht, Haeften, Stauffenberg, and Mertz were led out to the courtyard, where they met their deaths calmly. Witnesses reported that Stauffenberg shouted immediately before his turn, "Long live our sacred Germany." When the executions were complete, Fromm asked about Beck. When told he was still alive and in great pain but unable to complete his suicide, Fromm ordered a soldier to "help the old gentleman." Beck, now unconscious, was shot in the neck by a sergeant.

At 21 minutes past midnight, General Fromm sent out a teleprint to Wolfs-schanze and several command centers, claiming full credit for putting down the revolt in Berlin. The teleprint read:

> Attempted putsch by irresponsible generals suppressed with bloodshed. All leaders shot. Orders from Field Marshal von Witzleben, Colonel-General Hoepner, General Beck and General Olbricht not to be obeyed. I have resumed command after being temporarily held at gunpoint.
>
>   [signed] Fromm[18]

Fromm intended to continue the executions and rounded up another group of conspirators. Before he was able to see these executions through, however, SD Chief

---

*Fromm felt a sense of urgency in completing the executions of the leaders in the War Ministry. He knew that his own position was weak, and he wanted to do away with those who might testify against him. It didn't help. In the aftermath of the coup, Fromm was arrested and was sentenced to death in February 1945. He was executed by prison officials on March 19, 1945, uttering his last words, "Heil Hitler."

Kaltenbrunner arrived and ordered all executions halted immediately, on orders from Himmler. The remaining conspirators were handcuffed and taken away. Fromm was informed that Himmler was now head of the Reserve Army. The SD and Gestapo took control of the War Ministry in Himmler's name. Fromm went out to the street, mounted a truck, and gave a spirited speech to the soldiers, concluding with a call for three "Sieg Heil's." Fromm then left for Goebbels' house to take part in the investigation.

1:00 A.M. Wolfsschanze. The Deutschlandsender radio broadcast of Wagner's music was interrupted abruptly at 1:00 A.M. The announcer briefly introduced the Führer, Adolf Hitler:

> My German comrades ... you should hear my voice and should know that I am unhurt and well.... A very small clique of ambitious, irresponsible and, at the same time, senseless and stupid officers had concocted a plot to eliminate me and, with me, the staff of the High Command of the *Wehrmacht*. The bomb planted by Colonel Count Stauffenberg exploded two meters to the right of me. It seriously wounded a number of my true and loyal collaborators, one of whom has died. I myself am entirely unhurt, aside from some very minor scratches, bruises and burns.... The circle of these usurpers is very small and has nothing in common with the spirit of the German *Wehrmacht* and, above all, none with the German people. It is a gang of criminal elements which will be destroyed without mercy. I therefore give orders now that no military authority ... is to obey orders from this crew of usurpers. I also order that it is everybody's duty to arrest or, if they resist, to shoot at sight, anyone issuing or handling such orders.... This time we shall settle accounts with them in the manner in which we National Socialists are accustomed.[19]

Chapter 15

THE AFTERMATH

We were not born into the world of politics; we are not political fanatics
fighting to get power in the State for one party. That is not what we were
taught to do.

Hans Oster, statement to the Gestapo, 1944

Over the next few months, arrests numbered in the thousands. Besides conspirators, family members, friends and associates, anyone even remotely connected with those in the conspiracy, were subject to arrest, interrogation, imprisonment, and ultimately, execution.

Hitler's promise of revenge was swiftly implemented by the cool efficiency of Himmler's secret police. The official investigation of the conspiracy, the "Special Commission of 20 July," ultimately employed more than 400 investigators, whose findings were thoroughly reported and cataloged. They were published in 1961 in a massive document called *Spiegelbild einer Verschwörung* (Picture of a Conspiracy).

Interrogations of those arrested were not especially productive. Even under the most brutal treatment, few prisoners revealed information not already known to the Gestapo. Investigators discovered, however, files and records at the War Ministry and at Army Headquarters at Zossen that included the names of hundreds of men and women who were part of the resistance or were slated for positions in the new government.

The Nazi leadership undertook a carefully orchestrated campaign to convince the people of Germany that the conspiracy to overthrow the government had been very limited, while they were discovering, in fact, that it was quite widespread. The public relations campaign, led by Propaganda Minister Joseph Goebbels, began a mere three days after the coup failed. Goebbels issued an order on July 23, 1944, to propaganda offices throughout the Reich that read:

> Highly confidential: Over the next few days a wave of demonstrations of loyalty to the Führer must be organized in all *Gaue* and districts of the Reich as a spontaneous reaction of our people to the nefarious assassination attempt on the Führer. Full participation of local military units must be secured through collaboration with the appropriate military headquarters....

The German press will receive daily instructions to provide effective publicity of the demonstrations…. The speakers at the demonstrations must emphasize … only a small group of reactionary traitors are behind the assassination attempt and putsch…. The most experienced speakers must be employed so as to guarantee the decisive success of the wave of demonstrations.[1]

In an especially fiery radio broadcast of July 26, Goebbels denounced the conspirators as a "small clique of traitors" and "despicable creatures with German names."* The rhetoric was not limited to German pronouncements. The American press, in its editorial pages, found more to criticize than to praise in the attempted coup in Germany. Taking sides with Hitler, the intended victim, rather than those who tried to rid themselves of him, the *New York Herald Tribune* reported on August 9, 1944, that

American people as a whole will not feel sorry that the bomb spared Hitler from the liquidation of his Generals. Americans hold no grief for aristocrats as such and least of all for those given to the goosestep and, when it suits their purpose, to collaboration with low-born, rabble-rousing corporals. Let the Generals kill the Corporals, or vice versa, preferably both.[3]

The same day, the *New York Times* editorialized that the news of the attempt on Hitler was more like that of

the atmosphere of a gangster's lurid underworld [than of what] one would normally expect within an officers' corps and a civilized state. [For a whole year some of the highest officers in the German Army had plans] to capture or kill the Head of State and the Commander-of-Chief of the Army. [They put their plan into effect] with a bomb, the typical weapon of the underworld.[4]

Negative civilian reaction to the bomb attempt was genuine even without the propaganda effort. On July 21, 1944, the Reichssicherheithauptamt (Central Security Department, abbreviated RSHA) polled public reaction and cited a sense of "shock, disturbance, deep disgust and rage" among the people. Even those who were not Nazis expressed virtually unanimous opposition to the idea of assassination of the country's leader.[5]

The same reaction was observed in German soldiers captured by Americans during the month of July 1944. From July 1 to July 17, American intelligence reports showed that 57 percent of the prisoners expressed confidence in Hitler. During August the percentage grew to 67 percent.[6]

The first trial, held August 7, 1944, was arranged solely for publicity, with the outcome predetermined. The large courtroom was draped with swastikas and sound-track

---

*In spite of his public pronouncements, Goebbels knew all too well that Hitler had not been realistic in his running of the war. To close friends, Goebbels confided, "It takes a bomb under his ass to make Hitler see reason."[2]

Roland Freisler, judge of the People's Court, was famous for humiliating defendants for propaganda purposes. The plan backfired badly, only showing the mockery the Nazi regime made of the justice system (Photo: National Archives).

cameras were concealed behind the flags. The audience consisted of hand-picked soldiers and members of the SS, SA, and Gestapo.

The judge, Roland Freisler, tried to make a great show of degrading the defendants. He interrupted them with constant loud tirades, often obscene, accusing them of the worst character flaws and crimes. Defendants included Field Marshal Erwin von Witzleben, General Paul von Hase, General Helmuth Stieff, General Erich Fellgiebel, Fritz-Dietlof von der Schulenburg, Peter Yorck von Wartenburg, and General Erich Hoepner. All had been subjected to the most brutal treatment during interrogation. They maintained their composure during the mock trial, however, and went to their deaths with dignity. The plan was "to break them down psychologically and present them as miserable, morally worthless criminals actuated by base motives."[7]

The plan backfired badly. Freisler's loud demeanor did not impress Witzleben, who calmly told the judge:

> You can hand us over to the executioner, but in three months' time this outraged and suffering people will call you to account and drag you alive through the mud of the streets.[8]

Freisler struggled to prevent the defendants from having their say in court, without success. Schulenburg spoke when his turn came:

> We have accepted the necessity to do our deed in order to save Germany from untold misery. I expect to be hanged for this, but I do not regret my action and I hope that someone else in luckier circumstances will succeed.[9]

General Fellgiebel's response to his death sentence was to tell Freisler, "You had better hang us in a hurry, otherwise you will hang before we do."[10]

The outcome in these show trials was never in doubt. The method of execution was determined in advance. Hitler had ordered that the conspirators "must all be hanged, hung up like carcasses of meat," instructing that they be slowly strangled with thin wire suspended from meat hooks. Hitler also ordered that the executions be filmed. He intended to show the film to soldiers as an example and a warning of how traitors were dealt with in the Third Reich. When the film was shown to cadets at the training school at Lichterfelde, the soldiers were so disgusted they walked out and refused to view it. So negative were the responses in all circles that Hitler finally ordered all copies of the film destroyed.[11]

Field Marshal Erwin Witzleben at his trial. The effects of ill treatment on the elderly Witzleben were obvious. He was sentenced to death at his trial on August 7, 1944 (Photo: National Archives).

Some conspirators avoided interrogation and execution by committing suicide. Given the nature of the Nazi regime, they had no illusions of what awaited them at the hands of the Gestapo. One of the more prominent of these was General Henning von Tresckow, who had tried to organize an assassination plan from Smolensk in 1943. He knew that his name would be linked to the conspiracy. On July 21, 1944, he told his aide, Fabian von Schlabrendorff, that he planned to take his own life. Schlabrendorff recounted Tresckow's parting words:

General Erich Hoepner, who on July 20, 1944, asked Fromm to delay his execution so that he could explain his actions in court (shown here at his trial). He was sentenced to death by strangulation at his August 7, 1944, trial (Photo: National Archives).

> Now they will all fall upon us and cover us with abuse. But I am convinced now as much as ever, that we have done the right thing. I believe Hitler to be the arch enemy, not only of Germany, but indeed of the entire world.... The moral worth of a man only begins at the point where he is ready to sacrifice his life for his convictions.[12]

Tresckow then drove to an area near the front and, using his pistol, set off a rifle grenade, which killed him. The suicide was quick and certain. Others, intent on suicide as well, were not as fortunate.

General Stülpnagel, head of the coup attempt in Paris, was ordered by Hitler's aide Keitel on July 20 to report to Berlin. The general said he would report the following morning at 9 A.M. As his car drove near the site of the First World War battleground of Verdun, where many of Stülpnagel's comrades had died, he ordered the driver to detour, giving precise directions to the old battlefield. He left the car and ordered it to proceed to the next village, saying he wanted to walk alone for a while.

The driver followed his orders. A short distance up the road, he heard a gunshot. Returning, he found Stülpnagel floating in a canal. The driver, assuming partisans had shot the general, rushed him to the hospital at Verdun. Doctors were able to save him, although the sight in both eyes was destroyed in the attempted suicide. Stülpnagel, like many of his comrades, would face a show trial and a gruesome execution for his part in the conspiracy.

Verdun was also the site of General Kluge's suicide. Although not part of the conspiracy, Kluge was under suspicion by the Gestapo. On August 18, he was relieved of his command in France and ordered to Berlin for questioning. He stopped near the old battlefield, lay on a blanket under a tree, and took poison. He left letters to his wife, his son, and his leader, Hitler. To Hitler, Kluge wrote:

> Führer, I have always admired your greatness ... your iron will to maintain yourself and National Socialism.... You have fought an honorable and great fight.... Show yourself now always great enough to put an end to a hopeless struggle.... I depart from you, my Führer, as one who stood nearer to you than you perhaps realized.[13]

Even Erwin Rommel, Hitler's favorite field marshal, became a victim of the investigations. Although sympathetic to the goals of the resistance, Rommel was not directly involved. Injured before July 20, he was still recovering at his home in Ulm when Hitler sent two emissaries to inform him on October 14 that he had been implicated in the July bomb plot. According to the messengers, Rommel's name had been given during interrogation. Rommel was given a choice: suicide or trial before the People's Court. If he chose suicide, he was promised that his family would not be harmed and that he would be given a military funeral with full honors. Rommel, who was escorted from his house by SS men, took poison. The official cause of death was given as brain hemorrhage resulting from his wounds. Hitler kept his word. Rommel was given a proper funeral, and his family remained unharmed.

Only a handful of those involved survived to tell their stories. The majority were executed in prison or later in concentration camps. Approximately 7,000 people were arrested altogether, according to Gestapo files. Based on files found after the war, there were 4,980 documented executions for involvement in the July 20 bomb plot. Many others were summarily executed by the Gestapo or murdered in the concentration camps or in prison.

While most resistance members fell to the efficiency of the Gestapo, one who did survive was General Tresckow's aide, Fabian von Schlabrendorff. In 1943, Schlabrendorff had helped Tresckow disguise a bomb so that it looked like a bottle of Cointreau, in an unsuccessful attempt on Hitler's life.

On August 17, Schlabrendorff was arrested at his post on the eastern front and taken to Berlin, where he was placed in solitary confinement. For several months, Schlabrendorff was questioned and brutally tortured but refused to implicate anyone. He did finally admit that General Tresckow had been involved in resistance activities. With Tresckow dead, Schlabrendorff's admission did no harm, and the concession satisfied his interrogators for the moment.

Schlabrendorff came to trial on February 3, 1945, in the court of Roland Freisler. As the trial was about to begin, aid raid sirens went off. A direct hit caused a partial collapse of the building, and a falling beam struck Freisler, killing him.

At a rescheduled trial held March 16, Schlabrendorff's case was heard by Judge Dr. Wilhelm Crohne, who allowed the defendant to speak without interruption. Schlabrendorff detailed his mistreatment at the hands of the Gestapo, pointing out that torture had been outlawed in Germany by Frederick the Great two hundred years before. The argument gained Schlabrendorff an acquittal. As he was leaving court, the Gestapo took him back into custody, explaining that the judge had obviously made a mistake. Schlabrendorff was taken to Flossenbürg concentration camp where he was kept in chains in solitary confinement, awaiting execution. Because of the rapid advance of the American army, he was moved to Dachau and then to South Tyrol, where he was freed in the last days of the war.

Ironically, many innocent people were arrested because of information provided by Carl Goerdeler, one of the leading members of the resistance. When arrested, Goerdeler, believing that logic and intelligence would prevent drastic measures toward any of the conspirators, revealed in great detail the political plans of the resistance. Although many resistance members believed that Goerdeler must have broken down under torture, that had not been necessary. Goerdeler simply believed that he and the other resistance leaders were so valuable that the Nazis would never execute them.

Goerdeler was not in touch with the reality of his own situation. Shortly after his arrest on August 12, 1944, he wrote a note to Hitler asking for the release of all the conspirators so that they could form a political front to prepare for a rebuilding of Germany after the war. A visionary who ignored the brutal reality around him, Goerdeler dreamed of a United States of Europe, with Germany the financial and economic leader, existing in a world of prosperity, peace, and good relations between countries.

His vision was positive, his timing a half century too early. Goerdeler's position had always been that a political solution to the war was possible and that Hitler would ultimately agree. Goerdeler, a stern Christian, had opposed assassination. Unfortunately, his willingness to provide the Gestapo with names led to the arrest and execution of many people only marginally involved with the resistance movement.

Goerdeler's trial was held On September 7 and 8, 1944. Even when found guilty, Goerdeler believed he would not be executed, that his political abilities were so valuable that his death sentence would not be carried out. On February 2, 1945, he was proven wrong.

The wrath of the Nazi regime extended to the families of conspirators. On August 3, 1944, Himmler announced the infamous doctrine of *Sippenhaft*, "blood guilt." Under this doctrine, guilt was hereditary because of "diseased blood." Guilt extended to all members of the family, including the aged and the very young. Himmler specified, for example, that every last member of Stauffenberg's family was to be extinguished.

The blood guilt doctrine, also referred to as "kith and kin," was put into effect without delay. Approximately 50 children, some infants, were housed in the Children's Concentration Camp at Bad Sachsa, where they were forbidden to use their real names.

The original plan was to keep the children in the camp until their relatives had been executed and then to adopt them out to SS families. As the course of the war degenerated, this plan was abandoned. The imprisoned children were liberated by the American army on April 12, 1945. They were allowed to again use their real names and were returned home on May 4, by which time most were orphans.

The initial reaction to the failure of the coup d'état was an almost universal vilification of everyone involved. History, however, softened its opinion after the war, when the entire story became known. Although the effort appeared as too little, too late, it was seen in retrospect as courageous, an action undertaken with an eye on history itself.

The last words of several condemned conspirators best summarize their own perspective on their efforts. Immediately before his execution, Fritz-Dietlof von der Schulenburg wrote to his wife:

> What we did was inadequate, but in the end, history will judge and acquit us.[14]

Insight is also provided in the last words of one of Stauffenberg's cousins, Peter Yorck von Wartenburg. In a last letter to his wife, Yorck wrote:

> I, too, am dying for my country, and even if it seems to all appearances a very inglorious and disgraceful death, I shall hold up my head and I only hope that you will not believe this to be from pride or delusion. We wished to light the torch of life and now we stand in a sea of flames.[15]

Appendix A

*N*AMES

Maurice **Bavaud,** theology student who attempted to assassinate Hitler in 1923.

General Ludwig **Beck,** chief of staff of the army and later the acknowledged head of the military resistance against Hitler. Suicide, July 20, 1944.

Dr. George **Bell,** bishop of Chichester, prestigious British clergyman and contact between representatives of the German resistance and the British government.

General Werner von **Blomberg,** minister of war and commander in chief of the armed forces in the early years of the Third Reich.

General Fedor von **Bock,** commander of Army Group B in the west at the start of the war, who protested Hitler's planned invasion of France; later commander of Army Group Center on the eastern front.

Colonel Georg **Boeselager,** commander of Cavalry Regiment Center, who volunteered to devise a direct assault on Hitler while the Führer was visiting the eastern front.

Dietrich **Bonhoeffer,** Protestant pastor prominent in the Confessional church, prolific writer and world traveler placed under a writing and preaching ban by the Nazis; one of the few clergymen in favor of removing Hitler by any means possible. Executed April 9, 1945.

Colonel Heinz **Brandt,** aide to General Heusinger, present at the bomb attempt in Smolensk and at the bomb attempt in Wolfsschanze the following year.

General Walther von **Brauchitsch,** commander in chief of the army in the early war years.

Colonel Eberhard von **Breitenbuch,** aide to the Army Group Center commander, Field Marshal Ernst Busch. Breitenbuch carried a pistol to a meeting, intending to shoot Hitler, but was prevented by guards from entering the conference room.

General Walter von **Brockdorff-Ahlefeldt,** commander of the Potsdam Division and a supporter of the German resistance.

Carl J. **Burckhardt,** League of Nations high commissioner for Danzig, who helped the German resistance by carrying messages to Switzerland.

Field Marshal Ernst **Busch,** Kluge's replacement as commander of Army Group Center on the eastern front. (Promoted to field marshal on February 1, 1943.)

Captain Axel von dem **Bussche-Streithorst,** officer who volunteered for a suicide-murder attempt on Hitler after witnessing atrocities on the eastern front.

Admiral Wilhelm **Canaris,** chief of the Abwehr (army counterintelligence) and a member of the German resistance. Executed April 9, 1945.

Neville **Chamberlain,** British prime minister prior to the war, who attempted to appease Hitler with visits to Germany in 1938.

Winston **Churchill,** British prime minister after the beginning of the war.

Ian **Colvin,** British journalist with influential contacts in the government and a key contact for the German resistance.

Hans von **Dohnanyi,** civil servant who reorganized the civilian resistance after 1938, working closely with Hans Oster. Executed April 9, 1945.

Johann Georg **Elser,** carpenter and electrician who nearly succeeded in assassinating Hitler in November 1939.

Dr. Hasso von **Etzdorf,** counselor in the Foreign Ministry who predicted that the invasion of France would fail.

Michael von **Faulhaber,** cardinal archbishop of Bavaria and leader of the Catholic opposition to the Nazi regime.

General Erich **Fellgiebel,** chief of Army Communications, whose task it was to delay messages being sent or received for as long as possible on the day of the coup d'état. Executed September 4, 1944.

Dr. Hans **Frank,** commissioner of justice in the Nazi government.

Roland **Freisler,** infamous Nazi judge in the People's Court who presided over trials of resistance members.

Wilhelm **Frick,** Nazi minister of the interior.

General Werner von **Fritsch,** commander in chief of the army before the outbreak of war.

General Friedrich (Fritz) **Fromm,** commander of the Reserve Army who refused to cooperate with resistance leaders. Executed March 12, 1945.

Cardinal Clemens August von **Galen,** bishop of Münster and an outspoken leader of the religious opposition to the Nazi regime.

Colonel Rudolf von **Gersdorff,** an intelligence officer with Army Group Center on the eastern front who helped General Tresckow by obtaining explosives for the Smolensk attempt on Hitler's life.

Dr. Eugen **Gerstenmaier,** employee in the Information Division of the German Foreign Ministry who, with his friend Fritz-Dietlof Schulenburg, tried on several occasions to organize a company of officers to assassinate Hitler.

Dr. Hans **Gisevius,** counselor in the Ministry of the Interior and ex-police officer, Gestapo officer, and member of the Criminal Police; member of the resistance who established and maintained contact with American OSS agents in Switzerland.

Dr. Paul Joseph **Goebbels,** head of the Ministry of Propaganda in the Third Reich.

Carl **Goerdeler,** politician and administrator and civilian leader of the German resistance. Executed February 2, 1945.

Hermann **Göring,** head of the Luftwaffe and one of Hitler's closest advisers.

Major Helmuth **Groscurth,** Abwehr officer who obtained weapons and explosives for the planned 1938 coup in Berlin and predicted disaster if Germany invaded France.

Lieutenant Werner von **Haeften,** Stauffenberg's aide present at the assassination attempt on Hitler. Executed July 20, 1944.

Colonel Kurt **Hahn,** chief signals officer reporting to General Fellgiebel and a member of the resistance. Executed September 4, 1944.

General Franz **Halder,** armed forces chief of staff who opposed Hitler but backed away from full participation in planning for a coup d'état.

Lord Edward Frederick Lindley Wood **Halifax,** foreign secretary in the British government and an important diplomatic contact for the German resistance.

General Kurt von **Hammerstein-Equord,** commander in chief of the Reichswehr who opposed Hitler's appointment as chancellor and was later a supporter of the German resistance movement.

General Paul von **Hase,** commander of No. 50 Infantry Regiment and a military supporter of the German resistance; his units were picked to play the key role in Berlin during the coup d'état. Executed August 8, 1944.

Ulrich von **Hassell,** German ambassador to Rome until 1937 and a member of the German resistance involved with numerous diplomatic contacts with the Western Allies. Executed September 8, 1944.

Major Friedrich Wilhelm **Heinz,** head of the raiding party organized to arrest Hitler in the planned 1938 takeover of the government in Berlin.

Wolf Heinrich von **Helldorf,** Berlin police president and a member of the German resistance. Executed August 15, 1944.

Nevile **Henderson,** British ambassador to Germany whose contacts with the German resistance led to several appointments between resistance members and officials in the British government.

Konrad **Henlein,** head of the Czech *Sudeten Deutsche Partei* and ally to Hitler before the Allies gave in to German demands.

General Adolf **Heusinger,** operations chief and deputy chief of the General Staff.

Reinhard **Heydrich,** Himmler's head of the SS Intelligence Service, Reichssicherheit-shauptant (R.S.H.A.), organizer of the "final solution."

Heinrich **Himmler,** leader of the SS and one of the most powerful men in the Third Reich.

Paul von **Hindenburg,** president of Germany at the time Hitler was appointed chancellor.

General Erich **Hoepner,** resistance member who assumed command of the Reserve Army during the coup d'état in Berlin. Executed August 8, 1944.

Dr. Cäsar von **Hofacker,** reserve Luftwaffe colonel and cousin to Colonel Stauffenberg, leading resistance member in Paris. Executed December 20, 1944.

Dr. Kurt **Huber,** professor and head of the philosophy and psychology departments at the University of Munich and adviser to the White Rose, arrested and executed by the Nazis.

General Alfred **Jodl,** chief of the Armed Forces Operational Staff.

Otto **John,** legal adviser to the airline Lufthansa who worked with the resistance and established diplomatic contacts for them in Madrid, including communications with General Eisenhower's headquarters, which the resistance intended to use for peace negotiations.

Jakob **Kaiser,** former head of the Christian Trade Unions slated by Carl Goerdeler to organize reconstruction under the new German government.

Field Marshal Wilhelm **Keitel,** chief of the High Command of the armed forces.

Albrecht von **Kessel,** who with Adam Trott approached General Alexander Falkenhausen in 1939 and suggested a plot to arrest or kill Hitler.

Captain Friedrich Karl **Klausing,** aide to Colonel Stauffenberg who attended a July 11 meeting where a planned attempt on Hitler was canceled at the last minute. Executed August 8, 1944.

Lieutenant Ewald Heinrich von **Kleist,** son of diplomat Kleist-Schmenzin, volunteer for a suicide-murder attempt on Hitler.

Ewald von **Kleist-Schmenzin,** diplomat who made numerous contacts in Britain, attempting to negotiate for support of the resistance movement. Executed April 16, 1945.

Field Marshal Günther von **Kluge,** commander in chief at Army Group Center and later commander in chief in the west, replacing Field Marshall Rommel. Suicide, August 19, 1944.

Erich **Kordt,** an employee in the ministerial bureau of the Berlin Foreign Ministry involved with establishing important diplomatic contacts for the German resistance.

Theodor **Kordt,** acting chargé d'affaires in the German embassy in London who established useful British contacts for the German resistance.

Carl **Langbehn,** lawyer and member of the diplomatic service, who aided the resistance by setting up a meeting between Popitz and Himmler. Executed October 12, 1944.

Julius **Leber,** Social Democrat and writer placed under a publishing ban by the Nazi regime; he was a prominent member of the German resistance. Executed January 5, 1945.

General Wilhelm von **Leeb,** commander of Army Group C at the beginning of the war who wrote to Hitler protesting the planned French offensive.

Wilhelm **Leuschner,** former minister of the interior in Hesse and firm anti–Nazi, one of Carl Goerdeler's important resistance allies. Executed September 29, 1944.

Lord **Lloyd** (George Ambrose), chairman of the British Council contacted by the German resistance before the start of the war.

Walter **Löwenheim,** founder of the underground group Neu-Beginnen who wrote and smuggled anti–Nazi literature into Germany using the pseudonym "Miles."

General Erich **Ludendorff,** head of the German High Command at the end of the First World War and a proponent of Hitler's 1923 putsch.

Colonel F. Noel **Mason-Macfarlane,** British military attaché in Berlin who volunteered to assassinate Hitler from his apartment, using a high-power rifle.

Hans **Meiser,** bishop of Bavaria and outspoken opponent of the Nazi regime.

Colonel Albrecht von **Mertz von Quirnheim,** conspirator present at the War Ministry on the day of the attempted coup d'état. Executed July 20, 1944.

Vyacheslav M. **Molotov,** Russian foreign minister who engineered the German-Russian nonaggression pact.

Helmuth von **Moltke,** young idealist who headed the Kreisau Circle and provided the intellectual leadership of the German resistance. Executed January 23, 1945.

Dr. Josef **Müller,** a civilian who established contact with the Vatican and produced the "X Report" establishing the pope's willingness to help the German resistance negotiate with the Allies after Hitler's removal.

Ludwig **Müller,** a dedicated Nazi appointed as Reich bishop in an attempt to unify German churches in cooperation with the Nazi regime.

Arthur **Nebe,** director of the Reich Criminal Police Office and member of the German resistance. Executed March 3, 1945.

Martin **Niemöller,** pastor of Dahlem and retired U-boat commander who spoke from his pulpit in opposition to the policies of the Nazi regime.

Sir George **Ogilvie-Forbes,** counselor in the British embassy involved in several unofficial contacts with the German resistance.

General Friedrich **Olbricht,** deputy commander of the Reserve Army who promised to issue orders launching the coup d'état. Executed July 20, 1944.

General Hans **Oster,** Abwehr chief of staff under Admiral Canaris and a leading member of the German resistance. Executed April 9, 1945.

Rudolf **Pechel,** editor of the ant-Nazi newspaper D*eutsche Rundschau* who delivered resistance messages to London.

Johannes **Popitz,** ex-Prussian minister of finance, one of the idealists of the Kreisau Circle and an experienced politician, economist, and scientist, perhaps the most intellectual member of the German resistance. Executed February 2, 1945.

Christoph **Probst,** member of the White Rose in Munich, arrested and executed by the Nazis.

Admiral Erich **Raeder,** naval commander who advised Hitler against invading Britain before the RAF could be destroyed.

Adolf **Reichwein,** Social Democrat and friend of Julius Leber; attended a meeting in June 1944 with a cell of Communists that was infiltrated by the Gestapo. Executed October 20, 1944.

Joachim von **Ribbentrop,** German foreign minister.

Ernst **Röhm,** head of the SA until 1934, when Hitler had him executed.

Captain Josef (Beppo) **Römer,** would-be assassin of Hitler in close contact with the underground "Robby Group."

Field Marshal Erwin **Rommel,** commander in chief of Army Group B in France in July 1944 who agreed to work with the resistance by contacting Eisenhower to negotiate a cease-fire after the coup d'état. Suicide, October 14, 1944.

Alfred **Rosenberg,** pseudo-philosopher and author of *The Myth of the Twentieth Century,* appointed by Hitler in 1941 to organize the management of civilian populations on the eastern front.

General Gerd von **Rundstedt,** commander of Army Group A in the west who protested Hitler's planned French offensive at the beginning of the war.

Dr. Karl **Sack,** judge-advocate general of the German army and opponent to the Nazi regime. Executed April 9, 1945.

Dr. Hjalmar **Schacht,** minster of economics in the early years of the Third Reich.

Fabian von **Schlabrendorff,** lawyer and Wehrmacht reserve officer who worked with the resistance in trying to establish diplomatic contacts and was involved with General Tresckow in the Smolensk attempt on Hitler's life.

Professor Friedrich Alfred **Schmid Noerr,** the author of the "Community of the People," a draft for a constitution for Germany after the removal of the Nazi regime.

Alexander **Schmorell,** member of the White Rose in Munich, arrested and executed by the Nazis.

Paul **Schneider,** pastor of Dickenschied and outspoken critic of Nazi policies, tortured and murdered in Buchenwald in 1939.

Hans and Sophie **Scholl,** students and founders of the White Rose, a group of students who wrote anti–Nazi literature in the Munich area. Both were arrested and executed for their writings.

Dr. Hans **Schönfeld,** research director with the World Council of Churches and a member of the Foreign Affairs Department of the German Evangelical church; carried messages from the German resistance to Dr. George Bell in Sweden.

Friedrich Werner von der **Schulenburg,** German ambassador in Moscow when the war began. Executed November 10, 1944.

Fritz-Dietlof von der **Schulenburg,** vice president of the Berlin police and a member of the German resistance who tried with Eugen Gerstenmaier to organize a party of officers to assassinate Hitler. Executed August 10, 1944.

Harro **Schulze-Boysen,** founder of the Red Orchestra underground group, arrested and executed by the Nazis.

Gerhard **Schwerin von Schwanefeld,** a career officer and aristocrat who helped the resistance by using his contacts in the British government to try and influence policies to discourage the Nazi regime before the outbreak of the war.

Captain Ulrich Wilhelm **Schwerin von Schwanefeld,** officer recruited to the resistance by Witzleben. Executed September 8, 1944.

Hanna **Solf,** hostess of a group of aristocratic Germans known as the Solf Circle who held discussion groups.

General Hans **Speidel,** chief of staff to Field Marshal Rommel and a member of the resistance.

Colonel Claus Schenk von **Stauffenberg,** chief of staff of the Reserve Army and, from the winter of 1943 onward, the undisputed leader and driving force of the German resistance. Stauffenberg planted a briefcase containing explosives beneath a conference table on July 20, 1944, injuring Hitler and killing four other officers. On the same day, he returned to Berlin and led the attempted coup d'état against the Third Reich. Executed July 20, 1944.

General Helmuth **Stieff,** headquarters staff officer who obtained explosives for an attempt on Hitler's life and hid them at Wolfsschanze; later supplied explosives to Stauffenberg for his July 20, 1944, attempt. Executed August 8, 1944.

Julius **Streicher,** publisher of *Der Stürmer* and one of Hitler's earliest supporters.

General Karl Heinrich von **Stülpnagel,** military governor of France and key member of the German resistance in Paris. Executed August 30, 1944.

General Fritz **Thiele,** chief of staff to General Fellgiebel and a member of the resistance. Executed September 5, 1944.

General Georg **Thomas,** chief of the Economics and Supply Group in OKW, who helped Hans Oster by drafting economic arguments against the plan to go to war.

General Henning von **Tresckow,** chief of staff at Army Group Center on the eastern front and leading resistance member in 1943 who organized the plan to place a bomb on Hitler's plane at Smolensk. Suicide July 21, 1944.

Adam von **Trott zu Solz,** a world traveler and intellectual of the Kreisau Circle who made efforts over many years to establish diplomatic ties for the German resistance, both in London and Washington, under the guise of his position as counselor in the German Foreign Office. Executed August 26, 1944.

Robert **Uhrig,** Communist activist opposed to the Nazi regime and founder of the "Robby Group."

Robert **Vansittart,** permanent undersecretary of state for foreign affairs in the British government and an important go-between for the German resistance.

Major Hans-Alexander von **Voss,** officer recruited to the resistance by General Witzleben and later transferred to Army Group C on the eastern front. Suicide, August 11, 1944.

Captain Alfred von **Waldersee,** operations officer for the commandant of Paris and a member of the resistance.

Ernst von **Weizsäcker,** secretary of state in the German Foreign Ministry who contacted the British government on behalf of the German resistance before the beginning of the war.

Sumner **Welles,** under-secretary of state in the Roosevelt administration.

Sir Horace **Wilson,** industrial adviser to the British government and confidant of Prime Minister Chamberlain.

Dr. Karl Joseph **Wirth,** ex-chancellor of Germany who contacted Prime Minister Chamberlain on behalf of the German resistance and received assurances from Britain to cooperate with a new government in Germany.

Field Marshal Erwin von **Witzleben,** officer slated to assume command of the armed forces in Berlin on the day of the coup d'état. Executed August 8, 1944.

Theophil **Wurm,** bishop of Württemberg and outspoken opponent of the Nazi regime.

Peter **Yorck von Wartenburg,** prominent member of the Kreisau Circle and cousin to Colonel Stauffenberg, idealist and economic adviser attached to the Wehrmacht at the beginning of the war. Executed August 8, 1944.

Appendix B

DOCUMENTS

Teleprint from Witzleben, July 20, 1944[1]

I The Führer Adolf Hitler is dead.

An irresponsible gang of Party leaders, far behind the front, has tried to exploit this situation to stab the hard-pressed army in the back and seize power for its own ends.

II In this hour of supreme danger the Reich government, to maintain law and order, has proclaimed a state of military emergency and has entrusted to me both supreme command of the armed forces and executive power in the Reich.

III I hereby order:

1. I transfer executive power, with right of delegation to territorial commanders:

In the Home Forces area to C-in-C Replacement Army who is at the same time appointed C-in-C Home Forces area

In western occupied territories to C-in-C West (C-in-C Army Group D)

In Italy to C-in-C South-West (C-in-C Army Group C)

In the south-eastern area to C-in-C South-East (C-in-C Army Group F)

In the occupied eastern territories to Cs-in-C of Army Groups South Ukraine, North Ukraine, Center, North and the Wehrmacht Commander Ostland, each in their respective areas.

In Denmark and Norway to the Wehrmacht Commanders.

2. The following are placed under orders of the holders of executive power:

   (a) all agencies and units in the area concerned of the armed forces including the Waffen-SS, the Labor Service and the Todt Organization;

   (b) all official authorities (of the Reich, the Länder and of communities), in particular the entire regular police, security police and administrative police;

   (c) all officials and branches of the National-Socialist Party and its affiliated organizations;

   (d) all transport and supply agencies.

3. The whole of the Waffen-SS is incorporated into the Army with immediate effect.

4. The holders of executive power and responsible for the maintenance of public order and security. They will pay particular attention to:

(a)   security of communications installations;

(b)   elimination of the SD

Any resistance to military authority will be ruthlessly suppressed.

5. In this hour of supreme danger to the Fatherland the first necessity is the unity of the Wehrmacht and the maintenance of discipline.

I therefore order all Army, Navy and Air Force commanders to use all resources available to them to support those given executive power in their difficult task and to ensure that their orders are obeyed by all subordinate agencies.

The German soldier is confronted with a historic task. The salvation of Germany will depend on his energy and morale.

All territorial commanders, the High Commands of the Services and the Army, Navy and Air Force headquarters immediately subordinate to the High Commands have identical instructions.

— The Supreme Commander of the Wehrmacht
v. Witzleben, Field Marshal

Teleprint from Stauffenberg, July 20, 1944[2]

1. In virtue of the authority granted me as Supreme Commander of the Wehrmacht I transfer executive power to Wehrkreis Commanders. The prerogatives of Reich Defense Commissars are also transferred to Wehrkreis Commanders.

2. The following measures are to be taken forthwith:

(a)   Communications installations:

The most important buildings and installations of the Post Office and Wehrmacht communications networks (including wireless transmitters) will be taken systematically under military protection. Forces employed must be strong enough to prevent unauthorized action or demolitions. The more important communications installations will be occupied under officer supervision. In particular the following will be guarded: Repeater stations, army transmitting exchanges, main radio stations, telephone and telegraph offices carrying vital lines, amplifier and battery rooms, antennae, transmission current and emergency current rooms, traffic offices. The railway communications network will be protected in agreement with transport agencies. A radio network will be set up using own resources.

(b)   Arrests:

Following will be relieved of their offices forthwith and placed in secure solitary confinement:

All Gauleiter, Reichsstatthälter, Ministers, Governors, Police Presidents, Senior SS and Police Commanders, heads of Gestapo and SD offices, heads of propaganda offices, Kreisleiter. Exceptions only by my special order.

(c)   Concentration Camps:

Concentration camps will be occupied at once, camp commandants arrested, guard personnel disarmed and confined in barracks. Political prisoners are to be instructed that, pending their liberation, they should refrain from demonstrations or independent action.

(d) Waffen-SS:

If compliance by commanders of Waffen-SS formations or by the senior Waffen-SS officers appears doubtful or if they seem unsuitable, they will be taken into protective custody and replaced by Army officers.

Waffen-SS formations whose unquestioned compliance appears doubtful will be ruthlessly disarmed. Firm action with superior forces will be taken to avoid further bloodshed.

(e) Police:

Gestapo and SD headquarters will be occupied. Otherwise the regular police will be used as far as possible to relieve the Wehrmacht. Orders will be issued by Chief of German Police through police channels.

(f) Navy and Air Force:

Contact will be maintained with naval and air force commanders. Measures will be taken to ensure combined action.

3. To deal with all political questions I attach to each Wehrkreis Commander a Political Representative. Until further orders he will be responsible for administration. He will advise the Wehrkreis Commander on all political matters.

4. The headquarters of the C-in-C Home Forces is the executive agency for all matters concerning the exercise of executive power. It will dispatch a liaison officer to Wehrkreis Commanders for the exchange of information and views.

5. In the exercise of executive power no arbitrary acts or acts of revenge will be tolerated. The people must be made aware of the difference from the arbitrary methods of their former rulers.

— Stauffenberg (For Fromm)

Appeal to the Wehrmacht from Witzleben (intended for radio broadcast, never aired)[3]

German soldiers!

More than four years of the most courageous struggle lie behind you. Millions of your comrades have died on the battlefields of Europe and Asia, in the air and at sea. Hitler's unscrupulous leadership has sacrificed whole armies made up of the flower of our youth in Russia and in the Mediterranean for his fantastic plans of boundless conquest. The wanton use of the Sixth Army at Stalingrad and the senseless sacrifice throw a harsh light on the grim truth. Capable officers who opposed this insane act were removed, the General Staff pushed aside. In spite of your heroism Hitler's self-imagined military genius is driving us to a fatal end.

At home more and more centers of family life and places of work are being destroyed. Already six million Germans are homeless. In the rear corruption and crime, tolerated from the outset and even ordered by Hitler, are assuming tremendous proportions.

In this hour of extreme trouble and danger German men have done their duty before God and the people; they have taken action and given Germany a leadership of experienced and responsible men.

The man who gave a timely warning, who resolutely opposed this war and for that reason was dismissed by Hitler, is Beck. For the present he has taken over the leadership of the German Reich and the Supreme Command of the Wehrmacht. The Government is composed of tried men from all classes of the nation, from all parts of the Fatherland. It has begun to work.

I have been entrusted with the command of the whole Wehrmacht. The Commanders-in-Chief on all fronts have put themselves under my orders. The German Wehrmacht now obeys my command.

Soldiers! We must secure a just peace which will make possible for the German people a life of freedom and honor, and for the nation voluntary and fruitful cooperation. I pledge you my word that from now on you will be called upon to make only those sacrifices necessary to achieve this end. All the strength of the nation will now be thrown in only for this task. The senseless squandering of strength, the half measures and tardy decisions which have cost so much human life are at an end.

Wherever you may be, at the front or in the occupied territories I call upon you to observe the laws of unconditional obedience, soldierly discipline and honorable, chivalrous conduct. Whoever has not observed these laws in the past or offends against them in the future will be severely called to account. At home too we are fighting for right and freedom, for decency and purity.

I expect each one of you to continue to do your duty loyally and bravely. On that depends the fate of our Fatherland, our own and our children's future.

Soldiers! What is at stake is the continued existence and the honor of our Fatherland, a true community within our own people and with the nations of the world.

Appeal to the German people from Beck (intended for radio broadcast, never aired)[4]

Germans!

In recent years terrible things have taken place before our very eyes. Against the advice of experts Hitler has ruthlessly sacrificed whole armies for his passion for glory, his megalomania, his blasphemous delusion that he was the chosen and favored instrument of Providence.

Not called to power by the German people, but becoming the Head of the Government by intrigues of the worst kind, he has spread confusion by his devilish arts and lies and by tremendous extravagance which on the surface seemed to bring prosperity to all, but which in reality plunged the German people into terrible debt. In order to remain in power, he added to this an unbridled reign of terror, destroyed law, outlawed decency, scorned the divine commands of pure humanity and destroyed the happiness of millions of human beings.

His insane disregard for all mankind could not fail to bring our nation to misfortune with deadly certainty; his self-imagined supremacy could not but bring ruin to our brave sons, fathers, husbands and brothers, and his bloody terror against the defenseless could not but bring shame to the German name. He enthroned lawlessness, oppression of conscience, crime and corruption in our Fatherland which has always been proud of its integrity and honesty. Truthfulness and veracity, virtues which even the simplest people think it their duty to inculcate in their children, are punished and persecuted. Thus public activity and private life are threatened by a deadly poison.

This must not be, this cannot go on. The lives and deaths of our men, women and children must no longer be abused for this purpose. We would not be worthy of our fathers, we would be despised by our children if we had not the courage to do everything, I repeat everything, to ward off this danger from ourselves and to achieve self-respect again.

It is for this purpose that, after searching our conscience, we have taken over power. Our brave Wehrmacht is a pledge of security and order. The police will do their duty.

Each civil servant shall carry out his duties according to his technical knowledge, following only the law and his own conscience. Let each of you help by discipline and confidence. Carry out your daily work with new hope. Help one another! Your tortured souls shall again find peace and comfort.

Far from all hatred we will strive for inward reconciliation and with dignity for outward reconciliation. Our first task will be to cleanse the war from its degeneration and end the devastating destruction of human life, of cultural and economic values behind the fronts. We all know that we are not masters of peace and war. Firmly relying on our incomparable Wehrmacht and in confident belief in the tasks assigned to man by God we will sacrifice everything to defend the Fatherland and to restore a lawful solemn state of order, to live once more for honor and peace with respect for the divine commandments, in purity and truth!

Statement to the press from Goerdeler (never released)[5]

Germans!

Since this morning, you know what is at stake, you know what our motives and intentions are. The law of extreme self-defense and the duty of self-preservation point the way both to you and to us. Our lot has not been the promised state, firmly and wisely led, but a terrible despotism. The bravery, the courage in dying and the skill of our soldiers have been shamefully abused; and our homeland has been unscrupulously exposed to misery and destruction.

As the final link in an unnecessary chain of oppression and violation of the law, Hitler in his Reichstag speech of April 24, 1942, described all Germans as being as free as the birds, while he claimed for himself the right to overturn every judgment according as he saw fit. Thus he called into being a depth of lawlessness such as was never before known among civilized peoples and which cannot be surpassed. From the proud Germany of equal rights for all he made a powerful community of slaves, in which the citizen had no longer the opportunity to defend himself against injustice.

The holders of the highest honors, even Adolf Hitler himself, have committed, ordered and tolerated countless crimes against the person and against life, against property and honor. Men in high positions have shamelessly enriched themselves from public funds or from money extorted from others, and chief among these is Field Marshal Göring! We do not wish to see German honor sullied by such parasites. We do not wish to be led by scoundrels who cannot distinguish between mine and thine, who abuse their positions to lead a sumptuous life in magnificent rooms even in wartime, when the people are suffering, while abroad sons, husbands and sweethearts are fighting and dying and at home the mad destruction of total war rages.

An adventurous foreign policy, thirsting for power, has brought our people to a situation the seriousness of which can no longer be overlooked. Considerations of war prevent us from calling things by their proper names. But you know or feel what pitch we have been brought to by unscrupulousness and madness. As soon as the situation allows, we will call upon good men from all classes and from all districts and we will tell you their names; they will carefully examine everything that has happened and will give you a detailed report on the situation as we found it.

One thing we can tell you now: the structure of the State which was built up on injustice, tyranny, crimes of all kinds, self-interest and lies will be torn down. The cornerstone of the new State will be the sure principles of human life, right and justice, truth, decency, purity, reason, mutual consideration and respect for the nations created by God and their vital interests.

If we do not want a repetition of November, 1918, this is the last moment at which we can put this plan into action. In the next few days we shall publicly call to account, irrespective of their position, those who are responsible for the ruin of the State and the people.

Hard work in all walks of life lies ahead. There is no magic formula for stopping the frivolous destruction of all the basic principles of life and gradually restoring them. Together we want to save the Fatherland and restore the fabric of duty and community. We cannot promise an alleviation in ordinary life during the war and during the period of reconstruction. Think what is at stake! For what do you want to live and die? What are our soldiers to fight and die for? For justice, freedom, honor and decency, or for crime, terror, shame and disgrace? If you answer these questions rightly, there is hope of ending this war, which has developed into a wretched Second World War, in such a way that Germany's vital interests can be preserved.

But this aim is not the only decisive one. The decisive factor for us is that we will no longer tolerate the dishonoring of our people and the sullying of our good name by insolent criminals and liars. For if they carry on their dirty work, then not even our children and our children's children would be able to restore the Fatherland on a healthy basis.

You shall learn of the criminals and the crimes as soon as possible. You yourselves will be in a position to see that terrible things have happened. But we shall also see to it that only just punishment in accordance with the laws is administered. None of you must allow himself to take precipitate action; for above all feelings of vengeance is the necessity to restore the state of equal rights for all under a just leadership.

Anyone who has an accusation to make on account of some wrong suffered, should make it either himself or through someone he trusts to any authority he thinks fit. It will be the duty of these agencies to pass on accusations made to them to the new Ministry of Justice, which will see to it that they are dealt with immediately. Each will receive an answer. Only those accusations will be dealt with in which the accuser states his name. All others will go unexamined where they belong: into the wastepaper basket. If the complaint is justified, the proper legal proceedings will be taken; but in the same way anyone who makes an accusation against his better knowledge will be held responsible; for we want the honor of our fellow men and our own moral sense to be taken seriously again.

No one whose conscience is clear need be afraid or worry. The question is not: Party member or not Party member. Away with these distinctions, which have been artificially grafted on to the German way of life! The question is not: SS, SA or any other organization. The question is: decent or corrupt!

Each must continue to do his duty where he is, obeying only the laws and decrees of the new administration. The fate of our soldiers who are fighting a hard battle depends on each one at home giving his best. We owe everything to them and to our beloved dead. They, the soldiers and the wounded, must come before all other cares.

It is understandable that you must feel extremely excited by what has at long last taken place. From now on, as far as considerations of war allow, you are again free to give unhampered expression to your thoughts and feelings and to follow the dictates of your own conscience. You yourselves will be responsible that our beloved Fatherland does not suffer by this, for the state of war still imposes restrictions on all of us. We will ensure that everything proceeds in a legal and orderly manner, as demanded by the well-being of the Fatherland.

The inner cleansing of Germany from corruption and crime, the restoration of law and decency regardless of the person, but at the same time without prejudice to those who hold other views can be achieved very quickly and very easily in accordance with the proud traditions of our people, if each makes his contribution. That we can expect from all right thinking men and women, for their personal happiness depends on the restoration of these benefits. Even those who previously thought they could or ought to deny this, are aware of this.

In wartime, no one can loosen the fetters of State control of economy. For the present we can only introduce simplifications and attack dishonesty for which State control has prepared the ground. But as soon as possible we will restore freedom and self-administration in economy and in family life, in the small community and in the State.

The most serious aspect is that of foreign policy. Here we must take account of the interests and the wishes of other nations. We do not yet know what will be the attitude of the outside world to us. We have had to act as our conscience told us. But we will tell you the aims we envisage in foreign policy.

We Germans are no more alone in this world than any other nation. We must therefore reconcile ourselves to the best of our ability with the presence, the qualities and the interests of other nations. We are convinced that this reconciliation will not be achieved by force of arms. The more God has allowed us, through the mental gifts which we owe to him, to make technical developments, the more destructive has war become. It destroys everything which those mental gifts are intended to build up. In the end it consumes itself.

Therefore, we desire a peaceful, just settlement of the conflicting interests which are determined not so much by men as by their environment. We are convinced that such a settlement is possible, because, considered calmly, it is in the interests of all nations. It can take place provided the nations respect each other and grant each nation the right to form and administer a State independently. Nations can best advance their physical and spiritual welfare when they work together and thus bring their various forces into a great harmonious whole, which benefits everyone. Such cooperation will lead to trade which will be as untrammeled as possible. With such trade the large and small States have flourished and thrived since the beginning of the nineteenth century. We must restore it as soon as possible. Every thinking person will realize that this restoration cannot take place overnight or without great disturbance. Thinking men of all nations must study how the surest and shortest way can be found which will allow each to attain his vital interests in the best possible way, in so far as he has the firm intention to work hard and to consider the interests of others.

We therefore think it is essential to end as quickly as possible further devastation and the further squandering of the national forces of each nation for the work of destruction. Each nation, whether involved in the war or not, will have a multitude of difficulties to overcome to repair the material losses caused by the way.

Such cooperation is possible only if it is built up on a stable system of acknowledged legal principles. Even a simple game cannot be ended without dispute unless each player observes definite rules of the game. How much more impossible it is if nations, living under the most widely differing conditions, will not cooperate in the greatest task of all, namely, the harmonious fusion of all forces. We believe that God wishes this. We therefore regard as the best bulwark to ensure these rules of the game in the life of nations purity of mind; the moral sense which springs only from religious conviction. We do not forget that these rules need to be formulated and that man's imperfection makes it necessary to entrust them in addition to a protecting power. Recognizing the independence of all States as it has developed in the course of history we are prepared to cooperate in this way in small as well as in big matters.

The quickest possible restoration of an ordered public economy in all countries is essential; for, without this, stable currencies cannot exist and without them the orderly and regular exchange of goods and services is impossible.

We shall not hesitate to transform these necessities into reality. In doing so we must take into account the facts of this terrible war. But we will see to it that, where foreign territory must still remain occupied, it will be made possible for the countries affected to be self-governing, and the presence of German troops as little of a burden as possible. We know from painful experience how deeply it enters into the soul of every nation to see the soldiers of another power on the sacred soil of their country.

So, not knowing what the attitude of the outside world towards us will be, we must continue our struggle. All of us have bitter experiences behind us. We are men who were accustomed to do our duty even in the most repugnant circumstances. We are men who took over an evil inheritance without complaining about the previous faithless arbiters of our fate. We do not want to lessen our own responsibility or to put ourselves in a better light by putting the blame on others and by slandering them. We wish to return to the language of civilized decency such as was the custom in every self-respecting German family.

We call upon you to practice self-searching and confidence and to be ready to make sacrifices. Do not hate, help rather! Accomplish the highest good: find the soul of our nation again. Thus you will gain strength to achieve more and to help even more effectively our brave soldiers on land, at sea and in the air. Let us unite with you, knowing in our hearts that no more German blood will be sacrificed to the thirst for power of an incompetent leadership, but only for the defense of our vital interests.

With God for right and freedom and the security of peaceful work!

Draft of a government statement
(intended to be read over radio, never aired)[6]

The principles on which Government will be conducted and the aims which we are pursuing have been announced. We make the following statement on this:

(1) The first task is the restoration of the full majesty of the law. The Government itself must be careful to avoid any arbitrary action, it must therefore submit itself to orderly control by the people. During the war this control can only be organized provisionally. For the time being upright and experienced men from all classes and from every Gau will be called to form a Reich Council; we will be accountable to this Reich Council and will seek its advice.

There was a time when we were proud of the integrity and honesty of our people, of the security and the excellence of German administration of justice. Our grief at seeing it destroyed must be all the greater.

No human society can exist without law, no one, not even those who think they can despise it, can live without it. For each man there comes the moment when he calls upon the law. In His ordering of the universe, in His creation and in His commandments God has given us the need for the law. He gave us insight and power to ensure human institutions within the framework of the law. Therefore the independence, irremovability and security of office of the judges must be restored. We know quite well that many of them acted as they did only under the pressure of extreme terrorization; but apart from that a strict investigation will take place to find out whether judges committed the crime of misapplying the law. Those guilty will be removed. In order to restore public confidence in the administration of the law, laymen will take part in passing sentence in penal cases. This will also apply to the courts martial which have been established temporarily.

Justice will be restored. It is not the business of the judge to make new laws. His duty is to apply the law and to do so in the most scrupulous manner. The law shall not be a rigid written code, but it must be definite and clear. It was a crime against the people and against the judge to give the latter vague ideas and so-called ideology as a guiding principle. It is intolerable that men should be condemned when they could not know that what they had done was punishable. In cases where the State has by law declared actions of its own bodies to be exempt from punishment, when in fact these actions were punishable, these exceptions will be canceled as being incompatible with the nature of the law and those responsible will be called to account.

The law will be applied to all those who have offended against it. The punishment deserved will be meted out to the offenders.

Security of person and property will again be protected against arbitrary action. According to the law only the judge can interfere in these personal rights of the individual which are essential for the existence of the State and for the happiness of men and women.

The concentration camps will be abolished as soon as possible, the innocent released and the guilty brought to justice.

But in the same way we do not expect anyone to carry out lynch justice. If we are to restore the majesty of the law we must energetically oppose personal vengeance, which, in view of the injustices suffered and the wounding of the souls of men, is only understandable. If anyone has a grudge, let him lodge an accusation with whatever public authority he likes. His accusation will be forwarded to the proper quarter. The guilty will be pitilessly punished. But the accusation must be genuine. False accusations will be punished, anonymous accusations will find their way into the wastepaper basket.

(2) We wish to restore the principles of morality in all spheres of private and public life.

Among our people who were once so upright, corruption has been practiced by high, even by the highest, officials of the Nazi Party to an extent never known before. While our soldiers were fighting, bleeding and dying on the battlefields, men like Göring, Goebbels, Ley and company were leading a life of luxury, plundering, filling their cellars and attics, urging the people to endure, and, cowards as they were, avoiding the sacrifice going on around them, both they and their entourage. All evil-doers will be called to account before the full severity of the law, their ill-gotten gains will be taken from them and restored to those from whom they were stolen. But the chief culprits shall pay with their lives and property. All their property and that which they have assigned to their relatives will be taken from them.

The reserved occupations established for political pretexts are abolished. Every man who is fit to fight can prove his worth and his will to endure at the front. We will tolerate no more fireside heroes.

An essential part of the safeguarding of law and decency is decent treatment of human beings. The persecution of Jews which has been carried out by the most inhuman, merciless and degrading methods and for which there can be no compensation is to cease forthwith. Anyone who thought that he could enrich himself with the assets of a Jew will learn that it is a disgrace for any German to strive for such ill-gotten possessions. The German people truly wants to have nothing more to do with pillagers and hyenas among the creatures made by God.

We feel it is a deep dishonor to the German name that crimes of all kinds have been committed in the occupied countries behind the backs of the fighting soldiers and abusing their protection. The honor of our dead is thereby sullied. There, too, we will see that restitution is made.

Anyone who has taken advantage of the war in these countries to fill his pockets or has departed from the rules of honor will be severely punished.

One of our noblest tasks is to restore the family as the nucleus of the community. For this we need the influence of the home, the power of religion, the cooperation of the Churches. Pure and healthy family life can only be built up on a serious and responsible conception of marriage. Immorality must be attacked if our children are not to be demoralized; for how can parents expect their children to be pure if they themselves do not exercise self-control and show their children the best example? The life of our nation will only recover when there is once more healthy family life.

We want no split in the nation. We know that many entered the Party out of idealism, out of bitterness against the Versailles dictate and its effects and against many national degradations, and others from economic or other pressure. The nation must not be divided according to this. All Germans who feel and act as Germans belong together. The only distinction which is to be made is between crime and unscrupulousness on the one hand and decency and integrity on the other. On this basis we will strive with all our might for the inner reconciliation of the people. For only if we remain united on the basis of justice and decency can we survive the fateful struggle into which God has placed our nation.

(3) We declare war on falsehood. The sun of truth shall dispel the thick fog of untruth. Our nation has been most shamelessly deceived about its economic and financial position and about military and political events. The facts will be ascertained and made public, so that everyone can examine them. It is a great mistake to assume that it is permissible for a Government to win over the people for its own purposes by lies. In His order of things God admits no double morality. Even the lies of Governments are short-lived and are always born of cowardice. Success in asserting the position of the nation, the happiness of the people, and the peace of mind of the individual can only be founded on integrity. The truth is often hard; but a people which cannot bear the truth is lost in any case. The individual can only summon up true strength if he sees things as they are. The climber who underestimates the height of the peak to be scaled, the swimmer who misjudges the distance to be covered, will exhaust his energy too soon. All untrue propaganda shall therefore stop; that applies first and foremost to the Reich Ministry of Propaganda. The abuse of the propaganda agencies of the Wehrmacht must also cease. The living and dying of our soldiers needs no propaganda. It is deeply engraved in the heart of every German wife and mother, in the heart of every German at home.

(4) The freedom of mind, conscience and faith which has been destroyed will be restored.

The Churches will again have the right freely to work for their faith. In future they will be completely separated from the State, because only by being independent and by remaining aloof from all political activity can they fulfill their task. The life of the State will be inspired by Christian thinking in word and deed. For we owe to Christianity the rise of the white races, and also the ability to combat the evil impulses within us. No community either of race or of State can renounce this combat. But true Christianity also demands tolerance towards those of other faiths or free-thinkers. The State will again give the Churches the opportunity to engage in truly Christian activities, particularly in the sphere of welfare and education.

The press will be free again. In wartime it must accept the restrictions necessary for a country in any war. Everyone who reads a newspaper shall know who is behind that paper. The press will not again be allowed to publish lies either deliberately or through carelessness.

By strict jurisdiction the editors will ensure that the rules of decency and of duty towards the welfare of the Fatherland are also observed in the press.

(5) It is, above all, German youth which calls out for truth. If proof of the divine nature of man is needed, here it is. Even the children with their instinctive knowledge of what is true and what is false turn away ashamed and angry from the falseness of the thoughts and words expected of them. It was probably the greatest crime of all to disre-

gard and abuse this sense of truth and with it the idealism of our young people. We will therefore protect it and strengthen it.

Youth and the education of youth is one of our main cares. First and foremost this education will be placed in the hands of the parents and the schools. All schools must implant elementary principles simply, clearly and firmly in the child. Training must again be general, embracing the emotions and the understanding. It must have its roots in the people, and there must be no gulf between educated and uneducated.

Education must again be placed deliberately on the Christian-religious basis, and the Christian laws of the utmost tolerance towards those of other faiths must not be broken. On this basis the educational and training system must again be conducted calmly and steadfastly, and must be protected against constant changes and disturbances.

(6) The administration must be reorganized. Nothing which has proved its value will be abolished. But it is essential to restore at once clear responsibility and the freedom to make independent decisions. Our once so proud administration has become a pile of machines and little machines working to no purpose. No one dares to make an independent and true decision. We will demand just the opposite from the civil servants. They will do right with the greatest simplicity and will little red tape.

The civil servant must again become an example in his whole way of life, official and private; for the people have entrusted him his public sovereign power. This power may only be exercised by those who are upright, who have acquired the technical knowledge, steeled their character and proved their ability. We will put an end to the civil servants who followed the Party rules. The civil servant shall once again obey only the law and his conscience. He must show himself conscious and worthy of the distinction of being assured of a secure livelihood by the community, while others must struggle for the barest necessities. Secure in his authority and in his rights he must proceed in the ideal endeavor to be worthy of his special position by special devotion to duty.

In order to make it possible for the civil servant to carry out his duties in this loyal way, and to spare the people from having public power exercised by unworthy persons, all appointments and promotions made since January 1, 1933, are declared to be temporary. Every individual civil servant will in the very near future be examined to find out whether he has offended against the law, against discipline or against the behavior expected of every civil servant. If this is found to be the case the proper measures will be taken, either by punishment, dismissal or transfer. The Civil Service tribunals will cooperate in this. Temporary civil servants, whose performance does not fulfill the demands of their office, will be transferred to positions for which they are fitted, or if this is not possible, they will be dismissed. Luxury is out of place in Government offices, but there must be comfort in the home of the individual. Heads of departments are instructed to take the necessary measures at once. Superfluous articles of furniture will be handed over to those who have suffered damage by bombing.

(7) The arrangement of the administration, the proper distribution and fulfillment of public duties are only possible on the basis of a Constitution. A final Constitution can only be drawn up with the agreement of the people after the end of the war. For the frontline soldiers have the right to have a special say in this. So for the time being we must all content ourselves with a temporary Constitution, which will be announced at the same time. We too are bound by this.

Prussia will be dissolved. The Prussian provinces, as well as the other German Länder, will be amalgamated into new Reichgaue. The Reichgau will in law again be given a life of its own. To a large extent they will be self-governing. Public duties which are in any way compatible with the unity of the Reich and the systematic conduct of the Reich will be handed over to the self-administration of these Reichgaue, Kreise and Gemeinden.

In all Reichgau authority will be exercised on behalf of the Reich by Reichstatthalter, who are to be appointed at once. As far as possible they will grant freedom of activity to the organs of self-government, but at the same time will preserve the unity of the Reich. Elected corporations in the self-governing body will guarantee liaison with the people.

(8) In wartime, economy can only be conducted in the form of State control and of control of prices. As long as there is a shortage of essential goods, a freer economy is, as everyone will realize, impossible, unless we want to pass over cold-bloodedly the vital interests of those with smaller incomes. We know quite well how distasteful this economy is, the abuses it fosters and that it does not, as is so often maintained, serve the true interests of the small consumer. For the time being, we can only simplify it, and free it from obscurities and from the confusion of different authorities and from the lack of a sense of responsibility. We will cancel all measures which have interfered too much with the freedom of the individual and which have destroyed livelihood in trade, handicraft, business, industry and agriculture without due consideration or where this was not absolutely necessary.

Furthermore, economy may not be unnecessarily disturbed by State interference nor may the joy of production or the possibilities of creation be stifled (economic freedom shall only be held in check by law, by the safeguarding of the integrity of competition and by decent intentions). In view of our country's poverty in raw materials and the fact that we cannot grow enough to feed ourselves, autarchy is a cowardly denial of the possibility of participating in the goods and services of the whole world by an exchange of services.

The aim of our conduct of economy is that every worker, every employee and every employer shall have a share in the benefits of our economy. It is not a question of establishing free enterprise for the employer and forcing him to struggle in competition. No, the German worker too must and will have the opportunity to take part in a creative capacity in the responsibility of economy, only we cannot free him from the effect of the natural laws governing economy.

Property is the basis of all economic and cultural progress; otherwise man gradually sinks to the level of the animal. It will therefore be protected not only in the hands of the large, but also in the hands of the small, property owner, who can only call his household goods his own. The abuse of property will be combated just as will the accumulation of capital, which is unhealthy and only increases man's dependence.

The organization of economy will be based on self-administration. The system so far employed of administration from above must cease. What must be done is to restore the beneficial functioning of independent decision and thus the responsibility of the individual. As far as possible the confidence of all, including the workers, in the justice of the organization of economy must be restored.

(9) From this arises the essence of the State policy directed towards equality — social policy. Those who through no fault of their own have fallen upon evil days or who are weak must be protected and given the opportunity of securing themselves against the accidents of this life. The State must also intervene where the interest in acquiring savings (capital) conflicts with the interest of assuring work for those now living. (Such conflicts of interest can arise in times of great political and economic tension. It would be very foolish to overcome them in such a way that only capital, i.e. savings, was destroyed. It would please the small saver just as little as it would serve the interests of the people as a whole if, for example, all farms and factories were suddenly without machinery. On the other hand, all these capital goods have no value unless they can be made to serve men living now.) Thus conscientiously and with a sense of responsibility we must find a just compromise, in which each individual knows from the outset that sacrifices must be made by him as well as by others.

In cases where the powers and responsibility of the individual branches of business and industry are not sufficient to make such compromises, all those citizens engaged in business must cooperate and in the last resort a just compromise laid on the shoulders of the people as a whole, must be assured by the State. In so far as social institutions affect the worker, they will have the right to full self-administration.

But we must realize that the State does not have inexhaustible means. Even the State can only exist on what its citizens do and give to it. It cannot give the individual citizens more than it receives from the efforts of its citizens. We therefore clearly and definitely refuse to make promises of economic well-being. Each of us knows that those who have wasted their savings must work specially hard to regain their accustomed standard of life. Thus it is with the family, in every company and also in the State. Any other idea is foolish. Cheap promises that the State can do everything are irresponsible demagogy. You with your resources are the State. We and the organs of the State are only your trustees. Each of you must stir up his resources. It is obvious that after the enormous devastation of this war we must all make special efforts to work hard to create replacements for clothing, for bombed homes and factories and for destroyed household goods. And finally we want to give our children the possibility of a better life. But we are convinced that we are all capable of doing this if we can again work in justice, decency and freedom.

(10) The basic condition for a sound economy is the organization of public funds. Expenditure must be kept within the real income which the State, the Gau, the Kreis, and the Gemeinde can draw from their citizens. Effort, character, renunciation and struggle will be requested to restore this order; but it is the most important and essential basis of an assured currency and of all economic life. The value of all savings depends on it. Without it, foreign trade, on which we have depended for more than a hundred years, is impossible.

Taxes will be considerable; but we will watch over their careful use all the more strictly. It is more important that the citizen should have the necessities of life than that the administration should provide itself with magnificent establishments and take upon itself duties which are in contradiction to the simple way of life of the individual.

We will also demand the same care from economy, which must again realize that expenditure in the administration only serves the comfort and the needs of the individual but must be borne by all in the shape of higher prices and by workers in the form of lower wages. The cessation of the enormous expenditure of the Party is a beginning of the remedy.

Since 1933, the principle of an orderly State economy was forsaken by constant and unscrupulous wasting of funds by increasing debts. It was inconvenient to pretend to the people that the general welfare had been successfully increased by extravagance. This method was in reality contemptible, for it consisted in piling up debts. Therefore, even in wartime when each State is forced to spend enormous sums, we will restore the utmost simplicity and economy in all public services. A real leveling out generally can only take place when this war is over.

We regard the mounting debts of all belligerent and natural States as an extremely great danger. They threaten currency. After this war every State will be faced with an extremely difficult task. We hope to be able to find ways of paying off the debts if we succeed in restoring confidence and cooperation between the nations.

(11) But we are still at war. We owe all our work, sacrifice and love to the men who are defending our country at the front. We must give them all the moral and material resources which we can summon. We are with them in rank and file, but now we know that only those sacrifices will be demanded which are necessary for the defense of the Fatherland and the well-being of the people, and not those which served the lust for conquest and the need for prestige of a madman; we know too that we will carry on this war until we obtain a just peace, fighting with clean hands, in decency and with that honor which distinguishes every brave soldier. We must all give our care to those who have already suffered in this war.

In our anxiety about the front we must reconcile the necessities with clarity and simplicity. There must be an end of the welter of bombastic orders which are incapable of fulfillment and which today demand from industry impossible numbers of tanks, tomorrow aircraft and the next day weapons and equipment. We shall only demand what is necessary and expedient. In contrast to the former despotic tyranny we expect from each who is called upon to carry out an order that he will on his own account point out mistakes and discrepancies.

(12) We gave a warning against this war which has brought so much misery to mankind, and therefore we can speak boldly. If national dignity at present prevents us from making bitter accusations, we will call those responsible to account. Necessary as this is, it is more important to strive for an early peace. We know that we alone are not masters of peace or war; in this we depend on other nations. We must stand firm. But at last we will raise the voice of the true Germany.

We are deeply conscious of the fact that the world is faced with one of the most vital decisions which have ever confronted the peoples and their leaders. God Himself puts the question to us whether we wish to live in accordance with the order of justice imposed by Him and whether we wish to follow His commandments to respect freedom and human dignity and help each other or not. We know that this order and these commandments have been gravely violated ever since, in 1914, the nations forsook the blessed path of peace. Now we are faced with the question whether we are willing to turn to good use the bitter experiences we have had to undergo and to turn to reconciliation, the just settlement of interests and the healing of the terrible wounds by working together.

In this hour we must tell our people that it is our highest duty bravely and patiently to cleanse the much dishonored German name. Only we Germans can and will fulfill this task. Our future, no matter what material form it takes, depends on our doing this pitilessly, seriously and honestly. For God is not there to be appealed to as Providence on each petty occasion, but He demands and ensures that His order and His commandments are not violated. It was a fatal mistake, the origins of which can be traced to the unhappy Versailles dictate, to assume that the future can be built up on the misfortune of other nations, on suppression and disregard of human dignity.

None of us wishes to malign the honor of other nations. What we demand for ourselves we must and will grant to all others. We believe that it is in the interests of all peoples that peace should be lasting. For this international confidence in the new Germany is necessary.

Confidence cannot be won by force or by talking. But whatever the future may bring, we hate the cowardly vilification of our opponents, and we are convinced that the leaders of all States want not only the victory for their own peoples but a fruitful end to this struggle, and that they are ready to alleviate at once with us the inhuman hardships, which affect all people, of this total war which was so thoughtlessly started.

With this consciousness and relying on the inner strength of our people we shall unwaveringly take those steps which we can take towards peace without harm to our people. We know that the German people wants this.

Let us once again tread the path of justice, decency and mutual respect! In this spirit each of us will do his duty. Let us follow earnestly and in everything we do the commands of God which are engraved on our conscience even when they seem hard on us, let us do everything to heal wounded souls and to alleviate suffering. Only then can we create the basis for a sure future for our people within a family of nations filled with confidence, sound work and peaceful feelings. We owe it to our dead to do this with all our might and with sacred earnestness — whose patriotism and courage in sacrifice have been criminally abused. To how many of you who have realized this did the fulfillment of your duty become the most bitter grief of conscience? How much beautiful human happiness has been destroyed in the world!

May God grant us the insight and the strength to transform these terrible sacrifices into a blessing for generations.

Notes

PROLOGUE: THE GROWTH OF CONSPIRACY

1. F. L. Carsten, in Hermann Graml, et al., *The German Resistance to Hitler* (Los Angeles: University of California Press, 1970), p. viii.
2. Joachim Remak, ed., *The Nazi Years* (Englewood Cliffs, N. J.: Prentice-Hall, 1969), p. 168.

CHAPTER 1—ROOTS OF THE NATIONAL SOCIALIST PHILOSOPHY

1. H. G. Haile, *Luther* (Garden City, N.Y.: Doubleday, 1978), p. 290.
2. Ibid.
3. E. Lingens-Reiner, *Prisoners of Fear* (London: Gollancz, 1948), pp. 1–2.
4. Lucy S. Davidowicz, *The War Against the Jews 1933–1945* (New York: Bantam, 1976), pp. 33–34.
5. Ibid.
6. Ibid.
7. Ibid., p. 41.
8. Ibid., p. 47.
9. Joachim Remak, ed., *The Nazi Years* (Englewood Cliffs, N. J.: Prentice-Hall, 1969), p. 4.
10. Ibid., p. 5.
11. R. J. Lifton, *The Nazi Doctors* (New York: Basic, 1986), p. 21.
12. Richard Grunberger, *A Social History of the Third Reich* (London: Weidenfeld and Nicolson, 1971), p. 466.
13. Ibid.
14. Marshall Dill, Jr., *Germany, A Modern History* (Ann Arbor: University of Michigan Press, 1970), p. 273.
15. René Albrecht-Carrié, *A Diplomatic History of Europe Since the Congress of Vienna* (New York: Harper, 1958), pp. 390–91; and William L. Langer, *An Encyclopedia of World History*, 5th ed. (Boston: Houghton Mifflin, 1972), p. 1121.

16. Harold Laswell, "The Psychology of Hitlerism," *The Political Quarterly* 4 (1933): p. 374.
17. Davidowicz, *War Against the Jews*, p. 62.
18. Karl D. Bracher, *Die Auflösung der Weimarer Republik* (Stuttgart: Ring Verlag, 1954), pp. 86–106.
19. *Statistisches Jahrbuch für das Deutsche Reich 1933* Berlin, 1934), p. 291.
20. Lifton, *Nazi Doctors*, p. 25.
21. Ibid., p. 27–28.
22. Remak, *Nazi Years*, pp. 146–48.
23. Ibid., p. 54.
24. Lifton, *Nazi Doctors*, p. 27.
25. Remak, *Nazi Years*, p. 151.
26. M. Gilbert, *The Holocaust*, (New York: Holt, Reinhart & Winston, 1985), p. 280–83.

CHAPTER 2—THE RISE TO POWER

1. William L. Shirer, *The Rise and Fall of the Third Reich*, (New York: Simon and Schuster, 1960), p. 68.
2. Robert Payne, *The Life and Death of Adolf Hitler*, (New York: Praeger, 1973), p. 221.
3. René Albrecht-Carrié, *A Diplomatic History of Europe Since the Congress of Vienna* (New York: Harper, 1958), pp. 392, 396.
4. Shirer, *Rise and Fall*, p. 138.
5. Payne, *Life and Death*, p. 239; and Shirer, *Rise and Fall*, pp. 158–59.
6. John Toland, *Adolf Hitler* (Garden City, N.Y.: Doubleday, 1976), p. 347.

CHAPTER 3—EARLY MILITARY RESISTANCE

1. Terence Prittie, *Germans Against Hitler*, (Boston: Little, Brown, 1964), p. 39; and William L. Shirer, *The Rise and Fall of the Third Reich* (New York: Simon and Schuster, 1960), p. 227.

2. Fabian von Schlabrendorff, *The Secret War Against Hitler,* (New York: Pitman, 1965), p. 223.

3. Pierre Galante, *Operation Valkyrie* (New York: Harper & Row, 1981), p. 9.

4. Richard Grunberger, *A Social History of the Third Reich* (London: Weidenfeld and Nicolson, 1971), p. 22.

5. John W. Wheeler-Bennett, *The Nemesis of Power* (London: Macmillan, 1953), pp. 224–25.

6. Shirer, *Rise and Fall,* p. 260.

7. Ibid., p. 303.

8. Wolfgang Foerster, *Generaloberst Ludwig Beck: Sein Kampf gegen den Kreig* (Munich: Isar Verlag, 1953), p. 120.

9. Schlabrendorff, *Secret War,* pp. 156–57.

10. Foerster, *Beck,* pp. 125–28.

11. Ibid.

CHAPTER 4— RESISTANCE IN GERMAN CHURCHES

1. William L. Shirer, *The Rise and Fall of the Third Reich* (New York: Simon and Schuster, 1960), p. 234.

2. Walter Consuelo Langsam, ed., *Documents and Readings in the History of Europe Since 1918* (New York: Lippincott, 1951), pp. 722–28.

3. Mary Alice Gallin, *German Resistance to ... Hitler* (Washington, D.C.: Catholic University of America Press, 1961), p. 166.

4. Herbert Molloy Mason, Jr., *To Kill the Devil* (New York: W. W. Norton, 1978), p. 94.

5. Terence Prittie, *Germans Against Hitler* (Boston: Little, Brown, 1964), pp. 73–74.

6. Ibid., pp. 74–75.

7. *Salzburger Chronik,* April 30, 1937.

8. *Statistisches Jahrbuch für Deutschland, 1939,* p. 29.

9. Prittie, *Germans Against Hitler,* pp. 79–80.

10. Ibid., pp. 85–86.

11. Peter Hoffmann, *The History of the German Resistance 1993–1945* (Cambridge: MIT Press, 1977), p. 167.

12. Ibid., p. 161.

13. Shirer, *Rise and Fall,* p. 235.

14. *New York Times,* January 3, 1942.

15. Shirer, *Rise and Fall,* p. 239.

CHAPTER 5— POLITICAL OPPOSITION

1. Terence Prittie, *Germans Against Hitler* (Boston: Little, Brown, 1964), pp. 137–38.

2. Ibid., pp. 131–33.

3. Walter Schmitthenner and Hans Buchheim, *Der deutsche Widerstand gegen Hitler: Vier historisch-kritische Studien* (Cologne: Kiepenheuer and Witsch, 1966), pp. 167–68.

4. East German Ministry of Defense, *History of the German Anti-Fascist Resistance Movement,* 1958.

5. Schmitthenner and Buchheim *Widerstand gegen Hitler,* p. 169.

6. Richard Grunberger, *A Social History of the Third Reich* (London: Weidenfeld and Nicolson, 1971), p. 185.

7. H. W. Koch, *In the Name of the Volk,* (New York: St. Martin's, 1989), pp. 232–34.

8. Franz Neumann, *Behemoth* (New York: Oxford University Press, 1942), p. 454.

9. Schlabrendorff, 1965, pp. 176–77.

CHAPTER 6— THE CIVILIAN OPPOSITION

1. Fabian von Schlabrendorff, *The Secret War Against Hitler* (New York: Pitman, 1965), p. 91.

2. Ian Colvin, *Vansittart in Office* (London: Gollancz, 1965), p. 223.

3. Leonard Mosley, *On Borrowed Time* (New York: Random House, 1969), p. 32; and Schlabrendorff, *Secret War,* p. 92.

4. Roger Manvell and Heinrich Fraenkel, *The Canaris Conspiracy* (New York: McKay, 1969), p. 39.

5. Carl J. Burckhardt, *Meine Danzinger Mission 1937–1939* (Munich: Verlag Georg D. W. Callwey, 1960), pp. 181–183.

6. Peter Hoffmann, *Hitler's Personal Security* (Cambridge: MIT Press, 1979), p. 99.

7. Ibid., pp. 110–12.

8. John W. Wheeler-Bennett, *The Nemesis of Power* (London: Macmillan, 1953), p. 446; and Albert Zoller, *Hitler Privat* (Düsseldorf: Droste Verlag, 1949), p. 177.

9. Herbert Molloy Mason, Jr., *To Kill the Devil* (New York: Norton, 1978), p. 87.

10. Imperial Palace Auto Collection, fact sheet, 1994.

CHAPTER 7— PLANS FOR A COUP D'ÉTAT: 1938.

1. René Albrecht-Carrié, *A Diplomatic History of Europe Since the Congress of Vienna* (New York: Harper, 1958), p. 522; and William L. Shirer, *The Rise and Fall of the Third Reich* (New York: Simon and Schuster, 1960), p. 359.

2. John Gunther, *Inside Europe* (London: Harper, 1938), pp. 103q–103r.

3. Peter Hoffmann, *The History of the German Resistance 1933–1945* (Cambridge: MIT Press, 1977), pp. 50–52.

4. Ibid., p. 87.

5. Albrecht-Carrié, *Diplomatic History,* p. 524.

6. Winston S. Churchill, *The Gathering Storm* (Boston: Houghton Mifflin, 1948), p. 313.

7. Keith Feiling, *Life of Neville Chamberlain* (London: Macmillan, 1946), p. 367.

8. Shirer, *Rise and Fall*, p. 389.

9. Churchill, *Gathering Storm*, pp. 303–4.

10. Shirer, *Rise and Fall*, p. 394.

11. Churchill, *Gathering Storm*, p. 315.

12. Shirer, *Rise and Fall*, p. 398.

13. Churchill, *Gathering Storm*, p. 317–18.

14. Ibid., p. 318.

15. Fabian von Schlabrendorff, *The Secret War Against Hitler* (New York: Pitman, 1965), p. 104.

16. Shirer, *Rise and Fall*, p. 421.

17. Schlabrendorff, *Secret War*, p. 103.

18. Eugen Spier, *Focus: A Footnote to the History of the Thirties* (London: Oswald Wolff, 1963), p. 127.

Chapter 8— On the Eve of War

1. Fabian von Schlabrendorff, *The Secret War Against Hitler* (New York: Pitman, 1965), pp. 208–11.

2. Eugen Spier, *Focus: A Footnote to the History of the Thirties* (London: Wolff, 1963), p. 127.

3. Herbert Molloy Mason, Jr., *To Kill the Devil* (New York: Norton, 1978), p. 77.

4. Allen Welsh Dulles, *Germany's Underground* (New York: Macmillan, 1947), p. 53; and Peter Hoffman, *The History of the German Resistance 1933–1945* (Cambridge: MIT Press, 1977), p. 113.

5. William L. Shirer, *The Rise and Fall of the Third Reich* (New York: Simon and Schuster, 1960), p. 456.

6. Ibid.

7. Ibid., p. 468.

8. William L. Langer, *An Encyclopedia of World History*, 5th ed. (Boston: Houghton Mifflin, 1972), p. 1132.

9. Hans Bernd Gisevius, *To the Bitter End*, trans. Richard and Clara Winston (Boston: Houghton Mifflin, 1947), p. 373.

Chapter 9— The Outbreak of War

1. Helmuth Groscurth, *Tagebücher eines Abwehroffiziers 1938–1940* (Stuttgart: Deutsch Verlags-Anstalt, 1970), pp. 498–503.

2. Ibid., pp. 211–15.

3. Jeremy Noakes and Geoffrey Pridham, *Documents on Nazism 1919–1945* (New York: Viking, 1974), pp. 302–3.

4. Peter Hoffman, *The History of the German Resistance 1933–1945* (Cambridge: MIT Press, 1977), pp. 116–17.

5. Hans Rothfels, *The German Opposition to Hitler* (Chicago: Regnery, 1962), p. 132.

6. Roger Manvell and Heinrich Fraenkel, *The Men Who Tried to Kill Hitler* (New York: Coward-McCann, 1964), pp. 40–41.

7. Gerhard Ritter, *The German Resistance* (New York: Praeger, 1958), p. 158.

8. Erich Kordt, *Nicht aus dem Akten: Die Wilhelmstrasse in Frieden und Krieg* (Stuttgart: Union Deutsche Verlagsgesellschaft, 1950), p. 371.

9. Winston S. Churchill, *Their Finest Hour* (Boston: Houghton Mifflin, 1949), p. 118.

10. William L. Shirer, *The Rise and Fall of the Third Reich* (New York: Simon and Schuster, 1960), p. 748, citing *Documents on German Foreign Policy* files of the German Foreign Office), vol. 9, pp. 550–51.

11. *New York Times*, June 25, 1940.

12. *New York Journal American*, June 14, 1940.

13. Churchill, *Their Finest Hour*, pp. 261–62.

14. Shirer, *Rise and Fall*, p. 752.

15. Churchill, *Their Finest Hour*, p. 281.

16. Ibid., p. 259.

Chapter 10— The War Turns Eastward

1. Adolf Hitler, *Mein Kampf* (Boston: Houghton Mifflin, 1943), p. 654.

2. William L. Shirer, *The Rise and Fall of the Third Reich* (New York: Simon and Schuster, 1960), p. 796.

3. Ibid., p. 801.

4. Ibid., p. 830.

5. Ibid., p. 831, citing Brauchitsch testimony at Nuremberg, "Trials of Major War Criminals," vol. 20, pp. 581–82, 593.

6. Fabian von Schlabrendorff, *The Secret War Against Hitler* (New York: Pitman 1965), p. 124.

7. Shirer, *Rise and Fall*, p. 833, citing Nürnberg trial document 2718-PS, "Nazi Conspiracy and Aggression," vol. 5, p. 378.

8. Sumner Welles, *The Time for Decision* (New York: Harper, 1944), pp. 170–71.

9. Shirer, *Rise and Fall*, p. 844.

10. Ulrich von Hassell, *The Von Hassell Diaries 1938–1944* (London: Hamilton, 1948), p. 208.

11. Hans Rothfels, *The German Opposition to Hitler* (Chicago: Regnery, 1962), 204–5.

12. Jeremy Noakes and Geoffrey Pridham, *Documents on Nazism, 1919–1945* (New York: Viking, 1974), pp. 320–22.

13. Schlabrendorff, *Secret War*, p. 136.

14. Robert Payne, *The Life and Death of Adolf Hitler* (New York: Praeger, 1973) p. 438–39.

15. Shirer, *Rise and Fall*, p. 867, citing Nürnberg trial document 1961-PS, "Nazi Conspiracy and Aggression," vol. 4, p. 153.

16. Rothfels, *German Opposition*, p. 112.

17. Roger Manvell and Heinrich Fraenkel, *The Men Who Tried to Kill Hitler* (New York: Coward-McCann, 1964), p. 229.

18. Rothfels, *German Opposition*, p. 135.

19. Manvell and Fraenkel, *Men Who Tried to Kill Hitler*, pp. 29–30.

20. Rothfels, *German Opposition*, p. 134–35.

21. Ibid., pp. 133–34.

CHAPTER 11— THE TURNING POINT

1. Warburg, *Germany— Bridge or Battleground*, pp. 259–60.

2. Hans Rothfels, *The German Opposition to Hitler* (Chicago: Henry Regnery, 1962), pp. 143–44.

3. Fabian von Schlabrendorff, *The Secret War Against Hitler* (New York: Pitman, 1965), pp. 248–49.

4. Ibid., pp. 245–48.

5. Rothfels, *German Opposition*, p. 86.

6. Peter Hoffman, *The History of the German Resistance 1933–1945* (Cambridge: MIT Press, 1977), p. 290.

CHAPTER 12— THE FORCES GATHER

1. Roger Manvell and Heinrich Fraenkel, *The Men Who Tried to Kill Hitler* (New York: Coward-McCann, 1964), pp. 67–68.

2. Ibid., p. 70.

3. Ibid., p. 86.

4. Allen Welsh Dulles, *Germany's Underground* (New York: Macmillan, 1947), pp. 135–36; and Hans Bernd Gisevius, *To the Bitter End*, trans. Richard and Clara Winston (Boston: Houghton Mifflin, 1947), pp. 477–78.

5. Dulles, *Germany's Underground*, p. 139.

6. Hans Rothfels, *The German Opposition to Hitler* (Chicago: Regnery, 1962), pp. 147–48.

7. Manvell and Fraenkel, *Men Who Tried to Kill Hitler*, p. 79.

8. Ibid., p. 89.

9. Dulles, *Germany's Underground*, p. 137.

10. Peter Hoffmann, *The History of the German Resistance 1933–1945* (Cambridge: MIT Press, 1977), p. 233.

11. Gerhard Ritter, *The German Resistance* (New York: Praeger, 1958), p. 540–541.

12. Manvell and Fraenkel, *Men Who Tried to Kill Hitler*, p. 67.

13. Herbert Molloy Mason, Jr., *To Kill the Devil* (New York: Norton, 1978), p. 171.

14. Manvell and Fraenkel, *Men Who Tried to Kill Hitler*, p. 90.

CHAPTER 13— VALKYRIE

1. John W. Wheeler-Bennett, *The Nemesis of Power* (London: Macmillan, 1953), p. 636, citing Jodl's testimony at the International Military Tribunal, June 2, 1946, Nürnberg Documents, vol. 15, p. 295.

2. Peter Hoffmann, *The History of the German Resistance 1933–1945* (Cambridge: MIT Press, 1977), p. 399.

3. Pierre Galante, *Operation Valkyrie* (New York: Harper & Row, 1981), pp. 20–21.

4. Herbert Molloy Mason, Jr., *To Kill the Devil* (New York: Norton, 1978), p. 189.

5. Terence Prittie, *Germans Against Hitler* (Boston: Little, Brown, 1964), pp. 244–45.

6. Roger Manvell and Heinrich Fraenkel, *The Men Who Tried to Kill Hitler* (New York: Coward-McCann, 1964), pp. 11–13.

7. Ibid., pp. 116–17.

8. Ibid.

9. Hoffmann, *German Resistance*, p. 422.

10. Manvell and Fraenkel, *Men Who Tried to Kill Hitler*, pp. 117–18.

11. Ibid.

12. Curt Reiss, *Joseph Goebbels: The Devil's Advocate* (New York: Ballantine, 1948), p. 280.

13. Hoffmann, *German Resistance*, pp. 754–55.

14. Hans Bernd Gisevius, *To the Bitter End*, trans. Richard and Clara Winston (Boston: Houghton Mifflin, 1947), pp. 539–40; Fabian von Schlabrendorff, *The Secret War Against Hitler* (New York: Pitman, 1965), p. 140.

15. Wheeler-Bennett, *Nemesis of Power*, p. 645.

CHAPTER 14— THE COLLAPSE

1. Herbert Molloy Mason, Jr., *To Kill the Devil* (New York: Norton, 1978), p. 202.

2. Roger Manvell and Heinrich Fraenkel, *The Men Who Tried to Kill Hitler* (New York: Coward-McCann 1964), pp. 133–34.

3. Peter Hoffmann, *The History of the German Resistance, 1933–1945* (Cambridge: MIT Press, 1977), pp. 426–427.

4. Pierre Galante, *Operation Valkyrie* (New York: Harper & Row, 1981), pp. 37–38.

5. Galante, *Operation Valkyrie*, p. 32; Manvell and Fraenkel, *Men Who Tried to Kill Hitler*, pp. 130–31.

6. Manvell and Fraenkel, *Men Who Tried to Kill Hitler*, p. 135; Mason, *To Kill the Devil*, p. 199.

7. Manvell and Fraenkel, *Men Who Tried to Kill Hitler*, pp. 135–36.

8. Hoffmann, *German Resistance*, 1977, p. 758.

9. Ibid., p. 755.

10. Ibid., p. 757.

11. Manvell and Fraenkel, *Men Who Tried to Kill Hitler,* pp. 144–45.

12. Ibid., pp. 145–46.

13. Galante, *Operation Valkyrie,* p. 41.

14. Manvell and Fraenkel, *Men Who Tried to Kill Hitler,* pp. 138–39.

15. John W. Wheeler-Bennett, *The Nemesis of Power* (London: Macmillan, 1953), p. 172.

16. Manvell and Fraenkel, *Men Who Tried to Kill Hitler,* pp. 148–49.

17. Wheeler-Bennett, *Nemesis of Power,* p. 661.

18. Hoffmann, *German Resistance,* p. 760.

19. William L. Shirer, *The Rise and Fall of the Third Reich* (New York: Simon and Schuster, 1960), p. 1069.

Chapter 15— The Aftermath

1. Jeremy Noakes and Geoffrey Pridham, *Documents on Nazism, 1919–1945* (New York: Viking, 1974), pp. 324–25.

2. Roger Manvell and Heinrich Fraenkel, *The Men Who Tried to Kill Hitler* (New York: Coward-McCann, 1964), p. 170.

3. *New York Herald Tribune,* August 9, 1944.

4. *New York Times,* August 9, 1944.

5. H. W. Koch, *In the Name of the Volk* (New York: St. Martin's, 1989), p. 190, citing *Spiegelbild einer Verschwörung, Die Kaltenbrunnerberichte,* Stuttgart, 1961.

6. M. J. Gruffein and M. Janowitz, "Trends in Wehrmacht Morale," *Public Opinion Quarterly,* (1946): p. 81ff.

7. Allen Welsh Dulles, *Germany's Underground* (New York: Macmillan, 1947), p. 83; Peter Hoffmann, *The History of the German Resistance 1933–1945* (Cambridge: MIT Press, 1977), p. 526.

8. Hoffmann, *German Resistance,* p. 526.

9. Ibid.

10. Fabian von Schlabrendorff, *The Secret War Against Hitler* (New York: Pitman, 1965), p. 298.

11. Dulles, *Germany's Underground,* p. 83.

12. Joachim Remak, ed., *The Nazi Years* (Englewood Cliffs, N. J.: Prentice-Hall, 1969), p. 161; Hans Rothfels, *The German Opposition to Hitler* (Chicago: Regnery, 1962), p. 80; Schlabrendorff, *Secret War,* p. 294–95.

13. Manvell and Fraenkel, *Men Who Tried to Kill Hitler,* p. 176.

14. Annedore Leber, *Conscience in Revolt* (London: Mitchell, 1957), p. 250.

15. Ibid., p. 186.

Appendix B— Documents

1. Peter Hoffmann, *The History of the German Resistance 1933–1945* (Cambridge: MIT Press, 1977), pp. 755–56; Herbert Molloy Mason, Jr., *To Kill the Devil* (New York: Norton, 1978), pp. 246–47; Rudolph Pechel, *Deutscher Widerstand* (Zurich: Eugen Rentsch Verlag, 1947), pp. 96–99; John W. Wheeler-Bennett, *The Nemesis of Power* (London: Macmillan, 1953), pp. 724–25.

2. Hoffmann, *German Resistance,* pp. 756–57; Mason, *To Kill the Devil,* pp. 248–50; Pechel, *Deutscher Widerstand,* pp. 96–99; Wheeler-Bennett, *Nemesis of Power,* p. 725.

3. Mason, *To Kill the Devil,* pp. 251–55; Pechel, *Deutscher Widerstand,* pp. 304–5; Wheeler-Bennett, *Nemesis of Power,* pp. 726–27.

4. Pechel, *Deutscher Widerstand,* pp. 305–9; Wheeler-Bennett, *Nemesis of Power,* pp. 727–30.

5. Pechel, *Deutscher Widerstand,* pp. 309–14; Wheeler-Bennett, *Nemesis of Power,* pp. 730–34.

6. Mason, *To Kill the Devil,* pp. 256–67; Pechel, *Deutscher Widerstand,* pp. 314–25; Wheeler-Bennett, *Nemesis of Power,* pp. 734–43.

BIBLIOGRAPHY

Abel, Theodor. *Why Hitler Came into Power.* Englewood Cliffs, N. J.: Prentice-Hall, 1938.

Abshagan, Karl Heinz. *Canaris: Patriot und Weltbürger.* Stuttgart: Union Deutsche Verlagsgesellschaft, 1949.

Albrecht-Carrié, René. *A Diplomatic History of Europe Since the Congress of Vienna.* New York: Harper, 1958.

Baigent, Michael, and Richard Leigh. *Secret Germany.* London: Cape, 1994.

Balfour, Michael, and Julian Frisby. *Helmuth von Moltke.* London: Macmillan, 1972.

Barnett, Correlli, ed. *Hitler's Generals.* New York: Grove Weidenfeld, 1989.

Bayles, Will D. *Caesars in Goose Step.* New York: Harper, 1940.

Baynes, Norman H., ed. *The Speeches of Adolf Hitler.* London: Oxford University Press, 1942.

Blake, Leonard. *Hitler's Last Year of Power.* London: Daker's, 1939.

Bracher, Karl D. *Die Auflösung der Weimarer Republik.* Stuttgart: Ring Verlag, 1954.

Brett-Smith, Richard. *Hitler's Generals.* San Rafael, Calif.: Presidio, 1977.

Brissard, Andre. *Canaris.* New York: Grosset & Dunlap, 1974.

Brown, Roger. *Social Psychology.* New York: Free Press, 1965.

Buchheit, Gert. *Ludwig Beck, ein preussischer General.* Munich: Paul List Verlag, 1964.

Bullock, Alan. *Hitler, A Study in Tyranny.* London: Odhams, 1952.

Burckhardt, Carl J. *Meine Danziger Mission 1937-1939.* Munich: Verlag Georg D. W. Callwey, 1960.

Cahen, Max. *Man Against Hitler.* New York: Dobbs & Merrill, 1939.

Carr, William. *A History of Germany 1815-1945.* New York: St. Martin's, 1969.

Carsten, F. L. *The German Resistance to Hitler.* Berkeley: University of California Press, 1970.

Casey, William. *The Secret War Against Hitler.* Washington D.C.: Regnery Gateway, 1988.

Churchill, Winston S. *The Gathering Storm.* Boston: Houghton Mifflin, 1948.

___. *Their Finest Hour.* Boston: Houghton Mifflin, 1949.

Ciano, Galeazzo. *The Ciano Diaries, 1939-1943.* New York: Doubleday, 1946.

Clark, Alan. *Barbarossa: The Russian-German Conflict 1941-1945.* New York: Morrow, 1965.

Clough, Shepart Bancroft, and Charles Woolsey Cole. *Economic History of Europe.* Boston: Heath, 1947.

Colvin, Ian. *Chief of Intelligence.* London: Gollancz, 1951.

___. *Vansittart in Office.* London: Gollancz, 1965.

Cooper, Matthew. *The German Army 1933-1945.* Chelsea, Mich.: Scarborough House, 1990.

Craig, Gordon A. *Europe Since 1914.* New York: Holt, Rinehart and Winston, 1961.

Davidowicz, Lucy S. *The War Against the Jews 1933-1945.* New York: Bantam, 1976.

Deuel, Wallace R. *People Under Hitler.* New York: Harcourt, 1942.

Deutsch, Harold C. *The Conspiracy Against Hitler in the Twilight War.* Minneapolis: University of Minnesota Press, 1968.

Dietrich, Otto. *12 Jahre mit Hitler.* Munich: Isar Verlag, 1955.

Dill, Marshall, Jr. *Germany, a Modern History.* Ann Arbor: University of Michigan Press, 1970.

Duffy, James P., and Vincent L. Ricci. *Target Hitler.* Westport, Conn.: Praeger, 1992.

Dulles, Allen Welsh. *Germany's Underground.* New York: Macmillan, 1947.

Dumbach, Annette E., and Jud Newborn. *Shattering the German Night.* Boston: Little, Brown, 1986.

Eden, Anthony. *Facing the Dictators.* London: Cassell, 1962.

Eich, Hermann. *The Unloved Germans.* New York: Stein and Day, 1965.

Ergang, Robert. *Europe Since Waterloo.* Boston: Heath, 1954.

Feiling, Keith. *Life of Neville Chamberlain.* London: Macmillan, 1946.

Fest, Joachim C. *Hitler.* New York: Harcourt Brace Jovanovich, 1974.

Finker, Kurt. *Stauffenberg und der 20. Juli 1944.* Berlin: Union Verlag, 1973.

Fitzgibbon, Constantine. *20 July.* New York: Norton, 1956.

___. *To Kill Hitler.* London: Tom Stacey, 1972 (originally published as *The Shirt of Nessus,* 1956).

Foerster, Wolfgang. *Generaloberst Ludwig Beck: Sein Kampf gegen den Kreig.* Munich: Isar Verlag, 1953.

Freiden, Seymour, and William Richardson, eds. *The Fatal Decisions.* New York: Berkley, 1958.

Fromm, Erich. *Escape from Freedom.* New York: Holt, Rinehart and Winston, 1941.

Galante, Pierre. *Operation Valkyrie.* New York: Harper & Row, 1981.

Gallin, Mary Alice. *German Resistance to ... Hitler.* Washington D.C.: Catholic University of America Press, 1961.

Gilbert, M. *The Holocaust.* New York: Holt, Reinhart & Winston, 1985.

Gisevius, Hans Bernd. *Bis zum bittern Ende.* Zurich: Fretz & Wasmuth, 1946: *To the Bitter End.* Trans. Richard and Clara Winston. Boston: Houghton Mifflin, 1947.

Gottschalk, Louis, and Donald Lach. *The Transformation of Modern Europe.* Chicago: Scott, Foresman, 1954.

Graml, Hermann; Mommsen, Hans; Reichhardt, Hans-Joachim; and Wolf, Ernst. *The German Resistance to Hitler.* Los Angeles: University of California Press, 1970.

Groscurth, Helmuth. *Tagebücher eines Abwehroffiziers 1938–1940.* Stuttgart: Deutsch Verlags-Anstalt, 1970.

Grunberger, Richard. *A Social History of the Third Reich.* London: Weidenfeld and Nicolson, 1971.

Gunther, John. *Inside Europe.* London: Harper, 1938.

Gutenberg, Buechergidle. *Deutsche Geschichte des 19. und 20. Jahrhunderts. The History of Germany Since 1789.* Trans. Marian Jackson. New York: Praeger, 1969.

Haile, H. G. *Luther.* Garden City, N. Y.: Doubleday, 1978.

Halder, Franz. *Hitler as Warlord.* London: Putnam, 1950.

Harris, Joseph P., ed. *Political Thought.* New York: McGraw-Hill, 1964.

Hassell, Ulrich von. *The von Hassell Diaries 1938-1944.* New York: Doubleday, 1947.

Heiber, Helmut. *Adolf Hitler: A Short Biography.* L. Wilson. Trans. London: Wolff, 1961.

Heiden, Konrad. *Der Führer.* Boston: Houghton Mifflin, 1944.

Henk, Emil. *Die Tragödie des 20. Juli 1944: Ein Beitrag zur politischen Vorgeschichte.* Heidelberg: Adolf Rausch Verlag, 1946.

Hilberg, Paul. *Perpetrators Victims Bystanders.* New York: HarperCollins, 1992.

Hitler, Adolf. *Mein Kampf.* Unexpurgated English translation. Boston: Houghton Mifflin, 1943.

Hoehne, Heinz. *Canaris.* Garden City, N. Y.: Doubleday, 1979.

Hoffmann, Peter. *The History of the German Resistance 1933–1945.* Cambridge: MIT Press, 1977.

Hoffmann, Peter. *Hitler's Personal Security.* Cambridge: MIT Press, 1979.

Jacobsen, Hans-Adolf, ed. *July 20, 1944.* Bonn: Press and Information Office, Federal Government of Germany, 1969.

John, Otto. *Zweimal kam ich heim: Vom Verschwörer zum Schützer der Verfassung.* Düsseldorf: Econ Verlag, 1969.

Johnson, Paul. *Modern Times.* New York: Harper & Row, 1983.

Keitel, Wilhelm. *Memoirs.* London: Kimber, 1965.

Klein, Burton. *Germany's Economic Preparation for War.* Cambridge: Harvard University Press, 1959.

Kleist, Petyer. *European Tragedy.* London: Antony Gibbs and Phillips, 1965.

Koch, H. W. *In the Name of the Volk.* New York: St. Martin's, 1989.

Kordt, Erich. *Nicht aus dem Akten: Die Wilhelmstrasse in Frieden und Krieg.* Stuttgart: Union Deutsche Verlagsgesellschaft, 1950.

Kramarz, Joachim. *Stauffenberg.* New York: Macmillan, 1967.

Krausnick, H. *Anatomy of the SS State.* New York: Walker, 1968.

Langer, Walter C. *The Mind of Adolf Hitler.* New York: Basic, 1972.

Langer, William L. *An Encyclopedia of World History.* 5th ed. Boston: Houghton Mifflin, 1972.

Langsam, Walter Consuelo, ed. *Documents and Readings in the History of Europe Since 1918.* New York: Lippincott, 1951.

Leber, Annedore. *Das Gewissen entuscheidet: Bereiche des deutschen Widerstandes von 1933–1945 in Lebensbildern.* Berlin: Mosaik-Verlag, 1960. *Conscience in Revolt.* Trans. Rosemary O'Neill. London: Valentine Mitchell, 1957.

Leithäuser, Joachim G. *Wilhelm Leuschner: Ein Leben für die Republik.* Cologne: Bund-Verlag, 1962.

Lewy, Günther. *The Catholic Church and Nazi Germany.* New York: McGraw-Hill, 1964.

Lifton, R. J. *The Nazi Doctors.* New York: Basic, 1986.

Lingens-Reiner, E. *Prisoners of Fear.* London: Gollancz, 1948.

Lipset, Seymour Martin. *Political Man.* New York: Doubleday, 1960.

Lochner, Louis. *Always the Unexpected.* New York: Macmillan, 1946.

Loewenstein, Karl. "Germany and Central Europe." In *Governments of Continental Europe,* edited by James T. Shotwell. New York: Macmillan, 1946.

Lowi, Theodore, ed. *Private Life and Public Order.* New York: Norton, 1968.

Manvell, Roger, and Heinrich Fraenkel. *The Canaris Conspiracy.* New York: McKay, 1969.

____. *The Men Who Tried to Kill Hitler.* New York: Coward-McCann, 1964.

Maser, Werner. *Adolf Hitler: Legende, Mythos, Wirklichkeit.* Munich: Bechtle Verlag, 1971.

____. *Die Frühgreschichte der NSDAP: Hitler Weg bis 1924.* Frankfurt: Athenäum Verlag, 1965.

Mason, Herbert Molloy, Jr. *To Kill the Devil.* New York: Norton, 1978.

Mason, John Brown. *Hitler's First Foes.* Minneapolis: Burgess, 1936.

Mosley, Leonard. *Dulles.* New York: Dial Press/James Wade, 1978.

____. *On Borrowed Time.* New York: Random House, 1969.

Neumann, Franz. *Behemoth.* New York: Oxford University Press, 1942.

Noakes, Jeremy, and Geoffrey Pridham. *Documents on Nazism, 1919–1945.* New York: Viking, 1974.

O'Neill, Robert. *The German Army and the Nazi Party 1919–1933.* New York: Heineman, 1966.

Payne, Robert. *The Life and Death of Adolf Hitler.* New York: Praeger, 1973.

Pechel, Rudolph. *Deutscher Widerstand.* Zurich: Eugen Rentsch Verlag, 1947.

Persico, Joseph E. *Piercing the Reich.* New York: Viking, 1979.

Picker, Henry, ed. *Hitlers Tischgespräche.* Bonn: Athenäum-Verlag, 1951. *Hitler's Secret Conversations, 1941–1944.* trans. Norman Cameron and R. H. Stevens. New York: Farrar, Straus and Young, 1953.

Pinson, Koppel S. *Modern Germany.* New York: Macmillan, 1966.

Prange, Gordon W., ed. *Hitler's Words, 1923–1943.* Washington, D.C.: American Council on Public Affairs, 1944.

Prittie, Terence. *Germans Against Hitler.* Boston: Little, Brown, 1964.

Remak, Joachim, ed. *The Nazi Years.* Englewood Cliffs, N. J.: Prentice-Hall, 1969.

Remer, Otto Ernst. *20. Juli 1944.* Hamburg: Verlag Hans Siep, 1951.

Riess, Curt. *Joseph Goebbels: The Devil's Advocate.* New York: Ballantine, 1948.

Ritter, Gerhard. *The German Resistance.* New York: Praeger, 1958.

Roon, Ger van. *German Resistance to Hitler.* London: Van Nostrand Reinhold, 1971.

Rothfels, Hans. *The German Opposition to Hitler.* Chicago: Henry Regnery, 1962.

Royce, Hans, ed. *Germans Against Hitler July 20, 1944.* Bonn: Press and Information Office, Federal Government of Germany, 1964.

Schacht, Hjalmar. *Confessions of "The Old Wizard."* Boston: Houghton Mifflin, 1956.

Scheurig, Bobo. *Claus Graf Schenk von Stauffenberg.* Berlin: Colloquium Verlag, 1964.

Schlabrendorff, Fabian von. *Offiziere gegen Hitler.* Frankfurt: Fischer Bücherei, 1959.

____. *The Secret War Against Hitler.* New York: Pitman, 1965.

Schmitthenner, Walter, and Hans Buchheim, eds. *Der deutsche Widerstand gegen Hitler: Vier historisch-kritische Studien.* Cologne: Kiepenheuer and Witsch, 1966.

Scholl, Inge. *Students Against Tyranny.* Middletown, Conn.: Wesleyan University Press, 1970.

Schramm, Wilhelm von. *Conspiracy Among Generals.* London: Allen & Unwin, 1956.

Shirer, William L. *The Rise and Fall of the Third Reich.* New York: Simon and Schuster, 1960.

Silfin, Paul Harrison. *The Völkish Ideology and the Roots of Nazism.* New York: Exposition, 1973.

Snyder, Louis L. *Hitler's German Enemies.* New York: Hippocrene, 1990.

Speer, Albert. *Erinnerungen.* Berlin: Propyläen Verlag, 1969.

____. *Inside the Third Reich.* New York: Macmillan, 1970.

Spier, Eugen. *Focus: A Footnote to the History of the Thirties.* London: Oswald Wolff, 1963.

Stein, George H., ed. *Hitler.* Englewood Cliffs, N. J.: Prentice-Hall, 1968.

Sumler, David. *A History of Europe in the 20th Century.* Homewood, Ill.: Dorsey, 1973.

Taylor, A. J. P. *From Sarajevo to Potsdam.* London: Thames and Hudson, 1966.

Taylor, Tedford. *Munich: The Price of Peace.* Garden City, N. Y.: Doubleday, 1979.

Toland, John. *Adolf Hitler.* Garden City, N. Y.: Doubleday, 1976.

Vogelsang, Thilo. *Reichswehr Staat und NSDAP.* Stuttgart: Deutsche Verlags-Anstalt, 1962.

Warburg, James P. *Germany — Bridge or Battleground.* New York: Harcourt, Brace, 1946.

Weiss, John, ed. *Nazis and Fascists in Europe, 1918–1945*. Chicago: Quadrangle, 1969.

Weizsäcker, Ernst von. *Memoirs*. London: Gollancz, 1951.

Welles, Sumner. *The Time for Decision*. New York: Harper, 1944.

Wheeler-Bennett, John W. *The Nemesis of Power*. London: Macmillan, 1953.

Young, A. P. *The "X" Documents*. London: Andre Deutsch, 1974.

Zeller, Eberhard. *The Flame of Freedom*. London: Wolff, 1967.

Zipfel, Friedrich. *Kirchenkampf in Deutschland 1933–1945*. Berlin: Walter de Gruyter, 1965.

Zoller, Albert. *Hitler Privat*. Düsseldorf: Droste Verlag, 1949.

INDEX